Adelina Patti

ADELINA PATTI, 1843–1919

Adelina Patti

QUEEN OF HEARTS

by

John Frederick Cone

Chronology by Thomas G. Kaufman
Discography by William R. Moran

SCOLAR PRESS

For permission to reprint from the following works, grateful acknowledgment is hereby made to the publisher, Dutton, an imprint of New American Library, a division of Penguin Books USA Inc.

Excerpt from *The Hotel New Hampshire* by John Irving. Copyright 1981 by Garp Enterprises.

Excerpt from *The Romantic World of Music* by William Armstrong. Copyright 1922 by E. P. Dutton.

Jacket front illustration courtesy Earl of Harewood Collection at Harewood House, Leeds.
Jacket back illustration courtesy M. E. Saltykov-Shchedrin State Public Library, St. Petersburg, Russia.
Frontispiece courtesy William R. Moran. Photograph by Bergamasco, St. Petersburg.

First published in the United Kingdom in 1994 by

Scolar Press
Gower House
Croft Road
Aldershot
Hants GU11 3HR

British Library Cataloguing in Publication Data

Cone, John Frederick
    Adelina Patti: Queen of Hearts
    I. Title
    782.1092

ISBN 1-85928-004-8

Contents

Illustrations follow pages 24, 40, 72, 88, 104, 136, 184, 232, and 248

To these special people—

my parents, Nina and Stephen Cone; Patti's niece and great-grandniece, Carin Cederström Ekelöf and Mary Barili Goldsmith; and my niece, Florence Taylor.

Foreword

Operatic history is the stuff of which legends are made, and singers and their stories are very much a part of those legends. Since Orpheus, with assistance from his lute, brought about those extraordinary gyrations among natural phenomena, singers have been celebrated for the power they have to move us. Adelina Patti was such a singer.

When I was very young and first started to go to the opera, our old family doctor told me that he had been at Covent Garden when Tetrazzini made her unheralded debut and had stood on his seat and yelled with everyone else and, even more romantically, that as a student in Edinburgh well back in the last century he had helped after a concert to pull Patti's carriage through the streets and back to her hotel. His stories may or may not have been fact, but I believed them and the point is that they had the ring of truth about them. That is how people have always reacted to the power of song.

What can one say about Patti at this distance? Her records were made when she was rather old but, however much they suggest she had not regularly looked at the music since she first learned it, they have a touching quality about them, and phrases every now and again flash in front of the listener to suggest how Verdi, even in distinguished maturity, may have been captivated by her art. The photographs, of which there are many, perpetuate the firm chin of a very determined young woman, and we can believe what contemporaries reported, that her secretary may have stood in for her at rehearsal but that the performance she gave was vivid and worth going miles to see and hear.

For my own part I remember how excited I was quite a number of years ago when I had the chance to buy a splendid portrait of her by a great Victorian artist and to know that it was being sold by the surviving widow of her last husband. In it she looks as though she was far from someone to be trifled with, but the picture (which appears on the present book's jacket) asserts she was beautiful and allows that she could also be the source of beautiful sounds. And it certainly suggests she could have been a legend, not only for us more than a hundred years after it was painted but in her own time too.

Lord Harewood
London
November 1992

Introduction

As we lurch towards the end of the twentieth century, the age of Adelina Patti, roughly 1850 to 1900, with its singers and composers, looks more and more like paradise. Of course, historians, Freudians, and common sense tell us it wasn't so. However, reading of Patti, perhaps the most gifted of all singers during that century and this, reinforces many prejudices about what was good then and what is questionable today.

Patti's early development may perhaps be credited to the extraordinary conjunction of heredity and environment she was privileged to enjoy. However, it is rare in the nineteenth century to find any female singer beginning in her late twenties and going on to have a significant career. Today, in contrast, an enormous industry has developed devoted to the care and training of singers. The vocal competition has become an entertainment to rival the opera performance, with stipends, grants, and awards theoretically making it possible for young or not-so-young singers to have lengthy careers without ever venturing further than the audition. Only pensions are lacking.

One of the first important singers to be photographed regularly, Patti quickly established the formula of what would be expected of a prima donna. The photos taken of her as a young girl are succeeded by the London *cartes de visite* that portray her in all her leading roles. Eventually, the opera portraits disappear and she was photographed simply as Patti, the most famous singer in the world. In the twentieth century, publicity photos from various news agencies show Patti arriving at Paddington Station, standing at the door of her London hotel, and visiting wounded Belgian soldiers in Swansea Hospital.

Photographs of the tiny Patti remind us that the nineteenth century has been much maligned in the matter of singers and weight. The cliché has long maintained that singers once were fat and now they are thin, one of those automatic sayings that overlooks our late-twentieth-century devotion to obesity. As recently as 10 June 1937, Zinka Milanov's first Metropolitan Opera contract obligated her to lose 10 kilos (roughly twenty-two pounds) before 1 September of that year. This would be unthinkable today. It is all but impossible in Victorian photography, with its limited skills in retouching, or in the Milanov iconography, to find singers with the proportions of the currently performing Mmes. X, Y, and Z. A corollary of this cliché has developed: if the singer is large, he or she must be either a dramatic soprano or a Wagnerian tenor.

Though regrettably late, recordings of Patti's voice permit us to know something of the tone, technique, and musicality of her singing. However, just as photography has increased in speed and flexibility since the daguerreotype, so the mechanics of recordings have brought with them greater fidelity but not necessarily greater truth. We know with certainty what Adelina Patti was able to achieve on specific days in 1905 and 1906. With commercial recordings today, however, we no longer have that assurance. The birth of cynicism for many of us probably dates to 2 January 1949, when a delayed Metropolitan Opera broadcast of *Lucia di Lammermoor* permitted engineers to substitute on tape one Lily Pons high note for another.

Even without her recordings, we would know from the critics how Patti sang. Her public could read about it the next day. This is no longer possible. Although technology makes it theoretically feasible for a newspaper to be printed simultaneously all over the world, this doesn't mean that what is printed is news. The idea of considering reviews as news has vanished. The typical performance, if noticed at all, is reviewed in print an average of six days after the event. This is not the unmitigated disaster it would have been were Richard Aldrich or W. J. Henderson, two of the finest from the early twentieth century, the critics involved. Today, the average reviewer practices on-the-job training with his most interesting statements frequently subject to correction soon after appearing in print. One has only to consider what was critically the most important subject of the mid 1980s—surtitles—to see how little thought is involved. Like intellectual junket hardening, surtitles became the answer to every operatic problem. Ignored in the process was accuracy of reporting and ability to describe. When the Metropolitan Opera Guild published the one-hundred-season *Annals of the Metropolitan Opera* in 1989, one of the reasons for omitting reviews that had been such a feature of the 1947 edition was the inability to find adequate material covering the most recent decades.

If the nineteenth century may be considered the time of the composer and the singer, the twentieth has become the age of the conductor and the director. The musical advantages are obvious, with greater polish of orchestral playing and performance coordination undeniable. The occasional disadvantage is in those extremes of control when a conductor makes decisions that are more properly the singer's. For some, the apogee of this kind of conductorial dictatorship was reached in a Philadelphia Orchestra performance of *Rigoletto* in Carnegie Hall when Riccardo Muti conducted Cecilia Gasdia through every note of the cadenzas of "Caro nome." High notes, of course, were proscribed.

The role of the director is more problematical. Since opera as we know it today is essentially an adaptation of a nineteenth-century phenomenon, considerable effort is expended on making works fresh, relevant, or timely. It is difficult to object to changes of time and locale so long as logic and credibility remain. After all, Verdi in *Rigoletto* and *Un ballo in maschera* proves that centuries and continents may shift without damage to integrity. What is almost impossible for the lover of voices and singing to accept is the rigidity that sets in when a director's book becomes as sacrosanct as the composer's score. Consider Verdi's *La traviata* in two Metropolitan Opera seasons. In 1933–34, the Violettas were Claudia Muzio, Rosa Ponselle, and Lucrezia Bori. In 1942–43, the role was shared by Licia Albanese, Jarmila Novotna, and Bidù Sayão. Would this kind of richness be possible if each soprano had to be guided through a Franco Zeffirelli production?

What is the underside of the nineteenth century that perhaps makes us happier to live today than then? Surely, most operatic performances, particularly on tour, were fairly ramshackle affairs that overlooked musical and dramatic niceties in the rush to present important voices to the public. More seriously, the vast operatic enterprise that we think of as profitable was in fact subsidized by everyone except the leading singers. Musicians, chorus, ballet, and stagehands—all contributed. Here are some salaries from 1896–97, the first season for which we have fairly complete pay records for the Metropolitan Opera. Jean de Reszke was paid $104,194 for his season of fifty-five performances. Nellie Melba received $1600 per performance, and Emma Calvé, $1560. The fifty members of the Italian Chorus were each paid $15 per week. The fifty members of the American Chorus, which performed everything except the Italian repertoire, were each paid $10 per week. Clearly, Patti and her slightly less-well-paid colleagues floated on top of a world whose only concern was sustaining the star.

Everything is different today, even though much of the repertoire from the nineteenth century remains the same. We can see and hear our favorite singers and music instantly. We know more of musical history than any audience in the past. But given a choice, wouldn't we gladly return briefly to see Adelina Patti sing Lucia at the New York Academy of Music in 1859, to hear Adelina Patti sing Aida in London in 1876, or hear one of her few performances at the Metropolitan Opera House in 1892? I, for one, would happily settle for a farewell concert, whatever the year, however many selections she was willing to dole out.

Robert Tuggle
Director of Archives
The Metropolitan Opera
April 1993

Acknowledgments

This biography would never have been realized without the kind assistance of many. To all I am deeply indebted and profoundly grateful. The pages of this book reflect their help and thus best exhibit my thankfulness.

I wish to acknowledge the gracious permission of Her Majesty Queen Elizabeth II to quote from Queen Victoria's journal, the correspondence of several of Queen Victoria's children, and the diary of King George V.

Then, too, I wish to acknowledge the generous assistance of Queen Elizabeth II's cousin the Earl of Harewood, who kindly gave permission for his Winterhalter portrait of Patti to be the jacket illustration as well as an illustration in the book and who most graciously provided the foreword. I also express sincere thanks to his son Mark Lascelles, who photographed the portrait.

Of the diva's relatives, Mary Barili Goldsmith, Patti's great-grandniece, constantly assisted and encouraged me. She also sent copies of letters Patti had written to family members. Through her, I was permitted to do research on the Patti holdings and correspondence at the Georgia Department of Archives and History. She further helped in sending photos of family members who had known the diva. Mary Barili Goldsmith's relatives of assistance were her husband, Wick; her sister, Anne Barili Carmichael; the late Alfredo Barili III; and Doris Elvington Barili. I also received inestimable help from Patti's niece by marriage to Baron Rolf Cederström, Carin

Cederström Ekelöf, who sent photographs from her collection and approximately 140 copies of letters dated from 1899 to 1918 that Patti wrote to her father and mother: Gustaf and Eleonore Cederström. She and her husband, Stig Ekelöf, were most gracious while I visited them in Sweden some years ago. Then, too, Baron Rolf Cederström's daughter, Brita Elmes, assisted as did her daughter, Christine Scott Plummer, and son, Lord Poltimore.

While engaged in research in Wales, I found the assistance of the following individuals especially helpful: Evans Arwyn, *The Brecon and Radnor Express*; Elizabeth Bennett, West Glamorgan Record Office, Swansea; Hilary Bulmer, Brecknock Museum; Lloyd Davies, Swansea Central Library; John Vivian Hughes, who sent the author copies of letters from Patti in his collection; Malcolm Johns, Brecknock Museum; John G. Rees, Welsh Office, Cathays Park, Cardiff; Jayne Southall, Swansea Central Library; Brian Thomas; and Jan Weeks, Swansea Grand Theatre.

The individual in Wales deserving most gratitude, however, is David Brinn, manager of Craig-y-Nos Country Park, who since 1985 has assisted in research and has graciously served as a link to the local scene. This gentleman provided material on Craig-y-Nos Castle as well as information on Patti he had amassed. Also, he photographed and sent copies of the diva's portrait at the Brecon Guildhall; her portrait at the Glynn Vivian Art Gallery, Swansea; pictures of Craig-y-Nos domestics at the Brecon Brecknock Museum; and recent exterior views of Craig-y-Nos. His patience, courtesy, and interest in the biography have been of inestimable help and are deeply appreciated. He was a kindred spirit in the creation of this book.

Although familiar with French, German, Italian, and Spanish, I sought help from those fluent in the preceding languages. Among these were Dr. André Dielwahr and William Todt, French; Walter Mannheim, German; Dr. Matilde M. Fava, Italian; and Alex Koharski, Judy Laurie, and Dr. Yolanda T. De Mola, Spanish. Mara Kashper, a native of St. Petersburg, translated correspondence in Russian. I am most grateful for these individuals' abiding interest and assistance.

I wish also to acknowledge the following persons, services, and institutions: Magda Helena Chaar Abdul-Khalek, Biblioteca Pública, Bélem, Brasil; Dr. J. R. Alban, Swansea City Archivist, Wales; American Institute for Verdi Studies at New York University; Marcel Bally; Rose Bampton; Richard Bebb; D. Bevan, University College of

Swansea; Biblioteca de Palácio, Madrid; Biblioteca Nacional, Buenos Aires; Biblioteca Nacional, Montevideo, Uruguay; Biblioteca Nazionale, Rome; Bibliothèque Municipale, Dieppe, France; Bildarchiv und Porträtsammlung der Österreichischen National-bibliothek, Vienna; S. Böhme, Der Magistrat der Stadt Bad Homburg; Carla Guiducci Bonanni, Biblioteca Nazionale, Florence; John W. Booth, who graciously shared with me Patti's and Baron Ceder-ström's British naturalization dates; British Broadcasting Corporation, Llandaff, Cardiff, Wales; British Museum Library; E. V. Brown, Immigration and Nationality Department, Liverpool; Frau Buchholz, Der Magistrat der Stadt Bad Homburg; California Historical Society, San Francisco; Chicago Historical Society; Chicago Public Library; Christie, Mason & Woods Ltd., London; Melanie Trifona Christoudia, Theatre Museum, London; Martin Chusid; P. M. Clark, Deputy Registrar, Royal Archives, Windsor Castle; Columbia University Theater Library; Birgitta Dahl, Musikmuseet, Stockholm; Christopher H. Talfan Davies, Christopher Davies Publishers Ltd., Wales; M. I. Demidova, Chief of Acquisitions Department, M. E. Saltykov-Shchedrin State Public Library, St. Petersburg; Paul-Charles Déodato, Avocat à la Cour, Paris; Eilis Ni Dhuibhne, National Library of Ireland; Eva Dillman, Kungl. Biblioteket, Stockholm; Roger Duce, National Library of Scotland; Francisco Echeverría; Owen Edwards, BBC Wales; Tim Egan, National Library of Wales; Rosemary Evison, National Portrait Gallery, London; Linda Fairtile, American Institute for Verdi Studies at New York University; Andrew Farkas; Jean Favier, Directeur Général des Archives de France; H. J. Faweus, Blenheim Palace Archives; Francesca Franchi, Royal Opera Covent Garden Archivist; Free Library of Philadelphia Music Division; Free Library of Philadelphia Newspaper Division; Gail L. Freunsch, Music Specialist, The Library of Congress; María Teresa Trueba Freire, José Marti National Library, Havana; Fundaçào Cultural de Pará, Belém, Brasil; Sr. Justa Moreno Garbayo, Royal Palace Archives, Madrid; Charles Neilson Gattey, who graciously recommended research sources in Mexico; Barbara R. Geisler, San Francisco Performing Arts Library & Museum; General Research Division, The New York Public Library, Astor, Lenox and Tilden Foundations; Georgia Department of Archives and History; Valeri Glotov, Director of the Theatre Museum, St. Petersburg; Norman Goodman, County Clerk and Clerk of the Supreme Court, New York

County; I. F. Grigorieva, M. E. Saltykov-Shchedrin State Public Library, St. Petersburg; Patricia Hall, San Francisco Public Library; Collin B. Hamer, Jr., New Orleans Public Library; Gladys Hensen, City Archivist, San Francisco Public Library; Christina M. Hanson, Beinecke Rare Book and Manuscript Library, Yale University; Jill Hanson, Royal Archives, Windsor Castle; Caroline Harden, Victoria and Albert Museum, London; Erica Harman, Royal Academy of Arts, London; Harvard University Library; Lic. Luz María Mendoza Hdez, México Biblioteca Nacional; Eckart Henning, Geheimes Staatsarchiv Preussischer Kulturbesitz, Berlin; Michael Henstock, who graciously sent information on Patti's South American tours; Historical Society of Pennsylvania, Philadelphia; Kathleen Hughes, National Library of Wales; John Humphreys, Craig-y-Nos Castle Co. Ltd.; Bernard Huys, Bibliothèque Royale Albert, Brussels; Dr. Eva Irblich, Österreichische Nationalbibliothek, Vienna; Jane Jackson, Royal Opera Covent Garden Archive Office; Richard Jackson; Charles Jahant; John Jenkins, Adviser in Music, West Glamorgan County Council, Wales; Ghislaine Jouen, Archives de la Région de Haute—Normandie; M. Joyce, Reference Librarian, Bath, U.K.; Paul W. Joyner, National Library of Wales; Martine Kahane, Bibliothèque et Musée de l'Opéra, Biblothèque Nationale, Paris; E. Kasinec, Slavic Division, New York Public Library; Thomas G. Kaufman; Herbert Kennedy, San Francisco Performing Arts Library & Museum; Danielle Kiey, Royal Botanic Gardens, Kew, London; Dr. Robert Kittler, Österreichische Nationalbibliothek, Vienna; G. A. Knight, Rothschild Archives, London; Kungl. Biblioteket, Stockholm; Lim M. Lai; Jane Langton, Registrar, Royal Archives, Windsor Castle; James A. Lea, Former Director, The Adelina Patti Hospital, Wales; Robert Leidner; François Lesure, Bibliothèque Nationale, Paris; The Library of Congress; Graham D. Llewellyn, Sotheby's, London; Concha Lois, Biblioteca Nacional, Madrid; Gisela J. Lozada, Louisiana State University, Baton Rouge; Gerard Lyne, National Library of Ireland; Ma Teresa Simarro Martinez, Biblioteca Nacional, Madrid; Jordan Massie; Rosanne McCaffrey, Historic New Orleans Collection, New Orleans; Adriana Méndez, Biblioteca Nacional, Montevideo; Metropolitan Opera Archives; Monmouth College Library; Margaret Moore, Coe Kerr Gallery, New York; Patricia Moore, Glamorgan Archive Service, Cardiff, Wales; William R. Moran; Mario Moreau, Lisbon; Michael Morton-Smith, Sotheby

Parke Bernet & Co., London; Virginia Moskowitz, Mount Vernon, New York, Public Library; Jean-Marie Moulin, Conservateur en chef, Musée National du Château du Compiègne; Museum of the City of New York; Musikhistoriska Museet, Stockholm; New-York Historical Society; New York Public Library Music Division; New York Public Library Newspaper Division; New York Public Library Slavic Division; New York Public Library Special Collections Division; New York Public Library Theater Division; New York University Library; Mildred Nijhove-Kerssenberg, Stichting Cultureel Centrum, Suriname; Nordica Memorial Association, Farmington, Maine; Richard Ormond, Director National Maritime Museum, London; Hofrat Mag. Dr. Franz Patzer, Direktor Wiener Stadt und Landesbibliothek, Vienna; Hofrat Univ.–Doz. Dr. Oskar Pausch, Österreichische Nationalbibliothek Theatersammlung; Prof. Pierluigi Petrobelli, Istituto Nazionale di Studi Verdiani, Parma; Julie Phillips, Newspaper Division, The British Library; W. G. Phillips, Town Clerk, Brecon Town Council, Wales; Andrew Phrydas, Georgia Department of Archives and History; Pierpont Morgan Library; Princeton University Firestone Library; the late Elsie Pritchard; René Rouveau, *Le Figaro,* Paris; Jean Rouffet, who assisted in research on the Marquis de Caux; Bengt Rur, Riksarkivet, Stockholm; Rutgers University Library; San Francisco Public Library Music Division; San Francisco Public Library Newspaper Division; San Francisco Public Library Special Collections Division; San Francisco Public Library Theater Division; Bidù Sayão; Service Culturel, Departemental de la Guyane; William Seward; Pedro Mendonça da Silveira, Director de Serviços, Lisbon; Stichting Cultureel Centrum Suriname; Stiftelsen Musikkulturens, Stockholm; Lord Swansea; Richard Taruskin; Brian Thomas, West Glamorgan County Council, Wales; Donald Thompson, whose research on Patti's concerts in Puerto Rico was of inestimable help; Edwin Tribble; Carol Troyen, Museum of Fine Arts, Boston; Donald H. Trueman, Curator, Powys County Council, Wales; Maria Twist, Birmingham City Council Library Services; the late Irving Wallace; Jan Wallace, National Portrait Gallery, London; Clifford Williams; Mag. Herwig Würtz, Direktor, Wiener Stadt-und Landesbibliothek; Yale University Music Library; and Julio Oscar Zolezzi, Biblioteca Nacional, Buenos Aires.

Of individuals who had known Patti, I especially remember a delightful conversation with an elderly member of the Cederström family. She primarily stressed the diva's appearance, her beautiful attire, flawless make-up, attractive coiffures, and jewels. Another who had known Patti was Mme. Pauline Donalda, who had appeared on a program featuring Patti as the star performer in the Diamond Jubilee Concert honoring Wilhelm Ganz, on 26 May 1908, at London's Queen's Hall. The connection I had with Mme. Donalda resulted from my writing the history of Oscar Hammerstein's Manhattan Opera Company. In its first season, she had been one of the impresario's brightest stars. For a considerable period I carried on a lengthy correspondence with the lady and finally met her in Montreal. At that time I asked her about Patti; Mme. Donalda's immediate response was an exclamation: "She was so *charming!*" The usual effusions concerning the diva's voice and artistry followed. In Wales I met several people who provided information they had gleaned from locals who had known Patti. Among the most informative were David Brinn; James A. Lea, former Director of The Adelina Patti Hospital; and the late Elsie Pritchard, who over the years had accumulated fascinating stories and details concerning Patti.

Of letters referred to in this biography, the majority of these are housed in the Bibliothèque Nationale, Paris; British Museum; Georgia Department of Archives and History; Louisiana State University, Baton Rouge; National Library of Wales; Music Division, New York Public Library; Rothschild Archives, London; Stiftelsen Musikkulturens, Stockholm; and Windsor Castle Archives. From the private collections of Carin Cederström Ekelöf, Mary Barili Goldsmith, and John Vivian Hughes, I received copies of Patti's letters. The Cardiff Public Library was another source of correspondence and relevant material. What I found there in 1985 had not been catalogued, filled two paper bags, and contained, above all, notes of Josiah Pittman, who may have intended their use for later publication.

As for the photographs, I should like to acknowledge the cooperation and generous help of the following individuals: John W. Booth, David Brinn, Walter Ernst, Karisa Krcmar, Vivian Liff, Robert Young Lock, William R. Moran, and Jesse Privett, who generously duplicated photos from Mary Barili Goldsmith's Collection. In the last phases in the writing of this book, I found invaluable the assistance of M. I. Demidova, Chief of Acquisitions Department, M. E. Saltykov-Shchedrin State Public Library, St. Petersburg, Russia. He sent microfilm copies of *Moskova Deutsche Zeitung, Baltische Tageszeitung, St. Petersburg Zeitung,* and the *Journal de St. Pétersbourg* as well as pictures of Patti from the St. Petersburg collection. Tanya A. Gozdavcic and Serge Gleboff, librarians in the Slavic Division of The New York Public Library, likewise offered invaluable assistance in locating old, obscure Russian publications while Nadia J. Shidlovsky translated these, material further shedding light on Patti's Russian experiences. Then, too, Robert Tuggle, archivist of the Metropolitan Opera, and his staff were helpful and cooperative. I am most thankful for such assistance. I am indebted to him most especially for providing the introduction to the book. I also gratefully recall the help of Maryse Ropars, of the Bibliothèque Municipale de Lyon, who sent me articles from the September 1864 issues of *Le Courrier de Lyon* concerning Patti's performances in that city.

I am most grateful to Henry Pleasants for allowing me to quote from his book, *Vienna's Golden Years of Music;* to Bill Moran for his many contributions to this biography; and to Gerry Trimble, who devoted hours to proofreading galleys.

Two ladies typed the manuscript and deserve my deepest gratitude: Mary Lou Cottingham and Kathy Van Dam.

Finally, I wish to acknowledge those friends who patiently endured much in both the creation and completion of this book. Among these are Carol and Gordon Berg; Bill Bernhardt; Jean Bowen Bloch; Ruth Brandt; Walter Ernst; Betty Hofmeister; Christian Howard; Mary Johnson; Renee Maxwell; Adonny Raphael; Ray Rhule, whose constructive critical comments regarding the manuscript provided needed balance and insight; Bruce Sherril; Sarah and Gerry Trimble; Susan and Ken Wallach; and Dr. Donald D. Warner, an educator and administrator with a keen sense of humor rousing requisite risibilities.

Adelina Patti

Prologue

Some years ago the distinguished American stage personality Cornelia Otis Skinner expressed indignation that the name and fame of a legendary French woman formerly universally acknowledged as the greatest actress of her time was virtually forgotten among educated adults and university students. "Who," various individuals asked her, "was Sarah Bernhardt?" Skinner ultimately responded with her fascinating biography entitled *Madame Sarah*.

In referring to the heroine of this book, I have often experienced a similar response from adults and students. "Who," I have repeatedly been asked, "was Adelina Patti?" In her own time she was globally renowned, a vocal star of the highest magnitude. Even her most formidable female rivals acknowledged Patti's preeminence and uniqueness.

She so inspired Emma Calvé, the greatest Carmen of them all, and Luisa Tetrazzini that they ranked her as the epitome of vocal perfection. Calvé said Patti's charm and artistry seemed "divine, almost miraculous"[1] and compared her voice to "a string of luminous pearls, perfectly matched, every jewel flawless, identical in form and colour"[2] while Tetrazzini from her earliest years considered Patti "a majestic being, more divine than human, so exalted that it was almost sacrilege to speak her name."[3] Nellie Melba, usually tempered in praise of other artists, declared that Patti had always been her goddess and that her voice was perhaps the most golden she had heard: "the *timbre* of it was exquisite, the diction crystalline."[4] Its

1

magic cast such a spell over Minnie Hauk and Frances Alda that they both felt unstrung, overwhelmed by its beauty and haunting quality. Marcella Sembrich always maintained that Patti was the most brilliant soprano of her time, and Emma Eames in her memoirs expressed like sentiments:

> Hers was the most perfect technic imaginable, with a scale, both chromatic and diatonic, of absolute accuracy and evenness, a tone of perfect purity and of the most melting quality, a trill impeccable in intonation, whether major or minor, and such as one hears really only in nightingales, liquid, round and soft. Her crescendo was matchless, and her vocal charm was infinite. I cannot imagine more beautiful sounds than issued from that exquisite throat, nor more faultless phrasing, nor more wonderful economy of breath. Her phrases were interminable.[5]

The legendary Wagnerian soprano Lilli Lehmann, of the loftiest vocal and artistic standards, acclaimed Patti the greatest Italian opera singer of the age. Of all the artists' tributes, perhaps Jenny Lind's was the most memorable: *"There is only one Niagara; and there is only one Patti."* [6]

The elderly Giuseppe Verdi in a conversation with the impresario Giulio Gatti-Casazza also ranked Patti as the preeminent singer of the age. To Verdi, she was the consummate prima donna.

That the name and fame of such a legendary figure is today virtually forgotten saddened me and ultimately prompted my action. A contemporary biography of this extraordinary woman and artist has been long overdue.

Its publication in 1993 occasions another celebration: the one-hundred-fiftieth anniversary of Patti's birth.

Adelina Patti . . . went up to a man, his hair parted in the middle and gleaming with pomade, who was stretching his long arms out across the footlights to hand her something— and the entire audience in the orchestra and boxes stirred, leaned forward, shouted and clapped. From his raised stand the conductor helped to pass over the bouquets.
> —Leo Tolstoy, *Anna Karenina*

You must come and dine with me, and afterwards we will look in at the Opera. It is a Patti night, and everybody will be there.
> —Oscar Wilde, *Dorian Gray*

On Saturday afternoon the Albert Hall was filled by the attraction of our still adored Patti. . . . The concert was a huge success: there were bouquets, raptures, effusions, kissings of children, graceful sharings of the applause with obbligato players—in short, the usual exhibition of the British bourgeoisie in the part of Bottom and the prima donna in the part of Titania.
> —Bernard Shaw, *Music in London 1890–94*

> *"Oportet pati."*
> *Les latinistes traduisent cet adage par*
> *"Il faut souffrir;"—*
> *Les moines par*
> *"Apportez le pâté;"*
> *Les amis de la musique par*
> *"Il nous faut Patti."*
> > —Hector Berlioz

And in one of Frank's opera books I read that Adelina Patti's
Lucia seemed fated for ... disturbance. In Bucharest, for
example, the famous mad scene was interrupted by a
member of the audience falling into the pit—upon a
woman—and in the general panic, someone shouted "Fire!"
But the great Adelina Patti cried, "No fire!"—and went on
singing. And in San Francisco, one weirdo threw a bomb onto
the stage, and once more the fearless Patti riveted the
audience to their seats. Despite the fact that the bomb
exploded!
                    —John Irving, *The Hotel New Hampshire*

Of all living singers she alone can execute the most difficult
forms of music with the unerring precision of an instrument
and a beauty of tone which no instrument can rival.
            —New York *Evening Post,* 19 November 1886

Probably no other singer ever remained on the stage so long
and none certainly ever succeeded so long in making every
bar she sang almost equal in value to a bar of gold.
            —New York *Evening Post,* 3 November 1903

Sonnet Dedicated to Patti and
Written by Eminent French Writers

Es-tu le rossignol, la rose, l'harmonie,
Jeune divinité du ciel italien?

Es-tu l'amour, l'esprit, le charme, le génie,
Étoile aux éclairs d'or de l'art cécilien?
—Théophile Gautier

Ô Diva radieuse! Ô musique infinie!
Tu nous suspens à toi d'un céleste lien,
Tu portes dans ton oeil le pleur d'Iphigénie,
La gaieté de Ninon et l'éclat de Tallien.
—Arsène Houssaye

Chante, Ô ma Lucia, chante, Ô mon Adeline,
Tressaille sous ton lys et sous ta mandoline,
Respire dans ta pourpre et dans ta floraison.
—Théodore De Banville

Ô brune Adelina, comme Vénus la blonde
De la pointe du pied boît l'écume de l'onde,
Tu sembles une fleur qui boît une chanson.
—Charles Coligny

5

Postlude/Prelude

Though but one of many rallying programs during the War to End All Wars, the patriotic concert of 24 October 1914 at London's Albert Hall, organized by Lady Randolph Churchill, was unique, as it marked an epoch in the life of its most celebrated performer: Adelina Patti. This artist was a vocal phenomenon, glamorous figure, and formidable legend renowned for both a nonpareil professional career and an intriguing private life. At the height of her career, she had been the world's singer of singers and its most highly paid entertainer.

For a time Patti, a septuagenarian seldom performing publicly, had deliberated over participating in the London event, reluctant to leave even briefly her third husband, forty-four-year-old Baron Rolf Cederström, who was recuperating from an operation. Daily her chauffeur drove her, bejeweled and swathed in scarves as protection against the elements, from their remote residence in Wales to his Swansea nursing home. The baron, however, insisted she appear at the affair, reasoning that his health was improving and that her performance at the benefit would generate tremendous response, as she still possessed infinite appeal, which neither age could wither nor custom stale. Fortunately his will prevailed, affording many the privilege of hearing a great voice perhaps for the last time.

At seventy-one, Patti had enthralled the music world for an unprecedented sixty-three years, having made her first concert appearance at the age of eight. Although time had taken its toll on her soprano voice, she still sang with exquisite style, perfect legato, a pure tone, and emotional expressiveness, occasionally nearly matching her golden days. To many she remained the supreme exponent of the art of grand singing, and her appearance at the patriotic concert was keenly anticipated.

After arriving in London, Patti conferred with her musical collaborator on the program, Sir Henry J. Wood, who later recalled his awe over her appearance and voice, neither suggesting her age:

> I was delighted when Lady Randolph engaged the Queen's Hall Orchestra and me for the concert at the Albert Hall on October 24, for I had always longed for the chance of accompanying Patti on the piano in a small room. The opportunity came when she asked me to meet her at the Carlton on the day before the concert.... Her wonderful little figure struck me at once when she entered her private sitting-room. Here was no low diaphragmatic breather, I said to myself, for Patti had a tiny waist and a very full bust. She had wonderful dark penetrating eyes that seemed to read your thoughts, and a delightful speaking voice. We rehearsed *Voi che sapete*. I felt the marvellous evenness of her warm quality. Her voice was not powerful but it excelled anything I had imagined in red-rose-like quality and voluptuous sweetness.... It was truly wonderful and I was entranced.[1]

Before the concert, as King George V and Queen Mary with their entourage entered the Royal box, His Majesty's Brigade of Guards played the National Anthem followed by the overture *Britannia*. The formal program included solo artists, the Royal Choral Society, the Queen's Hall Orchestra under Sir Henry's direction, and bands of the Brigade of Guards; but of these Patti stood apart, making the deepest impression with her singing of Mozart's "Voi che sapete" and her signature ballad, "Home, Sweet Home." The huge audience thunderously applauded, cheered, and gave floral tributes, all recalling the diva's past victories.

Hours later His Majesty noted the afternoon in his diary: "At 3.0. we all went to a Patriotic concert ... in aid of the Order of the Hospital of St. John of Jerusalem, there were 10,000 people present. Patti sang, wonderfully still."[2]

The performance marked a fitting postlude to an extraordinary career, to the legend of Patti beginning decades before in the circumstances of her birth.

Her father, Salvatore Patti, born in 1800 in Catania, Sicily, was the son of Pietro Patti and Concepcion Marino, the scion of an old Catanese family with roots in a Sicilian commune bearing the familial name. None of his relatives had ever been connected with the stage; but possessed of a fine voice, he found himself irresistibly drawn to it. A *tenore robusto*, Patti by his mid twenties was appearing in operas during the 1825–26 season at the Teatro Carolino in Palermo under the musical direction of composer Gaetano Donizetti, not yet thirty years old with a number of his operas already publicly performed. The season extended from May to February and evolved as one of the most trying for Donizetti while it foreshadowed Patti's professional life.

Scheduled to open on 11 April 1825, the Palermo season was postponed until 4 May, a postponement due to Donizetti's and principal performers' late arrivals, intrigues among opera house administrators, and casting problems. Stresses continued until the season closed on 19 February because of the quality of the orchestra and main artists, rivalries and jealousies, unresolved contractual issues, poor critical reviews, and insufficient funds for salaried personnel, with Donizetti himself in arrears. Writing to his old music teacher, the composer expressed his discontent:

> I am entirely convinced we will leave here with broken heads, that is to say with several months' salary owing. . . . I assure you, dear Maestro, that I suffer much from the type of beasts we have need of for the execution of our labors. . . . I am more than a little apprehensive. . . . And in the midst of all this I have had to play with music that requires some intelligence.[3]

Still, the season somewhat redeemed itself with several excellent productions, two including Patti. On 5 September he appeared as Pipetto in Donizetti's *L'ajo nell'imbarazzo,* a presentation lauded by public and press. Four months later, on 7 January 1826, he created the role of Ismaele in the world premiere of Donizetti's *Alahor di Granata,* also favorably received. These supporting roles presaged Patti's future; he was primarily a secondary tenor. He impressed audiences, however, as a competent performer, good actor, and conscientious musician, who was fortunately handsome, tall, and well-built.

Superior to her husband as singer and artist, Adelina's mother, Caterina Barili-Patti, was an illustrious soprano born in Rome, the daughter of Giovanni Chiesa and Luisa Caselli. For her, music cast its spell early; entering her teens, she had a promising voice. According to family tradition, one day in Rome, as she drew water from a well, singing all the while, vocal teacher and composer Francisco Barili heard her and was so impressed he urged her to study with him. At fifteen, she married this man and subsequently launched a career on stage and bore him three sons—Antonio, Nicolo, Ettore—and a daughter, Clotilda. As a young woman and mother, Caterina, according to an old Italian maestro, was beautiful, lively, daring, and vain, with a golden voice. Whatever dissipation or waywardness she indulged in, he said, never affected her singing. Then Barili died, leaving his widow and children devastated; but Caterina persevered and resumed her career, which provided Patti as a romantic colleague and ardent suitor.

As a leading artist, Caterina sang such principal and demanding roles as Elvira in Bellini's *I puritani* and the titular heroine in his *Norma*. Family tradition has it that at one performance she so overshadowed the internationally acclaimed soprano Giulia Grisi that Grisi refused to perform again on the same stage with this potential rival. Caterina's abilities so impressed Donizetti that he offered her the leading role of Isabella in his recently completed *L'assedio di Calais,* which premiered at the Teatro San Carlo in Naples on 19 November 1836. Though initially well received, this opera was not destined to join two earlier works ensuring the composer's lasting fame: *Lucia di Lammermoor* and *L'elisir d'amore*. That, however, the first performance of *L'assedio* had pleased Donizetti is evident in a letter he wrote three days later: "*L'assedio di Calais* went well. I was called out six times. . . . It is my most carefully worked-out score. Barroilhet, la Manzocchi, la Barili, Gianni, everyone applauded."[4]

As a colleague, Caterina at times left much to be desired with her irascibility and pathological jealousy occasionally creating havoc in the theater. One audience's enthusiasm for the great basso Luigi Lablache so aroused her envy that she seized a wreath intended for him and claimed it as her own. At another presentation, Caterina became so jealous of another soprano's reception that she told the woman her right eyebrow had fallen off, custom then being shaving off natural brows to replace them with artificial ones. Horrified, this soprano tore off her left eyebrow to match, no doubt stimulating quite a different audience reaction. Then, too, Caterina sometimes exploded on stage with fulminations and exclamations, a veritable virago, hurling apostrophes against an audience not giving her its undivided attention.

At home Caterina carried over this imperiousness. In her household her will prevailed, and in a rage "the extremely nervous madame" often "seized upon the fire-tongs or some other object at hand in order to enforce ... her will."[5] Caterina's jealousy, in an artist's world an emotion potentially stronger than even maternal love, extended to members of her own family. Thus, home life was often stormy. Her vehemence, nervousness, and resentments possibly increased after she and Salvatore became parents. Their first child, Amalia, was born in 1831; Carlotta in 1835; Carlo in 1842; and Adelina in 1843. The births, save the last two, were in different locales: Amalia's occurred in Paris; Carlotta's in Florence; and Carlo's and Adelina's in Madrid.

Apparently, while no unusual happenings heralded the first three Patti arrivals, several fanciful tales concern the fourth and place Caterina on stage in the demanding title role of Bellini's *Norma* moments before Adelina's birth. Suddenly indisposed, she was taken to the theater's greenroom, where she gave birth and where the principal tenor tore a portion of his wardrobe to provide baby wraps. The stories apparently originated in the fecund imagination of this tenor, José Sinico, with possible help from Adelina's brother-in-law and early manager, Maurice Strakosch, always keenly aware of the value of such publicity.

The new year 1843 found Salvatore and Caterina in Madrid, where she had been engaged as a principal prima donna at the Teatro del Circo. After several postponements Caterina appeared there on 31 January, according to Madrid journal *Revista de Teatros,* as Elena in Donizetti's *Marino Faliero* several weeks before giving birth to Adelina. That she, heavy with child, performed on this occasion no doubt reflected her proverbial iron will. She never assumed the part of Norma during this Madrid season. When *Norma* was presented at Circo in April, the Spanish soprano Cristina Villó sang the title role. The legendary birth occurred not in any theater's greenroom but at

11

number 6 Fuencarral Street, the house of a general's wife, doña Dolores Zárate de Rojas. Here at four o'clock Sunday afternoon, 19 February 1843, Adelina first appeared, presumably trailing not only sounds of vocal glory but intimations of the trills and cadenzas to come. Some six weeks later at the nearby church of San Luis, the vicar José Losada baptized her Adela Juana Maria while two sacristans served as witnesses and the aforementioned tenor and his wife, Rosa Manara Sinico, stood as godparents.

As for Adelina's birth date, various publications incorrectly marked it 10 February or 8 April, her christening day. Even Herman Klein in his biography, *The Reign of Patti*, published a year after her death, gives 10 February as the birth date, citing her biographical sketch in Dr. Hugo Riemann's authoritative *Dictionary of Music* and a copy of her baptismal register. The origin of this inaccuracy was perhaps due to a typographical error, but it is puzzling that Klein, having known Patti personally and aware she customarily celebrated her birthday on the nineteenth, failed to resolve the discrepancies. Spanish music historian Baltasar Saldoni, however, interviewed Salvatore at Adelina's opera debut in Madrid on 12 November 1863, and hastened to the church of San Luis on Montera Street, where he found her birth date in the baptismal register and quoted it in his forthcoming book *Diccionario Biográfico*.

In the year of Adelina's birth, thirteen-year-old Queen Isabella II of Spain pledged before assembled members of the Cortes to maintain the Constitution; citizen-king Louis-Philippe reigned in France, inspiring little admiration, while some eighty miles from Paris Emperor Napoleon I's nephew, having failed in a *coup d'état* to overthrow the monarchy, languished as a prisoner at the fortress of Ham; Queen Victoria of England had reigned for six years and her Prince Albert increasingly epitomized the model husband and father; in Prussia the government suppressed Karl Marx's writings; Austria's elder statesman Prince von Metternich resisted liberal policies, always the prime advocate of repression and immobility; in Russia Czar Nicholas I waged unrelenting war against change, determined to preserve autocracy and orthodoxy in an empire with millions of serfs; and John Tyler was America's lame-duck President, promoting immigration to the Northwest territories while Texas remained a republic and the abolition of slavery stirred up controversy throughout the twenty-six states. In opera among numerous world premieres were Wagner's *Der fliegende Holländer,* Verdi's *I lombardi,* and Donizetti's *Maria di Rohan, Dom Sébastien,* and *Don Pasquale.*

After Adelina's christening Salvatore and Caterina returned to Italy to pursue professional interests and familial duties. Clotilda Barili developed into an attractive young lady with a lovely soprano voice and began singing publicly. Not to be outdone, her brothers and the oldest Patti sisters sedulously applied themselves to musical matters. Carlo and Adelina no doubt awaited their time as well in this competitive household of emotional outbursts and even physical abuse.

However settled and routine the Pattis' life in Italy appeared, an individual from abroad ultimately altered it, prompting the family to plunge into a new life thousands of miles from home. The harbinger of change was an opera singer performing in the United States, basso Antonio Sanquirico, who had effected a favorable New York debut at Palmo's Opera House on Chambers Street in April 1844 and continued to make excellent impressions in the eight-hundred-seat theater. Proposing to manage an opera season there, he invited Salvatore and another Italian named Pogliani to direct the undertaking to begin after the new year 1847. This offer held powerful appeal, as both Caterina and Salvatore must have realized their singing days neared an end, while as an impresario, Salvatore might make an adequate living indefinitely.

At this time Italian opera was still comparatively new in New York, its first season having occurred there twenty-one years before, in 1825, beginning with Rossini's *Il barbiere di Siviglia,* featuring celebrated Garcia family members. The following two decades saw Italian opera gain popularity; but by the 1840s with the city's population near a half million, the demand for a permanent opera company had not increased. Salvatore no doubt looked forward to arousing interest in a change in this respect.

After the *Caledonia* docked in Boston on 5 December 1846, the Pattis and Italian opera members including Sanquirico made their way to New York. They were greeted upon arrival by this city's intense life with tides of mixed, crowded, hurrying humanity—over all, a noisy ebullience. Charles Dickens, visiting New York four years before Salvatore's arrival, described it thusly:

> Was there ever such a sunny street as this Broadway! The pavement stones are polished with the tread of feet until they shine again; the red bricks of the houses might be yet in the dry, hot kilns; and the roofs of those omnibuses look as though, if water were poured on them, they would hiss and smoke, and smell like half-quenched fires. No stint of omnibuses here! Half a dozen have gone by within as many minutes. Plenty of hackney cabs and coaches too; gigs, phaetons, large-wheeled tilburies.... Heaven save the ladies, how they dress! We have seen more colours in these ten minutes, than we should have seen elsewhere in as many days. What various parasols! what rainbow silks and satins! what pinking of thin stockings, and pinching of thin shoes and fluttering of ribbons and silk tassels, and display of rich cloaks with gaudy hoods and linings![6]

Edgar Allan Poe, living in Manhattan in the 1840s, provides a geographic picture of New York at the time of the Pattis' arrival with his description of the view from the Groton Reservoir at Fifth Avenue and Forty-second Street: "The prospect from the walk around the reservoir is particularly beautiful. You can see, from this elevation, the north reservoir at Yorkville; the whole city to the Battery; with a large portion of the harbor, and long reaches of the Hudson and East rivers."[7]

Potential competition for Salvatore's operatic productions were such attractions as forty-eight little girls named the Viennoise Children, who danced at the Park Theatre; Shakespearean actor James Murdoch in *Macbeth* at the Bowery Theatre; a London farce entitled *The Barber Bravo, or, the Inventor of Powder* at the Olympic; the circus of Sands, Lent & Company at the Chatham; and exotic, varied marvels at Barnum's Museum on Broadway and Ann Street. Among musical attractions were programs presented by the American Musical Institute; a final concert given by pianist Henri Herz before leaving the city for a tour of Cuba; and an orchestral gala by the Philharmonic Society featuring music by Mozart, Beethoven, Weber, Meyerbeer, and Bellini.

The new season at Palmo's began on 4 January 1847, with the American premiere of Donizetti's *Linda di Chamounix*, and closed on 31 March. Only three members of the family—Salvatore, Antonio, and Clotilda—participated in this series as well as in a supplementary one beginning on 7 April with Donizetti's *Lucrezia Borgia* and concluding on 7 June with a benefit for basso-profundo Antonio. In all, from January to June this company presented eight operas, one of the most popular being *Lucia di Lammermoor*. The diarist George Templeton Strong, attending a performance of this opera on 25 January with Clotilda as the title heroine, ranked the enterprise as capital, with a company that might "bear fruit in the building of a new opera house. The little Chambers Street concern is quite too small; 'twas more than full last night. The aristocracy were present *en masse*—Washington Irving among the rest."[8] Of leading artists, public and press acclaimed not only such old favorites as contralto Rosina Pico and Sanquirico, but also several new performers: tenor Sesto Benedetti, baritone Giuseppe Federico del Bosco Beneventano, and soprano Clotilda Barili, barely nineteen. Among secondary singers, Salvatore merited moderate praise.

Of Clotilda's New York debut in the title role of opening night's *Linda di Chamounix*, a critic wrote she was a delightful young artist singing "like an angel."[9] Historian Charles H. Haswell appraised her as charming and "esteemed a 'divinity' by the young men of our society."[10] Later Clotilda received special praise for Lucia and Griselda in *I lombardi*, the first Verdi opera to be staged in New York.

Salvatore made his New York debut on 26 February 1847, one week after Adelina's fourth birthday, as Henry in Coppola's *Nina pazza per amore*, substituting for an ailing Benedetti. One critic said Patti had sung "with a good expression, in good tune, and with an execution and style that prove him to be a well bred artist."[11] As Almaviva in Rossini's *Il barbiere di Siviglia*, he received mixed reviews, with the *Herald* considering him "an artist of excellent conception, a good actor, and by no means a mean singer.,"[12] while one pundit observed that "he was so plump, so like a middle-aged belle advanced into *embonpoint*, and in voice and person . . . suggestive of pinguidity, that when I laughingly called him *Patti de foie gras*, the name stuck to him for a long time."[13]

Parenthetically, an individual who owed much to this 1847 season and later attributed to it a change of attitude toward opera was poet Walt Whitman, then associated with the *Brooklyn Daily Eagle*. He reveled in various presentations at Palmo's, urged people to attend, and maintained the company would take root. Previously Whitman had preferred American singing groups, but Palmo operas stirred him. Of the poet's reversal, a biographer stated that the "operatic revival in New York in 1847 had worked a sea change . . .; the Whitman who in 1846 had seen the opera as a sequence of agonized squalls was not the Whitman who, on 13 December 1847 at the beginning of a brief announcement of two operatic troupes opening that week at the Park and Broadway theatres, put exclamation 'Good!'."[14] Years later the poet declared that without exposure to Italian opera he would never have been inspired to write his masterpiece, *Leaves of Grass*.

Successes at Palmo's so bolstered Salvatore's morale that he and Sanquirico invested a considerable sum of money to lease and manage the new Astor Place Opera House. When completed, this theater on Lafayette Street between Astor Place and Eighth Street accommodated eighteen hundred patrons in a spacious auditorium infinitely grander than Palmo's. On opening night, 22 November 1847, a presentation of *Ernani* attracted many of the city's first families. Years later a music critic recalled this event:

> So elegant and socially impressive a spectacle as that presented by the house on the rising of the curtain had not been seen before in New York. . . . It may safely be said that there was hardly a person present who was not known, by name, at least, to a very considerable number of his or her fellow auditors. A sociable feeling pervaded the assembly, . . . which added much to the glow of satisfaction with which they greeted one another and discussed the house and the artists.[15]

Diarist Philip Hone, attending an opera on 21 January, praised this new edifice as

> so advantageously situated and admirably adapted to contribute to the enjoyment of our citizens. . . . This opera of ours is a refined amusement, creditable to the taste of its proprietors and patrons; a beautiful parterre in which our young ladies . . . and . . . men . . . may . . . acquire a taste for a science of the most refined and elegant nature.[16]

During the five-month season Salvatore and Sanquirico

presented nine operas with a number of singers new to the city and several principals from Palmo's. Soprano Teresa Truffi's debut on opening night and her subsequent performances created a sensation with her impressive bearing, vocal expressiveness, and exceptional histrionics in tragic roles. Clotilda performed such parts as Elvira in *I puritani*; then, with Clotilda as Beatrice, sixteen-year-old Amalia made her New York debut as Agnese on 1 December 1847, in Bellini's *Beatrice di Tenda*. The critic for *The Albion* found her promising: "Her voice is very fine, her style good, and when she gains confidence we shall have a good deal to say in her favour."[17] Amalia appeared in only one other part this season: Fenena in the American premiere of Verdi's *Nabucco*. Caterina debuted in New York on 28 January 1848, as Romeo to Clotilda's Giulietta in Bellini's *I Capuleti e i Montecchi*, in its first New York performance, and the following day the *Tribune* said: "Her voice lacks steadiness and certainty, but her bearing and action are excellent."[18] *The Albion* concurred, commenting favorably on her mien and artistic powers, but said her voice, though beautiful, retained only a shadow of its original splendor. Caterina appeared as Romeo once again, on 31 January, in her last New York seasonal opera performance. Antonio assisted as accompanist and occasional conductor throughout the series, which by its conclusion in April signaled the end of Salvatore as an opera manager. His enterprise had become a financial failure. The New York *Spirit of the Times* summarized its failings: "There were too many stars and too little brilliancy.... The great variety that could have been presented was neglected, and two or three operas forced upon the subscribers. The *bon ton* or the *dilettanti*, or both, were *ennuied* to death."[19]

Seven months later Salvatore resumed his stage career at the Astor Place Opera House, where for over two years he generally performed only supporting roles, one of these being Di Fieschi in the American premiere on 10 December 1849 of Donizetti's *Maria di Rohan*, and where during these years his principal conductor and manager was Max Maretzek, who enlivened the American opera world as an enterprising impresario. Though Clotilda left New York City after her marriage in March 1848, Amalia repeatedly appeared at Astor Place in both leading and secondary parts, at times alongside her father. Caterina performed there in February 1850, in the title role in three presentations of *Norma*, with Amalia as Adalgisa. A year later Caterina made her final opera appearance in New York in a scene from Donizetti's *Marino Faliero*.

This Astor Place season ended with Maretzek having made considerable sums of money despite other musical competition, a success he attributed to the American debut (4 November 1850) and later performances of soprano Teresa Parodi. Salvatore, however, found himself in an antithetic fiscal situation, but before long discovered a means to solvency through his youngest child.

Adelina often said that before having learned how to talk, she had sung and trilled. Heredity and other familial influences played a remarkable part in her early artistic development. At a young age she revealed exceptional promise in music, seemingly having absorbed it from birth, if not in pre-natal life, possessing a preternaturally refined musical faculty duly blossoming in home surroundings where music and the theater pervaded daily existence as continual subjects as well as inspiration. In time she warbled melodies heard at home and the theater to entertain her dolls. Then, too, the presence of artists outside her family must have fostered her love of music and theater. Music critic Richard Grant White recalled visiting the Pattis' dwelling, where the dark, bright-eyed Adelina had repeatedly interrupted his conversation until irate Caterina reprimanded her, at which point "with the freedom of Italian childhood, she who was to be the '*diva Patti*' . . . half sat upon [his] knee, swinging one little red-stockinged leg as she glanced from her mother's face to [his]." White then asked Caterina whether she thought her child might some day become a singer. She replied:

> "*Lo spero; lo credo*" [I hope so; I believe so]. And then "*Canta . . . , Adelina, per il signore*" [Sing, Adelina, for the gentleman]; and she suggested something, whereupon the girl, without leaving her perch, sang, like a bird, a little Italian air . . . and soon ran away on some childish errand.[20]

Though deeply affectionate, young Adelina was also headstrong and difficult, already an individual to be seen and heard and the antithesis of idealized Victorian childhood.

Above all, Adelina was attracted to the experience of opera. Various artists, scenery, make-up, the chorus, orchestra, stage effects, costuming, and audience made profound impressions. She internalized much of what she saw and heard while attending a rehearsal or performance and when observing the comings and goings of her relatives and other artists.

In solitude, she relived performances:

> When, after being brought home, I had been put to bed, I used to quietly get up again, and, by the light of the night-lamp, play over all the scenes I had witnessed in the theatre. A cloak of my father's, with a red lining, and an old hat and feathers belonging to my mother, did duty as an extensive wardrobe, and so I acted, danced, and twittered—barefooted but romantically draped—all the operas. No, not even the applause and the wreaths were wanting; I used to play audience as well, applauding and flinging myself nosegays, which I manufactured by no means clumsily out of large newspapers crumpled up together.[21]

Adelina was especially inspired by Caterina's operatic moments, all of which she attended. Also inspirational, no doubt, were Clotilda, Amalia, and such leading women artists as Balbina Steffanone and Angelina Bosio, members of a company from Havana who made their New York debuts the spring of 1850. Bosio especially roused audiences and was later a sensation in London, Paris, and St. Petersburg. There was, however, a preeminent star, first appearing in New York the fall of 1850, who no doubt eclipsed all others in Adelina's early musical experience: Jenny Lind, whose name, fame, fees, philanthropy, and publicity (thanks to her American manager P. T. Barnum) had generated fantastic interest in the United States even before she sang a note.

Lind disembarked in New York on 1 September 1850, while some thirty thousand spectators manifested wild enthusiasm. By nightfall dense crowds blocked the area around her hotel. The *Tribune* celebrated Lind's frenzied reception with four columns on its first page, while the *Herald* found her presence as significant as would-be appearances of Dante, Tasso, Raphael, Shakespeare, Goethe, or Michelangelo.[22] Never before had a singer created such a furor in New York, a circumstance surely not lost on seven-year-old Adelina. She was soon singing songs Lind included in her concerts, and she identified herself with the singer in a photo, where she pointed to a picture of Lind on a piece of sheet music.

By the time Adelina heard the Swedish nightingale, she had begun singing lessons. Though in later life she maintained her stepbrother Ettore Barili had been her only vocal teacher, other individuals provided some initial instruction: her stepbrother Antonio and Italian opera singer Eliza Valentini Paravelli, who also taught Adelina how to read and write and whose husband said Adelina began studying with his wife in 1850. She received piano lessons from her sister Carlotta.

Her parents also assisted in music matters. Years later she especially remembered her father's admonition regarding vocal development after having heard her repeatedly singing F above high C:

> "Adelina," he exclaimed, with his utmost sternness, "if I hear you sing that note again I will never speak to you."
>
> "Oh, father," I rejoined, wholly unabashed, "that F is very easy for me."
>
> "Remember," he said solemnly, "that F, for which you try so hard and make so little of when you have reached it, is the enemy that lies in wait for all the beauty of your voice. Sing F above and your father tells you that you will become mute below."[23]

As a music student, Adelina responded well to instruction, making rapid progress. Legendary Wagnerian soprano Lilli Lehmann declared that Adelina possessed "unconsciously, as a gift of nature, a union of all those qualities that all other singers must attain and possess consciously. Her talent, and her remarkably trained ear, maintained control over the beauty of her singing and of her voice."[24]

Adelina sang ballads and opera arias well from the age of four, incredible as this seems. She later said that scales, trills, ornaments, and fioriture came naturally to her and that though she had always studied sedulously, she never laboriously toiled.

While amenable to musical instruction, Adelina could be uncooperative and unpleasant in other dealings, occasionally mirroring her mother's temperament. Years thereafter, Carlotta told her husband, cellist Ernst de Munck, that Caterina and Salvatore had always favored Adelina and inflated the child's ego.

An incident with the conductor/composer Luigi Arditi reveals her waywardness. One day, as her mother conferred with Arditi on an opera score, Adelina suddenly and inexplicably vented her ire or frustration on him by overturning an inkstand on a manuscript he had just composed for a current love interest, spoiling not only the composition but also his landlady's carpet. Shocked, then furious, Arditi spanked her to the sounds of Caterina's apologies. He wrote in his memoirs that she might

> enter the room as bright as a ray of sunshine, all smiles and sweetness; but if any one had had the misfortune to ruffle the pretty brows or thwart My Lady Wilful, her dark eyes would flash, her tiny fist would contract with anger, and clouds would speedily gather across the surface of her laughing face and burst forth in torrents of tears almost as quickly as a flash of lightning.[25]

When not involved in music or other studies, Adelina probably sewed, rolled a hoop down the street, shopped at such stores as Stewart's dry goods emporium on Broadway, or, in the winter, rode on a sled or public sleigh. Gene Schermerhorn, who grew up in New York in the 1840s, recalled Broadway sleighing: "The sleighs all had at least four horses and sometimes six, eight, or ten. I have known sixteen and twenty on some of the larger ones. People used to crowd in and hang on the outside, while there always seemed room for one more.... Every small boy who could not ride, seemed to feel like taking it out of those who could by pelting them with snowballs."[26]

For years Adelina could be seen around the small brick house Salvatore rented until the mid 1850s at 170 East Tenth Street next to Third Avenue, close to two landmark churches—St. Mark's in the Bowery and Grace Church—and to a Broadway stretch holding such childhood delights as Felix Effray's chocolate store, Dean's candy emporium, and Wagner's ice cream saloon, all between Seventh and Tenth streets.

On East Tenth Street the Patti family aroused indignation, for Italians were not welcomed by everyone in the then exclusive part of town. Long afterwards a former neighbor, Katherine Foot, recalled Adelina as a child victimized by discrimination, an exotic, tabooed playmate disapproved of by socially conscious mothers as a girl who was both Italian and the child of opera singers.

Katherine first saw Adelina standing in a window,

> balancing herself on the tips of her toes, and leaning over the iron guard in front of ... low French windows, to see how far she

could reach without falling over and out into the area. . . . When she finally concluded that she had reached over as far as she possibly could she stood up straight on the windowsill,[27]

whereupon the two stared at each other until Katherine, "quite satisfied as to exactly what an Italian looked like,"[28] continued to roll her hoop up and down the street.

Several later encounters were less reassuring. In one of these Katherine saw Adelina deliberately catch hold of a passing gentleman's coattails, insisting he let her propel him in the street. The passerby told her that she was naughty and should go home. At another time Adelina caused Katherine to receive a retribution. Though forbidden to cross Fourth Avenue, she disobeyed when joining Adelina on Broadway to see a band parade, at which event the two jumped up and down in excitement over the music. Afterwards, Katherine again gyrated, but to a different tune, when her mother dealt with the offence.

Katherine was awestruck at Adelina's ability to get what she wanted—for instance when her threats to harm herself resulted in a new doll like one of Katherine's: a wax doll with a wire under its petticoats for blinking the eyes.

Children generally enjoyed Adelina's company, but were fearful of provoking her because of her "passionate and . . . vindictive temper."[29] Nonetheless, she remained the source of much entertainment with her gift of languages, speaking English, French, and Italian; her mimicry of any unusual mannerisms; and her incredible tales of an opera house with its lore and personalities (girls were especially enthralled by descriptions of how the artists make up their faces). In her backyard she occasionally sang songs such as "Yankee Doodle," embellished with trills, and danced before her little neighbors perched on top of a fence, telling her audience when to applaud and when to throw bouquets composed of handfuls of grass or crumpled newspapers. Adelina early recognized the value of a claque.

Above all, some of these playmates admired her concern for the needy. Beggar girls often appeared on East Tenth Street asking for charity, with their stories invariably the same: dead father, sick mother, hungry brothers and sisters, no money—or "hapo" as they called it. Adelina responded with "her own slender means, with her warm-hearted, childish kisses, and her simple words of endearment."[30]

Still, her time away from studies remained limited. Occasionally rebelling, she

> would escape into the yard and climb to the very top of the grapevine trellis, and sit and sing at the top of her lungs. Then her mother and her sisters, Amalia and Carlotta, would go to the windows and call, "Adelina, Adelina," and pour out volleys of Italian in a vain attempt to keep her from singing out-of-doors, and injuring her throat. She was perfectly safe on the top of the trellis, for . . . nothing brought Adelina down, except her own will and desire.[31]

Nonetheless, practicing and studying did not harm her vocally. This is substantiated in the words of Arditi, who first met the child when he was concertizing with contra-bassist Giovanni Bottesini in New York in the late 1840s:

> The first time I ever set eyes on Adelina was in New York, when she and her mother visited the hotel at which I lived, in order to eat the macaroni which was always excellently prepared by an Italian *chef* of renown; and her determined little airs and manners then already showed plainly that she was destined to become a ruler of men. . . . Adelina's mother was anxious that I should hear the child sing, and so she brought her little daughter to my rooms one day.[32]

Arditi and Bottesini noted the

> air of importance with which the tiny songstress first selected a comfortable seat for her doll in such proximity that she was able to see her while singing, and then, having said, "*Là, ma bonne petite, attends que ta Maman te chante quelque chose de jolie*" [There, my good little one, wait while your Mama sings you something pretty], she demurely placed her music on the piano. [33]

Adelina's selection was not a child's simple song but the difficult aria "Ah! non giunge" from *La sonnambula*. Upon its completion Arditi and Bottesini "wept genuine tears of emotion, tears which were the outcome of the original and never-to-be-forgotten impression her voice made."[34] After having heard her sing several other arias, Arditi concluded that Bottesini and he had been "simply amazed, nay, electrified, at the well-nigh perfect manner in which she delivered some of the most difficult and varied arias without the slightest effort or self-consciousness."[35]

Even then, Adelina seemed ready for public acclaim and begged for an opportunity to help her parents financially, aware that various valued objects had already been pawned.

Caterina and Salvatore must have been amazed by the rapid progress Adelina made in her musical and vocal studies and by the quality of her voice with its extensive range. Her tenacious memory, musical ear, and the uncanny way she imitated melodies as sung by veteran performers did not escape their attention; nor did the enthusiastic responses of Arditi, Bottesini, Maretzek, and various personalities associated with the Astor Place Opera House, where she often sang a Verdi aria or one of Jenny Lind's songs "to the delight and astonishment of the singers and other persons present."[36] If they needed absolute proof of Adelina's ability, her rendition at home of the aria "Casta diva" from *Norma* held them spellbound, its execution virtually flawless.

To promote a professional appearance, Salvatore asked Maretzek to include her on a forthcoming program. Maretzek responded enthusiastically, remembering her singing at Astor Place and a rehearsal of *Norma* he had conducted with Caterina in the title role and Amalia as Adalgisa, when Adelina, on stage as one of Norma's children, persisted in singing with her mother and sister the duet "Mira, o Norma!" until exasperated Caterina gave the would-be trio member a spanking.

Adelina was all of eight, not seven as some have mistakenly reported, when on 22 November 1851, she debuted in New York's Tripler Hall, singing Eckart's "Echo Song" and "I Am a Bayadère." Years later she recalled this occasion:

> I didn't care for much to eat that evening, but nobody paid any attention to my want of appetite. I coaxed my mother, and she braided my hair and powdered my tiny brown face. We burned candles in those days, and I can still see myself looking for many

1 A young Salvatore Patti. As a secondary tenor, he created the role of Ismaele in the world premiere of Donizetti's *Alahor di Granata.* Courtesy The Billy Rose Theatre Collection, The New York Public Library for the Performing Arts, Astor, Lenox and Tilden Foundations.

2 Also an opera singer, Patti's mother, Caterina Barili-Patti, had already borne four children and been widowed before she married Salvatore Patti and started a second family of four, of whom Adelina was the youngest. Courtesy Mary Barili Goldsmith.

3 Patti in 1851, the year she made her concert debut at New York's Tripler Hall on 22 November. Courtesy Murry & Leonie Guggenheim Memorial Library, Monmouth College.

4 Patti points to a picture of Jenny Lind on a sheet of music, 1851. During her 1852–54 concert tour, Patti was billed as "La Petite Jenny Lind." Courtesy The Billy Rose Theatre Collection, The New York Public Library for the Performing Arts, Astor, Lenox and Tilden Foundations.

5 Patti in 1853, when she toured North America with Ole Bull; her brother-in-law, pianist Maurice Strakosch; and her father. Courtesy Stuart-Liff.

6 Maurice Strakosch married Patti's sister Amalia then toured with Patti as accompanist and manager from 1852 to 1854. Courtesy Murry & Leonie Guggenheim Memorial Library, Monmouth College.

7 Norwegian violin virtuoso Ole Bull was already a household name when he joined Patti on her first American tour. In Norway he had helped to support young playwright Henrik Ibsen and served as inspiration for *Peer Gynt.* Courtesy Murry & Leonie Guggenheim Memorial Library, Monmouth College.

8 Patti's stepbrother Ettore Barili created the title role in Verdi's *Rigoletto* in its American premiere. Patti credited him with establishing her method of vocal production. Courtesy Mary Barili Goldsmith.

9 Ettore Barili's wife, Antoinetta Barili. She and Ettore and their son, Alfredo, lived with the Pattis in New York City and in Westchester County. Courtesy Mary Barili Goldsmith.

10 The house the Pattis built in 1855 and sold in 1867. Patti lived here from time to time between 1855 and late 1860. This recent photo of the house at 4718 Matilda Avenue, Bronx, shows a latter-day change to the original red-brick facade. Author's Collection.

11 Patti's nephew Alfredo Barili at the age of three. He became a superb pianist, a source of pride for his aunt. Courtesy Mary Barili Goldsmith.

12 Patti and violin prodigy Paul Julien, who together toured Cuba in April and May 1856. Courtesy Murry & Leonie Guggenheim Memorial Library, Monmouth College.

13 Louis Moreau Gottschalk, piano virtuoso and composer, toured the Caribbean with teenage Patti and her father, who served as chaperone. A notorious womanizer, Gottschalk may have given Salvatore some difficult moments. Courtesy Murry & Leonie Guggenheim Memorial Library, Monmouth College.

15 Salvatore became a naturalized U.S. citizen on 28 August 1855. Like his wife, he was eager for Patti's opera debut but deferred to the judgment of his son-in-law, Maurice Strakosch. Courtesy Stuart-Liff.

14 Caterina Barili-Patti disagreed with Maurice Strakosch over the timing of Patti's opera debut. She would have set the date earlier than 1859, when Patti made her debut at the age of sixteen. Courtesy The Billy Rose Theatre Collection, The New York Public Library for the Performing Arts, Astor, Lenox and Tilden Foundations.

16 Patti made her opera debut as Lucia on 24 November 1859 at New York's Academy of Music. Patti said that night she was "thoroughly up in several parts, and ... did not know what stagefright meant." Courtesy William R. Moran.

minutes into the mirror of my bedroom, with the heavy shadows behind me, before we set out for the theatre. . . . [The] curtain went up, and I came on. I think everybody in the house must have applauded, for, besides having a great many friends there, it would have been hard of anybody not to have been interested in so young a *cantatrice*. They told me afterward that from those first notes nobody had any doubt that I was a success and a born prima donna. . . . When the curtain went down . . . I saw a great number of men and women clapping and waving their hands and crying "Brava, brava!" and even the gods in the gallery tried to whistle as loud as they could, and . . . the gods were my personal friends. There are no street arabs like those of New York. They had long before nicknamed me "The Little Chinese Girl" because of my black eyes and yellowish features.

Then I remember my father catching me up in his arms and kissing me, and my mother and all the members of the company petting me as if I had done something wonderful indeed; but it was not more than I expected to do.[37]

Besides Adelina the gala featured two solo instrumentalists, illustrious opera singers, and the orchestra of the Astor Place Opera House under Maretzek's direction. Surrounded by such an array of talent, the prodigy began where she remained throughout her career: at the top.

Of her contributions the *Tribune* reported:

The peculiar feature of the evening was the debut of Adelina Patti, a mere child . . . yet a Jenny Lind in miniature, a petite nightingale, whose performances were indeed surprising. She sang the difficult and eccentric "Echo Song" with remarkable effect, and entirely astonished her audience not only by her powers of voice, but by the self-possession and ease which could not have been looked for in one so young.[38]

The next day a number of neighborhood children including Katherine Foot gathered at Adelina's house to congratulate her. Katherine recalled that when she and others had earlier gone out to play,

the little girl next door told us that her father and mother had taken her to that very concert the night before on purpose to hear Adelina sing, and that she had sung one of the songs that we had often heard her sing . . . and that she had had a bouquet

25

given her, all to herself, and that she had [curtsied] herself backward. We all felt her reflected glory . . . and presently she spied us and came dancing out and asked us all in to see her flowers.[39]

In the following seven months Adelina appeared in seven more New York concerts, astounding audiences with such arias as "Ah! non giunge" from *La sonnambula*. At some of these affairs, she stood upon a table so that the public might get a better view of her, a veritable singing doll. Adelina said that Signora Valentini Paravelli used to make her take this position to sing.

About this time a boy born the same year as she first heard her. Decades later he recalled "the image of the infant phenomenon Adelina Patti . . . in a fan-like little white frock and 'pantalettes' and a hussar-like red jacket, mounted on an armchair, its back supporting her, wheeled to the front of the stage and warbling like a tiny thrush even in the nest."[40] The writer of these words was Henry James.

Adelina's successful New York concerts inspired Salvatore to plan a tour for her beginning in the fall of 1852, a risky venture due to the hardships of travel by train, steamboat, and stagecoach as well as the physical and psychological strain for a nine-year-old under pressure to perform in unfamiliar settings. Nonetheless, Salvatore, still financially pressed, proceeded with arrangements, assisted by Amalia's husband, Maurice Strakosch (they married on 8 May 1852).

Born in 1825, Maurice Strakosch made his debut as a concert pianist at age eleven, subsequently gaining fame in Austria and Germany. Then, finding his interest shifting to singing, he studied in Italy with legendary soprano Giuditta Pasta, for whom Bellini had written *Norma* and *La sonnambula*. Maurice failed, however, as an opera tenor and returned to the concert stage as a pianist. He met Salvatore in October 1843, appearing in a musical event in Vicenza, Italy, that also featured Clotilda Barili. Maurice was a flamboyant personality, piano virtuoso, and astute artist manager, who after immigrating to the United States in 1848 concertized throughout the republic and who, while in New York, renewed his friendship with Salvatore and fell in love with Amalia.

In this series, Maurice served as both soloist and Adelina's accompanist, also supervising her daily vocal practice, never allowing her to forego exercises and scales, a circumstance that later gave the impression he had been her vocal teacher. He coached Adelina in the arias and songs she regularly performed and added new pieces to her repertoire along with embellishments and cadenzas for arias. In the first programs on tour Maurice also accompanied young violin prodigy Miska Hauser. Adelina's contributions generally consisted of an opera aria or two and several ballads, such as "Comin' thro' the Rye," "Robin Adair," and "Home, Sweet Home." With these songs she often brought tears to the audience.

A man who visited her backstage and later heard her sing a ballad told of his experiences:

> She was playing with a doll, in company with a little girl of her own age, and was sitting in the artist's anteroom during the progress of a concert at which she had to sing. Our friend was fascinated by her charming and unaffected *naiveté,* and told her he should certainly go round to the front as soon as her time arrived to sing. "Oh, that *is* kind!" said the child; adding, "If you like, I'll make the people cry. Would you like to see me make the people cry? Well, when I'm encored (they are sure to encore me!), see if I don't make them cry!" As she had predicted, her first song, which was a brilliant "air and variations," was encored. On her return to the platform, she gave a glance at her new acquaintance, and sang an old English ballad, with such intensely pathetic expression, that he, as well as "the people," found it impossible to refrain from tears. On his return to the anteroom, he found the little singer, who so lately before had appeared to be overpowered with emotion, already re-possessed of her doll, and romping with her playmate; ceasing her play, for a moment only, to give him a merrily triumphant glance, as she said, "Well, the people *did* cry, *didn't* they? I told you so! And you cried, too! I saw you!"[41]

Whatever Adelina sang, so advertisements trumpeted, had been made famous by such great artists as Malibran, Lind, and two other distinguished singers appearing in the United States in 1852: Marietta Alboni, Rossini's pupil and the contralto Walt Whitman considered the most glorious singer of all, and the soprano Henriette Sontag, a classic beauty and exquisite artist. Alboni's presence was especially welcomed by the Patti family, since she had engaged in

Europe Caterina's son basso Nicolo Barili as a member of her opera company.

Adelina, billed as La Petite Jenny Lind, began touring early in September 1852 with concerts in New Haven and Hartford, Connecticut, and Springfield, Massachusetts. From the 21st to the 30th she, Maurice, and Hauser performed on five occasions in Philadelphia, where a local critic described her voice as "wonderfully clear, strong and sympathetic in its tones,"[42] adding that the upper register was especially powerful and effective, that she brilliantly sang several difficult songs Jenny Lind had performed in Philadelphia, and that her amazing vocal flexibility enabled her to render easily trills, chromatic scales, and complicated cadenzas "with almost the sweetness of facility with which a nightingale would warble its notes."[43] At Baltimore, the next tour site, the three performers protracted their stay, giving nine concerts from 5 to 20 October. Adelina's reviews echoed earlier ones, the *Sun* reporting that "the most prominent prima donna might take a lesson in style and execution from the exquisite warblings of this gifted child."[44]

Then the unexpected occurred and altered Salvatore's plans. Forty-two-year-old Norwegian violin virtuoso Ole Bull, who, like Jenny Lind, had become a household name in the United States and whose playing appealed to the unmusical as well as to connoisseurs, was then in Baltimore and, aware of the young singer's box-office appeal, contracted with Adelina and Maurice to join him on tour. In past American seasons he had made large profits, earning as much as $3000 at a concert.

The three became a formidable attraction in travels lasting until spring 1854 and extending from the East Coast and Canadian cities to as far South as New Orleans and to the Western towns of St. Louis and Chicago. At times Amalia Patti Strakosch joined them in concerts. Of their many programs, an unforgettable one occurred on 7 November 1853, when President Franklin Pierce was present at a Washington gala.

Years later, Maurice wrote in his memoirs that Adelina had occasionally exhibited prima donna airs, was temperamental, capricious, and imperious, getting her own way by refusing to sing until others met her requirements. In Cincinnati he placated her by purchasing a doll, and once, after Bull had refused her a second glass of champagne, Adelina slapped his face. Decades thereafter she said that Bull had been "a gentle, kind old man, and like a mother" to her. She then added: "What a little child I was to be going about with only those men! Not a woman . . . only papa—poor papa!—and Maurice and Ole Bull, and I was a little tyrant, I dare say, to all three of them."[45] By the end of the tour Adelina's, really Salvatore's, share of profits amounted to $20,000.

During months on the road she presented a dazzling image, a golden child blessed with a glorious voice. Music historian George Upton, hearing her at a Chicago concert, remembered the young star as "a somewhat delicate, pale-faced, dark-browed child, with thick glossy black hair hanging in two long braids down her back, dressed in rose-colored silk, pink stockings, and pantalettes," singing arias at an age when other children rendered "Twinkle, twinkle" if any song whatsoever. Upton also recalled Adelina as an imperious child who loathed encores: "When they were called for, she would refuse to give them. The insistence of the audience at last would exasperate her, and she would shake her head vigorously. Thereupon the amused audience would redouble its efforts, only ceasing when she began to manifest anger by stamping her little foot."[46]

American humorist Artemus Ward portrayed "little Patti" in his own inimitable style:

> When Mister Strackhorse led her out I thawt sum pretty skool gal, who had jest graduatid frum pantalets & wire hoops, was a cumin out to read her fust composishun in public. She cum so bashful like, with her hed bowd down, & made sich a effort to arrange her lips so thayd look pretty, that I wanted to swaller her. . . . When she opened her mowth a army of martingales, bobolinks, kanarys, swallers, mockin' birds, essettery, bust 4th & flew all over the Haul.[47]

Occasionally Adelina dropped the public persona. While singing at one concert, she caught sight of two little girls sitting near the stage and impulsively cried out to them that as soon as she finished, they should join her outside and play. She did the same at a Chicago program, publicly telling her little friend Nellie to visit her after the concert.

Privately, Adelina presented quite a different image: often miserable, experiencing periods of intense dreariness and loneliness, longing for home and the companionship of other children. To keep up her spirits, Bull occasionally participated in childish games, while Maurice invited other children to visit. An episode in a Southern town reflects his efforts in this respect while revealing her in a pathetic light.

One morning Maurice introduced Adelina to two blonde girls whose parents approved their spending time in her hotel room. She devised a game whereby she was a photographer taking their pictures, telling them how to pose. Then reversing her role, she assumed such droll faces and positions that the two girl photographers exploded in fits of laughter. After lunch the three played another game, also devised by Adelina: opera. She outlined plots, gave instruction as to playing the various parts, and directed them in their histrionic efforts. Her own dramatic examples chilled them. If the scene required mourning over the body of a late beloved, she performed it with gusto, even going mad *à la* Lucia, raving and ranting over the body of one of her newfound friends playing dead.

Later the girls were present while Adelina was dressed for the evening's concert:

> Oh, the wonder of it! To see the little pink silk robe, with its graduated bands of black velvet and lace, spread out upon the bed, not by a mother's careful touch, but by a father's hand; the tiny boots laced up neatly, and the tumbled locks braided, looped around the little ears, adorned with velvet rosettes, and diamonds hung therein; then a pair of kid gloves coaxed on the dark, little hands, and by degrees, before their eyes, the lassies beheld their little, frowsy, careless romp of the play-room transformed into a wonderful young lady in silk and jewels—a prima donna.[48]

At the concert the girls marveled even more at Adelina's transformation and found her singing exquisite. When the program concluded they waited to congratulate her and found her in tears: "We are going away to-night . . . and I never knew it!" cried the child, throwing her arms around her two little friends. "And Maurice says I must say good-bye, and I shall never see you again. Promise me you will never forget me!" With passionate embraces and tears, she repeated over and over, "Promise me you will never, *never* forget me!"[49]

This was one of many such situations for Adelina:

If the journey was at night, . . . my father would turn over a seat, bundle me up in a shawl, and I would go off to sleep. Sometimes we would arrive at our destination late at night and no supper was to be had. Then I would eat my bread and cheese with a glass of water and feel quite content if they would only let me have my doll.[50]

Years later Adelina recalled an element in these early experiences with righteous indignation: "I was always very serious and unhappy as a girl. Everybody was making money out of me and I was a mere prey to every mercenary person around me."[51]

By the end of the tour in the spring of 1854, she began to show strain in her singing, her voice beginning to tremble as a result of fatigue and exploitation. To avoid ruining it, for months she rarely sang in public. In early 1855, however, Adelina concertized in New York on 20 and 27 January and 27 February, singing several selections per program.

Since her voice needed rest, there followed a time when she rarely uttered a note. Perhaps Adelina then discovered her life's motto: "*Chi va piano va sano e chi è sano va lontano* [Who goes slowly goes safely; who goes safely goes far]."[52] Looking back, she said, "While I was suffering this enforced but necessary silence I used to go often to the theatre and [met] my operatic heroines there."[53] Most were probably portrayed by the soprano Giulia Grisi, who with her "husband," the great tenor known simply as Mario, appeared in New York opera from September 1854 to late February 1855 and who was occasionally assisted by Amalia and Salvatore.

Grisi and Mario had long reigned supreme in Paris and London and other European music centers, captivating audiences by their glorious singing, dramatic interpretations, and personal beauty. Both excelled in a variety of roles in the Rossini-Bellini-Donizetti repertoire, Mario also in Meyerbeer operas.

Adelina was most likely at Castle Garden when on 4 September 1854 these celebrities made their New York debuts in *Lucrezia Borgia* with a cast including Amalia and Salvatore. Adelina may also have seen their performances of *Norma* and *I puritani*, in whose world premieres Grisi had created the roles of Adalgisa and Elvira. Then the two began a season in the new and sumptuous Academy of Music at Irving Place and Fourteenth Street—a setting that dominated New York's opera world for three decades thereafter—opening on 2 October in *Norma*, with Salvatore in the cast.

The Academy's auditorium presented a handsome effect: extending eighty feet from floor to dome, brilliantly painted with mythological figures; lighted throughout by gas; decorated with ornamented fronts on the first two tiers, supported by pillars topped with busts; and holding some forty-six hundred people. At each side of the gilded proscenium were eighteen elegant boxes topped with three large figures holding trumpets. The stage was forty-eight feet wide and seventy feet deep. In all, the house was an impressive venue with perfect acoustics.

Adelina always remembered an episode related to or in the Grisi-Mario series, occurring after a performance and revealing her vulnerability:

> I hurried behind the scenes, and, approaching Grisi, in my childish admiration offered her a few simple flowers. But to my infinite mortification the *cantatrice,* with the deafening applause of the audience in her ears, brushed me aside. The tears welled up in my eyes, and I turned and proffered the poor little blossoms listlessly to Mario. He at once took them graciously and fastened them to his coat. Then, lifting me in his arms, he kissed my cheek and said: "I shall keep these always, little one, in memory of you."[54]

Grisi's rudeness may have resulted from the presence of an English lady who attended that and every presentation in which Mario performed. Idolizing him, this creature customarily sat in a spacious box easily seen from stage and had shadowed Mario for over two years. The jealous Grisi resented such an obsession and was so enflamed by her *bête noire* that she scarcely knew what to do or say.

Meanwhile, Adelina took singing lessons from her stepbrother Ettore Barili, who had recently disembarked in the United States with his wife, Antoinetta, and their four-month-old son, Alfredo, and settled at the Tenth Street dwelling. Having sung in opera in Italy, Ettore hoped to continue his operatic career in the New World; and for a number of years he did so without achieving much acclaim. He did, however, assume the title role in Verdi's *Rigoletto* in its American premiere on 19 February 1855, at New York's Academy of Music in a short-lived company which Ole Bull managed. In this production the *Times* reviewed his voice and acting favorably:

> Signor Barili has a good baritone, highly cultivated, impressive and finished. If he would avoid dragging the time, and resist the temptation of a *crescendo* or *diminuendo* occasionally, (he can execute these things very well, though) he would be much more enjoyable. The upper part of Signor Barili's voice is exceedingly clear and powerful; he phrases well, and possesses some dramatic ability.[55]

This premiere also featured stepsister Amalia, assuming the role of Maddalena. Ultimately Ettore's greatest contribution to music was the instruction he gave Adelina, who always acknowledged him as the teacher providing the foundation and finish of her vocal method. "It was he," she said, "who saved my voice. He never forced it; he never permitted me to strain it. And yet he taught me all that could be learned in the Italian school of singing."[56] Earlier lessons with Antonio Barili and Eliza Valentini Paravelli had been merely diversions or a spasmodic succession of lessons. Ettore's instruction, by contrast, was given, according to Adelina, "quite systematically, and not as a mere amusement or by fits and starts."[57] Years later pianist Wilhelm Kuhe, among others, declared that she had never required a singing teacher: "I maintain that Adelina Patti would still have been all that she was . . . and is . . . even if no one had trained her in voice production—scales, shakes, and all the other departments of vocal tuition. In her, all accomplishments of that kind were inborn."[58]

Some months after Adelina had begun lessons with Ettore, the family moved from New York City to a small town near the metropolis, Wakefield in Westchester County. Here Caterina bought land in May 1855 for $625 with profits from Adelina's tour. Caterina and Salvatore later erected the first brick house in the area, a dwelling now located at 4718 Matilda Avenue in the Bronx. This property remained in the family's possession until May 1867. Before Adelina's departure from the city, Katherine Foot recalled seeing her on East Tenth Street for the last time: "I remember perfectly how she looked that afternoon with two long, black braids hanging far below her waist, very black eyes and a slightly protruding under jaw. Her manners were quiet and modest, and she seemed more like the other girls."[59]

In Wakefield Adelina continued studying with Ettore and briefly attended school, where at times her piano playing and singing in music classes so intrigued other students that they paid attention to little else. At home she looked after her young nephew, Alfredo, who recalled that she sang to him and that when the elders were absent, she ate porridge she had been told to feed to him. Often, she and other children played in nearby fields and wandered by the banks of the Bronx River. Quite athletic, Adelina enjoyed bucolic pleasures and activities which ended when, in the early months of 1856, Salvatore determined that she was ready to make a tour of Cuba with Ettore Barili, pianist August Göckel, and violin prodigy Paul Julien, whose mother, like Salvatore, accompanied her teenage phenomenon.

Adelina arrived in Havana via New Orleans on 7 April 1856 and made her local concert debut seven days later to critical and popular acclaim, having sung a duet with Ettore, the aria "Ah! non giunge," the air "La calesera," and Eckart's "Echo Song." After a second Havana concert on 18 April, a critic of *Prensa de la Habana* wrote that Adelina had given new proofs of her musical genius in her renditions of "Casta diva" from *Norma* and "Una voce poco fa" from *Il barbiere di Siviglia,* and that she was destined to become the world's greatest singer. Later they performed seven concerts in other Cuban cities, most often in Havana. This whirlwind tour abruptly ended with disagreements between Julien's mother and Salvatore, so rumors ran, and on 14 May, Adelina, Ettore, and Salvatore embarked for New York, followed a few days after by Paul Julien, his mother, and Göckel.

Several months later Salvatore made arrangements for yet another tour outside the United States, this to feature, alongside Adelina, the hedonistic and flamboyant twenty-seven-year-old American piano virtuoso and composer Louis Moreau Gottschalk, who was a European and American matinee idol, Chopin's and Berlioz's friend, and an inveterate womanizer. Such an arresting personality required Salvatore's watchful eye as his daughter's chaperone.

Leaving the United States on 7 February 1857, Adelina, Salvatore, and Gottschalk arrived in Havana on the twelfth, one week before her fourteenth birthday. After some sensational programs there they toured Cuba for several months before giving lucrative concerts on the island of St. Thomas and in Charlotte Amalie. In St. Thomas they experienced a minor earthquake during a concert, at which Adelina did not panic and urged the audience to remain in the hall. They arrived in San Juan in July, and Puerto Rico so enchanted them they remained on the island for months. From November to February Adelina and Gottschalk gave a series of concerts in Ponce, where, reported *El Fénix*, they royally entertained and were entertained in return. In his journal, Gottschalk remarked on the gracious hospitality of a wealthy man and his wife on their plantation in Plazuela:

> I have spent four weeks on the plantation of Mr. K. There I found that cordial and assiduous hospitality which has become proverbial when we speak of Plazuela. But what cannot be imagined is the grace, the distinction, and the cordiality with which Monsieur and Madame K. do the honors of their comfortable mansion.... Frequently some visitors came from Manati, Arecibo, or some of the neighboring plantations.... I played or improvised according to the caprice of my imagination; Adelina and Madam K. sang a duet.[60]

In May Adelina and Gottschalk concertized in San Juan, where she met her first romantic suitor, José Rios:

> I was sitting on the balcony waiting for my turn to sing when this tall, handsome young fellow first came under my notice. I don't know why he should have found any attraction in me, for I was a plain little girl with sallow skin, two black plaits hanging down my back, and eyes that, in an uncanny way, seemed much too big for my face. He was most kind to me, and in those days, when we had little of the world's goods, his consideration made a great impression on me ... and when ... Rios asked my father for my hand I had little idea of even the meaning of marriage.[61]

Though met with refusal, this man did not lose hope, but awaited an opportunity to renew his suit.

Months after her return to New York on 27 July 1858, Adelina wrote Rios that he had not been forgotten despite his protests to the contrary; that she hoped he would write often; and that she wished he would come to New York during the summer. Her only amusement for the past two months had been sleigh riding. Music studies and lessons dominated hours of each day. Adelina ended her letter with two pasted-in verses cut from a newspaper:

> My heart is with thee night and day,
> In sunshine and in shower,
> And languidly I'd fondly say,
> How much I own his power.
>
> Oh could I hear thee once declare,
> That fond affection lives for me,
> Oh, could I once delighted share,
> The sweet return of love from thee.[62]

Though her heart may have been with Rios in sunshine and shower, what increasingly occupied Adelina was not romance but her music studies and determination to make her operatic debut as soon as possible. While still looking like a child, she had already become a strong woman in her career aspirations.

Though for months Caterina and Salvatore had thought Adelina ready for her debut, Maurice opposed it, convinced she needed more time for vocal development. He persuaded them to postpone such a venture for a year, but later played a great part in realizing her dreams.

Since 1857 Maurice had been partner to veteran music agent and manager Bernard Ullmann in presenting opera at New York's Academy of Music. In their first series they introduced eminent conductor Karl Anschütz and basso Karl Formes, both well received, as was the following season's soprano Marietta Piccolomini, making her New York debut on 20 October 1858 as Violetta in *La traviata*, a role she had earlier introduced to London and Paris. Financially pressed for a third year, Maurice and Ullmann obtained a loan of $12,000 from twenty-four patrons. Maurice then engaged several European singers for the 1859–60 season, which saw a number of misfortunes in its first weeks. Convinced Adelina was ready for her opera debut, Maurice urged Ullmann, who favored European celebrities, to engage her as a principal singer.

At first Ullmann adamantly refused to consider her. According to Adelina, his refusal was primarily due to her inexperience in opera: "He objected . . . to allowing a beginner like me to come out in a leading part in New York; and I would not listen to anything about secondary parts."[63] Maurice nonetheless persisted until finally his partner reluctantly agreed to her debut before the end of 1859 with a salary of $100 per presentation. His decision was partly based on the audition she gave Emanuele Muzio, the principal conductor at the Academy and Verdi's pupil. Overjoyed, Adelina could hardly wait for her debut: "My passion for the stage and my talent had waxed wonderfully. I was thoroughly up in several parts, and I did not know what stagefright meant."[64] She already realized what was required:

> so much of everything: voice, knowledge of singing and acting. Everything has to be calculated; even a wrong step or two during a phrase will bring one into the wings instead of to the front of the stage. Ease of movement, dramatic instinct and feeling are all necessary of response with the opera singer. . . . Not alone on the stage but in the auditorium, incidents are continually arising that demand of a singer an absolute self-control, command of memory and vocal powers in the face of distractions and of danger.[65]

Meanwhile, at Amalia's and Maurice's 343 West Twenty-second Street residence between Ninth and Tenth avenues, Adelina studied with Muzio, who coached her in the part of Lucia, the opera heroine of her debut. Maurice also "altered some passages in which her voice was too severely taxed, and introduced cadenzas which enabled her to employ her marvellous upper register in the two operas of *Sonnambula* and *Lucia*."[66] Another musician at the Academy, Signor Manzocchi, later instructed her in other operatic parts.

In the days preceding her late November debut, Adelina knew only hard work and such excitement she hardly slept at night. Muzio later recalled rehearsals just prior to the event at which other principals and supporting cast members, chorus, and orchestra expressed enthusiasm for her singing. At the general rehearsal, which many guests attended, she created a sensation.

Throughout this time Adelina felt increasingly confident of success, a confidence partly based on a curious experience in New York during the past winter:

She and her sister Carlotta were present one evening at a party. By some mistake it had been neglected to order a carriage to take the young ladies home. It had been snowing heavily all day. The Misses Patti were in evening attire, their feet protected only by white satin slippers. It was two o'clock in the morning; no convenient way of getting a conveyance; the greater part of the guests had left. What could be done? Finally a gentleman had the ingenious idea of procuring a sleigh which stood before a grocery store at the corner. The Misses Patti, well wrapped in shawls and covered with blankets, got in it. The clotheslines were fetched, fastened to the sleigh; a number of gentlemen placed themselves in front of it, and drew the ladies to [Amalia and Maurice's Twenty-second Street residence].... "Never," she said afterward, "will I forget this incident, which I look upon as a good omen for my future career."[67]

CHAPTER II

Superstar

Adelina made her opera debut on 24 November 1859 as Lucia at New York City's Academy of Music with the tenor Pasquale Brignoli as Edgardo and a Signor Ferri as Ashton. A *New-York Illustrated News* critic reviewing the event declared that "the most fastidious could find no flaw" in her voice and that "the most experienced could remember no superior."[1] At sixteen she became a celebrity overnight. Hereafter, Adelina Patti became Miss Patti, or, later in Europe, Miss, Mlle., or Mme. Patti, and ultimately Diva, a title then reserved for only the supreme female opera vocalist.

Though young for such acclaim, Patti had the qualities of a finished artist, with a brilliant voice and an ease of execution that bordered on the miraculous and that in bravura passages electrified the house. She took E-flats and Fs above high C with ease while perfectly executing staccato passages and trills. The day after her debut, the *Tribune* declared: "Her voice is clear and excellent; the brilliant execution which she begins with at the outset of her career—she is only turned of sweet sixteen—ranks with that where the best singers end. This is saying a good deal, but it is not an overstatement. . . . There is in her as much sentiment as we ought to look for in one so young."[2] The *Herald* concurred but deplored her excessive embellishments and variations not of the composer's making, liberties "only pardonable in an artist who has already assured her position." The same paper, nonetheless, conceded that hers had been one of the most extraordinary debuts New York had ever seen with the

39

audience in a "positive *furore,* which was demonstrated in the usual way—recalls, bouquets, wreaths, etc., etc."[3]

With her vocal gifts, Patti created a "more profound impression than Jenny Lind,"[4] whose first New York appearance had occurred nine years before. Patti's acting and mien were less impressive but required, according to the *Times,* "nothing but a little stage practice."[5] Some reviews also revealed pride in the debutante's having reached eminence without "a transatlantic puff,"[6] the *Herald* crowing that Americans needed no longer "look to Europe for . . . singers, any more than for . . . painters, or . . . sculptors."[7] Her success also momentarily lifted the pre–Civil War gloom: "It is very refreshing . . . this oasis in the desert of politics. People are beginning to be a little tired of the . . . Union destroyers."[8]

A member of the audience later described the event and its aftermath:

> The house was crowded to excess. Miss Patti's friends and admirers, who were very numerous at that time . . . were of course all present and full of hope; but great as their expectations were, they were far surpassed. She took the house by storm; she not only sang as only she can sing, but looked lovely and acted well. Though a little timid at first, she displayed her great dramatic powers in the Mad Scene. She was simply dressed in gray silk trimmed with plaid, looked beautiful and modest. . . . The day after the performance I called to see her; her parlour looked like a flower garden, . . . so many floral tributes she was at a loss where to place them.[9]

Katherine Foot also recalled the exciting debut:

> Through my glass I saw Madame Strakosch in a proscenium box, and I thought that I recognized Carlotta also. The curtain rose and "Lucia" came in from the upper left with her attendant. She wore a gray gown . . . , and I kept my glass close to my eyes. Could that be Adelina—that slender little creature walking so calmly down to the prompter's box? It certainly was. To me that début was something personal. "Lucia" was familiar to me, but I rejoiced and sorrowed with a new "Lucia" that night, for behind all was Adelina, the little child that had been tabooed on our block.[10]

On 1 December, Patti assumed a second role for which Muzio had coached her, Amina in *La sonnambula*; it confirmed previous

17 Illustration of the young soprano. Courtesy William R. Moran.

18 & 19 Exterior and interior of New York's Academy of Music at the time of Patti's opera debut, 1859. At the Academy Patti essayed ten leading roles in the year following her debut, when she was sixteen and seventeen years old. Courtesy Murry & Leonie Guggenheim Memorial Library, Monmouth College.

20 Salvatore posing as an admonishing father to Patti, a part he often played in life, at home and abroad, during the first seasons of his daughter's operatic career. Courtesy William R. Moran.

21 & 22 Covent Garden as it appeared in May 1861, when Patti made her London debut in her "lucky" role of Amina in *La sonnambula*. She would appear on this stage for twenty-five consecutive seasons. Exterior courtesy General Research Division, The New York Public Library, Astor, Lenox and Tilden Foundations; interior courtesy Murry & Leonie Guggenheim Memorial Library, Monmouth College.

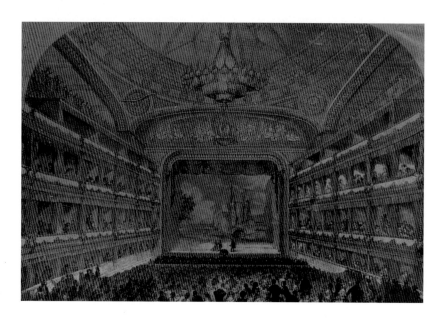

23 Patti as Amina in *La sonnambula*. London's *Illustrated Sporting and Dramatic News* reported that with her Covent Garden debut in this role, she "leaped with one bound, from comparative insignificance, to the highest pinnacle of popularity." Courtesy Stuart-Liff.

24 Patti as Violetta in *La traviata,* a role in which she triumphed at Covent Garden on 4 July 1861. Courtesy Stuart-Liff.

25 As Zerlina in *Don Giovanni*, a role Patti first performed for London audiences on 6 July 1861. Courtesy Stuart-Liff.

26 Patti's performance as Harriet in *Marta* impressed Hector Berlioz, who abhorred the opera itself. Courtesy Murry & Leonie Guggenheim Memorial Library, Monmouth College.

27 Patti always ranked Rosina as one of her favorite parts. She told Herman
Klein, "I love the comedy and the constant fun. . . . I revel in the 'Lesson Scene.' I
can do just as I please there, and . . . it always amuses me when I introduce music
that was written years after Rossini wrote the opera." Courtesy Stuart-Liff.

28 Patti's first Covent Garden appearance as Rosina took place 27 July 1861. Later, seeing Patti in the role at the Théâtre-Italien in Paris, Rossini declared her *"adorable, adorable!"* Courtesy Stuart-Liff.

29 Patti studied the part of Dinorah with the composer, Meyerbeer, and some critics considered her superior to all other artists in this role. Courtesy Stuart-Liff.

30 Patti added Leonora in *Il trovatore* to her Covent Garden repertoire in 1863; the portrayal received superb reviews. Courtesy Stuart-Liff.

31 Patti first assumed the role of
Ninetta in Rossini's *La gazza
ladra* on 6 June 1863, before a
Covent Garden audience, so
impressing the severe critic
Henry F. Chorley that he
declared it the best of her serious
characters. Courtesy Stuart-Liff.

32 Ninetta was the tenth part
Patti undertook at Covent Garden
in the two years following her
debut there. Courtesy William R.
Moran.

33 Patti as Adina in *L'elisir d'amore,* a role she assumed for the first time in an 1863 performance at Covent Garden. Courtesy Stuart-Liff.

34 The soprano as Maria in *La figlia del reggimento,* the only part Patti first assumed in Brussels and the final addition to her Covent Garden repertoire during the 1863 season. Courtesy Stuart-Liff.

impressions. She sang the florid music with marvelous facility as well as with a "delicacy of expression . . . seldom heard equaled."[11] She scattered "staccato notes about, with a toss of her little head, like a child at play."[12] Her acting was impressive, except in the second act, which required more than she offered, as she was "too young to give any dramatic significance"[13] to it. When later debuting in European cities, she invariably chose the role of Amina, a part and opera she thought particularly displayed her abilities. Then before the end of the month, Patti essayed the role of Zerlina in *Don Giovanni*, a part she had first assumed in Philadelphia on 19 December before appearing in it on the 27th at New York's Academy of Music. *The New-York Times* reported her performance "thoroughly excellent" with exquisite singing combined with "an elegance of phrasing which is rarely heard."[14]

From 3 January to 3 February 1860, Patti was in Boston, where she repeated the roles presented in New York and Philadelphia and where she introduced two parts to her repertoire, Rosina in *Il barbiere di Siviglia* on the seventeenth and Elvira in *I puritani* eight days later. A local critic wrote:

> Adelina Patti has gained a place in the esteem of the Boston public . . . seldom accorded to the most cultivated singers and actors. . . . Popular sympathy and appreciation, the impression produced by artlessness and modesty, arch and winning manners, combined with unparalleled vocalism considering the age of the performer, have made Adelina the pet of the Boston musical community.[15]

She then appeared in seven new roles at New York's Academy of Music, these being, successively, Elvira (*I puritani*); Rosina; Harriet (*Marta*); Norina (*Don Pasquale*); Anaïde (*Mosè in Egitto*); Violetta (*La traviata*); and Linda (*Linda di Chamounix*). Appearing with her in some of these productions were tenors Brignoli, Stigelli, and Errani; baritone Amodio; bass Karl Formes; and family members Amalia, Ettore, and Nicolo Barili. In all, from the debut of 24 November 1859 to her final New York performance on 8 October 1860, Patti essayed ten leading roles, an achievement remarkable, if not unprecedented, for an artist in her sixteenth and seventeenth years.

According to *The New York Herald*, Patti, by then "fairly enthroned as a popular pet,"[16] received a grand ovation as Elvira. The

Tribune evaluated her Rosina as vocally and dramatically superb with her young age "just the thing"[17] for the role. Her trim figure elicited praise from the *Times,* commenting that unlike the shapes of matronly prima donnas, Patti's bearing exemplified an ideal and should also "bring burning blushes to the cheeks of some of the male members of the company, whose angularities increase in the precise ratio of their popularity."[18] According to the *Herald* critic, Patti, as Harriet, was impressive with her soulful rendition of the ballad "The Last Rose of Summer." It combined rare sentiment, sympathy, true feeling, and elaborate execution. The *Times* ranked her performance as Norina "in every way a success,"[19] and the *Herald* reported that as Anaïde, Patti sang a role quite different from those previously essayed in New York, adding that she "made a distinguished success in it."[20] Her Violetta, which she had initially performed in Philadelphia on 24 September and in New York on 3 October, was more vocally than dramatically impressive—the *Times* described her throwing herself "entirely upon the music, and [conquering] it with that facile grace which is the chief characteristic of her style, and her best letter of operatic credits"[21] while her "reckless ecstasy of the first act, and her despair of the *finale,* [smacked] more of the boarding-school than of life, and it would be idle to say that she either comprehended or pretended to create the *rôle* in its dramatic aspects."[22] She first assumed the part of Linda, in New York, only two evenings after her appearance as Violetta, an accomplishment not lost on the *Times:* "One new part in a week might well content an ordinary singer—but Miss Patti is no ordinary singer; on the contrary, she is an extraordinarily willful little siren. She chose to sing two new parts in a week. . . . Miss Patti last night attacked part number two, and conquered it."[23]

Her audiences were often as notable as she. She gave one concert on 31 March 1860 in Washington, D.C., that was supported by members of executive and legislative branches of government. This opportunity Patti considered "a compliment of the highest character inasmuch as a similar tribute has never been tendered to any other artist."[24] On 24 August, she sang at a Grand Musical Festival in Montreal honoring the Prince of Wales (later King Edward VII), and ended the long concert at 1 A.M. with "God Save the Queen." Then, as she portrayed Harriet in *Marta* on 10 October 1860 at Philadelphia's Academy of Music, the young prince was again in attendance and was so impressed he wrote of her to his mother, Queen Victoria.

Patti must have been satisfied with her professional life and no doubt at this time also found pleasure in a private life that included, above all, devoted men of "very diverse sorts."[25]

One such admirer was New York's affluent Leonard Jerome, a married man and father (later the American grandfather of Winston Churchill). Earlier Jerome had taken an interest in Jenny Lind that was said to be neither solely nor soully musical, and when his second daughter was born in 1854, he named her after the Swedish nightingale. An inveterate Don Juan, Jerome particularly enjoyed the company of female vocalists and reportedly fathered an illegitimate daughter, later known to the opera world as Minnie Hauk, one of the greatest Carmens. As for Patti, Jerome attended her performances, reveled in what he heard and saw, and found himself fascinated. In his mansion on the northeast corner of Twenty-sixth Street in Madison Square, he directed architects to construct a private theater that he placed at her disposal. One of Jerome's descendants wrote of the infatuation:

> She was so young and her gift, so perfect. What could any man have to offer? Flowers, jewels? No! No! That, to use the favorite adjective of the age, would be vulgar. Only kind Mr. Jerome could produce a toy out of the ordinary for a little prima donna. His private theater was placed entirely at her disposal for the trying of new roles. And who gave her the most stimulating criticism? Who spoke of a woman's soul as well as of her technique? And who was always ready to drive her home in his superb sledge? New Yorkers saw them often together and gossip began.[26]

Though Jerome's interest in Patti created gossip, an incipient romance with Maurice Strakosch's brother Max did not. He was eight years older than she, and several of her early letters to him attest to an intense affair. Caterina, however, did not share her daughter's fervor for Max and was vehemently opposed to marital plans with him, as she had earlier objected to Amalia's marriage to Maurice. A devout Catholic, Caterina preferred that her daughters not marry Jewish men.

After New York, New Orleans provided Patti with the most career opportunities. From 19 December 1860 to 22 March 1861, she amazed local operagoers not only in roles she had assumed elsewhere but also in four successive new ones: Leonora in *Il trovatore,* Gilda in *Rigoletto,* Valentine in *Les Huguenots,* and Dinorah in the American premiere of Meyerbeer's *Le pardon de Ploërmel*—all testaments to her fantastic stamina and discipline.

After having studied the part of Leonora for only eight days, Patti triumphed in this role on 2 January. Hours later a *Daily Picayune* critic marveled that her performance had been "almost faultless throughout, both in the singing and the acting,"[27] and considering the brief preparatory time, "only a little short of miraculous."[28] As Gilda, she won more laurels and seemed to soar "higher in excellence with every new demand."[29] Patti scored another success in her portrayal of Valentine, singing in French and giving one of the "most remarkable operatic performances ever seen or heard"[30] in New Orleans. She studied the part of Dinorah for just three weeks before substituting for an ailing colleague at the opera's American premiere, on 4 March. With great self-possession, she brilliantly executed difficult passages even veteran singers might fear, achieving "a success as perfect and indubitable as it was remarkable, and, we may almost say, phenomenal."[31]

The New Orleans appearances proved epochal:

> Hitherto, for many years past, Italian operatic engagements, even under the most auspicious circumstances, have not lasted longer than ten or twelve representations. . . . But M'lle Patti, for three months and over, has been the leading and most compensating attraction at our Opera House, giving nearly forty representations, all of them to good, and most of them to great audiences. She has sung in [seven] operas, in four of which she appeared for the first time, having studied them since her arrival. We have heard it credibly stated that her share of the proceeds of this season amount to the very handsome sum of ten thousand dollars. This demonstrates, of course, that her engagement must have resulted most profitably to the management, whose season, it is not too much to say, has been saved by this fortunate conjunction. All things considered, we think we may safely say that the annals of the lyric drama do not furnish so remarkable and triumphant a success as this.[32]

From New Orleans, Patti, Salvatore, and her manager, Maurice, originally planned to go to Mexico, where Max Maretzek had planned an opera season around her. Overjoyed to count her a member of his company, Maretzek "concluded definitely all... engagements, paid the usual advance on salary to every one employed, bought new dresses for the operas to be performed, and engaged the passages to Vera Cruz."[33] Everything appeared promising until Patti heard of robberies occurring on the road between Mexico City and Vera Cruz, where she would disembark. Instead of Mexico, Patti determined to go to England, where she had received some operatic proposals. On 23 March, Patti, Salvatore, and Maurice left New Orleans for Havana. There she appeared in three programs with scenes from *Lucia, Rigoletto,* and *Il trovatore*; and on 7 April they boarded an English steamer for London.

Five days later off the coast of South Carolina, Southern rebels fired on Fort Sumter in Charleston's harbor, inciting the war that had been anticipated over the past months. Its imminence had not been lost on Patti, as South Carolina had seceded from the Union the day after her New Orleans debut.

Aware of Patti's American successes, English music agent and manager James Henry Mapleson had negotiated for her services on behalf of English impresario E. T. Smith and offered her an engagement at Her Majesty's Theatre for 200 pounds (approximately $1000) a month. Europe seemed a golden opportunity; but soon after arriving in London, Patti, Salvatore, and Maurice received news that Smith had canceled his opera season.

Apparently unperturbed, Patti suggested Mapleson present a series of performances with her as a principal artist since she felt certain she would attract an audience. Mapleson then asked Patti to sing for him, and, thrilled by the beauty of her rendition of "Home, Sweet Home," he resolved to form a company with her as one of its stars, subsequently securing the Lyceum Theatre and going abroad to engage other artists.

Mapleson was an entrepreneur in the grand manner; a peppery individualist with boundless energy, enthusiasm, panache, and irresistible charm; and a manipulator of people and events to serve his own purposes. According to prima donna Minnie Hauk, he appeared wily and wide-awake, more so in this respect than any other impresario she had encountered. His strategies and politesse served him well with artists and—at times even more amazing—with creditors. Arditi recalled Mapleson's finesses in placating feral prima donnas with past-due salaries. Furious when entering his office, these ladies, marveled Arditi, sallied forth "after awaiting his leisure for some considerable time, with their angry looks transformed to absolute serenity, and actually feeling, to all appearance, as though [he] were conferring a considerable favour upon them by continuing to owe them their hard-earned salaries."[34] Such a person required wary watching.

Not one to be caught napping, Maurice explored another possibility for Patti in Mapleson's absence and conferred with veteran English impresario Frederick Gye, manager of the Royal Italian Opera at Covent Garden, at the behest of opera enthusiast Willert Beale, who, knowing Gye well, urged him to audition Patti and who later recalled their conversation.

> "Too late; it's quite impossible," said Gye, taking the plan of the season from his desk; "every night is filled up, as you see. It would alter my arrangements, and I should have to keep my most expensive people idle—for what? To try an experiment."
> "You will be wrong," I replied, "not to try the experiment. Others will be glad to do so. Strakosch is a good authority, and he is very confident of a great success. Why not increase the number of your extra nights?"
> "And add to my expenses? Besides, it's most unusual. However," continued Gye, reflecting, and looking over the arrangements for the season again, "it would be the only way."
> "I shall tell Strakosch to come and see you this evening."
> "If you like," said the courtly manager, rising; "terms, you know, must be very moderate. Covent Garden Theatre carries great prestige with it."[35]

Mapleson subsequently revealed what had transpired while he was away from London:

> Maurice Strakosch told me that as their last £5 note had been spent he had been obliged to borrow £50 of Mr. Gye, which intelligence at once reduced my height by at least two inches;

and after a deal of difficulty I ascertained that he had signed a receipt for the said loan in a form which really constituted an engagement for the Royal Italian Opera, Covent Garden.[36]

Though foiled in his plans concerning Patti, Mapleson later played a great part in her career.

The contract Gye made with Patti stipulated that her first three performances were on a trial basis without pay; that if she did not win public and critical opinion, he would nullify the engagement; and that, if successful, she was to appear thereafter twice weekly for five years with the salary of 150 pounds a month the first year and increased monthly increments each succeeding year until the payment reached 400 pounds a month the fifth year. Decades later she received 1000 pounds a performance in the United States and even more in South America.

Gye set the date for Patti's first London appearance the evening of 14 May; and that morning, meeting with his old friend Wilhelm Kuhe, the impresario confided he anticipated a sensation, urging him not to miss it: "Come to Covent Garden to-night and hear *Sonnambula*. A little girl is to sing Amina, and I shall not be surprised if she makes a big hit."[37] Other principals included tenor Mario Tiberini as Elvino, Joseph-Dieudonné Tagliafico as Rodolfo, and Mme. Tagliafico as Lisa. Michael Costa conducted.

Hours later London operagoers initially reacted coldly, few knowing anything about Patti, who was virtually unheralded in the press. Kuhe gave another reason for the frigidity:

> The little girl turned out to be a pretty child—to all seeming, of about fourteen. On making her first entry she had no reception, for, amazed at the sight of a mere child stepping on to the stage to essay the part identified with . . . great stars of the operatic firmament, the audience was too much taken aback to applaud.[38]

Their reaction, however, changed within moments. Patti shone as a revelation, quickly establishing herself as worthy of a place on Covent Garden's stage with her singing of the first-act aria "Come per me sereno" and its coruscating cabaletta "Sovra il sen la man mi posa." The audience went wild, electrified by her presence and voice,

> equal, fresh, and telling in every note of the medium, the upper "E flat," and even "F" at ready command; admirable accentuation of the words; considerable flexibility; dashing and effective

use of "bravura"; expression warm, energetic, and varied, while never exaggerated; and, last, not least, an intonation scarcely ever at fault.[39]

She capped the performance with vocal pyrotechnics in the rondo finale "Ah! non giunge," given with

> wonderful brilliancy, at the second verse rendered still more brilliant by a variety of new ornaments . . . , the high E-flat and the F again successfully attacked, and the whole crowned with a neat, equal, and powerful shake upon the penultimate note— which, considering that the air was sung in the original key (B flat) was a feat of no small peril.[40]

The Illustrated London News said that throughout the performance the audience seemed spellbound, enthralled by

> the magic of her acting, so full of truth, refinement, and simplicity; by the charm of her voice, so fresh and lovely, and at the same time so flexible and brilliant, and by her most marvellous powers of execution, unrivalled even by the greatest singers of the day.[41]

The *Musical World* predicted only the greatest destiny awaited her.

In the afterglow she succumbed to powerful emotions: "So far . . . from feeling any sense of triumph or elation, I returned to our little hotel in Norfolk Street in the Strand and burst into tears."[42]

In London the reign of Patti had begun. Charles Dickens celebrated it in a memorable tribute:

> And now has come the youngest *Amina* of all, and at once . . . has stirred up the tired town to an enthusiasm recalling the days when . . . Lind breathed out her whole soul of sadness over the flowers as, leaf by leaf, they mournfully dropped on the stage. Born in Madrid, Italian by parentage, trained exclusively in America, Mlle. Adelina Patti, on her first evening's appearance at our Italian Opera—nay, in her first song—possessed herself of her audience with a sudden victory which has scarcely a parallel.[43]

Dickens claimed that she was already a perfect artist and that she would inevitably sweep all before her throughout Europe.

Despite this Dickensian puff, not all agreed Patti was a perfect artist. Though decidedly in the minority, several critics noted that among defects her voice was somewhat weak in the middle and lower registers, that she interpolated embellishments not in the composer's score and overused staccato, and that her acting occasionally seemed inappropriate. The most adverse criticism came from the powerful, caustic *Athenæum* critic Henry F. Chorley, who thought her voice sounded tired, commenting that a blind person "might have fancied it the property of a singer past her prime."[44] But in time he, too, became an admirer.

James Davison of the *Times* struck the right note:

> "Is . . . Patti"—it will naturally be asked—"a phenomenon?" Decidedly *yes*. "Is she a perfect artist?" Decidedly *no*. How can a girl of scarcely 18 summers have reached perfection in an art so difficult? It is simply impossible. We are almost inclined to say that she is something better than perfect; for perfection at her age could be little else than mechanical, and might probably settle down at last into a cold abstraction, or mere commonplace technical correctness. . . . Patti has the faults incidental to youth and experience; but these in no single instance wear the semblance of being ineradicable.[45]

Time vindicated Davison's view. Through constant study and arduous work, Patti ultimately scaled such heights of excellence that critics found themselves occasionally struggling for adequate words of tribute.

One inspiration for her pursuit of excellence was Covent Garden's principal conductor, Michael Costa. A martinet, he demanded the best from everyone at the opera house. He allowed Patti few prima donna caprices, and while in later years she often refused to attend rehearsals except for new productions (her contracts stipulated her exclusion from them if so desired), Costa did not tolerate such license with her or anyone else. His effect on Patti was evident even in her first London season, at the end of which she expressed gratitude for his impact on her career, writing in a note dated 24 August 1861:

> I really feel sad and mortified—when I think how much you have done for me, and that I am so utterly incapable to reciprocate your favors. I called to see you with my father as I desired to express to you myself all this, but unfortunately I never found you at home.[46]

On 25 May, Patti portrayed her second Covent Garden role, Lucia, before a packed house, confirming the impression she had made as Amina, singing with ease and brilliance and overwhelming the audience in the Mad Scene. *Musical World* reported that she carried "the whole house with her by her natural and earnest acting and her really admirable singing."[47] Davison, however, missed the intensity of feeling she had displayed in *Sonnambula*. Still, he thought her entire performance exceptional while Chorley, by contrast, found little to praise, continuing to hear a fatigued voice; but he did concede that Patti was already "more intensely the fashion than any singer who has till now sung at Covent Garden."[48] Sharing honors with Patti on this occasion were Tiberini as Edgardo and Francesco Graziani as Ashton.

A month later, on 28 June, Patti took part in her first State Concert at Buckingham Palace by Royal command. Members of the Royal Family attending were Albert, Queen Victoria's Prince Consort; the Prince of Wales; Crown Prince and Princess of Prussia; Princess Alice; the Duke and Duchess of Cambridge; and Princess Mary, mother of future Queen Mary, all accompanied by the elite of British aristocracy. Queen Victoria, absent, remained in mourning for the death of her mother. During this program composed of selections from sacred music, Patti sang "Jerusalem! Jerusalem!" from Mendelssohn's oratorio *St. Paul*, "Hear ye, Israel" from the same composer's *Elijah*, and Hummel's air "Alma Virgo." Other eminent soloists included glorious dramatic soprano Thérèse Tietjens, English baritone Charles Santley, and distinguished tenors Italo Gardoni and Antonio Giuglini. According to the Royal Library at Windsor Castle, Patti sang at many other State Concerts in the next twenty-five years with such artists as Tietjens, Santley, Graziani, mezzo-soprano Zélia Trebelli, sopranos Christine Nilsson and Pauline Lucca, tenors Victor Capoul and Ernest Nicolini, baritone Victor Maurel, and basso Édouard de Reszke.

At these solemn affairs attended by royalty, peers, ambassadors or representatives, and members of the Court and held in the Buckingham Palace ballroom, artists often waited an interminable, dreary time for the arrival of the Royal Party. Upon their approach, artists stood, curtsied, and then remained standing until the Royal Party took their seats. All men in the audience wore ceremonial dress— knee breaches, silk stockings, and elaborate upper garments—with the ladies in magnificent gowns and sparkling gems. Once the concert began there was no applause, Royal etiquette forbidding it; and once the Prince and Princess of Wales were seated, no one dared rise, regardless of provocation. At the end of each program, after the singing of "God Save the Queen," the Prince and Princess of Wales with lesser royalties greeted the artists, extending congratulations and pleasantries. Then, upon their departure, guests noticeably relaxed and the atmosphere became less formal and strained.

On 4 July, Patti essayed the role of Violetta in *La traviata* after having repeated in June a number of Aminas and Lucias to enthusiastic, crowded houses with the *Musical World* marveling that she had achieved "greater popularity in a briefer space of time than any singer since Jenny Lind."[49] All London's opera world clamored to see and hear Patti; and Gye obliged with more presentations of his new star, offering her 100 pounds a performance over the weekly two specified in their original agreement. As for her portrayal of Violetta, the *Times* reveled in the "genuine, piquant, original, and attractive" interpretation and evaluated her acting as "more elaborately finished than any previous impersonation of the character we remember."[50] A duet with Tiberini as Alfredo was a "genuine triumph of expression,"[51] which even if she had "done nothing else remarkable would have fixed her performance in the memory of the audience."[52] In the last act, Patti's affecting acting and singing manifested many tears.

Before the end of this London season on 3 August 1861, Patti added three roles to her Covent Garden repertoire: Zerlina in *Don Giovanni* on 6 July, Harriet in *Marta* on the 13th, and Rosina in *Il barbiere di Siviglia* on the 27th.

In the revival of Mozart's opera she appeared for the first time with Giulia Grisi, who was portraying Donna Anna. During this season, Grisi made a series of farewell performances at Covent Garden, where, as prima donna *assoluta*, she had been a favorite for almost three decades. Patti's presence and potential no doubt lessened the sadness surrounding Grisi's farewells. Gye outdid himself with the galaxy of extraordinary singers he had assembled for *Don Giovanni*: in addition to Patti and Grisi there were Jean-Baptiste Faure as Don Giovanni, Enrico Tamberlik as Don Ottavio, Giorgio Ronconi as Masetto, Karl Formes as Leporello, Tagliafico as Il Commendatore, and Rosa Csillag as Donna Elvira. Some considered this Covent Garden's opera event of the decade.

As Zerlina, Patti elicited wild public and critical acclaim (excepting Chorley). Her acting, singing, and expert delivery of recitative were irreproachable; for many Patti as Zerlina remained ideal. *Musical World* said that in her "previous essays she had shown both natural gifts and artistic acquirements . . . but in no instance to such a degree of perfection as in Zerlina" and that "she gave an exquisite charm to everything she sang by the sweet and sympathetic quality of her voice, her pure intonation, graceful phrasing, and truth of expression."[53]

Her Harriet in *Marta* also received paeans and she reminded Mario, appearing as Lionel, of the time, years before in New York, when she had given him flowers Grisi had rejected. He said that his memories of this incident remained vivid and that he had kept the flowers as cherished souvenirs.

As Rosina, Patti, with Mario as Count Almaviva and Ronconi as Figaro, achieved yet another great success, she and Rosina seemingly indissoluble, a fitting climax to a series of twenty-five presentations deserving only the adjective "epochal."

Some months later en route to St. Petersburg, Constance Nantier-Didiée, who had appeared in *Marta* as Nancy to Patti's Harriet, highlighted the season to music historian H. Sutherland Edwards:

> "No one," she said, "paid the least attention to any of *us*. We are all crushed by that little Patti."
>
> "Who," I asked, "is 'that little Patti?' " For I thought I had never heard of her, though, on reflection, I remembered that this was the name of the vocalist whose first appearance I had missed.
>
> "You must have been living in the desert," exclaimed the vivacious mezzo-soprano. "But you said you had been in Poland; it's the same thing. Adelina Patti is a young artist with a light soprano voice, brilliant execution, and engaging manners who has driven the London public absolutely wild. Nothing but Patti goes down with them now."[54]

Several weeks after the end of this Covent Garden season, Patti sang at the Birmingham Festival, first appearing on 27 August. She also sang at three other concerts there. Sharing laurels with her at these affairs were Tietjens, Charles Santley, and tenors Sims Reeves and Antonio Giuglini. Prior to this engagement, Patti had appeared in concert at Brighton, that, according to Wilhelm Kuhe, being her first public appearance on the concert platform in England. In following months she fulfilled engagements in Dublin, Berlin, Brussels, Amsterdam, and The Hague, triumphant in each place. After a performance of *Marta* in Dublin, Trinity College students cheered her at the stage door then, as a token of esteem, unleashed horses from her carriage and drew her to her hotel, where they and others refused to disperse until Patti appeared on a balcony and thanked them and showered them with flowers torn from her bouquets. Later she experienced similar enthusiasm in Berlin, where King Wilhelm, not yet Emperor, attended her performances and where Patti first met celebrated Viennese soprano Pauline Lucca, a Meyerbeer protégée and a potential rival. From the beginning, however, the two enjoyed a friendly relationship, any rivalry existing, according to Maurice Strakosch, "only upon the stage, for outside the theatre they were always upon the best terms of *camaraderie*."[55] After Berlin Patti made her debut at Brussels in January 1862, when a local critic stressed, above all, her individuality: "Her style is peculiar to herself; it is impossible to compare it, with justice, to anything ever heard before; she resembles no one."[56] In Holland Patti became a virtual affair of state over a situation concerning the king. Before agreeing to payment of the exorbitant sum of 120 pounds for her concert in the Royal Palace, His Majesty met with members of a Council of Ministers for their approval, which they gave only after due consideration.

For months her return to London had been eagerly anticipated. The metropolis was in a festive mood as the scene of an International Exhibition, and as part of the festivities Covent Garden offered an interesting list of operas with Patti as a major attraction. She made her seasonal entrance on 5 May 1862, once again as Amina, singing with greater spontaneity and power, her voice having gained in volume and her acting displaying more proficiency. In the following weeks, she added two roles new to her Covent Garden repertoire, Norina in *Don Pasquale*, with Mario as Ernesto, and Dinorah in *Le pardon de Ploërmel*; but of these two the latter created the greater effect. The *Times* thought it "the most elaborately studied, the most carefully wrought out ... the most seemingly spontaneous of her performances."[57] The *Standard* likewise evaluated her Dinorah a great triumph:

> She sang indeed enchantingly, and with as much ease and self-possession as if the part had been as often essayed by her as Amina or Zerlina. . . . The success of the young artiste in a new character was triumphant; so much so, indeed, as to lead to the belief that she will retain the character of Dinorah for the future at the Royal Italian Opera.[58]

Other chief characters included Jean-Baptiste Faure as Hoel and Italo Gardoni as Corentino. Throughout this series Patti nights became the rage; in all, there were thirty-four.

Verdi, in London during April and May for performances of his new cantata *Hymn of the Nations*, first saw her at this time, years later recalling the effect she had had on him:

> I was stupefied not only by her marvelous performance but by several dramatic traits in which she revealed herself to be a great actress. I recall her chaste and modest demeanor when in *La Sonnambula* she lay down on the soldier's bed, when in *Don Giovanni* she left the libertine's room as though contaminated. I recall a certain byplay in Don Bartolo's aria in the *Barbiere*.[59]

At the end of this 1862 Covent Garden season Patti prepared for her debuts in Paris and Vienna as Amina, appearances awaited with both keen anticipation and skepticism over her abilities.

In Paris a *Musical World* correspondent wrote that the Parisians had never been more suspicious, foreseeing a failure, if not a waterloo, and that she would see no laurels:

> As the fog and smoke of London had, on a certain May-morning, proclaimed her famous who was previously obscure, so would the sunshine and clear atmosphere of Paris, on a certain November morning, proclaim her obscure who was previously famous.[60]

Some christened Patti the *Bohémienne*, while jealous London artists spread abroad malicious reports concerning her voice, appearance, and character. French critic B. Jouvin in *Le Figaro* called these detractors a conspiracy of vocal invalids, singers past their prime. Patti duly learned to deal with such individuals, considering them plagues and their envy and jealousy inevitable.

Debuting in Paris on 16 November 1862, Patti may have been wary of the operagoers filling the Théâtre-Italien in the Salle Ventadour; but contrary to any foretold fiasco the evening was a complete triumph. After the last act the house erupted into cheers, and she was presented to Emperor Napoleon III and Empress Eugénie in the Imperial box, where the Royal couple greeted her warmly and offered congratulations.

Patti was not obscure the next day, but received many paeans—a delightful one from French composer Daniel-François Auber: "I was twenty years old throughout the entire performance, which is exactly sixty less than the truth."[61] To Hector Berlioz, Patti was "Goddess of Youth, Hebe, in person."[62] Le Figaro considered her debut so newsworthy and its triumph so emphatic that the 20 November issue splashed the event across the entire front page in an article concerning her early years, career, voice, and portrayal of Amina. La Revue et Gazette Musicale de Paris, like Le Figaro, devoted much space to this debut and maintained that it had been effected with unusual éclat. Paul Bernard in Le Ménestrel praised her as a great singer, "a consummate actress ... an artist of the first rank."[63]

Still, there were adverse comments from such critics as Guy de Charnacé and Pierre Scudo. To some she seemed excessively self-conscious and awkward; but most disturbing were threats of blackmail from a well-known French critic who terrorized artists into giving him almost half their salaries to avoid public censure in his articles for French and foreign publications.

This execrable man met with Maurice before Patti's second performance and offered to review her favorably if he received a mere 60,000 francs. He assured Maurice that he had the power to put upon her head either "a crown of laurels or one of thorns."[64] Unimpressed, Maurice replied that his sister-in-law at this phase of her career needed not pay any critic for puffs. He would, however, consider such a proposal when she was older with a worn-out voice. The critic left in a huff, swearing vengeance, but his subsequent doings were to no avail.

Soon after this debut, Patti met seventy-year-old Gioachino Rossini at one of his celebrated Saturday soirées held at 2 rue de la Chaussée d'Antin, where the attractions were "the conversation, the music (particularly when it meant new music by the host), the skits prepared and performed by such talented entertainers as Gustave Doré and Eugène Vivier, and Rossini's acidulous comments."[65] Since 1858 many well-known musicians, artists, political, social, and commercial people had attended these Parisian gatherings. During the evening of her first visit, Patti sang the aria "Una voce poco fa" from the composer's *Il barbiere di Siviglia*. Camille Saint-Saëns recalled the aftermath:

> Unhappily, I was not present at the soirée during which Patti was heard at Rossini's for the first time. It is known that when she had performed the aria from *Il Barbiere,* he said to her, after many compliments: "By whom is this aria that you just have let us hear?" I saw him a few days later: he still had not calmed down. "I know perfectly well," he told me, "that my arias must be embroidered; they were made for that. But not to leave a note of what I composed, even in the recitatives—really, that is too much!"[66]

Rossini also commented that the rendition reflected Maurice Strakosch's efforts; it had been, according to Rossini, Strakoschonized. In another version, Rossini used a play on words and said it had been *extra-cochonnée*, with *cochonnée* meaning mucked-up. In the 7 December 1862 *Figaro*, B. Jouvin said that one should reproach the singer for substituting music of Patti for music of the composer.

Though annoyed by the Rossini incident, Patti knew better than to make him an enemy. Saint-Saëns reported what subsequently followed: some days later she "went repentantly to ask for his advice. It was wise of her, for at that time her astonishing, fascinating talent was not yet perfected."[67] Ultimately they became friends and he delighted in going over her scales and providing musical advice. Approximately two months after their first meeting, Patti sang arias from his *La gazza ladra* and *Semiramide* with Rossini accompanying on piano; at that time, wrote Saint-Saëns, she coupled "with her brilliant qualities the absolute correctness that she has always displayed since then."[68] Rossini further favored the young star by attending a performance of *Il barbiere* featuring her as Rosina, afterwards declaring her delineation *"adorable, adorable."*

While this Rossini affair had ended well, a concurrent romantic one did not. Early that fall Puerto Rican suitor José Rios appeared in Bath, England, on 6 September to renew his marriage proposal while Patti was there on tour. After pressing the issue, he then traveled to

France and awaited her arrival. Meanwhile she wrote to him from Scarborough and Liverpool.

A letter from Scarborough reassured him as to her devotion:

> We have just had your letter, and we are much surprised to hear that you have written before for we have not received it. Whatever you said in the missing letter, Papa says you are to repeat in the next, for that he is perfectly satisfied that you could have said nothing that would in any way offend him. I wrote to you yesterday and directed it to the Hotel de la Paix, if you can, you had better fetch it from there.
>
> We have only thirteen more places to go to after which I am happy to say, I shall soon be in France.
>
> When you write, direct to Covent Garden and put "Immediate" on it . . . I shall write to you as often as I can and you must not think all sorts of unhappy things, for I never know where we go next and we only stay a day or two in each place.[69]

In a missive from Liverpool, Patti wrote of her regret in not having received mail from him and of an illness:

> I expected a letter from you during my stay here, but not having one, I hope to hear from you in Manchester.
>
> You have only written me one letter and this is my third to you. I have been very ill indeed, and have been keeping my bed this last week, in consequence of which [we] were obliged to leave out some of the concerts, I caught a violent cold in my chest, which prevented me from singing and as Papa is so very careful of me, he certainly would not allow me to sing untill [*sic*] I was quite well. I hope that you do not find my letters too difficult to read and that that was not the reason you did not write to me. As I am writing this in bed, you must excuse the style.[70]

At last came their reunion in France, where, upon her arrival on Tuesday, 11 November, Patti dashed off a note to him: "We have arrived in Paris this evening and we are ready to receive you either tonight or tomorrow morning whichever suits you best."[71] She followed this message with another written on her personal card bearing the address Rue Neuve des Capucines 5, près de Place Vendôme: "As I have forgotten to send you the address in the note, I thought it best to write it on this card at once."[72]

Two days after her Paris debut, Patti, in another letter, apologized for not being able to see him that evening, 18 November, but suggested he visit her the following night, pointedly adding not to be late:

> I should have asked you to come this evening only that Dr. Strakosch has had a consultation about some important business with some gentlemen and having to remain in my bedroom of course I could not receive you there but tomorrow evening come precisely at half past 7 o'clock and do not come an hour and a half after that time. I was so glad you went to the theatre last night I have had so many visitors today who brought me such beautiful bouquets I have read the letter you sent me & I am indeed surprised to find so much difference in the writing of former times & now.[73]

In her next letter, Patti again apologized for not being able to receive Rios. She finished with some interesting personal matters.

> I am sorry not to be able to receive you this evening as my friend Alice has been taken very suddenly ill, and is my duty to remain with her all the evening. I have also a little rehearsal of the Barbiere and renders it impossible for me to see you. I am so so sorry but hope you will not feel offended and rest assured that as soon as I can receive you again it will be such a great pleasure for me. I have spoken to Papa lately and must still hear from him the answer, and when you come I shall tell you all about it. I was happy to see you last night at the Opera, I thank you very much for the ring, I shall always wear it as a dear keepsake from you.[74]

In three letters and a card written towards the end of November, she complained of suffering from a cold, but in each communication Patti assured Rios that she longed to see him though she was unable to do so because of chest pains, coughing, and excessive fatigue. Nonetheless, she would send for him as soon as possible. In one letter Patti closed with a sentiment that must have thrilled him: "I *love* you Joseph."[75]

The affair finally ended with irreconcilable differences. Portions of yet another letter suggest her disappointment:

> I sent three times last evening to know if you were at home and each time you were out I sent afterwards for the answer to the card as I got up expressly to see you & you had no sooner finished the letter than you *went out* which shows how little you cared about my illness I suppose you did not believe it in the first place

Perhaps you want a certificate from my doctor Another thing, I hear that you spend your time very well and come home *very late*. I hope you amuse yourself nicely. Is that what *you call staying at home to think of me?* Let me give you a little advice. People in delicate health should not stay out at the "*café*" quite so late—If that is the way you amuse yourself *don't talk* to me about *dying* if you have to wait for me *two years*. . . . I am in bed today & my cold is very bad. I am afraid I shall not be able to sing on Saturday This time I shall not trouble myself to get up because you don't come.[76]

Patti lost faith in Rios, who never gave her what she really wanted: his undivided attention, loving devotion, and keen admiration for her as woman and artist.

Meanwhile, she had become the toast of Paris and was, according to the 4 January 1863 issue of *Le Ménestrel*, charming not only ears but also eyes and hearts. By the end of this season the Patti craze crescendoed, "the chief topic of conversation in every circle."[77] No doubt most comments centered on her successes as Amina, Lucia, Rosina, Norina, and Zerlina in *Don Giovanni*; or perhaps they related to her earnings. For each of her thirty-seven performances, she had received 1500 francs (60 pounds) a night. In the next several years Patti's fee at the Théâtre-Italien doubled per performance.

Especially contributing to her renown was Royal patronage: Emperor Napoleon III and Empress Eugénie had attended six of her performances. An individual at one of these recounted their enthusiasm:

At the end of almost every phrase, both the Empress and the Emperor applauded, and on one occasion the Empress cried so loudly and so frequently, "Brava, bravissima," that the whole audience took it up, and burst out into such a tremendous shout of applause as I never remember hearing. When the opera was over, the Empress sent, through Count Bacciochi, . . . her kind compliments, together with a magnificent bouquet which she had worn all the evening, stating, moreover, that she . . . intended very shortly to get up a private concert at the Court for her to be presented.[78]

The Royal couple even graced her benefit performance in February, when she again enchanted a crowded house with her portrayal of Mozart's Zerlina. After the second act they invited her to

the Imperial box, where the empress gave her a golden bracelet with
large emeralds and diamonds. Patti's season in Paris thus concluded
in glory.

Before leaving, she granted *Le Figaro* its first interview with a
prima donna at a time when journalistic dialogue was an innovation.
Her brief responses may be due to warnings to say little to the press.
Musical World later published the interview in translation:

> "Patti!" exclaims the Parisian *Figaro*. You are introduced to
> Patti, and find that she is a little girl of nineteen, who looks
> fourteen—a child who might have a doll and know nothing of
> life. "Do you ever read the newspapers?"
>
> "No; I never see them," she replies. "If there is anything nice,
> my brother-in-law reads it to me. If not, I don't hear of it."
>
> "What do you read, then?"
>
> "Thackeray, Dickens—nearly all the English authors."
>
> "Do you like Paris?"
>
> "Yes, but I like London better. The French are changeable, I
> am told; whereas the English—"
>
> "Well?"
>
> "When they have taken a liking to you it lasts for ever. I was
> much quieter in London; and if you only knew how fond I am of
> quiet. Here people talk so fast and so much, it confuses me."
>
> "How can that confuse you?—you who can speak English,
> French, Italian, and Spanish equally well?"
>
> "Not being accustomed to it, I suppose." . . .
>
> "Shall you sing much at Vienna?"
>
> "I don't know."
>
> "How is that? Don't you know what your engagements are?"
>
> "No; I never know. My papa arranges everything. As for me,
> they tell me I must start, and I start; they tell me to sing, and I
> sing."
>
> "And Italy, when are you going there? It is not its fault that it
> is not your native land."
>
> "Oh, I am very sorry I have not been there already. I shall be
> delighted to see Italy."[79]

Musical World then editorialized:

The . . . depicting the character of the great singer of the day
through an ordinary conversation, well arranged, appears to us
an immense improvement on the old-fashioned memoir. . . . In
future, when this method has become generally known, ladies of

celebrity, instead of being asked to sit for their portraits to photographers, will be asked to talk for their portraits to writers, and the great art will be to make them talk characteristically and well.[80]

Little time remained before Patti's Viennese debut. Accompanying her were, as usual, Salvatore and Maurice and also a German lady named Louisa Lauw, who since 6 January 1863 had become a companion and intimate, replacing the Englishwoman Alice, who was unexpectedly obliged to leave. A lady of approximately Patti's age, Lauw remained with her for the next fourteen years, thereafter writing an exposé infuriating Patti as it contained gossip on her private life.

Before assuming this position, Lauw, whose uncle had been Maurice's friend, had met Patti socially and had seen her as Rosina only several weeks before. The day following this performance she visited the singer to express her boundless admiration. Then the evening of 5 January, during an opera intermission, Lauw heard about the departure of Patti's companion Alice. Suddenly her uncle appeared, exclaiming, "My child, Patti wishes to see you: come immediately with me, and try to cheer her up a little, as she is very sad at the departure of her friend."[81] She then found the singer inconsolable, and regarded Patti "still as half a child whom one must coax, or tell stories in order to comfort."[82] Soon her small talk and anecdotes lifted the gloom, and Patti showed her some personal valuables: ornaments, several picture-books, and fashion journals. When Lauw proposed leaving, Patti, again tearful, persuaded her to stay and thereafter shared confidences for hours. The following day Lauw began a long association of sensational, unforgettable moments.

One of these was her introduction to Rossini and his wife, Olympe, followed by a dinner party he gave in Patti's honor on 14 February, the night before her Parisian seasonal farewell. During this meal, Rossini's Little Pattina sat between him and Auber, and afterwards a Rossini protégé, Louis Diémer, entertained at the piano with virtuosity.

Upon arrival in Vienna, Patti found that it, like Paris, housed disbelievers; but despite the ill will, gossip, and an illness requiring bed rest for several days before the debut, she once again demonstrated at her initial performance, on 28 February 1863, that her abilities were as reported to the audience filling the Carl Theater, where illustrious tenor Antonio Giuglini was Elvino to her Amina. The well-known and severe critic Eduard Hanslick wrote glowingly of this evening:

> If Patti's singing, acting, and personality are regarded as a whole, one must confess to having hardly ever met a more charming individual on the stage. I have heard greater artists as singers, and more brilliant voices. I recall more sophisticated actresses, and more beautiful women. But Patti's charm consists in making one forget them. What she offers is so completely hers, so harmonious and lovable, that one allows oneself to be captivated and accepts capitulation with pleasure.[83]

Later Hanslick found himself attacked as a gullible enthusiast by an anti-Patti faction of the Viennese press.

Her subsequent performances duplicated the triumph of her debut with a succession of ovations, to which Emperor Francis Joseph and his family contributed, often initiating the applause. Her Norina in *Don Pasquale* particularly aroused H. Sutherland Edwards, then in Vienna, who maintained she outdid herself in this part:

> I had been told on her own authority that she played it, not as in London, where Costa would allow no upsetting of furniture, no vigorous slaps in the face, administered to "Don Pasquale" by his insubordinate ward, his rebellious bride; but with an impulsiveness and a self-abandonment which she herself thought natural in the character, and which she, in any case, practised—to the entire satisfaction, it must be added, of the Viennese public. Never, indeed, did I see the charming vocalist and actress play with so much gaiety, so much vivacity, so thoroughly in the spirit of Italian comedy, as on this one occasion at Vienna.[84]

Her singing in St. Augustine's Church attracted enormous crowds both inside and out; and the press of the throng outside the church after the service so terrified Patti that she fainted. With the greatest difficulty, Maurice and several other men forced their way through to carry her to a nearby mansion where Count Zichy and various onlookers, having seen the demonstration from the windows, admitted them seconds before the mob pursued.

Throughout the entire series of performances, her hold on the Viennese never wavered. Among the most enchanted was Hanslick, who soon became a friend and daily visited the apartment where she,

Salvatore, Maurice, and Lauw received him cordially. In this milieu Hanslick described Patti as "a child of nature, half timid and half wild ... good-humored and violent, inclined to sudden, quickly passing fits of temper, directed usually against Strakosch, who tried to appease her."[85] Often a guest at mealtimes, he would entertain Patti afterwards by playing some of her favorite waltzes at the piano until exhausted, at which time she would insist he dance with her and had Maurice accompany them at the keyboard. Occasionally Maurice admonished Patti to conserve her energies (she danced with great abandon), reminding her she was to sing at the opera that evening. " 'For heaven's sake, Lina,' he would cry, 'you must sing tonight.' 'Leave that to me,' she would answer, laughing, and the waltz would go on."[86]

No doubt Hanslick would have been more enchanted had the young star possessed broader intellectual interests. He regretted that at that time she took little or no interest in subjects other than music and theater and was not concerned, for example, "for higher questions of humanity, for science, politics, religion, or even for literature." He decided to further her education and gave her a copy of Dickens's *Great Expectations*, which includes the tale of an old woman for whom time had stopped years before when her fiancé jilted her at the altar. The shock of his desertion left the woman unbalanced. Several days later, when Hanslick asked Patti what she thought of the novel, her reply surprised him: "It's nothing but lies which nobody will make me believe. That an old woman wouldn't give up her old bridal dress and her old wedding cake can't be true and isn't possible. I am no longer a child to whom one can give such things to read."[87] She had probably read only the beginning of the novel, which for her may have been enough. On that note the critic let the matter of her education rest.

Still, Hanslick obviously enjoyed this friendship and was one of few on intimate terms with Patti, who rarely admitted people into her inner circle or accepted social invitations. One she did accept in Vienna ended disastrously. The proprietor and editor of a local journal had implored her to attend a musical soirée at his residence, an invitation that, after first declining, she finally agreed to, provided she not be asked to sing. No sooner had she arrived at his house, however, than the host's wife begged for a song. Patti's refusal then resulted in adverse comments from the host's journal. Like the

Parisian blackmailing critic, this Viennese editor vowed to ruin her in print. Needless to say, he never succeeded.

Some Viennese held Maurice responsible for Patti's exclusivity as he constantly protected his sister-in-law from fatigue. Then there were accusations, later undenied in his memoirs, that he often took her place at rehearsals to save her vocal and physical exhaustion and would act and sing her various parts to the annoyance or amusement of those present. Such services and attendant gossip inspired a farce entitled *Adelina and Her Brother-in-law,* which played at a minor Viennese theater and showed his impersonating her on some interesting occasions. In one, Maurice said to a photographer wishing to take Patti's picture that though she could not oblige, he would gladly take her place; his response to an ardent suitor wanting to express his emotions was similarly outrageous: "She is too much engaged to listen to you . . . but anything you may have to say can be addressed to me."[88] All was grist for the publicity mill.

To the *Athenæum,* the Viennese successes evoked memories of Jenny Lind's triumphs in the United States: "Mdlle. Adelina Patti has been, during her stay in Vienna, as much assailed (the word is not too strong) with honours, cataracts of gold, and inroads of popular curiosity and rapture, as was Mdlle. Jenny Lind in America."[89] The cataracts of gold included Patti's fee of 80 pounds a performance while Impresario Merelli realized a 4000-pound profit from her engagement.

Among the Viennese experiences Patti long remembered was a dinner party at which she met the composer called the Schubert of Dance: Josef Strauss, brother of Johann. During this evening he sat at the piano and played some of his waltzes, whose melodies delighted her.

In Paris for a short stay before the Covent Garden season, Patti once again attended a Rossini soirée in her honor, at which the composer accompanied a duet she sang with baritone Antonio Tamburini from *Il barbiere* and the aria "Bel raggio" from *Semiramide,* Rossini having written new passages in it expressly for her. She also sang music by Meyerbeer and Auber, with both composers enjoying her renditions. The musical portion of this evening concluded with music from Rossini's *Mosè in Egitto*, in which Patti, Marietta Alboni, and Italo Gardoni took part.

During the 1863 Covent Garden season, beginning on 7 May, Patti added four roles to her repertoire at that opera house—Leonora in *Il trovatore*, Ninetta in *La gazza ladra*, Adina in *L'elisir d'amore*, and Maria in *La figlia del reggimento*. As Leonora, she displayed a remarkable dramatic ability, providing, said *Musical World*, "a living presentment of the object of the troubadour's ill-fated love which for power, pathos, and genuinely human reality has never known its equal."[90] Chorley, mellowing in his reviews of Patti, considered Ninetta the best of the serious characters she had thus far essayed, while another critic thought her conception of Adina "faultless in itself and wrought out with a rare intelligence."[91] As Maria, she was "an incomparably perfect representation of Donizetti's charming and vivacious heroine."[92]

Also creating a sensation at this time was a legal affair known as Patti v. Patti that received considerable press coverage. In this suit the pseudo-plaintiff was the singer; the defendants were Salvatore and, by association, Maurice. It alleged that the defendants had treated Patti cruelly; tampered with her liberty of action; appropriated her valuables, such as jewelry; and kept sufficient sums of money from her. Ostensibly acting on Patti's behalf and providing affidavits was her so-called "next friend," Henri de Lossy, Baron de Ville, who claimed to be her fiancé.

Although at first attracted to this young man, she later spurned him; he thought her rejection was due to Salvatore's and Maurice's influence and interference and retaliated with the lawsuit. At the court hearing, Patti's counsel submitted an affidavit sworn by her on 11 May 1863, in which she declared that the Bill of Complaint and affidavit of Baron de Ville were submitted without her sanction and knowledge and that the allegations were wholly false, whereupon Baron de Ville's solicitors advised him to drop the suit and in a letter to the editor of the London newspaper *The Morning Star*, published on 3 June 1863, made clear their part in what had become a sensational issue:

> In justice to ourselves we feel bound to state that we should not have advised a bill being filed by any one, whoever he might be, on behalf of Mdlle. Patti, without being first well satisfied by

authentic information that there were good *prima facie* grounds for taking the proceedings. What that information was we have now no need to detail, but the publication of her affidavit compels us to say that, although Mdlle. Patti has thought fit to deny any material allegation in the bill, these allegations, especially of ill-treatment by her father and brother-in-law, are founded strictly upon statements in her own letters, in which, moreover, she implored the protection of deliverance she has now refused to avail herself of.

Our proceedings have given her an opportunity of expressing, and us of learning, her present sentiments . . . and as soon as we ascertained that she . . . chose to deny the truth of the complaints she had repeatedly made, and on the strength of which our client proceeded, we at once advised [him] to discontinue further proceedings on her behalf, and to dismiss, as he had a right to do, his own bill; and that course was adopted.[93]

This affair afforded a rare opportunity to glimpse Patti's private life. Then, several weeks later, a letter written by Louis Moreau Gottschalk appeared in the French publication *L'Art Musical*; and it, too, created a stir with information about her family perhaps unknown to European admirers. With Max Strakosch as his manager on some tours, Gottschalk had concertized in the United States, excluding the Confederacy, from time to time assisted by Amalia Patti Strakosch, then mother of a boy and girl and still a renowned mezzo-soprano, and Carlotta Patti, whose high soprano voice had been creating a sensation since her first New York concert on 25 October 1860. Two years later, however, she made an unsuccessful debut as Amina at New York's Academy of Music on 22 September 1862, with the disadvantages of a lameness suffered since childhood and a temperament unsympathetic for the stage. Carlo Patti had also joined Gottschalk on his tours and was a Don Juan whose good looks and violin playing enraptured young women. Of this family, Gottschalk wrote:

This Patti family is truly a dynasty of distinguished singers. The father, Salvatore Patti, was still, some twenty years ago, an excellent tenor *di forza*. His wife (the mother of Adelina) was a fiery lyrical tragic actress, whose name of Barili (for her first husband was Signor Barili) is still celebrated in Portugal, in Spain, and at Naples, where she achieved some great triumphs. . . . Her eldest daughter, Clotilde Barili (who died four or five years ago), was eminently successful at New York, and in all Spanish America, especially at Lima and San Francisco. Her sons, Ettore Barili, a distinguished baritone; Antonio, *basso profundo*; and Nicolo Barili, *basso chantante*, bravely support the family name.

The children of the second (Patti) marriage are: Amalia Patti, married to Maurice Strakosch, . . . whose compositions deserve to be better known; Carlotta, whose extraordinary voice and marvellous flexibility have fanaticised the United States, and been a second edition of the enthusiasm excited there by Adelina. After Carlotta come Carlo and Adelina. As for the latter, all Europe already knows her. With regard to Carlo, he is a handsome fellow, with something of the Bohemian about him . . . and is at present enjoying the health the Pattis usually enjoy, for among other enviable privileges, they have the privilege of never being ill. What a family! Do you know of many others in art whose quarterings of nobility are better than those I have just enumerated?[94]

In the late summer and early fall of 1863, Patti fulfilled a number of engagements in Germany, where she appeared as Rosina in August at the Frankfurt Conference—attended by various German princes; Kings of Hanover, Saxony, and Bavaria; the Grand Duke of Baden; the Duke of Coburg; and Emperor Francis Joseph. She took part in a series at Hamburg, where her performance as Marguerite in Gounod's *Faust* created a sensation, and sang in Berlin with the king and entire Court present at every presentation. Patti, whom the monarch called a little fire-ball of the explosion, canceled an appearance before him at a gala concert, subsequently explaining that

> the King of Prussia, later the German Emperor William I, had arranged a court concert in which I was to sing. Although everything had been prepared at the palace, when the day arrived I did not feel well and refused to go. To Meyerbeer was given the unpleasant task of conveying my refusal. But the King did not resent it, for he came to hear me when I next appeared. During the performance he asked,
> "Miss Patti, what caused you to be so ill?"
> "Your royal climate, Your Majesty," was my reply.[95]

From Germany she proceeded to Paris and remained briefly before departing for a series of performances in Madrid. The morning of her departure, Rossini called to wish her bon voyage, and finding her not ready to receive him, he announced his presence by playing an old French song on the piano with one finger. Its playing produced immediate effect, with Patti rushing to greet him, and as a going-away present he gave her a piece of parmigiana cheese which he had received from Pesaro.

On 12 November 1863, she effected a brilliant debut in her birthplace, where many considered her one of their own, another Madrileña. Among her enthusiasts was Queen Isabella II, who later received Patti and her father at the Royal Palace, dispensing with the usual rigid formalities of the Spanish Court, inviting them to sit at her side. She wanted to know about Patti's nationality, birth date, and career as the journals she had read disagreed on these matters, whereupon Patti responded in considerable detail, reviewing aspects of her life in the United States and in opera, to which Salvatore added his comments. At the end of this audience, Her Majesty called Patti her countrywoman, proud of what she had accomplished with her art.

At a benefit performance in Madrid in December, she received not only many wreaths and bouquets from such aristocrats as the Duke of Alba and the Countess of Montijo (Empress Eugénie's mother), but also sapphire and diamond earrings from Queen Isabella II. A further tribute was the release in her honor of two hundred canary birds flying towards the stage.

Looking back on this year about to end, Patti no doubt rejoiced in her triumphs, having scaled great heights, catapulted into celebrity by her meteoric successes. Looking ahead, she no doubt hoped for more of the same in a new year about to begin.

CHAPTER III

Celebrity of Celebrities

Patti returned to Paris's Théâtre-Italien for the first four months of 1864, with the newspaper *Le Temps* announcing: "Beat drums! Sound horns! Mlle Adelina Patti, the grand, illustrious, incomparable, prodigious Patti has returned!"[1] During this series she appeared as Harriet in *Marta*, first presented on 21 February with Mario as Lionel, Enrico Delle Sedie as Plunkett, and Emilie de Méric Lablache as Nancy. She also sang at another Rossini soirée and at a concert before the Imperial Court in the Tuileries. On 16 February, Rossini copied several bars from *Il barbiere* and wrote words of admiration in her autograph album: "Nothing is easier than to fling a thought [*jeter une pensée*] into your album. The thought that runs in my head, to love you as an adorable creature . . . , to admire your surpassing talent, to be forever your friend."[2]

After Paris Patti went to London to begin her fourth successive Covent Garden season from May to August, and she then heard of Meyerbeer's death on 2 May. He had often visited Patti in Paris, promised to write her an opera, and gone over his various scores with her, particularly for the role of Dinorah. Apparently Patti's singing of this part so impressed his daughter, not overfond of her father's compositions, that she thereafter appreciated his music.

During this London season, Patti performed, for the first time at Covent Garden, the role of Marguerite in *Faust*, a part not initially assigned to her. Originally Gye had engaged Lucca for it, but after

69

her first appearance, some unfavorable reviews so enraged the prima donna that she left the city in a pique.

Faust was first presented at Covent Garden on 2 July 1863, with Marie Miolan-Carvalho as Marguerite, a role she had created four years before at the opera's world premiere in Paris. Many considered her the ideal interpreter. Lucca, her successor in the role, was far from satisfactory, outrageously flippant and coquettish, besides striking, according to critics, some unladylike postures.

Patti's Covent Garden debut of the role occurred on 6 June, with some critics considering it her finest achievement, an opinion shared even by Chorley:

> We are as much delighted as surprised by the last of the *Margarets*. The part is read after the fashion of Madame Miolan-Carvalho, but "with a difference." It is less dreamy than hers, without the added amount of spirit and life taking any of those forms which were so questionable in Mdlle. Lucca's personation. . . . Obviously, every note of the music, every word of the text, every change of the situation, had been thought over, and been felt by the artist.[3]

At the end of this season, Patti returned to France and enjoyed a brief holiday at Boulogne-sur-Mer before concertizing there towards the end of August and at Le Havre. Leaving France momentarily, she performed at the Birmingham Musical Festival in September with such illustrious artists as Tietjens, Sims Reeves, and Charles Santley. She made her first appearance on the 7th there in the world premiere of Michael Costa's oratorio *Naaman*, in the part of Adah. The chorus and orchestra numbered almost five hundred participants, and Jenny Lind, one of the world's greatest oratorio singers, attended.

Shortly thereafter, Patti appeared in opera at Lyons, where her initial reception on 17 September as Lucia was from a cold, if not hostile, house. Although annoyed, she determined to win them over. By the end of the first aria, the house "broke forth into indescribable shouts of joy, and the musicians of the orchestra had great difficulty in restraining the people from rushing from the parterre upon the stage, over their heads."[4] After the opera a throng of enthusiasts surrounded Patti's carriage, shouting themselves hoarse and accompanying her to her hotel in homage.

That evening Patti also received compliments from the late tragedienne Rachel's relatives, who had found her acting and deportment as Lucia riveting. In a letter dated 19 September, she expressed her pleasure:

> The greatest satisfaction I had . . . was the compliment paid to me by the father and brother of the great Rachel, [who] said . . . I reminded them so much of their lost treasure. . . . The brother, who is the director here, wishes to make another engagement with me for next year and offers to pay me double the amount if I only wish to accept and also he wishes to take me to Russia, where he thinks we can make a great deal of money.[5]

Still, what she no doubt treasured most while in Lyons was an eagerly awaited reunion with Max Strakosch.

When Patti heard of Max's proposed trip to Europe, she immediately wrote him a letter, on 5 March 1864, from Paris:

> I dare say these few lines from me will surprise you very much, but as a gentleman came to-day, to see us, and who has just arrived from America, brought us the . . . news that you will come to London, next May, if it be true, dear Max, you can never imagine how *exceedingly* happy you have made us all, as I have been anxiously waiting for you this long while. Maurice is so happy about it . . . Do dear Max answer this by return of post if it is no trouble. . . . God bless you and may you ever be happy, and also may you ever love your little *Lina*.[6]

A few days later, writing to Max's sister in Vienna, Patti declared that being with him in Europe would make her the world's happiest woman. His subsequent response, however, was cold and distant. Perhaps the widely publicized Baron de Ville episode or some news of José Rios had affected his attitude. She again wrote his sister on 8 May and shared the contents of his letter, soliciting her advice.

Max arrived in Europe in September but had little time to be with her as he represented Pasquale Brignoli. Patti learned he would have to hasten to a Madrid engagement with the tenor. She addressed a letter to him in Paris dated 16 September:

Oh! Max *dear* can't you remain near me? do you wish to go? I can assure you, I cryed [*sic*] to Maurice about it, and when he saw my tears, he promised me faithfully that he would try and arrange something about your big fat Tenor, so that we may still remain a little longer together.[7]

Several days later Max joined Patti—at long last—in Lyons. No doubt he found her excruciatingly enchanting.

Berlioz was also in Lyons at that time, having come in quest of a woman he had idolized for decades. A widower in his sixties, he craved her affection but found the lady unwilling to give it. After leaving her, the despondent Berlioz unexpectedly met Maurice, who greeted him warmly:

> "Berlioz! how fortunate! Adelina will be delighted to see you. She is giving performances here. Would you like a box for the *Barber of Seville* to-morrow night?"
> "Thanks, but I shall probably be leaving this evening."
> "Well, at any rate, come and dine with us to-night; you know how pleased we always are to see you."
> "I can't promise, it will depend. . . . I am not very well. . . . Where are you stopping?"
> "At the Grand Hotel."
> "So am I. Well, if I am not too unsociable this evening, I will dine with you, but don't expect me."[8]

Berlioz did attend the dinner and recalled the evening in his memoirs:

> I turned my steps towards the hotel in the hope of dining fairly quietly with Mdlle. Patti. On seeing me enter the salon she uttered a cry of delight, clapping her hands like a child.
> "Oh, how delightful! there he is! there he is!" And the fascinating *diva* rushed up to me after her usual fashion and presented her virgin forehead to be kissed. I sat down to table with her, her father, her brother-in-law, and some friends. During dinner she overwhelmed me with charming civilities, continually repeating: "There's something the matter with him. What are you thinking about? I don't like you to be in trouble." When the hour for my departure arrived, they determined to go down with me to the station; the charming creature herself, one of her lady friends, and her brother-in-law came with me in the carriage. We were all allowed on to the platform. Adelina would

PATTI . MARIO . FAUR

35 Patti as Marguerite, Mario (right) as Faust, and Jean-Baptiste Faure as Méphistophélès in Gounod's *Faust.* Patti's Covent Garden debut in this role took place 6 June 1864. Courtesy Stuart-Liff.

36 Patti as a remorseful Marguerite, betrayed by Faust. She studied this role
with the composer, Gounod. Courtesy Stuart-Liff.

37 The diva as a mad Marguerite in prison. Courtesy Stuart-Liff.

38 As Linda di Chamounix,
Patti occasionally interpolated
her signature song, "Home, Sweet
Home," into the opera. Courtesy
Stuart-Liff.

39 This print appeared in a local
Florentine newspaper following
Patti's Italian debut at Teatro
Pagliano on 11 November 1865.
Author's Collection.

40 Patti as Caterina in Meyerbeer's *L'étoile du Nord*, a role she first assumed on 26 June 1866, at Covent Garden. Courtesy Stuart-Liff.

41 In *L'étoile du Nord*, Patti underwent several changes of costume and character. According to H. Sutherland Edwards in *The Prima Donna*, one saw six Pattis: a waiting-maid at an inn, a fortune-telling gypsy, a young recruit, a sentinel, "a young lady clothed in melancholy and white muslin, and finally a princess... decked in robes of splendour." Courtesy William R. Moran.

42–44 Patti in three versions of Annetta in *Crispino e la comare,* a role she first assumed during the 1866 Covent Garden season. Right, courtesy William R. Moran; left and opposite, courtesy Stuart-Liff.

45 Patti and Mario as the star-crossed lovers in Gounod's *Roméo et Juliette.* They premiered the opera for London audiences at Covent Garden on 11 July 1867. Courtesy Stuart-Liff.

46 Patti in the title role of Verdi's *Giovanna d'Arco*. After the 28 March 1868 performance at the Théâtre-Italien in Paris—in the local premiere of the work and also Patti's first assumption of the role—her portrayal and the libretto were lambasted by a French critic. Courtesy Stuart-Liff.

47 The armor Patti wore as the Maid of Orleans was later displayed on a wall of her Welsh country estate. It was an apt costume during performances at the Théâtre-Italien, where she received death threats and encountered poisoned water, poisoned gloves, and a bouquet containing a lead ball—thrown at her head during a curtain call. Fortunately it missed its mark. Courtesy Stuart-Liff.

48 A slight smile and intricately embellished cape well suit the young singer. Courtesy Carin Cederström Ekelöf.

49 Offstage, Patti appears serene. Courtesy Carin Cederström Ekelöf.

50 Carlotta Patti's singing had impresse Europeans by the late 1860s, and h triumphs at times rivaled those of her mo famous sibling. Courtesy William R. Mora

51 Salvatore Patti (left) and his children Carlotta, Adelina, and Carlo were reunited in 1864 in Paris. Carlotta's career as a singer was then flourishing; Carlo had come to Europe to study violin. Courtesy The Billy Rose Theatre Collection, The New York Public Library for the Performing Arts, Astor, Lenox and Tilden Foundations.

With Maurice Strakosch, Salvatore ti continued to manage his daughter's eer through most of the 1860s, but his e in her life changed in 1868 when Patti rried the Marquis de Caux. Courtesy art-Liff.

53 Caterina Patti left the United States in the late 1860s to live in Rome. She saw Patti infrequently. Nonetheless, the diva financially supported Salvatore and Caterina until the ends of their lives. Courtesy Stuart-Liff.

54–56 Patti in various gowns, which became richer as her celebrity grew. She emulated Empress Eugénie's attire—the crinoline skirt and plunging neckline. Courtesy William R. Moran.

57 By the age of twenty-five, Patti contemplated marriage despite the opposition of her father and brother-in-law, Maurice Strakosch. Courtesy William R. Moran.

not leave me till the last moment, when the signal was given for the train to start. When we had to part, the mad creature jumped up and put her arms round my neck.

"Good-bye, good-bye till next week. We shall be returning to Paris on Tuesday; you will come and see us on Thursday. It's settled, isn't it? You won't fail?"[9]

Though flattered by her affection and attention, Berlioz left Lyons in misery:

During all the coaxings and caresses of the melodious Hebe, I felt as if a marvellous bird of paradise were whirling round my head, perching on my shoulder, pecking at my hair, and singing its gayest songs. I was dazzled, but not touched. The fact was I had no *love* for the young, beautiful, radiant, and celebrated artist who ... had brought all the musical world of Europe and America to her feet; whereas my whole soul went out to the aged, saddened, and obscure woman, to whom art was unknown, as it had ever done, ever will do to my dying day.[10]

Berlioz's description of Patti reflects a degree of joie de vivre on her part, no doubt due to Max's presence in Lyons and, more importantly, his marriage proposal. Despite Caterina's opposition to him as a husband for her daughter, the two were secretly engaged.

Max's quick departure for Spain left Patti disconsolate as revealed in her letter of 29 September, sent to him in Madrid:

Since you left ... I have been very sad indeed, always thinking about your true love for me and how good you are to your *dear* little Ady, who feels that she can never love anyone else but you in this world, and wishes very ardently to clasp you once more to her heart, and keep you there forever.[11]

On 2 October, Patti, then in Paris, responded to a letter from Max that concerned trust between them:

Now my love I suppose you know that our happiness depends entirely on confidence, and that you ought to have in me, but I am sorry to say, that very often, I noticed your mistrusting smile; but now I hope you will for the future look upon me as a woman that loves you sincerely and not as a foolish child, that likes to flirt.[12]

Ten days later she responded to another of Max's letters, telling him of her latest successes at the Théâtre-Italien, adding that she had conferred with its manager as to Brignoli's engagement there and that he had assured the tenor would be sent for in December, in time for them to share Christmas. Without him, Patti said, days seemed long, empty, and wearisome: "I feel I cannot be happy so far away from you. *E tu, mio caro angelo, dici che voi morir per me, ma no! Tu devi vivere per far mi felice. Non è cosi, Max mio?* [And you, my dear angel, say you will die for me, but no! You must live to make me happy. Isn't it so, my Max?]"[13] She added a postscript: "Mama does not torment me any more and even if she did *nothing* can make me love [underlined four times] you any the less."[14] Inside the envelope flap she wrote: "*Write soon*, my dear little husband!!!"[15] On 16 October she once again assured Max of her love: "I have just received your dearest letter which I passionately pressed to my lips and heart, it seemed to me already an age since I heard from my dear betrothed ... the only sweet dream of my happiness."[16] Max had become "*Mio tesoro!* [My treasure!]," an exclamation Patti underlined nine times. Three days later she wrote she could not go to sleep without telling him of her devotion, and that he was her main thought day and night. Patti concluded with the message that she was miserable away from him and that she would not be happy until she again clasped him in her arms.

Still, in several months' time these effusions ended. Perhaps Patti, always a prima donna, demanded too much, with Max unable or unwilling to satisfy her emotional needs. At any rate, once again, there was a lovers' quarrel with each going a separate way. Years later when asked why their engagement had ended, Max replied:

> I've forgotten. I suppose we quarreled; we often did, and boys and girls in love always do. Besides, I could never have been the husband of a great prima donna. I am a domestic creature. My only happiness is with such a wife as I have now: a good mother, who gives me always something nice to eat and keeps the buttons sewed on my shirts. Patti could never have done that![17]

During the Théâtre-Italien season extending from October 1864 to March 1865, Patti occasionally appeared with Brignoli, who had made his Parisian debut as Lionel in *Marta* to her Harriet not long after the beginning of the series. In December Berlioz attended a performance of this opera, later responding to it negatively except for her contribution:

> I went to hear that delicious little Patti sing *Martha* the other day: when I came out I felt I was crawling with fleas, as one does after coming out of a dove cote. I told the marvellous creature that I would forgive her for making me listen to platitudes—that was the most I could do! Fortunately it has that exquisite Irish air "The Last Rose of Summer" in it, and she sings it with such poetic simplicity that its perfume is almost enough to disinfect the rest of the score.[18]

A highlight of the season was Patti's portrayal of the titular heroine in *Linda di Chamounix*, a role that she performed for the first time in the French capital on 18 December and that created a sensation. Another highlight was her studying the role of Marguerite in *Faust* with its composer, Charles-François Gounod, who expressed great satisfaction in her interpretation. However, perhaps the event most profoundly affecting her occurred in January after a concert at the Tuileries. Among those contending for an introduction was an equerry of Napoleon III: the Marquis de Caux.

According to Maurice Strakosch, both the evening and the marquis left an indelible impression:

> There was the Emperor beaming in health and at the very zenith of his popularity and power—then the arbiter of Europe; the Empress in all her beauty and literally covered with diamonds, and the young Prince of whom they were so proud; all the marshals and dignitaries of the Empire hanging on the will of their imperial master as if he were something more than human. It was in the Salle [des] Maréchaux. These concerts went off generally, in consequence of the great ceremony observed, in a rather cold way; but on this occasion, to the surprise of everybody, the Emperor was quite enthusiastic, and himself as well as the Empress were so very liberal in their applause that they carried the whole audience with them in a great storm of delight which seemed to send a thrill through all present. . . . After the concert the Emperor and Empress, with the Prince Imperial, came to Adelina and complimented her in the kindest manner. . . . As the imperial party were leaving an *ecuyer* who stood behind them, after adding his compliments in a very enthusiastic manner, offered to escort Adelina to her carriage. This gentleman was the Marquis de Caux.[19]

A second meeting, Maurice said, occurred the following afternoon:

> The marquis came with a splendid pair of diamond earrings—a
> present for Adelina from the Emperor—and a superb bracelet,
> the gift of the Empress, neither of whom, the marquis said, could
> suffer a day to pass before sending Adelina some token of their
> appreciation of her beautiful singing.[20]

In the next several years this marquis's interest in Patti
increasingly alarmed Salvatore and Maurice while it more and more
intrigued her.

Meanwhile, Madrid operagoers had impatiently awaited a series
of Patti performances scheduled for late March and April. By the
time she arrived, the season had suffered a series of reverses with
pundits and a public critical of the artists, orchestra, and productions. Political unease also affected the city's atmosphere, with many
Spaniards then so openly opposed to Queen Isabella II that her
abdication seemed imminent. Patti, however, remained undisturbed
by the political current and was self-possessed even at performances
that might have been disastrous.

Despite the audience's hostile reaction to Queen Isabella II's
presence at a presentation of *Il barbiere di Siviglia,* Patti manifested
equanimity throughout the evening, scoring her usual triumphs as
Rosina. Later, however, she was less composed—trembling before a
benefit concert to aid poor students. Earlier that evening gunshots,
mob roars, and rumors of barricades in the city center had made her
question the advisability of participating. She nonetheless did appear
to an audience's ovation.[21] No doubt Patti felt relieved when the
series ended in late April. Before departing, she was once again
received by Queen Isabella II, who praised her highly and as a token
of esteem gave her a brooch: an amethyst cameo surrounded by forty
pearls.

Back in London for her fifth Covent Garden season, Patti
repeated a number of former successes while appearing, on 6 June
1865, in only one new role: the titular heroine in *Linda di
Chamounix*. Davison in the *Times* considered it an example of the
highest art and was doubtless astounded anew by her vocal power
and control, as evidenced by her singing a trill of seventeen bars in
one breath. Appearing with her here, as in Paris, was Brignoli, having
made his Covent Garden debut approximately a month before. She

might have appeared in another new role during this series had Gye had his way, but she decided against it: "Gye wants me to sing 'Norma.'—Must it always be the drudgery of hard work? I thought I should get a respite from new parts this season. Shall I never rest a little?"[22]

During and after the Covent Garden series, Patti participated in two special musical events. The first occurred on 5 July at St. James's Hall: a concert including Lucca, Mario, Brignoli, and Graziani. It was an affair typical of later Patti concerts with a miscellaneous program featuring various artists. Her associates at these events were other vocalists as well as instrumentalists, with Wilhelm Ganz a frequent accompanist. The second event in which she took part was a Handel Festival in August at the Crystal Palace, where she sang on three occasions and was a skilled interpreter of oratorio, though some thought her better suited for opera and the dramatic expression she obviously preferred.

Then, after making a tour of various music centers in France, Belgium, Holland, and Germany, Patti traveled to Italy, where in six weeks she gave ten performances in Florence and four in Turin. She made her Italian debut at the Teatro Pagliano in Florence on 11 November 1865 in the role of Amina. Among the enthusiastic on this occasion, for which prices had become exorbitant, were Grisi and Mario, who flung a wreath at her feet from their box. At the end of this performance Grisi came onstage to congratulate her erstwhile London colleague, embracing her before the entire company. The following day she and Mario entertained Patti at a dinner party at their Villa Salviati, filled with priceless works of art. Patti followed her sensational debut with performances of Lucia and Rosina. The eminent critic A. Filippi in *Perseveranza di Milano* especially praised her singing:

> Her voice is not only of an extraordinary compass, but is of a rare softness ... delicate and even as well in colour, as in strength. ... And then it is a clear and embellished agility, a thrill which is perfect, an elegance of phrases unique, a taste for passages, which is seldom false ... and of so pure an intonation that she never is at fault.[23]

Subsequently the King of Italy, Victor Emmanuel, and the King and Queen of Portugal received Patti during a performance of *La sonnambula,* lavishing praise for her glorious singing, while in Turin operagoers filling the Teatro Regio were enthralled by what they saw and heard.

After Italy Patti returned to France, where at Marseilles she met with fantastic receptions, her final one bordering on insanity:

> The last evening a perfect ovation was prepared for her on quitting the theatre. Ten thousand individuals were crowded in the very small space which separates the theatre from the Hôtel de Luxemburg. Her carriage and horses proceeded at a foot pace; people threw themselves almost under the wheels, the glasses were smashed, her bonnet fell in the confusion and was instantly torn to atoms, the smallest shred thereof being seized as a relic. On reaching her hotel she was compelled to appear on the balcony, where the crowd obliged her to remain one hour and a half, clamorously beseeching her to throw down some of the flowers under which she had been almost smothered on the stage. Each leaf as it fell was caught and treasured as though it had been the love token of *la diva* to each separate individual of the dense mass of human beings over which her genius swayed with almost supernatural power.[24]

Such acclaim never ceased in the next several years when Patti's professional activities centered in Paris and London, where she sang in some operas new to her repertoire, such as two novelties in Paris: Prince Giuseppe Poniatowski's *Don Desiderio* and Verdi's *Giovanna d'Arco.* She triumphed on 9 November 1867 in the former work, lavishly produced at the Théâtre-Italien with audience response highly favorable. According to a review in *Le Figaro,* the role she portrayed seemed to have been written for her. As Verdi's heroine, however, Patti failed to achieve glory when, on 28 March 1868, she appeared in it for the first time. Though singing superbly, Patti roused little interest in her portrayal of the Maid of Orleans. French critic A. de Gasperini maintained that the failure was not hers but was in the role itself as well as in the music and incondite libretto.

Patti's new parts at Covent Garden included Caterina in *L'étoile du Nord,* on 26 June 1866, with Naudin (Danilowitz), Faure (Peter), and Ciampi (Gritzenko); Annetta in *Crispino e la comare,* on 14 July 1866, with Ronconi (Crispino); and Juliette in *Roméo et Juliette,* on 11 July 1867, with Mario (Roméo), Cotogni (Mercutio), and Tagliafico (Friar Lawrence), this performance being its London premiere. Of Patti's new roles, critics especially lauded her assumption of Gounod's Juliette, citing not only exquisite singing but also her acting—her grace and timidity in opening scenes and a later impassioned tenderness, love, and resoluteness in the death scene. According to the *Athenæum,* Patti as Juliette had "deservedly raised herself higher than she has till now stood by this performance."[25]

In July 1868 a *Pall Mall Gazette* critic evaluated the diva's artistic development since her first European engagements:

> Her career has been as honourably industrious as it has been uniformly successful. Richly endowed, she has not the less perseveringly studied to attain the perfection of detail indispensable to true art, and the defects observable when she first appeared among us have, with laborious and resolute striving, been conquered one by one. Her voice has grown richer and more flexible through constant use—a proof that its use has been legitimate; her vocalization is as fluent and correct as it is brilliant and expressive. As an actress, both in the comic and serious range of characters, she has reached that acme of perfection which makes acting seem no acting at all, but rather truth idealized. Nothing can be more natural, graceful, and spontaneous than her comedy, nothing more deeply felt and touching than her tragedy. In short, she now presents to us the very *beau idéal* of a lyric artist.[26]

A contemporary issue of *Saturday Review* evaluated her similarly:

> In comic opera, in melodramatic opera, in serious opera, she is equally at home; and her repertory probably surpasses in variety and extent that of any singer we could name.... [Her] progress during the brief period of seven years ... is almost, if not quite, unexampled. To have matured herself from the imperfect though richly promising artist she was then into the perfect artist she is now, must have cost no end of thought and persevering study. But these have brought their fruits; and Mlle. Patti enjoys her reward in the unanimous opinion that now places her in the position she holds both as singer and as actress.[27]

In Paris, Albert Vizentini recalled Patti performances at the Théâtre-Italien after her debut there in 1862. Her portrayals of Amina, Lucia, Ninetta, Gilda, Violetta, Norina, Rosina, and Annetta had especially impressed him. He maintained she never played a part; she lived it. He compared her singing to that of a heavenly bird (*un oiseau céleste*) and to a violin virtuoso's playing a Stradivarius.

No other singer in London (or in Europe for that matter) merited such acclaim. At Covent Garden, Patti had more than held her own despite such other highly regarded sopranos in this company as Marie Miolan-Carvalho and Pauline Lucca. Then, too, during these years she prevailed against competition Mapleson provided season after season at a rival London house with his star sopranos Thérèse Tietjens, Ilma di Murska, Clara Louise Kellogg, and Christine Nilsson, whose appearances in Paris at the Théâtre Lyrique had often coincided with Patti's at the Théâtre-Italien. Even her sister Carlotta Patti, singing in London and in other European music centers during the 1860s, did not significantly challenge the diva's sovereignty.

To attain these lofty heights, Patti concentrated on her career, determined to become the world's greatest singer. Her accomplishments were due not only to perseverance and self-discipline, however, but to Maurice Strakosch's influence as both manager and coach. He obtained the best terms possible in professional engagements, regularly went over opera scores with her, enlarged her repertoire, and worked not as singing teacher but as a coach to eradicate flaws the critics had detected. Maurice served in another indispensable way: taking her place at rehearsals of familiar operas, though not generally substituting for her at formal dress rehearsals or at rehearsals for new productions. In short, he acted the part of Svengali, watching that his little sister-in-law took proper care of herself and that she avoided any troublesome situations or people. Years later she said: "Maurice's idea of hygiene was to keep the mind clear of all unnecessary worry and the body clear of all unnecessary food— to live with great regularity and greater moderation."[28] With his direction, she became extremely careful not to exhaust her vitality: conserving her energies on all occasions, keeping herself cheerful, and practicing positive thinking. American soprano Clara Louise Kellogg marveled at this way of living:

> Such a life! Everything divided off carefully according to *régime:*—so much to eat, so far to walk, so long to sleep, just such and such things to do and no others! And, above all, she ... allowed herself few emotions. Every singer knows that emotions are what exhaust and injure the voice.[29]

Still, Patti more and more found time for other pursuits, especially in socializing, and gradually widened her circle of acquaintances and friends, primarily in London and Paris, where her engagements extended over some months.

Since the 1863 Covent Garden season, Patti, Lauw, Salvatore, and Maurice had lived in the quiet London suburb of Clapham Park, approximately a half hour's drive from Charing Cross. Originally they had occupied part of a dwelling at 22 High Street; but in the 1864 season and for the next four successive ones they lived in Pierrepoint House on Atkins' Road, a residence Patti christened Rossini Villa, after the Villa Rossini that the composer occupied during warm months in the Parisian suburb of Passy. Here she relaxed in a spacious dwelling with its adjoining garden, a well manicured lawn, and towering trees. She enjoyed long walks, horseback riding, and driving a one-horse vehicle, though once the horse reared and overthrew the wagon, slightly bruising her. The Rossini Villa afforded an escape from pressures of the opera house and London excitements. Here, too, she entertained as a perfect hostess and socialized with such notables as James Davison and his wife, concert pianist Arabella Goddard; Irish composer Michael William Balfe; Grisi and Mario; soprano Desirée Artot; tenor Alessandro Bettini; mezzo-soprano Zélia Trebelli; and composer Arthur Sullivan.

In Paris Patti also extended her hospitality, though with more care, avoiding, among others, Prince Nariskine, whose attentions annoyed her. During a season at the Théâtre-Italien he sent her a bouquet every evening containing a brooch or bracelet or necklace with his portrait attached and with these words: "It is I, it is I again, it is I always." Each time Patti returned these "too material proofs of an ardent passion."[30] Among those she welcomed, however, on Sunday evenings were celebrated illustrator Gustave Doré; Christine Nilsson, introduced to Patti by Rossini's wife, Olympe; Russian Baron

Thal; Vicomte Paul Daru; Baron de Saint Amant; the Marquis de Caux; and the handsome French actor Jean Mounet-Sully, with whom, so some gossiped, she was having an affair. At these gatherings she charmed her guests with her presence and sartorial panache and received them dressed in the latest fashion—magnificent gowns with crinoline skirts and plunging necklines by couturier Charles Frederick Worth, her hair often done à l'Impératrice Eugénie with jewels blazing in it, as well as around her neck and on her arms and fingers—all flattering her five-foot-two-inch figure and seventeen-inch waist. Her shoes were size two.

Then, also, Patti went out more than before, especially in Paris. Soirées at Doré's house on rue St. Dominique particularly appealed to her, as he was a grand host and provided evenings "famous for their elaborate staging—such as dressing a whole meal à la Post Office in honour of the visiting Postmaster."[31] She sometimes joined him in song as he had a fine voice or listened to his excellent violin playing and yodels or applauded his acrobatic skills or participated in tableaux vivants, the rage at that time. According to gossip, Doré was so much in love with Patti that he threatened to kill himself in her boudoir if she would not have him, an act appropriate to scandalous Second Empire Paris. Ultimately, however, he found solace in the arms of the great French actress Sarah Bernhardt. Patti also spent evenings at the theater, lured by highly emotional dramas that reduced her to tears. Opera bouffes by the clever, cynical Jacques Offenbach delighted her as did one of his greatest stars: Hortense Schneider in his Grand Duchess of Gérolstein at the Théâtre des Variétés. Some speculated that Patti would create a role in his next comic opera.

One evening at Giuseppe Verdi's Paris dwelling was particularly memorable. On 14 February 1866, the composer entertained her and other artists in honor of the sculptor Jean-Pierre Dantan, who had sculpted Verdi's bust. Two days afterwards the composer wrote:

> Strictly speaking it was not a party, for I issued no invitations; but some close friends visited me the other evening to view this bust. They wanted to make music, but I did not permit it, because I wished to avoid publicity—which I managed to do as success-fully as I had found peace and quiet in the Champs-Élysées! We could certainly have made excellent music with Patti, Fraschini, Delle-Sedie, Ronconi, etc., etc.[32]

Perhaps it was on this evening that Verdi signed Patti's autograph album, which already contained entries from Mario, Grisi, Rossini, Meyerbeer, Berlioz, Alboni, Tietjens, Giuglini, Gardoni, Ronconi, Tamberlik, and Arditi, among others. Several weeks later, Rossini hosted a gathering on 9 March, with various artists entertaining. Patti sang excerpts from his operas *Mosè in Egitto, Otello,* and *Il barbiere.*

Hanslick, visiting Paris in the spring of 1867, may have heard her at a Rossini affair. At this time he noted her social climb:

> She had an elegant apartment on the Avenue de l'Impératrice. There were visitors galore and even brilliant parties, where I met a number of celebrities. I made the acquaintance, among others, of the gifted illustrator Gustave Doré and of that famous sportsman the Marquis de Caux, both of whom were infatuated with her. She treated them both with the same friendliness and impartiality—and without a thought of serious involvement.[33]

Perhaps her aloofness was due to yet another romantic affair that had ended disastrously. During the 1866 Covent Garden season at the residence of an elderly Italian gentleman, she met a young man from Milan. Returning home, she amazed Lauw, who was not present at the party, with her emotional reaction:

> She told me even to the slightest details of the interesting acquaintance which she had made . . . with an ardor and an enthusiasm which made me immediately divine that Adelina . . . was desperately in love with the young Signor M——. I had to promise her to seize the first occasion to make the acquaintance of this "interesting young man," as she wished to know the impression which this apparition from the ideal world would make upon me.[34]

Upon meeting him at a dancing party, Lauw admitted that Patti had not exaggerated his charms and attractiveness. He even impressed Salvatore, who invited this Milanese merchant to the Rossini Villa, "a favor of which only a few could boast, and of which the one now in his good graces made the most ample use."[35]

This impetuous, fiery Italian soon gained Patti's favor and asked for Salvatore's blessings on their union. Salvatore said yes provided they not marry for several years. He opposed an early marriage for two reasons: the prospective bridegroom lacked the funds to support a great singer in style, and she did not yet have the capital to "be indifferent to the question whether the business of her husband produced anything or not."[36] Meanwhile, Salvatore decreed that his daughter and her beloved might see each other twice weekly at the Rossini Villa, an arrangement frustrating for the young Milanese. Increasingly tortured by jealousy, this man soon found himself unable to tolerate any Patti-enthusiast or any opera scenes requiring affectionate or amorous displays directed towards her, at which times "his eyes flashed flames and daggers in all directions."[37] Ultimately he gave Salvatore an ultimatum for an early marriage. Salvatore's response then so enraged the man that they had a violent dispute causing him to end his affair with Patti, who, though deeply hurt, reconciled herself to this turn of events and doubted the sincerity of his love.

She remained not long, however, without a love interest: a man she had known for several Parisian seasons, the Marquis de Caux. Seventeen years older than she, this nobleman and ladies' favorite had an inflated ego and a cynical attitude.

As a young man, the marquis, whose Christian name was Louis-Sébastien-Henri de Roger de Cahuzac, had inherited a considerable fortune; but he spent most of it in several years and turned to diplomacy as a career, becoming attached to French embassies at Florence and Rome. Later at the Imperial Court in Paris the marquis served as an equerry to Napoleon III and beguiled the ladies of various Royal palaces with the latest gossip and scandals, second in this respect, said the Count de Soissons, only to Princess de Metternich, the wife of the Austrian ambassador. His stories were "more than risqués."[38] Another Frenchman maintained that the marquis was "never more keenly appreciated by the ladies than during those intervals when conversations were held behind scented fans, and grave indiscretions committed behind kindly screens."[39] De Caux also participated in amateur theatricals often arranged by the Princess de Metternich in the great châteaux of Compiègne, Saint-Cloud, and the Villa Eugénie at Biarritz. He also took part in the Hunt during the Court's sojourns at Compiègne and Fontainebleau. To many, however, he was above all an expert dancer, and for several successive seasons he conducted cotillions at State balls in the Tuileries, where as many as three thousand assembled and where he appeared resplendent in his green and gold uniform. As the leader, De Caux opened the dance with his partner, performing any figure they desired, which other dancers followed. He enjoyed "a reputation for inventing, apparently off-hand, the most striking and at the same time graceful figures of this favourite dance."[40] One American said that his presence at a ball or dinner party assured its success and that he was the most sought-after man in Paris.

Even with their passion for music and dance as mutual interests, Patti and the marquis did not form a romantic attachment until late summer 1867 at Baden-Baden, where she had gone for a holiday. There, one September evening after a dinner at the old castle the marquis had arranged, they became infatuated with each other as a full moon set. Afterwards she declared she had never known such happiness. Daily visits followed, but soon Patti regretfully left him to fulfill engagements at Wiesbaden and Mainz. Observers noted that they parted looking deeply perturbed and sad. They were soon briefly reunited in Paris until the marquis was required to accompany the empress to Biarritz, where he would remain for weeks. He implored her to write him, saying he would initiate the correspondence and continue it faithfully. She enlisted Lauw as intermediary, with his letters to be addressed to her and in turn answered by her with news of Patti, a scenario intended to keep Salvatore and Maurice ignorant of the romance. Lauw not only served as intermediary but championed the marquis's suit, citing him as an eloquent conversationalist, superb horseman, and incomparable dancer.

His return in October overjoyed Patti, who received him daily in her residence on the Champs Élysées, where he ingratiated himself with Salvatore and Maurice while becoming more and more indispensable to her. Two months passed in this manner before the inevitable occurred, with Patti, according to Lauw, initiating it:

> One evening—it was after a performance of *Traviata*—the marquis remained with us—after some friends had retired from Adelina's dressing-room. As he always conscientiously told us the gossip of the day, Adelina turned toward him smilingly and asked: "Now, marquis, what is new; what is Paris talking about?" "The very newest," was the answer, "is that we are engaged." I must admit that I was very much struck with this answer, and that I looked with intense curiosity at Adelina. Her features seemed irradiated by an indescribable love charm. Smilingly she said to the marquis, "And why not? I hope surely that this would not be unpleasant to you?" At first embarrassed, then joyfully agitated,

the marquis could only stammer out the words: "No, certainly not! I should be the happiest of mortals if it were really so!" Blushing sweetly, Adelina extended her hand to the marquis, who was completely disconcerted with joy, saying to him: "And I also should be happy!" Passionately the marquis pressed the offered hand to his lips, drunk with joy he folded Adelina in his arms, and without uttering a word rushed from the room. Adelina, however, whispered in my ear, in a long, ardent embrace, the sweet confession: "I am very happy!"[41]

The next day Patti feared the marquis might not have taken her seriously. Knowing that they and Lauw were to be guests at a dinner party hours later, she implored Lauw to assure him of her sincerity. At the soirée Lauw related Patti's concern to the marquis, who declared that her initiative had made him extremely happy, since as a nobleman without property he would never have dared a marriage proposal.

For a time thereafter, this romantic affair, like others, seemed doomed. When the engagement became public knowledge, Salvatore and Maurice received anonymous letters that "stamped the marquis, who certainly had the reputation of a fast liver, as the most terrible of future husbands, calculated to a sou the dissipation of his fortune, and narrated the most piquant adventures, and at last wound up with the assertion that the marquis was going to marry Adelina 'only on account of her millions.'"[42] To lead his lavish life, the marquis had lived beyond his limited yearly income, at times overextending his financial means even at one of Paris's most exclusive restaurants, Maison-Dorée, where the owner ultimately refused him further credit. Appalled by such accusations and reports, Salvatore determined to break the engagement and sent the marquis a letter to that effect.

Undeterred by Salvatore's wishes, however, the marquis persisted in being as near his beloved as possible for the next three weeks, daily promenading before her residence or occupying a nearby box or seat in every theater she, Lauw, Salvatore, and Maurice patronized. He instructed his coachman to follow Patti and inform him of her whereabouts. Though unable to prevent his presence at a playhouse or his neighborhood walks, Salvatore and Maurice decreed an end to theatergoing.

As for Patti, she stormed and raged daily and resolved to marry the marquis, being then of age to accept marital proposals herself. In the midst of the tribulations, Baron Thal and his family played matchmakers and invited her and the marquis to a dinner party, where they reveled in each other's company. The baron and his wife thereafter invited the two to meet at their residence whenever they desired. Soon they found another rendezvous setting: in the Bois de Boulogne at the fortification.

Empress Eugénie also played a part after De Caux had confided in her, and she encouraged Patti "to go on working for five more years, until she had made an independent fortune, since the marquis had only 10,000 francs (£400) a year; and ... when the income derived from her new fortune secured her an independence, the Empress [Eugénie] would receive her at court as a *dame d'honneur* with some palace honorarium, a position which, so long as she sang for money, she could not hold without wounding a number of vanities and prejudices."[43] As another token of affection for Patti, the empress sealed the proposal with a gift of diamonds and pearl earrings.

The tribulations lessened somewhat when Patti asked for and received the present she most desired for her twenty-fifth birthday: permission from Salvatore for the marquis to visit Rossini Villa upon her arrival in London, where she had been engaged for her eighth successive Covent Garden season. Later Salvatore also reluctantly consented to her marriage to De Caux, after having to deny newspaper reports that it had already been performed: "My attention having been called to a paragraph respecting my daughter, Mdlle. Adelina Patti, which appeared in the *Morning Post* of May 6, copied from the Paris *Figaro*, I beg to say that the statement as to my daughter having been married is totally untrue."[44]

During the 1868 London series, Patti assumed no new opera parts, but impressed the audiences, as always, in familiar ones, especially those with Mario in *Roméo et Juliette*, *Marta*, *Don Giovanni*, and *Il barbiere*. She was, however, preparing for the great new role of the Marquise de Caux.

CHAPTER IV

The Famous Marquise

Shortly before marriage, Patti and the marquis experienced difficulties, one being that De Caux wanted her to leave the stage so he might continue as equerry to the emperor and empress. The Imperial Court would not allow him to retain the position while his wife performed in opera; but financial needs prevailed. They decided she would continue her career for at least several more years. He would resign as equerry. Another problem was his mother. De Caux, whose father had died years before, wanted his mother's blessing. She was, by remarriage, the Duchess de Valmy and an aristocrat from one of France's oldest noble families. Although originally opposed to the match, his mother was swayed by her daughters Princess Ginetti and Countess Reculot into offering her blessing. Then, too, Salvatore and Maurice created ill will by placing a clause in the marriage contract ensuring that Patti's savings and investments before the marriage, a sum said to be from 300,000 to 400,000 francs, were to be deposited in the Bank of England solely in her name, a settlement which the marquis resented as it showed a lack of confidence in him as a gentleman and husband. The marriage contract also stipulated the disposition of her future earnings: "One third . . . was to go to her personally and two-thirds were to go to their joint account after having paid their expenses."[1] Finally, two days before nuptials, Patti, who had been reared a Catholic, belatedly received first communion and the sacrament of confirmation with Grisi's officiating as godmother.

The marriage took place Wednesday morning, 29 July 1868, at

58 The Patti and De Caux wedding party in the garden at Pierrepoint House in
Clapham Park, which Patti called Rossini Villa, 29 July 1868. Salvatore Patti is to
the bride's right. Courtesy of the Board of Trustees of the Victoria & Albert
Museum.

59 As Juliette, Patti created a sensation in St. Petersburg when she first performed the role there in 1872. One of those present described the evening as "one continuous ovation." Courtesy Stuart-Liff.

60 French tenor Ernest Nicolini was Patti's Roméo during the 1872 Russian season. Though Patti initially claimed annoyance with his vanity, womanizing, and boasting, and though each was married, they became the most publicized stage romance of the latter nineteenth century. Courtesy Stuart-Liff.

61 Patti's first assumption of the role of Desdemona in Rossini's *Otello* took place at St. Petersburg's Imperial Theater in January 1871. She repeated her portrayal at Covent Garden later that spring. Courtesy William R. Moran.

62 Patti as Valentine in Meyerbeer's *Les Huguenots,* a part she performed infrequently as, she said, it required all her strength. Her Covent Garden debut of the role occurred in July 1871. Courtesy William R. Moran.

64 Also during the 1873 London season, Patti added Elvira in Verdi's *Ernani* to her Covent Garden repertoire. As a child, she had publicly sung the soprano aria from this opera, "Ernani, involami." Courtesy Stuart-Liff.

63 In the 1873 Covent Garden season, Patti triumphed in her first assumption of the role of Caterina in Auber's *Les dia- mants de la couronne.* Courtesy Stuart-Liff.

65 When Patti first sang Aida—at Covent Garden on 22 June 1876, in the long-awaited London premiere of Verdi's great work—she astounded critics with her emotional resources for this dramatic soprano role. By this time she had changed her mind about the once-annoying Nicolini—eight months later she left her husband. Courtesy Stuart-Liff.

66 Nicolini as Radames, a role he performed opposite Patti at Covent Garden while the two conducted their romance on and off the stage. Many critics thought him ideal in the part, though others tempered their praise. Courtesy Stuart-Liff.

67–69 As the Marquise de Caux, Patti amassed striking attire for social affairs with the Prince and Princess of Wales and other European aristocrats. Courtesy William R. Moran.

70–72 Patti's dresses were handmade by Worth and other famed dressmakers of the time. Courtesy William R. Moran.

73 A fashionable Patti of the 1870s in profile. Courtesy M. E. Saltykov-Shchedrin State Public Library, St. Petersburg, Russia.

74–77 Patti's hair was often arranged in elaborate coiffures, some adorned with flowers or jewels. Courtesy William R. Moran.

78 & 79 Among hair ornaments, lace was a favorite. Courtesy William R. Moran.

80 & 81 Patti's hats varied in size and complexity. Some may actually have offered protection from the elements. Courtesy William R. Moran.

the Roman Catholic Chapel on London's Clapham Park Road. As bridesmaids Patti chose Louisa Lauw; Rita di Candia, Grisi and Mario's daughter; Maria Harris, daughter of the Covent Garden stage manager; and Alexandrine Zanzi. All dressed in white with blue wreaths on their hair, blue ribbons on necks, and blue sashes on gowns. Accompanying De Caux were his cousin French ambassador Prince de la Tour d'Auverge; M. Muro, Secretary of the French Consulate in London; and other friends. The edifice was full with invited guests occupying reserved places, most prominently, Grisi and Mario, composer Prince Giuseppe Poniatowski, Michael Costa, the Duke of Manchester, Frederick Gye, singers from Covent Garden, and eminent music critics. Of Patti's family only Salvatore and Maurice were present. Other members, for one reason or another, were unable to attend, several still living in the United States while Caterina, Amalia, and Carlotta, then in Europe, were conspicuously absent. Outside a throng gathered, extending from Rossini Villa to the chapel, a light rain not dampening their enthusiasm.

When Patti entered, wedding guests beheld her in a white satin dress created by Worth, with a long lace veil and a crown of orange blossoms in her hair. Salvatore accompanied her to the altar, where she knelt and was joined by the marquis. The marriage ceremony was short and when the priest, the Very Rev. F. Plunkett, son of the Earl of Fingal, asked Patti whether she accepted De Caux as her husband, she "uttered so full and clear a 'Yes,' as though she wished to bind herself beyond the grave, to her beloved husband."[2] After he placed a gold ring on her finger, the two went into the vestry-room, signing civil and ecclesiastical registers witnessed by the Prince de la Tour d'Auverge, M. Muro, Michael Costa, and the Duke of Manchester. Returning to the chapel, the newlyweds participated in the marriage mass. Afterwards the marquis and marquise left amid plaudits, driving off in a coach to the Rossini Villa, where a breakfast awaited for about sixty guests.

In the garden workers had pitched a large tent decorated with flowers and the flags of Italy, France, Spain, England, and the United States. During the repast the Duke of Manchester offered the first toast; others followed with Mario commenting to music historian H. Sutherland Edwards that "the Marquis, much as he might be attached to his fascinating bride, had never made love to her so much as he, her constant lover, had done."[3] Afterwards in the garden, well-known photographer Southwell photographed the wedding party.

The wedding presents included a sapphire and diamond bracelet from the marquis's mother, a bracelet of diamonds and rubies from the Duke of Manchester, a coral set mounted in gold from Mario, a white lace fan from Grisi, much beautiful glassware, and many art objects. Later the most intimate friends remained to observe the custom of throwing old shoes and slippers for good luck at the newlyweds' departing coach. This custom perhaps reassured De Caux, who had earlier lost a diamond setting from a ring Patti had given him and who considered it a portent of bad luck.

As evening approached, the two left London for a Paris honeymoon in a furnished Moorish mansion rented to them by the French writer and wag Arsène Houssaye. This place appealed to Patti, who had attended a party there. As their neighbor, Houssaye remembered the first days of the honeymoon:

> I was delighted with my new neighbor because often in the morning the lovely Marquise opened the connecting door to let me witness her morning trills and flourishes. She was a true nightingale. Everything about her sang; her eyes, her smile, the curve of her throat and the shimmer of her hair. Fortunately for me, I was not in love with her no matter how much I was charmed by her; moreover, in addition to my well-known virtue—and hers—her husband was always at home.[4]

On the second day in the mansion, the Duke de Valmy came to offer his congratulations and to invite them to a dinner party the following evening. Patti dreaded meeting her mother-in-law, fearful she would be subjected to chilling condescension, as the Duchess de Valmy was known for strong aristocratic principles. Her apprehension proved groundless, however, when the noblewoman, "a lady of exceptional intelligence and fascinating amiability, folded her so affectionately in her arms, and called her her dearest daughter."[5] During the evening Patti sang, and one guest expressed an opinion that the marquis would never be a satisfactory partner for an artist and that the diva had yet to experience grand passion.

Their time in Paris was brief, with Patti soon resuming her career at the fashionable spa at Homburg. A local paper *Der Taunusbote* celebrated her return as Lucia, on 15 August, in a cast including

Naudin as Edgardo with Luigi Orsini as conductor. A week later Patti appeared as the titular heroine in Rossini's *Semiramide,* a part she had first essayed in 1866, and towards the end of September she returned to Paris for a short season. Many Parisians were curious about the spectacle of a marquise upon the boards. Even Patti wondered what her reception as a member of one of France's noblest families would be and whether she would create a scandal as a noble-woman daring to appear on stage for vile mercenary reasons.

She need not have worried, however. Opening this season as Lucia on 1 October, she received only cheers, recalls, and torrential applause. During the series she appeared in a number of her familiar roles to great acclaim and mounting revenue.

Socially, during these first months of marriage, Patti also created a sensation among elegant society. Regarding her association with nobility, New York's *Spirit of the Times* commented: "This is a great company, indeed, for the little girl whom we recollect so well, singing at Maurice Strakosch's concerts when she was scarcely taller than the piano."[6] Some wondered whether this social position might change her character or whether she might find it and the life of an artist incongruent. De Caux thought not, but preferred to separate the title of nobility from her professional calling. In time Paris society received an invitation from him making this point clear: "The Marquise de Caux will be at home from nine to twelve on Saturday next. La Patti will sing."[7] This invitation spoke volumes.

The marquis gradually assumed the new role of entrepreneur and managed Patti's career and property. An excerpt from a letter he wrote in 1874 reveals his attention to details as well as a patronizing air:

We intend leaving London August 1st for Dieppe, where we shall stay the whole of the month. From Dieppe we go to Paris, and September 20th we come back to England for a few con-certs in the North—the Liverpool Festival, September 29 and 30; and a concert at Brighton, October 2nd, *en route* for Paris. October 22nd we leave Paris for Moscow, where my wife will sing from October 31st until December 1st. On the 7th Decem-ber, she will make her [reentry] at St. Petersburgh, and will stay there till the end of the season, March 7th. On the 15th she will begin her Vienna season, which will conclude May 3rd; and on the 10th May . . . she will, by God's help, make her [reentry] at

Covent Garden, very happy to find herself in dear old England. I hope she will bear all this hard work as bravely as she has done for many years; and, for my own part, . . . [the] only prayer I have to address to God is, to keep her in good health.[8]

Meanwhile, Patti received alarming news concerning Rossini, who beginning several months after her marriage had suffered from a rapidly spreading cancer. Two operations in the first part of November did not relieve him from constant pain, and his condition so worsened that his wife implored Abbé Gallet to dispense last sacraments. Patti and other devoted friends were present when he administered Extreme Unction. After the final benediction she collapsed.

Late the evening of 13 November 1868, Rossini died. His funeral took place on 21 November, in the Église de la Trinité, where more than four thousand mourners participated in a service that included music by Jommelli, Mozart, Pergolesi, Beethoven, and Rossini. The duet from Rossini's *Stabat Mater*, "Quis est homo qui non fleret," sung by Patti and Alboni, was described by Gounod as the "most heavenly and touching musical moment of his whole existence."[9] Outside, the sky seemed draped in mourning and Paris, to many, had never looked so devastated.

Patti treasured memories of this great man, always kind and considerate, her staunch admirer. When Hanslick visited Rossini in the previous year, the composer spoke of Patti with much admiration, singling "her out as an exception when deploring the extinction of truly great singers."[10]

Rossini's death ended a remarkable phase in her European experiences and career. She would never again know its like.

In the next two years, Patti's professional activities centered in St. Petersburg, Paris, and London. The Russian capital and Paris applauded and cheered her in a number of familiar parts, while London operagoers saw her in several new roles.

The financial terms for engagements in St. Petersburg were generous: 200,000 francs a season as well as 30,000 francs from two benefits, the series usually extending over three winter months. The fiscal picture had never looked brighter. Contracts with chief European opera houses for the next three years amounted to 1,600,000 francs—approximately 64,000 pounds or $320,000.

Arriving in St. Petersburg soon after the new year of 1869, Patti was greeted at the railway station by members of the Imperial Opera as well as by wildly cheering fans. From there she went to the Hotel Demouth, where impresario Intendant Excellenz Guedeonoff had engaged a suite of twelve rooms, all superbly furnished and ornamented with flowers and exotic plants. In preparing for her, the owner of this establishment had expended 80,000 francs.

The following day, Patti received many visitors, the first being Pauline Lucca, who also resided in this hotel, then Minister Count Alexander Vladimirovich Adlerberg, Czar Alexander II's companion and closest friend. Later she was obliged to appear at a rehearsal of *La sonnambula,* the opera she, as usual, chose for her debut in new surroundings. Orchestra members greeted her enthusiastically, a preview of the reception she received at her initial public performance.

When it occurred on 14 January 1869, the house erupted with Czar Alexander II, Czarina Maria Alexandrovna, and members of the Imperial Court among those leading the welcome. Patti took her bows in a storm of flowers costing 6000 rubles, all thrown or handed to the diva (a single camellia at that time cost four rubles). At the end of this debut the audience lingered and called her out over forty times. Outside an enormous crowd surrounded her Imperial carriage, provided by the czar, and with only the greatest difficulty, she entered it and left the scene.

At a later performance of *Il barbiere di Siviglia,* the czar and other Russian aristocrats received Patti in the Imperial loge. In the lesson scene she had included, among other selections, a song sung in Russian, pronouncing the words clearly and faultlessly and bringing the house down.

In time the fifty-year-old Czar of All the Russias and the czarina took much interest in Patti, who, decreed the czar, was to address him as papa and his wife as mama. At some intermissions thereafter the czarina maternally offered Patti tea, while the czar, always attracted to beautiful young women, looked on approvingly and presumably evinced only paternal concern.

For many and, no doubt, for Patti herself, the last performances

came too soon. Before their end, however, she appeared at a gala as
Norina in *Don Pasquale*, followed by a reception at her hotel. During
intermissions she received many baskets of flowers, a set of diamond
studs from the czar, and a brilliant diamond brooch from her adoring
public, the central stone of which was valued at between 60,000 to
80,000 francs, and which Catherine II had once given to a favorite.
Returning to the hotel, Patti discovered surprises: a flourish of
trumpets sounded from an invisible band in the vestibule; twelve
young girls threw flowers; and six generals placed the diva in a chair
of blossoms, bearing her in solemnity and triumph to her suite while
the band played the overture to *Don Pasquale*. Afraid these generals
might drop her, De Caux kept calling out, in his words, not to break
her. In the suite, friends and admirers joined Patti for a festive supper
and many toasts until four in the morning.

For her final St. Petersburg performance she intended to portray
Amina but after vocalizing several hours before the performance
found her voice husky. Conferring with a homeopathist and the
opera's conductor, she determined to sing not in *La sonnambula* but
in *Don Pasquale*. Patti managed to get through the first two acts fairly
well but then realized she could not continue. Though Director
Guedeonoff and the Grand Dukes Vladimir and Alexis (Czar
Alexander II's sons) encouraged her to finish the opera, Patti's voice
by then had completely failed her. Meanwhile, intermission having
been prolonged, the audience became restive, some murmuring that
the wait was due to a prima donna caprice.

At this moment Director Guedeonoff recognized in one of the
boxes a soprano who had appeared with his company: Elisa Volpini.
Without further ado, he begged this artist to replace Patti. Volpini,
whose contract for the following year had not been extended,
declared she would finish the opera provided that he renewed her
contract and raised her salary by 5000 francs. Moments later he
announced the change, an announcement that

> put the public in a state of boundless excitement, and divided
> them immediately into two camps. The Patti-ites hissed, the
> Volpini-ites clapped and cried "Bravo!" at the top of their lungs.
> Before, however, Madame Volpini appeared upon the stage, [the
> diva] had to show herself in the simplest house-toilet to the
> public, which manifested its warmest sympathy for her, cer-
> tainly not without a counter-demonstration on the part of the
> Volpini-ites.[11]

Looking back on this series, Russian operagoers had a wealth of Patti memories. One critic in the *Journal de St. Pétersbourg* especially remembered that golden voice:

> In Adelina Patti we find virtuosity *par excellence*. We have here, in the first place, an exceptional and unrivalled voice, ... an admirable method, and miracles without number of agility and wonderful feats of mechanical skill. This is not perhaps the result of any great application on her part; it is the result of a most happy and peculiar organisation—it is the natural singing of a bird created to sing.... The first time you hear her you are astonished; you are dazzled by the vocal pyrotechnic display, the flute-like arabesques in the highest register possible to the human voice (going up to the high F) are something so striking, and then, suddenly forming such a contrast to them, the full, sonorous phrases of a mellow voice in the lowest notes of a genuine soprano. A moment afterwards you find yourself under the spell of a beautiful, perfect style of execution.[12]

As for Patti, she recalled St. Petersburg happily:

> It is worth ten years of one's life to be a favourite for one night in St. Petersburg. They avalanche their applause upon you after a successful effort until you feel as happy as an angel. I have been called out again and again until I had no strength to stand any longer, and then was obliged to sit on a chair upon the stage and wait until the audience would let me go.[13]

Such boundless enthusiasm inspired her to hyperbole: "Oh, those Russians! They would rip the Tropic of Capricorn off the earth and fling it to you for a belt."[14] Of various tributes given her there, she especially appreciated student offerings:

> On the occasion of my benefit ... I ... stood ankle deep in flowers that were flung upon the stage—hundreds of them—flung, not by the rich, but by the poor, hungry students; and that at a time of the year when a rosebud, tied to a simple fern leaf, cost $1.25 at the florist's.[15]

Patti's second season in St. Petersburg extended from November 1869 to March 1870, when she appeared in the roles of Violetta, Zerlina in *Don Giovanni*, Linda, Dinorah, and Amina, among others. Czar Alexander II, appointing the diva a Court singer, awarded her the Order of Merit for exceptional talents said to be valued at about

10,000 francs. She also received costly gifts from members of nobility, gifts prompting her to write: "London is good, Paris is better, St. Petersburg best. Never such enthusiasm. . . . Emperor exceedingly kind. My collection of jewels is growing fast. Such diamonds as they present one with here!"[16] An author who knew her well commented: "The diamonds she carried away from Russia constituted in themselves a small fortune."[17] At her benefit on 3 March, she received a superb brooch with a pearl in the center surrounded by twenty large diamonds valued at 70,000 francs. During this evening Patti appeared in the first acts of *Crispino e la comare* and *La traviata* and in the Mad Scene from *Lucia*. Later a journalist recalled this occasion: "The worthy singer has had many glorious triumphs in her life as an artist, but here the enthusiasm, the frenzy of the multitude defy all description and have mounted to a pitch as yet unknown in the annals of the theater."[18]

In 1869 and 1870 at the Théâtre-Italien in Paris, Patti enjoyed artistic triumphs and many social events. With the marquis, she was a guest at the Tuileries as well as at other great châteaux. In turn they offered their own receptions. At one of these Auber, not a flatterer, compared her voice to the singing of past great artists: "I have seen and heard many singers. I remember Catalani, Pasta, Malibran, Grisi, and Sontag. But I never heard so perfect an artist as Patti. As for her voice, it is without a flaw."[19] At another soireé, this one given in honor of the Crown Prince of the Netherlands and including members of the highest French nobility, Patti and her sisters Amalia and Carlotta sang the trio from Cimarosa's opera *Il matrimonio segreto*.

In November 1869 Patti especially endeared herself to a number of Parisians when she participated in a benefit performance for Sarah Bernhardt, who had recently lost all her possessions in a fire. Years later the actress recalled the occasion:

> This benefit was a wonderful success, thanks to the presence of the adorable Adelina Patti. . . . Her husband [De Caux had been one of Bernhardt's "protectors"] came during the afternoon, to tell me how glad she was of this opportunity of proving to me her sympathy. As soon as the "fairy bird" was announced, every seat in the house was promptly taken, at prices which were higher than those originally fixed. She had no reason to regret her friendly action, for never was any triumph more complete. The students greeted her with three cheers as she came on the stage.

She was a little surprised at this noise of bravos in rhythm. I can see her now coming forward, her two little feet incased in pink satin. She was like a bird hesitating as to whether it would fly or remain on the ground. She looked so pretty, so smiling, and when she trilled out the gem-like notes of her wonderful voice the whole house was delirious with excitement. Everyone sprang up and the students stood on their seats, waved their hats and handkerchiefs, nodded their young heads, in their feverish enthusiasm for art, and encored with intonations of the most touching supplication. The divine singer then began again, and three times over she had to sing the *cavatina* from the "Barber of Seville," *Una voce poco fa.*

I thanked her affectionately afterwards, and she left the theater escorted by the students, who followed her carriage for a long way, shouting over and over again: "Long live Adelina Patti!"[20]

During the 1870 Paris spring season at the Théâtre-Italien, Verdi and Auber attended two performances. After a presentation of *Rigoletto,* Verdi sent her a card reading: "*Alla mia unica e vera Gilda* [To my unique and true Gilda]."[21] She most impressed him in the recitative preceding the quartet in the last act, when, as Verdi wrote in a letter to the Milanese publisher Giulio Ricordi, her father "points out her lover in the tavern and says 'And you still love him?', and she replies 'I love him'. Words cannot express the sublime effect of these words, when sung by her."[22] After returning to his home in Italy, Verdi wrote to his friend Clarina Maffei on 20 April that he had found nothing good at the opera except for one artist—Patti! Following another performance, Auber responded to her question as to whether he liked her new stud of diamonds, presumably the ones the czar had given her: "The diamonds you wear are beautiful, but those you put in our ears are a thousand times more beautiful."[23]

In her London 1869–70 engagements, Patti appeared at Covent Garden for the first time as Gilda in *Rigoletto*; the titular heroine in Fabio Campana's *Esmeralda*; and Elvira in *I puritani*. Here, too, she and De Caux moved in the highest social circles. These two seasons in London's opera world saw some notable changes, however. Eschewing their rivalry, Gye and Mapleson joined forces at Covent Garden for a series of performances in what were called "coalition seasons." In 1869 Gye ended his professional relationship with Costa as principal conductor, replacing him with Luigi Arditi and Signor Li Calsi. In 1870 Gye also engaged Auguste Vianesi as conductor, formerly of the Imperial Opera in St. Petersburg. Leading singers during these "coalition seasons" included sopranos Di Murska, Lucca, Nilsson, Patti, and Tietjens; mezzo-soprano Sofia Scalchi; tenors Mario, Mongini, Naudin, and Tamberlik; and baritone and basses Ciampi, Cotogni, Foli, Graziani, and Santley. London operagoers saw and heard virtually all the world's greatest singers at Covent Garden during this time.

Patti's first appearance there as Gilda, on 21 July 1869, merited high praise vocally and dramatically, with her having acquired a great "force in the expression of tragic pathos and emotion, without losing any portion of that genial grace and charm which were heretofore considered her chief characteristics."[24] The following year, before assuming the title role of *Esmeralda,* she had a disagreement with the German tenor Theodor Wachtel resulting in some sensational publicity to her disadvantage. In a letter to the editor of *Musical World,* Wachtel gave some intriguing details:

> Before leaving London I feel myself compelled to give the following explanation, in order to avoid all future misunderstanding. During the last representation of *Don Giovanni* ... Madame Patti (Marquise de Caux) believed herself insulted by me, and in consequence informed Mr. Gye that she should decline to sing again with me. Although afterwards it was proved that the alleged insult was the result of a misunderstanding on the part of Madame Patti, and as such acknowledged by her, yet I felt it due to my reputation as an artist, and also to my personal honour, to request Mr. Gye to release me from my engagement, which he has accordingly done. [25]

Patti's singing as Esmeralda was about the only feature critics liked in Campana's opera, first given at Covent Garden on 14 June 1870. They thought the libretto a travesty of Victor Hugo's *The Hunchback of Notre Dame* while the score, said *The Illustrated London News,* aimed more at "prominence of melody and florid vocalization ... than at depth of expression or intense dramatic effect."[26] *Musical World* described the score as "the work of a composer whose ambition has outgrown his powers and placed him in a false position."[27] Patti's final new role at Covent Garden, first performed there on 5 July 1870, was Elvira in *I puritani* with new tenor Vizzani as Arturo, replacing Wachtel. According to the *Illustrated London News,* her conception of Elvira was "admirable in every respect, dramatic and vocal."[28]

As for London social triumphs, Patti and De Caux were included in engagements hosted by the Prince and Princess of Wales, one being a party in their honor after their arrival for the 1869 Covent Garden season. The prince led Patti to the table and placed her at his right while De Caux offered his arm to the princess and took his place at her right. On 26 June Patti sang after a dinner party at Marlborough House, the Prince and Princess of Wales's London mansion, given in honor of the Viceroy of Egypt. Then, several weeks later they attended a ball at Marlborough House, where the Princess of Wales received Patti for a private, farewell audience, as she was departing for a short season at Homburg. Her Royal Highness introduced the diva to the Royal children and gave her a bracelet of turquoises and diamonds, which she clasped on Patti's arm.

Months later, during the 1870 opera season, the Prince and Princess of Wales continued to receive Patti and De Caux with utmost cordiality. The prince, enjoying practical jokes, once invited Nilsson, Lucca, and Patti to a party, requesting they sing the scolding trio in *Il matrimonio segreto,* convinced the three prima donnas would try to upstage one another and provide great amusement. Divining his purpose, Patti outwitted him and plotted with her singing colleagues to draw out the piece with such a funereal air that "the whole company, with the joke-loving royal host at their head, helplessly stared at this hand-organ trio."[29]

Later Patti and De Caux were flabbergasted to discover the prince had made a surprise visit to their London residence when they were not there. Failing to recognize this august caller, a servant asked for his card. Not having one, the caller told the servant to tell his master and mistress that the Prince of Wales had been to see them and regretted his having missed them at home.

Still, in the midst of artistic and social triumphs, Patti and De Caux experienced personal disasters. Berlioz died on 8 March 1869. Five months later Salvatore Patti succumbed to a stroke. After Patti's marriage he had gone to Paris to live with Amalia, Maurice, and their two children; and there, on 23 August 1869, he breathed his last. Approximately a year later, on 7 September 1870, Caterina Patti died in Rome. A final tragedy involving Patti and De Caux as well as many,

many others was the Franco-Prussian War, which began in July 1870. By the time it ended six months later, the Second Empire had fallen; Napoleon III was a prisoner in Germany; Eugénie had fled to England; and Patti's and De Caux's dream of a future life at the Imperial Court had vanished forever.

During the 1870s Patti performed primarily in Moscow, St. Petersburg, Vienna, and London and reached the zenith of her vocal and artistic powers. Early in this decade, she first appeared in Moscow for several presentations. Before the first of these, she brushed too close to a spirit-lamp at the base of a looking glass, and her dress burst into flames. Fortunately she remained calm while others extinguished the blaze. Afterwards, however, Patti fainted but, soon revived, proceeded to the stage and sang as gloriously as ever.

In Moscow and St. Petersburg, as formerly in Paris and London, Patti was compared to Christine Nilsson, both sopranos engaged for a series in the two Russian cities. The public insisted there was intense rivalry between the two, who did not appear in the same city simultaneously, an arrangement, according to an article in an 1872 journal, precluding any immediate assault: "Whilst Madame Nilsson is in St. Petersburg, Madame Patti will be in Moscow; and when she has completed her engagement she will go to St. Petersburg, and Madame Nilsson will go to Moscow. The contending stars will not, therefore, be in immediate collision."[30] Not long thereafter, collision occurred with Nilsson's initiating it:

> Madame Nilsson opened fire . . . in a telegram to Paris from St. Petersburg, addressed to her teacher, . . . informing him that she had achieved, as Ophelia, a grand triumph. . . . Her agent, or her husband, supplemented this new news by telegraphing that the fair Swede had been recalled thirty times. These despatches roused the Parisian agents of Madame Adelina Patti, and they at once published counter-telegrams, stating that Madame La Marquise de Caux had been recalled thirty-six times in Verdi's . . . *Traviata*.[31]

Later Tolstoy gave this rivalry some passing attention in *Anna Karenina*.

According to the *St. Petersburgh Gazette,* Patti was now at the apogee of her career, but the *Gazette*'s music critic conceded that she still might "surpass all provisions and baffle all calculations."[32] Tchaikovsky expressed his admiration by deriding her critics:

> As soon as anyone enjoys a reputation for musical knowledge, he holds it for his duty to proclaim that Patti leaves him cold, sings without expression, like a bird, or—to be more severe—like a clarinet become flesh. And there are singular coots who describe her as a stick of wood. I assure you that this is the sheerest nonsense, the meanest slander. . . . Aside from the artistic purity of her coloratura and the accuracy of her intonation, all the registers of her voice are of like strength and beauty; she sings with exceeding taste, and she possesses sufficient warmth and native, genuine animation in her performance.[33]

Another Russian admirer was director Constantin Stanislavsky:

> My impressions of the Italian opera are sealed not alone in my visual or aural memory,—for I still feel them physically with my entire nervous system. When I remember them I experience again that physical state which was created in me by the super-normally high and silvery note of Adelina Patti, by her coloratura and technique which made me hold my breath, by her full chest tones which caused my spirit to swoon and brought a smile of satisfaction to my lips. Together with this [there] is sealed in my memory her exquisite little figure and her profile that seemed to be cut from ivory and had something porcelain-like about it.[34]

The eminent Russian critic Vasili Lenz, writing in the 17 January 1873 issue of the *Journal de St. Pétersbourg,* described her as the greatest contemporary artist of the lyric stage. Still, Alexander Serov's and critic F. M. Tolstoy's admiration of Patti made anyone else's seem ridiculous. Observing such enthusiasm, Mussorgsky satirized Italian opera and Patti in his musical lampoon *Peepshow,* written in 1870. Lyrics in one song included such lines as "O Patti, Patti, / O Pa-pa-Patti, / Wonderful Patti, / *Marvelous Patti,* / O Patti, Patti, / O Ti-ti Patti. / Wonderful Patti, / Glorious Patti!"[35]

Both in Moscow and St. Petersburg, she experienced unprecedented successes, whether in familiar roles or in such unfamiliar ones as the titular heroine in Gounod's *Mireille* (1874) and Caterina in Auber's *Les diamants de la couronne* (1876). Among roles that especially pleased Russians was her portrayal of Gounod's Juliette, beginning 8 February 1872 in St. Petersburg with tenor Ernest Nicolini. An individual at this performance wrote:

> Patti surprised and astounded the warmest admirers of her talent and of herself individually, that is to say: the entire public. It was one continuous ovation. . . . The audience applauded with tears in their eyes. . . . By the side of such a Juliette, Nicolini really surpassed himself. He acted and sang his fine part to perfection. The last scene, that of the death of the two lovers, gave the finishing touch to the enthusiasm of the public. . . . The Emperor and the Empress, with all the Imperial Family, sent for . . . them. The Empress herself expressed a wish for the opera to be repeated next Wednesday, as she wished to see it again.[36]

Though another work had been scheduled for that day, the impresario altered all arrangements.

Patti as Juliette created a problem in the Imperial Family that she later recalled:

> One day . . . after a concert at the winter palace, Czar Alexander II . . . said to the little grand dukes, Paul and Serge, "Kiss the hand of the greatest singer of her day." The little boys would regularly come to the opera to hear me sing. But one night Paul came alone. "Mother would not let Serge come to-night," he said, in reply to my inquiry.
> "Why?" I asked.
> "Because, the other morning, after he had heard you sing in *Romeo and Juliet,* they found some verses under his pillow written to Mademoiselle Patti as 'Juliet.' So mother won't let him come."[37]

Czar Alexander II outdid the rest of the Imperial Family in Patti-worship, and his appearance onstage at the Imperial Opera after her 1873 benefit in St. Petersburg to present a diamond coronet shaped as wild roses shocked many who did not consider such a public display *de rigueur*. An unfavorable press comment soon followed:

> At the inspiriting sight of the Czar of all the Russias making a present on the public boards to an undoubtedly charming prima donna the loyal audience rose as one man and applauded with enthusiasm; though what they applauded, whether the Emperor or the prima donna, or the homage done by the former to the

latter, does not appear. This seems to us the most extraordinary performance in which royalty has taken part since the days of Louis XIV, who, though he acted and danced on the stage, did so only at Court entertainments, where he was more or less among acquaintances.[38]

The czar's tribute on this occasion and later ones inspired largesse from others, giving such gifts as a gold circlet ornamented with a star of diamonds, a locket covered with diamonds and rubies, an enormous jeweled butterfly in diamonds, and a brooch with twenty-seven large pear-shaped pendent pearls surrounding scrolls of diamonds. At Patti's 1873 benefit in Moscow, where Muscovites called her "Little Mite," she received

> monster bouquets, enormous baskets of white camelias [sic], hundreds of wreaths and ditto of bouquets, and ladies waving their handkerchiefs; the students up aloft yelling her name with deafening cheers; the curtain being pulled up and down every three or four minutes. She had over 80 calls during the evening. At last she was so fearfully fatigued, it was proposed to carry her on a chair to acknowledge their calls, but the little lady resisted, and stood it like a martyr.[39]

The following year Moscow operagoers presented her with a golden crown; five diamond stars with a ruby in the center of each star; a pendalock of diamonds; a gold cup, saucer, and spoon inlaid with precious stones; a pearl fan; a ruby and diamond ring; and quantities of enormous baskets and bouquets of flowers.

Then, attending a British ambassador's reception, Patti left another indelible impression:

> At the soirée, at which "everybody" who was "anybody" at St. Petersburg was present, I was more than mildly thrilled when . . . "Madame Patti" was announced. The representative of Queen Victoria received the Opera Queen at the entrance to the great salon. As she passed slowly and majestically between the "hedge" she bestowed her smiles on all. She sparkled with diamonds on her head, round her neck, and on her corsage and hands. "A charming vision," murmured austere diplomats.[40]

Patti was also present in St. Petersburg on 23 January 1874, when the czar's only daughter, Grand Duchess Marya Alexandrovna, married Queen Victoria's son the Duke of Edinburgh. British ambassador Lord Loftus described the marriage ceremony in the chapel of the Winter Palace and a banquet afterwards at which Patti, Canadian soprano Emma Albani, and Ernest Nicolini sang:

> The Greek service was performed with due impressiveness. The deep tone of the choir, the thrilling force of the chants mingled with the grand voices of the clergy, the magnificent dress and jewelled ornaments of the priesthood, and the impressive forms of the Greek service, gave an imposing and solemn effect to the ceremony. The Emperor, who took his usual place on the right of the altar, looked pale and appeared deeply moved, no doubt feeling acutely his separation from his only daughter, to whom he was devotedly attached—who had been his daily companion— his idol of love and affection. The Empress, who had been in delicate health, and showed symptoms of suffering, both physical and mental, stood on the right of the Emperor and next Her Majesty the Crown Princess of Germany, as sister of the bridegroom. Then came the Cesarevna and the Princess of Wales, the two sisters, beaming with beauty and delight at being together, and on whom the eyes of all rested with admiration and pride. . . . Immediately behind the bride and bridegroom stood the three brothers of the bride, . . . and Prince Arthur, who relieved each other in turn in holding . . . the golden crowns over the heads of the bride and bridegroom. . . . At half-past four the grand banquet took place at the Winter Palace, when 700 guests were seated at table. On this occasion I was seated immediately opposite the Emperor, having on my right Prince Gortschakoff and on my left Prince Reuss, the German Ambassador. Nothing could exceed the grandeur of this banquet. The display of magnificent jewels, the brilliancy of the uniforms, the mass of ornamental gold and silver plate, the priceless value of the rarest Sèvres china, added to the vocal talents of Patti, Albani, and Nicolini, who sang the most lovely airs during dinner, gave a charm and perfection to a scene, which, for its unrivalled beauty, is quite indescribable.[41]

After a nine-year absence from Vienna, Patti reappeared there as Lucia on 19 March 1872 at the Theater an der Wien and remained until the end of April. She returned each season through 1877, adding to the roles in which she had enthralled the Viennese in her first engagement there—Amina, Lucia, Rosina, Norina, Violetta, and Zerlina in *Don Giovanni*—leading parts in *Il trovatore, Dinorah, Les*

Adelina Patti
A Color Portfolio

Patti in her favorite color, pink, in an 1873 portrait by Frossard. It was said her "name, her personality, the circumstances of her public and private life were discussed in every drawing-room." Courtesy Stuart-Liff.

Winterhalter portrait of Patti as Rosina in *Il barbiere di Siviglia,* commissioned by Empress Eugénie and completed in 1862. Courtesy Brita Cederström Elmes.

Also by Winterhalter, this painting dates from the 1860s, when Patti kept an elegant apartment on the Avenue de l'Impératrice. Courtesy Earl of Harewood Collection at Harewood House, Leeds.

Noted artist Gustave Doré, infatuated with Patti, painted two portraits of her in 1867. Again, she is dressed *à l'Impératrice Eugénie,* who epitomized chic in Second Empire society. Courtesy Christine Scott Plummer.

This portrait by Doré reveals a dreamy, contemplative Patti. Courtesy Glynn Vivian Art Gallery, Leisure Services Department: Swansea City Council/David Brinn.

Patti as Desdemona in Rossini's *Otello,* by Steinhardt. For years this portrait hung in the Patti Theatre at Craig-y-Nos. It is now at the National Museum of Wales, Cardiff. Courtesy Mike Cooper and David Brinn.

Portrait of Patti by H. Schadow, 1895. It hangs in the Guildhall, Brecon. Courtesy Brecon Town Council/David Brinn.

Huguenots, Roméo et Juliette, Faust, Linda di Chamounix, I puritani, Marta, Semiramide, Rigoletto, Ernani, Rossini's *Otello,* and *Mireille.* One of her conductors was Luigi Arditi, who recalled the furor she created:

> It was Patti, Patti, Patti, and nothing but Patti. All the enthusiasm, all the excitement, was concentrated on her. People followed her carriage for miles just to catch a glimpse of her, and I have heard tell that some of her admirers took rooms in the Hotel Munsch (where she invariably stayed) in the hope of being privileged to meet her on the stairs, or to see her coming from or going to her room.[42]

Emperor Francis Joseph, also an enthusiast, appointed her Court Singer.

In 1879 Hanslick recorded his impressions of Patti as singer and artist. She possessed, said this critic, three extraordinary operatic assets: "refinement of hearing, quickness to grasp and to learn, and a secure memory."[43] Her intonation was faultless: at a benefit performance of Gounod's *Faust* on 1 May 1877, she responded to an ovation of fifteen minutes by repeating the "Jewel Song," beginning without orchestral support on the correct pitch. In learning a new role, Patti, to Hanslick's amazement, needed to sing it only two or three times *sotto voce.* Before her marriage, Maurice had played new parts on the piano while she, busy with other matters, listened from an adjoining room, and after her marriage she continued in that fashion, engaging an accompanist for this purpose. As for her secure memory, she rarely forgot what she had learned. Hanslick recalled only a few seconds of uncertainty during an intermission of *Don Pasquale*:

> In the final performance . . . I visited her in her dressing room after the first act. In the course of the conversation she asked to see a piano score of the opera. She opened it to the second act, sang two measures *sotto voce,* and laid the book aside, continuing with the conversation. "What was it?" I asked. "Nothing," she answered. "I know the opera by heart all right, although I sang it last a year ago. But I sang *Linda* day before yesterday, and I just remembered that a certain part in *Linda* starts exactly like a part in the second finale of *Don Pasquale.* I just wanted to make sure that I would not fall into the wrong theme."[44]

As for Patti's repertoire, Hanslick most admired her in such half-serious, cheerful roles as Rosina, Norina, and Zerlina in *Don Giovanni,* her physical appearance lending credibility to these parts. He noted that she increasingly preferred more serious, heavier roles. Of these, he admired her as Leonora in *Il trovatore* and praised her singing of the principal arias, her dramatic gestures, and facial expressions. He also found her Violetta praiseworthy:

> When Patti enters in the first scene, bubbling with childlike gaiety, the camellias in her corsage seem transformed into lilies. Her rendering of the first aria resembles a shower of flowers, and in the last act she finds the most touching accents. Such delicate shading from piano to expiring pianissimo, as in the death scene, such remarkable transitions from *mezza voce* to fortissimo, as in her duet with Alfredo, I have never heard before.[45]

Hanslick liked Patti's Valentine and Marguerite in *Faust* less. Though she sang these parts superbly, he thought her individuality inappropriate for those characters, Valentine requiring excessive dramatic passion and Marguerite an introspective soulfulness foreign to her sensibilities. She admitted that performing Valentine required unusual physical and vocal stamina and that this was the reason she seldom appeared in it.

Hanslick noted that Patti retained abundant charm and inexhaustible joy in performing, while having grown

> not only musically but also dramatically. Her understanding seems to have deepened, her acting to have gained in refinement, her ever-attractive pantomime to have become exemplary. . . . Her voice, too, has gained strikingly; one enjoyed especially the greater fullness and beauty of the low notes. They sounded immature nine years ago; now they remind one of the dark tones of a Cremonese viola.[46]

Hanslick considered her someone all younger singers should study, particularly her "tone formation, portamento, scales, and interpretive art right down to the smallest mordent. There is no more perfect model."[47]

In London, after the 1870 "coalition season" under the aegis of Gye and Mapleson, Gye remained sole manager of Covent Garden until his retirement at the close of the 1877 season. Though his sons Ernest and Herbert assumed direction of this house the following year, in 1879 Ernest became sole manager, retaining that position for five years thereafter.

Another change at Covent Garden concerned Mario's retirement in 1871. He had performed in London for thirty-two years, and his farewell, on 19 July, as Fernando in *La favorita* made that season, according to Wilhelm Kuhe, an exceptionally memorable series. In some final performances, Patti was his leading lady as she had often been during the past decade at this opera house.

Throughout the 1870s, only one singer offered serious competition to Patti: Emma Albani, whose debut as Amina in *La sonnambula* on 2 April 1872 impressed a *Musical Times* critic with her "facile and unexaggerated execution, and remarkable powers of *sostenuto* in the higher part of her register."[48] Later appearances that season as Lucia, Lady Harriet in *Marta*, Gilda, and Linda di Chamounix made Albani a great attraction and rival to Patti. In August 1878 she married Ernest Gye, who the following year assumed sole directorship of Covent Garden. Her position at that opera house then seemed unassailable. Nonetheless, Patti gave it little regard. Her opinion of Albani was not flattering as revealed in a letter she wrote to the wife of opera conductor Enrico Bevignani: nobody, she said, could accompany Albani's way of singing, with the soprano forgetting "all time completely—which every Conductor will not,—and *cannot* accept!"[49] To accompany Albani, in the diva's opinion, required forbearance. Years later while on tour of the British Isles, she saw a framed picture of Albani in a theater where she was concertizing and ordered her manager to turn it to the wall.

Rocketing from one triumph to the next, Patti held her own against Mapleson's star sopranos at London's Drury Lane and Her Majesty's Theatre: Tietjens, until her death in 1877; Nilsson; and Etelka Gerster, whose London debut as Amina in *La sonnambula*, on 23 June 1877, created a sensation. She later became Patti's *bête noire* during an American engagement.

Parenthetically, early this decade, the diva owed Nilsson gratitude for an increase in her fee at Covent Garden. Having discovered in 1872 that Mapleson paid Nilsson 200 pounds per presentation, Patti demanded an increase from her 100-pound rate. Unwilling to settle for Nilsson's fee, she finally agreed to 200 guineas a performance.

Patti's sister Carlotta also challenged her supremacy and won laurels in the 1870s, but had limited appearances in London. Her lameness, however, precluded an opera career, a situation embittering the singer more and more. Her feelings toward Patti once surfaced in the press in Birmingham, England, in 1874, when Carlotta's manager had advertised her as the sister of the celebrated Adelina Patti. Learning of this, Carlotta became furious and momentarily refused to sing there. On regaining her composure, though, she decided to fulfill the engagement, but explained her indecisiveness to the editor of the *Birmingham Gazette*:

> I did indeed think it strange that under my name on the placards, as well as on the programs, should have been placed the words "Sister of Adelina Patti." Though but a twinkling star by the side of the brilliant planet called Marchioness de Caux, I am nevertheless too proud of the humble reputation which Europe and America have confirmed to allow anybody to try to eclipse my name by the dangerous approximation of that of my dear sister, to whom I am bound by the tenderest affection.[50]

Despite all competition Patti remained the stellar attraction at Covent Garden, one reason being the enlargement of her repertoire. In the decade after the close of the last "coalition season" in 1870, during which she had appeared as the titular heroine in *Esmeralda* and as Elvira in *I puritani*, Patti added nine roles she had not hitherto presented at Covent Garden: Desdemona in Rossini's *Otello* and Valentine in Meyerbeer's *Les Huguenots* (1871); the title heroine in Prince Giuseppe Poniatowski's *Gelmina* (1872); Caterina in Auber's *Les diamants de la couronne* and Elvira in Verdi's *Ernani* (1873); the titular heroines in Verdi's *Luisa Miller* (1874) and *Aida* (1876) and Rossini's *Semiramide* (1878); and Selika in Meyerbeer's *L'africaine* (1879). A contemporary journal praised her for not confining her repertoire:

> The laudable ambition of Madame Patti . . . is to increase her list of parts, and her hearers may always rely on a novel reading, and a display of strong individuality. Above all, this accomplished artiste never presents herself before the public without being completely prepared for her work. She is always note as well as letter perfect, and so cleverly does she contrive to conceal her art, that she seems to the "manner born."[51]

Of these new roles, all well received with the possible exceptions of

Valentine and Selika, perhaps the ones most identified with Patti in later years at Covent Garden as well as elsewhere were Aida and Semiramide.

The world premiere of *Aida* occurred on 24 December 1871 at Cairo's new opera house in celebration of the opening of the Suez Canal. Its first European production followed some two months later at La Scala, Milan, on 8 February 1872, with Teresa Stolz (Aida), Maria Waldmann (Amneris), Giuseppe Fancelli (Radames), and Francesco Pandolfini (Amonasro). After that it was produced in various opera houses throughout the world with tremendous acclaim, critical opinion generally being that Verdi had surpassed himself. London operagoers thus awaited its first performance at Covent Garden on 22 June 1876. Some wondered whether the title role suited the diva histrionically and vocally, as it required the voice of a dramatic soprano, but she held no such doubts: "I am in love with the part—it is so beautiful and dramatic. It calls upon every fibre of one's being. I shall sing it often if they will let me, though they say it is too sad to be popular. They evidently got me to sing it to try and make it popular."[52]

At the initial performance, Patti's assumption proved doubters wrong and she showed as never before her tragic power and pathos. This portrayal, said the *Athenæum* critic, placed her among the greatest tragediennes:

> Her make-up was picturesque; her bearing shrinking and retiring as the slave, but dignified and forcible as the royal maiden; it was interesting to watch her facile expression, so well did it indicate the passing action. Her voice, so equal in its *timbre* throughout her register, came out with electric force at times, towering above the *fortissimo* of her colleagues, band, and chorus.[53]

Herman Klein maintained that she had surpassed herself in this part:

> There was a new note of tragic feeling in the voice; there were shades of poignant expression in the "Ritorna vincitor," the "Cieli azzuri," and the three superb duets . . . that seemed to embrace the whole gamut of human misery and passion. Such tragic depths Adelina Patti had never plumbed before.[54]

Other principals included Ernesta Gindele (Amneris), Ernest Nicolini (Radames), and Francesco Graziani (Amonasro).

Patti first performed the role of Semiramide in Rossini's opera at Covent Garden on 11 July 1878, experiencing another triumph. Her principal associates on this occasion were Sofia Scalchi as Arsace and Victor Maurel as Assur. Years before, Rossini had urged the diva to undertake this role, even composing special ornamentations for her, but in past London seasons Thérèse Tietjens had often appeared as the Assyrian queen and had been considered the model interpreter. It was only after her death that the diva agreed to add this part to her Covent Garden repertoire. According to *The Illustrated London News*, as Semiramide Patti revealed "transcendent powers of execution," rendering elaborate fioriture with "an ease and certainty that formed a rare display of vocal art."[55] The *Athenæum* critic wrote at length on Patti's latest success, among the greatest of her career:

> In the singing of the cavatina . . . "Bel raggio," the execution of the *bravura* passages was perfect, and the emotional expression she threw into the duets, "Serbami ognor" and the "Giorno d'orrore," has never been surpassed. There is not a vocalist in the Covent Garden company except Madame Patti who could have conquered the complexities of the *cadenzas* with such taste, tact, and precision. Madame Patti is also loyal to her colleagues in the cast, identifying herself with the assumed character and disregarding the audience before her. This self-abnegation, this freedom from singing and acting at the stage lights, enable her hearers to watch every gesture, to follow every movement with intense interest.[56]

Long afterwards Herman Klein recalled this performance:

> I remember the night well, more especially for two things— Patti's magnificent singing of "Bel raggio" with the new Rossini changes and cadenzas; and the extraordinary effect that she created with Scalchi in the famous duet, "Giorno d'orrore." I thought the audience would bring the roof down.[57]

By now the diva had successfully assumed roles in light comedy and deep tragedy, her versatility remarkable. In 1877 a London critic marveled at her artistic development and rare abilities:

> The voice . . . was always sweet and sympathetic, the tones clear as a bell, and produced amongst large and mixed audiences that indescribably thrilling sensation of which the word "charm" conveys but a comparatively weak notion. She could always

reach the F in alt; but, fortunately for her, it was not the brilliancy of the upper octave which alone formed the basis of her vocalization; her register was rich in the medium notes, the real working instrument of a truly great *prima donna,* and, as the artiste has advanced in life, she has acquired the use of lower notes, so that she has gained increase of facility and volubility, and has been enabled to meet difficulties with the certainty of attack and surety of intonation of the most expert violinist. Her gifts have tempted her to go beyond the routine of a *bravura* singer, in the delivery of scales, shakes, and brilliant *fioriture,* and she has created hazardous caprices and intervals most complex and dazzling, which some vocalists have essayed to imitate in vain. What is so specially captivating in her style is not simply her fluency and accuracy, but that hearers feel there is no peril in her flights of fancy. It is a delight to have the confidence that she can accomplish her dexterous feats, without any apparent exertion; there is no facial distortion, and not only does she appear to be singing *con amore,* but it seems mere child's play to her to display such masterly embroidery. It would be, however, a mistake to consider her superiority in vocal effects the sole or main ground of her triumphs. Madame Patti possesses histrionic ability of the highest order. There are no signs of art in her dramatic displays, she is seemingly to the manner born, although, of course, she contrives to conceal the mechanism in her irresistible appeals to the sympathies of her hearers.[58]

All this time Patti's uniqueness as artist and vocalist had attracted thousands of admirers in London. Among them were various members of the Royal Family, with the Prince of Wales one of the most ardent. He attended many Patti nights at Covent Garden. One of his brothers—Prince Arthur—had done the same. After a performance of *La sonnambula* he wrote: "I never heard her sing better & she was received with the loudest applause, this being her first appearance this season."[59] Later Prince Arthur saw her as Dinorah, sharing some of this experience with his mother: "Patti sang most beautifully & had quite an ovation—bouquets rained upon the stage from all sides of the house."[60] Queen Victoria's youngest son, Prince Leopold, thought the singer "really too lovely for anything."[61]

In this decade Patti may have most treasured a "command" to sing before Queen Victoria at Windsor Castle. Since the death of her husband, Prince Albert, on 14 December 1861, Her Majesty had become a recluse. Nonetheless, her children's enthusiasm for the diva piqued Queen Victoria's curiosity, and Patti first sang before the monarch on 4 July 1872, rendering several solos as well as a duet with French bass-baritone Jean-Baptiste Faure.

Later Queen Victoria wrote in her journal:

> I was charmed with Patti, who has a very sweet voice & wonderful facility & execution. She sings very quietly & is a very pretty ladylike little thing. The duet with Faure was quite lovely & her rendering of "Home Sweet Home" was touching beyond measure & quite brought tears to one's eyes.[62]

While Patti's professional life was highly successful, her private life had become more and more unhappy because of irreconcilable differences between her and De Caux, beginning as far back as her first seasons in Russia.

Ironically, her devotion to the marquis reached a high point in Russia during the 1874 winter, when he was suffering from inflammation of the lungs. "Day and night," wrote Lauw, "Adelina watched by the side of her suffering husband: all her thoughts were directed to him."[63] She would leave him only for her performances at the Imperial Opera and at their end would rush back to his side.

Nonetheless, there were those who had always expressed the opinion that her emotional involvement with De Caux had never gone deep. Hanslick observed her with De Caux before and after nuptials and maintained that the diva had not married for love: "She had no knowledge of love," he wrote, "in the sense of *la grande passion*. Thus, she was able to believe that she could marry a man without this unknown element, a man in whom she saw an accomplished gentleman and whom she knew to be her enthusiastic admirer."[64] There were those, too, who had always believed she loved the marquis's coronet more than the man.

With the overthrow of the Second Empire, De Caux, like various other intimates of Napoleon III, lost his place at the Imperial Court and, in a sense, his reason for being, merely serving as an agent for his wife. An acquaintance noted this metamorphosis at a London party given by the Duke and Duchess of Sutherland: "The Marquis de Caux . . . looked rather out of place. It seemed queer to see him again, not as the brilliant Marquis of the Tuileries (the 'beau' *par excellence*), but simply as the husband of Patti."[65] He had become a mercenary agent, offending her after performances with "well, another show in the bag."[66] Aware of De Caux's avarice, Franz Liszt commented that Patti's appearances in Budapest during the 1874 Easter week would, financially speaking, "in no way bother her spouse."[67] In time, according to Arsène Houssaye, De Caux regretted "he had a wife and took a mistress who resembled Patti and who sang a little like her."[68] In this activity he emulated his cousin the French ambassador to Great Britain, Prince de la Tour d'Auverge, whose mistress had been the Italian beauty Virginie, Comtesse di Castiglione. (Earlier she had served in a similar capacity for Napoleon III, who before and after his marriage to Eugénie had numerous affairs.) Like De Caux, Patti became dissatisfied with marriage and took interest in a married man and father of five children: the French tenor Ernest Nicolini. For a number of years she had performed with him in Europe. The press subsequently called their affair the century's greatest stage romance.

Nine years older than Patti, Nicolini first appeared in opera in 1857 at the Opéra-Comique in Paris, afterward singing in some performances at La Scala. In the 1860s he fulfilled engagements at the Théâtre-Italien, often with Patti, and on 29 May 1866 made an unsatisfactory Covent Garden debut in *Lucia* with Patti as the titular heroine. Five years later Nicolini returned to London, performing at the Drury Lane, there meriting both critical and public acclaim. In 1872 Gye reengaged him at Covent Garden, where his mien, acting, and voice were impressive, especially in such roles as Lohengrin, Faust, Roméo, and Radames. Wilhelm Kuhe, in his *Musical Recollections*, noted Nicolini's physical resemblance to Mario while also evaluating his voice and acting:

> He was very handsome, his voice was a real tenor of exceeding beauty and most artistically managed, while his acting was both manly and graceful. Nicolini had been originally trained at the Paris Conservatoire as a pianist, but making the discovery that he possessed a voice of fine calibre, he wisely devoted himself to its cultivation.[69]

In their initial contacts, the diva found Nicolini obnoxious. During a Homburg season, Patti and De Caux occupied Victoria Villa and discovered their next-door neighbors were Nicolini, his wife, and their children. What especially aroused Patti's ire concerned Nicolini's excessive vanity and his willing disclosures of extramarital affairs and names. Still, observing Victorian propriety, Patti and De Caux returned Nicolini's visits, though as infrequently as she could manage. She did, however, enjoy his spouse's company, except when the wife was enflamed over her husband's tom-catting. The couple's quarrels were as cacophonous as their reconciliations, with Nicolini firing off fireworks once he had been restored to his wife's good graces.

Several seasons later Patti and De Caux again lived in close proximity to Nicolini and his wife, in the Hotel Demouth in St. Petersburg. As in Homburg, the diva remained cool to the tenor. She particularly loathed singing Juliette to his Roméo because of the love scenes. By contrast, De Caux maintained that the two artists seemed ideally paired upon the boards, with his voice admirably supporting hers and their handsome effect on the stage. In time De Caux became friendly with Nicolini and enjoyed his company and conversations.

After this St. Petersburg season, Patti and Nicolini fulfilled engagements in Vienna, where he had come alone, having sent his wife and ill daughter to Paris. Here, he further ingratiated himself with De Caux, who often invited him to play écarté with his wife and him, though she invariably protested against the invitations. When a Viennese in-law of Maurice Strakosch informed her he intended to give a party in her honor and to include Nicolini, Patti said if he were invited, she would forego the affair.

Her attitude towards him hardened when Nicolini sought De Caux's advice on how to rid himself of a Russian woman who had followed him from St. Petersburg and with whom he had had an affair. Patti threatened to tell his wife, but decided against it. She nonetheless did not refrain from reproaching him for deceiving his spouse. Nicolini finally persuaded the Russian to return to St. Petersburg, where society ostracized her.

Nicolini had another adventure to which the diva was privy, when he, wearing a false beard, gained access to one woman's apartment with his own key while her jealous husband waited outside his wife's room with a loaded revolver for the entire night to no avail. On a later occasion a friend discovered Nicolini hidden in the same apartment:

> This friend, on one occasion when the young wife with her husband had gone to a *soiree,* had been detained in making his visit,

and became aware that a man, a stranger to him, had glided into the apartment of the young lady. Without giving the matter any consideration, he ordered the servants of the absent family to search with him through the apartments. Arrived at the dressing-room of the lady, he was struck immediately by two extraordinarily well-hung clothes-horses. Entertaining the suspicion that there the intruder might be concealed, he called out vigorously: "Monsieur! Step out—in order to avoid a scandal!" As no answer followed, he ordered the servants to remove one of the horses—and behold, the man sought for stood revealed—as the tenor Nicolini![70]

Patti's protests, however, may have been a smoke screen for her true feelings, and in time she changed her attitude towards Nicolini. One day in Moscow Patti and Lauw were walking in Petrovski Park when Nicolini, alighting from a carriage, pressed a note into Patti's hand and rode away. It contained love sentiments Patti told Lauw she could not reciprocate. Though sharing its contents with Lauw, Patti did not mention them to De Caux. In time Lauw noted that the diva's attitude towards Nicolini changed, that she expressed compassion for him and felt he had been greatly abused.

Though receiving anonymous warnings regarding Nicolini, De Caux dismissed them as malicious gossip. What finally aroused his suspicion was his wife's newfound delight in singing with Nicolini and her unbridled enthusiasm for him. Nicolini's actions in the balcony scene of *Roméo et Juliette* during a public performance confirmed De Caux's suspicions: he kissed Patti twenty-one times, fifteen more than the libretto stipulated.

Then De Caux determined to end Nicolini's appearances with his wife and canceled her engagement for the 1876–77 season in St. Petersburg, declaring she needed a rest and would spend the winter in Naples. Hearing this, Nicolini broke his Russian contract and agreed to one in Naples, whereupon De Caux consented to his wife's performing in Moscow and St. Petersburg after all.

In Moscow all went fairly well between Patti and De Caux except when Nicolini's name came up in conversations. The marquis controlled himself, however, when he discovered a missive from Nicolini addressed to one of his wife's maids. Though not opening the letter, he kept it in anticipation of a time when its disclosure might be required.

Towards the end of the Moscow engagement, De Caux heard that Nicolini intended to leave Naples for St. Petersburg and had offered to sing twelve presentations gratis to make amends for his broken contract. De Caux responded by declaring that his wife would never appear on stage in St. Petersburg with Nicolini. The impresario swore he would comply, but the two artists exerted so much pressure on this poor man he eventually acceded to their demands to sing together in *La traviata*. De Caux, again, swore his wife would not appear in this opera unless another tenor replaced Nicolini, and though the impresario promised that Angelo Masini would sing opposite Patti throughout the run, the curtain rose at least once with Nicolini onstage.

Scenes between Patti and De Caux so intensified that Lauw left a nervous wreck. Several years later, she penned a biography of the diva full of gossip, an exposé that greatly annoyed the singer. According to the St. Petersburg *Golos,* the final rupture between Patti and De Caux occurred in February 1877 in her dressing room at the Imperial Opera. Although the article did not give names, referring to Patti as an actress and to De Caux as the husband, those in the know recognized the real subjects:

> She was said to be invulnerable to love, yet lately she was seized with a passion for a tenor applauded by the same public. When young she had espoused a Lord, Count, Viscount, or Marquis, one knows not what. She was greatly taken with him. This husband administered in his own way the windpipe of his wife, which became for him a mine of gold. He adored his spouse; he was the first to arrive at the theatre, armed with his telescope, and it was he who gave the signals for applause. The young tenor finally came to cloud a sky that had thus far been serene. The husband, jealous, and not without reason, it is said, wished to prevent his wife from playing with the lover in question. It was even made one of the verbal conditions when the engagement with the Diva was signed. The director had promised; but how could he resist when the popular tenor came to him and offered him his talents gratis? ... An explosion was inevitable; it took place day before yesterday. The actress was in her dressing-room, her diamonds spread about, when the husband burst in like a bomb. Immediately was heard through the partition incoherent words, uttered in a furious tone. All about the theatre came up to listen. Husband and wife screamed together, each

trying to outscream the other. Finally these words were heard:
"I gave you—*you*—a noble title; you have acted with me like
a—"

A screaming voice responded:

"Here! Your title—ah, it's paid for!" and at the same time a
storm of jewels fell upon the husband's head. An instant after, a
crac, sounding like the boxing of ears, and then loud screams for
aid:

"Help! help!"

The director had to break in the door. When the husband
was ordered out he refused to go, saying that he was with his
wife.

"Take him out!" the latter cried, "he is no longer a husband
for me."

He was put out, and the actress called upon those present to
witness what had transpired. She should demand a separation;
she had offered the half of her annual income to be left in peace.
She demanded protection, and a Police agent was stationed at
her door.[71]

The press blared that Patti's "running away with a common tenor,
after being for so many years a titled and respected lady, held up as a
model to all young ladies upon the stage, was almost beyond conception."[72] In short, the Victorian world shuddered.

Like Tolstoy's Anna Karenina (from the novel written during the
1870s), Patti soon experienced social ostracism for her infidelity. An
incident with Karenina at a St. Petersburg opera house is analogous to
some Patti was to endure.

In the literary work, Anna, a member of Russian aristocracy who
leaves her husband and young son for a lover, returns to St. Petersburg disgraced by a patrician society. She goes to an opera in which
the star is the diva. Tolstoy describes the scene after the end of an act:
"On the stage Adelina Patti, her diamonds and bare shoulders
glittering, bowing low and smiling, with the help of the tenor who was
holding her by the hand, was collecting the bouquets that came
clumsily flying across the footlights."[73] Tolstoy then relates that those
occupying the most elegant seats talk not of opera nor of Patti's
singing, but of Anna, who had created a scandal by her presence. A
lady in an adjoining box, incensed by Anna's effrontery, declares she
will not remain in the presence of an adulteress and leaves.

During some Patti and Nicolini performances, such morally upright women would turn their backs to the stage when Patti appeared on the boards. She likely shared with Anna the "feelings of someone being pilloried."[74]

The Infamous Marquise

On 26 February 1877, one day after arriving in Paris from St. Petersburg, Patti read several items in *Le Figaro* concerning her by then notorious affair. Later that day, she wrote a letter to the editor:

> Sir: I began on the 15th of the present month suit for a judicial separation against the Marquis of Caux. The matter being before the courts, I shall make no further observation upon a subject on which the legal authorities will have to pronounce. I was shown this morning certain articles published in your paper on the 21st and 22d of this month, and I take the earliest opportunity in my power to protest against a story which is absolutely incorrect. I arrived at St. Petersburg . . . December last. My husband and myself took up our residence in a suite of apartments in the Hotel [Demouth], which I then occupied for the ninth time. I remained there until the 22d of this month, passing my life in the sight of all, enjoying the consideration that has always been given me, surrounded even to the last hour of my stay by numerous and honorable friends and escorted by them to the very carriage which brought me straight to Paris accompanied by my maid, my theatrical agent, and two servants. I arrived in Paris yesterday for the purpose of attending to my suit and in order that I might appear tomorrow before the President of the tribunal. I request you to publish this in your earliest number.[1]

Gossip and allegations soon mushroomed, with her receiving the brunt of criticism. Interviewed soon after the scandal broke, Maurice Strakosch expressed no surprise:

> There was a radical difference in their feelings, and this made me always fear that there could be no lasting happiness in such a union. The Marquis de Caux comes of a very noble family, who, like the Bourbons, have forgotten nothing of their past importance, though they may not have either land or gold to support their claims to a public consideration of their assumed superiority. He is an aristocrat . . . to the tips of his nails, while Adelina is a republican to the heart's core, and has so much veneration for her art that she will not admit a great artist could possibly have a superior, whoever he may be.[2]

Maurice concluded that there would be no reconciliation.

In a letter to Verdi, soprano Teresa Stolz expressed disgust at this headline-grabbing sensation, criticizing both Patti and Nicolini, labeling the former a woman without heart and the latter an imbecile without feelings for his wife and five children. To some Patti had shamefully abandoned "husband, honour and social position to gain:—a Nickel!"[3] American soprano Emma Thursby maintained that nobody in Europe then received Patti socially, while another American prima donna Clara Louise Kellogg recalled that ladies had snubbed her at a State concert at Buckingham Palace:

> So much has been said about the Victorian prejudice against divorce and against scandal of all sorts that no one will be surprised when I say that, on one occasion when I sang at the Palace, I was the only woman singer whom the ladies present spoke to, although the gentlemen paid much attention to the others. . . . My fellow-artists on that occasion were Adelina Patti and [Zélia] Trebelli . . . and, as each of them had been associated with scandal, they were left icily alone.[4]

Various publications bristled with items on the sensation. Among the first was *Le Figaro*, on 22 January 1877, in a lengthy front-page article giving full details of the quarrel between Patti and De Caux in St. Petersburg. Then the article moved on to Nicolini, whose original last name was Nicolas: *"Nicolas! c'est vulgaire, n'est-il pas vrai? On ne peut prononcer ce nom sans penser 'à quelque coq de village'* [Nicolas! it is vulgar, is it not true? One cannot pronounce this name without thinking of a 'cock of the walk']."[5] A correspondent of *The New-York*

Times wrote that Nicolini was "a man of no great personal attractions and of no breeding or education . . . a very common fellow indeed beside the aristocratic De Caux."[6] On 15 March, after his wife had separated from him because of his liaison with Patti (a separation he had asked for the previous June), Nicolini wrote a public letter saying that the adverse publicity had compromised his interests "as well as those of another person."[7] An English publication entitled *Truth* sarcastically commented that Patti "must have that absolute liberty which many think needful to the development of gifted women," that whenever "she chooses to appear in the wrong, she wants freedom to do so" and that when at the age of thirty-four, "a spoilt woman's imagination goes on the tramp she will pursue her fancy, at all risks, to the end."[8] Some months later various American papers speculated that Patti was pregnant, a report indignantly denied in the 18 August 1877 issue of *Music Trade Review.* Later the press seized upon a story emanating from Naples, where a hotel proprietor had turned Patti, Nicolini, her maids, and her thirty-five trunks away as he feared losing his aristocratic guests. From Milan came the tale that Nicolini's brother-in-law had knocked him down in a row. More impressive were the reports that Patti intended to renounce the world and to take the veil in a Brittany nunnery.

De Caux was also in the news, reportedly saying he did not challenge Nicolini to a duel because he felt a marquis could not fight a duel with a cook's son (the tenor's father had been an innkeeper and chef). A San Francisco periodical uttered the last word on the affair and maintained that people went to the diva's performances "not to hear a great artist, but to see a great wanton—a beautiful sensualist the fame of whose adulteries has overspread the globe."[9]

Parenthetically, some thought Patti then portrayed Violetta in *La traviata* as never before. After all, her life was mirroring the operatic one: a fallen woman willing to sacrifice all for the man who had awakened her passion, a woman flouting convention while enjoying a luxurious life. Even Clara Louise Kellogg, whose judgment of the diva bordered on the severe, granted that

> her *Gran Dio* in the last act [of *La traviata*] was sung with something like passion, at least with more passion than she ever sang anything else. Yes: in *La Traviata,* after she had run away with Nicolini, she did succeed in putting an unusual amount of warmth into the *rôle* of Violetta.[10]

On 3 August the Judge of the First Civil Chamber at Paris approved an official separation between Patti and De Caux, a judgment favoring him. Her contentions primarily concerned verbal abuses, physical threats, denials of money for personal expenses, and De Caux's jealousy. According to her deposition, she could no longer live with him, citing that

> the Marquis (she deposes) is a man of a disposition not only hasty (*vive*), but violent. . . . He has repeatedly addressed his wife in terms of the grossest injustice, and has even struck her. . . . He always treated and considered her, as he used to say himself, as "a gold mine." . . . Not only did he treat her in this fashion, but he sought on all occasions to make her feel in the cruellest manner the difference of their station and origin. Many a time he said, "Cursed be the day that I married a strolling actress (*cabotine*) like you." Further he frequently said to her, "[that] he had picked her out of the gutter (*la boue*), that she was nothing, and that he had made her position." Not only did he thus reproach her, but he was constantly lifting his clenched hand and threatening to strike her. The rule of the Marquis was so absolute that . . . when she demanded money from him for absolutely necessary expenses of toilet, *coiffure,* or service, he always refused, and she had infinite difficulty to obtain it from him. When she exhibited any concern about the disposal of the large sums which were always banked by him, he used to reply, "You sing, and leave the rest to me." In this way their conjugal existence . . . became absolutely unbearable when he pretended to become jealous. That jealousy . . . was displayed towards different *artistes,* who had sung in various scenes with the applicant. Not only did the Marquis de Caux conceive these sentiments of an absurd jealousy, but he took for his confidants in reference to this subject various persons to whom he spoke of his wife in language of the grossest kind, recounting the private details of his life with her, saying that . . . she had fallen in the mud; that she had a lover . . . and . . . that he had all the proofs necessary against the Marquise.[11]

The deposition then gave an example of De Caux's violence:

> One evening, on their return from the theatre at St. Petersburg, a quarrel arose between them after supper, when the Marquis reproached his wife in loud tones, and at last, giving way to all the violence of his character, attempted to strike her in the face. She

turned and received the blow on the shoulder, and then fled, terrified, into the *couloir* of the hotel.[12]

Later Patti benevolently intervened, so the deposition read, to prevent his prosecution before Russian tribunals.

De Caux countered his wife's contentions with a number of his own. For years, he said in his deposition, their union had been a happy one; but, beginning in January 1876, her attitude towards him changed, and she became cold, cantankerous, reproachful, and disputatious. Their relationship deteriorated with scenes more and more offensive, culminating in the episode at the Hotel Demouth in St. Petersburg, in which his wife conceived to provoke him to an act of violence and in which she had pretended to be insulted and to have been struck. He then cited what he considered her true intentions:

> The Marquis having quitted St. Petersburg on Feb. 18, after the imaginary scene . . . , received immediately on his arrival at Paris on the 22nd of the same month a citation to appear before the Civil President of the Seine for preliminary proceedings respecting a *separation*. . . . It is sufficient to compare the date of the President's mandate—Feb. 15—with that of the pretended scene said to have occurred at St. Petersburg on the 14th to show that everything had been arranged and carried out in advance. The nearness of these two dates is most significant. Moreover, if a doubt could exist with regard to the intentions of Madame de Caux, it would be dispelled by accounts in certain journals, the *Morgen Post*, of Vienna, amongst others, which on October 1, 1876, announced that a process for separation between M. and Madame de Caux was about to take place at the request of the latter, and for an object which that journal took no pains to conceal.[13]

De Caux referred to an account entitled "Patti's Divorce Suit" in the 1 October 1876 issue of *Morgen Post* that read, in part, as follows:

> The headline above is not a typographical error; the diva is presently engaged in a divorce suit, and none other. We are informed from Paris that the suit to free the Marquise de Caux from her wedding bonds, which were not rosy, will be decided in the near future. Already last winter Patti officially cancelled two engagements because of illness. Informed sources assure us that it was anger over differences taking place within the four walls of

her home. Herr Nicolini is already said to have been an effective comforter and consoler on all sad occasions. We are assured that this has not changed up to this very day. During her stay in London, the aforementioned differences are said to have come to a head. . . .

The lady, yearning for release from her chains, is said to believe that she is able to petition the Pope for an annulment, a doubtful hope, of course. This kind of thing occurs most rarely, because it is against Canon law, which demands, above all, that the marriage be not yet consummated. . . . In addition, we are notified that the artist wishes to compensate the Marquis de Caux for the loss of his marital happiness by means of an annuity. The method by which her goal of maintaining her connection with Nicolini . . . is still not clear. Possibly, being a good Catholic, she would perhaps decide to change her religion. There is still nothing like Divine Love![14]

De Caux ended his deposition by citing press reports about Patti:

Being notoriously and publicly accused of maintaining culpable relations with a lyric artist, the first care which her personal dignity, as well as the respect due to her name imposed upon her, should have been to protest by irreproachable conduct against such grave imputations. Far from so doing, she has justified such reports by her conduct, and by persisting in appearing in public, in travelling, and occupying the same hotels—and, in a word, living in apparent intimacy with the person pointed out by the press of all countries as her lover.[15]

Further, he possessed correspondence from Nicolini to her, which left no doubt about their intimacy.

The judgment read on 3 August 1877, by President Aubepin before the Civil Tribunal of Paris, favored De Caux with Patti's having to pay all the expenses for the suit. Aubepin read,

whereas, touching the Marquise de Caux, she has in no wise established or even offered to prove the facts she has alleged in her petition; and whereas, touching the Marquis de Caux, inasmuch as a correspondence addressed to her, and articles inserted with her privity in the *Morgen Post*, constitute an offense of the gravest nature to her husband, we hereby rule the separation of persons and of goods which he asks for in his petition.[16]

President Aubepin named lawyer Champetier de Ribes and Judge L'Évesque to liquidate Patti's property, said to be worth approximately 100,000 pounds ($500,000). Her financial records, now in the Rothschild Archives in London, indicate that her monetary assets were in various currencies. Other valuables included jewels, furs, and household goods. Half her wealth was awarded to De Caux. Though legally separated, they were not divorced, a divorce being virtually impossible in the 1870s in France. For some time De Caux contemplated pressing charges against Patti for adultery but was prevailed upon by friends opposed to an action that might call for her imprisonment. He decided against prosecution, a decision shedding a favorable light on him while further damaging her reputation. A journalist commented:

> She is now thoroughly discredited... and the manly and generous course taken by the Marquis de Caux has turned society against her throughout Europe. No one knows this better than Mme. Patti herself, and a woman of her high spirit is not at all likely to brook the insolent sneers and coldness of European society.[17]

Later, interviewed by a reporter of the Paris *Matin,* De Caux said:

> I had only to say a word and she would have been sent to prison; I did not utter the word. You see that we are far from being in accord with the chronicler who depicts Mme. de Caux as a victim of the marriage-law and M. de Caux as a tyrant, a man without bowels of compassion, incapable of a sentiment of pity.[18]

Patti then sued for the nullification of her marriage on the ground that the Very Rev. F. Plunkett had not been a licensed priest, a circumstance, she claimed, making her marriage illegal. Her suit, however, was not acceptable to French courts; marriage in France was based on a civil contract, which she had signed at the time of her union with De Caux.

Long after these legal skirmishes there followed, according to Arsène Houssaye, a curious episode involving Patti and De Caux:

I often had dinner with the Marquis de Caux, at the Moulin Rouge and at the Ambassadeurs. He told me a huge number of stories about strange events in the Tuileries, and he told stories well. People who make it their task to be clever are all too ready to believe that all the rest have no wit; that is where they often go wrong. The Marquis also did wrong not to write his memoirs once he had retired from the conjugal battlefield.

He could, for example, have told about that comedy of mistaken identity. Here it is, in a few words: One day I was invited to dinner at an elegant house where I had been given the lovely Adelina Patti as my partner. She was then in the possession of the tenor Nicolini. We knew each other from long ago, as she had been my neighbor during the first days of her marriage. Well, on that evening I reminded her of her days as a bride and asked her why she had replaced Caux with Nicolini.

"Because Caux always said the same one thing to me."

"And Nicolini does not say the same thing all the time?"

"Yes, he does; he says he loves me."

I tried to defend the Marquis: "I have seen him cry no matter how he tried to hide it."

"Don't be sorry, he consoled himself very fast. Would you believe that he paid court to Nicolini's wife because she looks like me?"

On the following evening, another dinner—this time with the Marquis de Caux in the garden of the Ambassadeurs. And what do I see—Adelina Patti with her arm in his! But it seemed to be her only from a distance because, when they came closer, I saw that it was an illusion, and moreover a particular illusion for Caux. He had caught in clear water . . . a false Patti who made him believe in his luck. But that is not the end of the story.

On the next evening I dined at the house of Count Kowalsky. . . . I was seated between the lady of the house and Adelina Patti.

"Well—are you still in love with Nicolini?"

"He is a monster—I am suing him for divorce."

I took a look at the lady—the lady was Mme. Nicolini, a true replica of Patti but a little more worn by time.

"Oh, how you resemble Patti!"

"I can well believe it—the Marquis de Caux is always at my heels."[19]

Although there were those who thought the scandal would ruin Patti's career, it actually had little effect on her professional life and none at the box office. Instead, she created a greater sensation than ever. Only months after the publications of her infidelity, audiences in Vienna and London received her enthusiastically. Hanslick noted that Viennese operagoers idolized the diva as an artist, forgetting or forgiving all else. In London, according to the 16 May 1877 issue of the *Pall Mall Gazette*, her reception upon her reentry at Covent Garden was unprecedented, with "a welcome so cordial, so pronounced, and so prolonged."[20] Author G. M. Dalmazzo recalled the evening:

> It was thought by some people that she must have met with a cold and indifferent reception on the part of the English public as the natural effect of what had happened in her private life, and in fact, some coldness was remarked at her first appearance on the stage, although the applause had been great and prolonged; but scarcely had she exhibited her talent as an opera singer, than the welcome she received became spontaneous and universal, as nothing more charming, more perfect, more exquisitively rendered, could have been expected from an experienced singer, than the Dinorah she played on the 15th of May. We ourselves saw H.R.H. the Prince of Wales, who was in a pit box, get up and warmly applaud the singer, when she boldly launched herself into the splendid Meyerbeer's music.[21]

The prince's support spoke volumes. A womanizer, he knew about calumny and its effects. Later he made a point of going backstage and declared that he wanted Patti reengaged for coming seasons. Rumored American engagements should never, in his opinion, preclude Covent Garden appearances. In the last years of the 1870s, London saw no diminution of interest in or enthusiasm for the diva. At the same time she was wildly extolled by critics and the public in other cities from which she had been long absent or which had not heard her before. Though absent for more than a decade, Patti fulfilled engagements in Italy from November 1877 to the early months of 1879. Some lambasted the singer for the outrageously high prices demanded for her performances. Nicolini often appeared onstage with her, generally receiving favorable reviews. He also increasingly took charge of Patti's professional affairs as well as her private life, going so far as to superintend what she ate and drank. Maurice

Strakosch, managing the Italian tour of 1877–78, described some of its unforgettable moments:

> One cannot imagine the enthusiasm that the Italians displayed towards the diva; it sounds more fairylike than real. . . . In the towns which Patti passed through the hotels were crowded to excess; the people from the country round about simply rushed to hear her; they slept literally in the streets and in the public places. However vast the theatres in which she sang, the stage every night was completely strewn with flowers. The price of entrance alone cost 20 francs; it might be impossible to see Patti, but she could be heard from a corridor, and that was enough— the public was delighted. Stalls cost 50 francs and private boxes any price up to 2,000 francs (£80). The average receipts always exceeded 40,000 francs (£1,600). . . . Nicolini, whose tenor voice was of beautiful quality, shared with Mme. Patti the applause of the spectators. He had previously left pleasant memories in Italy, and the cordial reception accorded him . . . proved that he had not been forgotten.[22]

The highlight of this tour was her debut as Violetta, on 3 November 1877, at La Scala. Verdi predicted she would first be received coldly by the Milanese, unwilling to accept others' opinions concerning her voice and artistry. Verdi characterized this audience as "ignorant when it doesn't judge by its impressions, this . . . public, which has repeatedly applauded its approval of so many mediocre mediocrities, will hardly grace la Patti with one call after the *cavatina* in *Traviata*. An incomparable performance. . . . Ah public, public, public!!!"[23]

Patti's La Scala audience initially reacted as Verdi had predicted, but soon the magic of her voice and acting cast a spell, the house warming to Patti's matchless singing and art and becoming highly enthusiastic as her performance proceeded. The next day the *Gazzetta Musicale di Milano* rhapsodized:

> *Vi hanno certe emozioni, le quali sono impossibili a potersi descrivere anche nella loro centesima parte: fra queste emozioni rare assai nel corso di una vita, collochiamo in prima linea quella provata ieri sera nell'udire, e nel vedere* Adelina Patti!! *sublime, affascinante.* [There are certain emotions, which are impossible to describe, even in their smallest parts: among these emotions quite rare in the course of a lifetime literally we place in front

that which we felt last night when we heard and saw *Adelina Patti*!! sublime, fascinating.][24]

Though originally engaged for four performances, Patti doubled this number and especially enchanted La Scala audiences with her Violetta and Rosina.

Then in December, Verdi wrote of her successes in Genoa:

Nothing new here, except that there were three performances by Patti, who was received with indescribable enthusiasm. She deserves it, for she is an artist by nature, so perfect that perhaps there has never been her equal. . . . A marvelous voice, a very pure style of singing, a stupendous artist with a charm and naturalness which no one else has.[25]

Early in 1878, Patti reappeared at La Scala, where in March she and Nicolini were sensational in a number of presentations of *Aida*. Before these performances, though, she had visited Verdi to request his permission for a cut in the third act of that opera. He replied that she should confer with the authorities at La Scala, then wrote in a letter to Giulio Ricordi, who was the ultimate power at La Scala, that he would not tolerate any changes in his score:

And yet there is nothing to cut, not even the ugly *cabaletta* of the tenor-soprano duet. It is part of the situation, and it must, or should, remain; if not, there is a *hole* in the canvas. You know that I am the greatest enemy of *cuts* and *transpositions*. It's better not to perform the operas. If la Patti finds this role difficult, why does she do it? What need does she have to do *Aida*? And as I have said to her personally many times: "*Why a new opera when you have so many old ones to choose from*?" La Patti has no need for new operas, for *Aida*, or for other operas.[26]

Verdi thereafter wrote in praise of Patti:

I myself didn't need to be *baptized* by the audiences to realize what a marvelous *actress-singer* she was . . . when I heard her for the first time in *Sonnambula, Lucia*, the *Barbiere*, and *Don Giovanni*! She was then what she is now—except for some changes in her voice, especially in the low register, which was then somewhat empty and infantile and is now very beautiful. But the talent, the dramatic instinct, the singing—perfectly equal, equal, equal, equal.[27]

Patti was also well received at this time in Belgium and Germany. She was at the pinnacle of her career, astounding audiences anew by her voice, which had gained in brilliance, mellowness, and power. A Brussels correspondent marveled at its uniqueness:

> Certain transformations generally mark the successive phases in the career of singers. As a rule, when the voice becomes best suited for dramatic expression, it loses somewhat of its lightness and flexibility. On the other hand, perfection of method often comes together with a diminution of the voice's volume and a deterioration of its quality. But such is not, however, the case as regards Madame Patti. Her voice has undergone no transformation; it has only completed itself. The qualities she has lately acquired are only an addition to those she possessed already.[28]

German critic Ferdinand Gumbert in *Neue Berliner Musikzeitung* echoed the Brussels correspondent:

> One fact alone suffices to prove her genius—the fact that, as years have passed, she has correctly and closely marked the change in her voice, and, with extraordinary musical feeling, understood how to alter her style and florid ornamentation accordingly. In the kingdom of song Adelina Patti will be for all time one of the most brilliant.[29]

Patti's acting, too, received high praise. In an 1878 publication of *The Theatre*, critic Henry Hersee maintained she was successful in both comedy and tragedy, with life-like impersonations. Hersee also commented on the originality and spontaneity of her conceptions, citing her performance in the "Miserere" scene from *Il trovatore*:

> When the voice of her imprisoned lover, Manrico, was suddenly heard ..., she gave one gasp of wondering horror and fell suddenly to the ground, helpless. How she was recalled to life by the tones of her lover's voice—how she raised herself on one elbow to listen—how, too faint to walk, she crawled to the prison-door—how she tried to dislodge the stones of the prison walls with her slender fingers, will never be forgotten by those who saw her play Leonora on that memorable occasion. She subsequently declared that she had not premeditated this startling effect, and could hardly remember what she had done.[30]

If other singers, Hersee said, possessed Patti's acting ability, opera presentations would be more credible. George Bernard Shaw, on the other hand, took an antithetic view of her histrionics:

> She seldom even pretends to play any other part than that of
> Adelina, the spoiled child with the adorable voice; and I believe
> she would be rather hurt than otherwise if you for a moment lost
> sight of Patti in your preoccupation with Zerlina, or Aïda, or
> Caterina.[31]

In October 1878, Patti acquired a Welsh estate located midway on the main road between the towns of Swansea and Brecon. It was thereafter a source of much pleasure. Just prior to its purchase she and Nicolini had lodged in nearby Bridgend, at Waterton Hall, where a *Western Mail* reporter noted that they neither made nor received calls and that she, perhaps penitential, often went to a local Catholic Church accompanied by her maids. The previous year she had lived in much the same fashion. During the 1877 Covent Garden season, Patti resided in a neighborhood she had known before marriage, Clapham Common, rarely going out socially, receiving few visitors, and reevaluating professional plans—she canceled one lengthy Paris engagement. The old neighborhood provided a retreat and time to consider a new private life.

For years the diva had shuttled about season after season from one dwelling to another. The Welsh estate afforded a refuge she had long sought while also offering Nicolini such outdoor activities as fishing and hunting. Patti named the Victorian country house Craig-y-Nos. Later she invariably referred to it as a castle.

Its sale first came to the couple's attention while they were staying at Cadoxton Lodge in Neath, when Sir Hussey Vivian, later Lord Swansea, and his brother Graham advised her to purchase it. Craig-y-Nos was in a picturesque setting in a valley surrounded by steep high hills and noted for its pure air and springs effective for curing throat ailments. Initially what Patti purchased for 3500 pounds was a tall, solid, gray-stone building designed by T. H. Wyatt, with about seventeen adjoining acres. Later she added extensively to the structure and bought hundreds of acres with an expenditure estimated at 100,000 pounds ($500,000). Local gossip charged that Patti had obtained some of the added acreage by getting a reluctant seller tipsy.

An account written several years after this purchase described the property:

Craig-y-Nos Castle is situated in a wild and romantic spot, amid the hills and mountains which rear their heads majestically above the valleys between Brecon and Neath. . . . The structure . . . is of goodly proportions, and the architectural features are diversified and imposing. The building is of native stone, and its pinnacles and towers give it quite an air of antiquity. . . . There is scarcely another habitation in sight, and if there be a charm in solitude it is surely to be found in the "Rock of the Night," which is the English rendering of Craig-y-Nos. . . .

Running below the terraces in the front of the castle, which overlap each other in symmetrical proportions, is the River Tawe, whose waters now afford fine sport for the angler. . . . Madame Patti soon after taking up her residence at the castle gave instructions for the river to be stocked with fish, and this was done under the personal supervision and control of Mr. Heck, the agent of the estate. He procured his fish and ova from Scotland, and now the stream is alive with lusty trout, who jump joyfully to the fly of the fishermen. The estate is not what one would call a large one . . . but the owner of the castle has secured the right of shooting over immense tracts of land up and down the valley. The game is plentiful, thanks to careful attention in stocking and preserving. . . . At one portion of the estate the river, which is about 60 ft. wide, is spanned by a bridge. . . . The estate is laid out chiefly in coverts, with walks running through them; while conservatories effectively disposed here and there give diversity to the picture. There is, too, an artificial lake with a rustic bridge, and a boat for those of the visitors . . . who care to diversify the outdoor amusements of walking, shooting, and fishing by a little aquatic exercise.

The interior of the building is most luxuriously furnished, all the furniture, upholstery, &c., being specially manufactured by the order of Madame Patti by Messrs. B. Evans and Company, Swansea. The drawing-room, which looks out on the river and a fine landscape beyond, is arranged with much artistic skill, the silk tapestries, satin wood furniture, the exquisite fittings, being suggestive of richness combined with taste. The other principal apartments are the dining-room and the billiard room, which run on each side of the drawing-room, and the furnishing and decorations here are all characteristic of luxury in appointments by which the owner has surrounded herself in her delightful retreat. Madame's boudoir is at the rear of the pile, and in the same quarter is the well-stocked library and the music store-room, &c. A passage running through the centre of the building divides the chief apartments from those appropriated to domestic uses. There is an English and a French kitchen, each presided over by skilful *chefs de cuisine*. Perhaps the pleasantest portion of the building is the winter garden and conservatory, which continue the building away to the left. These are immense glass structures full of the rarest flowers and profuse with the choicest plants. Here is also a miniature lake, or huge aquarium, which has been very effectively laid out with rocks, in which there is a cascade and a fine fountain, and shoals of gold fish are seen disporting themselves beneath clear waters.

The house has just been fitted with the electric light which supplies a beautiful illumination by means of Swan lamps, with coloured globes. The effect is particularly fine in the drawing-room where there is a magnificent chandelier, covered with artistic globes. The light is also supplied to the conservatory and winter garden, the lamps being suspended in fantastic positions amongst the flowers and ferns. . . . The principal entrance is from the back, and a circular drive from here . . . and past the range of stables leads out to the turnpike road.[32]

Patti's estate ultimately included such dependencies as various hot houses where grapes, pineapples, strawberries, vegetables, and flowers were grown; servants' quarters; a gashouse; an electric light plant (Craig-y-Nos being among the first private residences in Britain, if not the first, to be electrified); an ice-making plant; tennis lawns and pavilions; stone and slated outbuildings; fruit, flower, and vegetable gardens; eighteen cottages; a farmyard with cows and chickens; stone-built and slated dog kennels; a brick and stone laundry; a coach house; stables with numerous horses; limestone quarries; a clock tower with chimes tolling each quarter hour; and a private theater.

To assist at Craig-y-Nos, Patti at first employed twenty servants, not including gamekeepers, a gasman, laundresses, and extra gardeners. Chief among these were two women who had been with her for a number of years—Patro, a loyal Black domestic, and Karoline Baumeister, "Karo," a faithful companion who acted as Patti's shield from unpleasantries, human and otherwise, and who

133

managed the household and arranged her mistress's gowns, costumes, and jewels—and William Heck, responsible for the estate's lighting, heating, ventilation, and sanitation; he also took care of all correspondence related to its business matters. Years later when the diva and Nicolini were in residence, the staff numbered over forty domestics, more on festive occasions.

Patti said: "All the time I don't spend at Craig-y-Nos seems to me time lost. I should not give a snap of my finger for my brilliant career had it not procured me a delicious country retreat and the kind of anchorage that exactly suits me."[33]

While away, Patti always looked forward to returning to Craig-y-Nos. Originally she did so via a private saloon railway car to Cray station; later she rode to Penwyllt, closer to Craig-y-Nos (with a waiting room built exclusively for her use) and near the private road which she had had constructed to her estate. When she would return from abroad, a grand reception invariably awaited. A journalist described one early homecoming:

> About 4 o'clock in the afternoon, Cray station being near, where we were to leave the train, a roar and a crash were heard away to our right. "That's the Krupp," explained Madame Patti, and she went on to tell us that the head keeper always fired it in salute whenever she returned home. At Cray, which is but a mile or so from the castle, we found a dozen or so carriages of every description, from a dog cart to a landau, in waiting, and a crowd of people, who cheered like a Republican rally. I have not had much experience in regal receptions, but I am sure a queen could not have been more heartily welcomed than Patti was by those whom she affectionately calls "her people." There were arches of flowers across the road, more arches at the castle gates, flags flying, flowers filling the air, guns booming, and people shouting, until we began to appreciate the fact that Patti was *la diva* at her home as well as on the stage. As soon as Patti's carriage turned into the driveway the band struck up "Home, Sweet Home." The tears came into Patti's eyes then.... Footmen in livery were stationed on the porch and assisted Madame—as I find she is always called here—and her five guests to alight. There was a marked absence of ceremony, and every one was made to feel at home at once. Wood fires burned in the great open fire-places, and there were maids and men servants in every room while the unpacking was going on. At dinner, over

which Patti presided with wonderful grace and tact, there were fireworks and music by a band from Swansea, the festivities continuing until midnight.[34]

In the early 1880s Patti presented European audiences with her familiar repertoire while assuming a new role at Covent Garden. She also performed again in Madrid and Paris, where her appearances had become infrequent. An engagement at the recently erected opera house in Monte Carlo created tremendous interest, attracting cosmopolitan society and the press from various foreign countries. It was then, too, that plans materialized for a United States tour.

In London on 3 July 1880, Patti assumed the title role in Jules Cohen's *Estella*, an opera originally entitled *Les bleuets* when it debuted in 1867 at the Théâtre Lyrique in Paris with Christine Nilsson. Though critics praised Patti, the opera itself they found unoriginal and unimpressive. Nicolini as Fabio merited considerable adverse criticism as he had sung with effort and excessive tremolo.

By then Nicolini was receiving a number of poor notices as well as demonstrations of disapproval at Covent Garden, where he was, at times, hissed. William Beatty-Kingston, however, wrote an article for *The Theatre* in which he said that this hissing was due solely to envy of the tenor, who had "the supreme good fortune to be beloved by a beautiful and gifted woman."[35] The *Illustrated Sporting and Dramatic News* responded with a different explanation for the adverse demonstrations:

> Signor Nicolini's "supreme good fortune" in obtaining possession of Mme. Patti's person and property at the expense of her social position and character may not in all eyes be so supreme as Mr. Kingston supposes. The only way in which the Patti element affects the matter is that audiences may possibly feel some extra dislike to Signor Nicolini . . . because it is known that by Mme. Patti's influence he retains a position which he would not retain for one single night by his own—that is what remains of his own—ability.[36]

Patti returned to Madrid in December 1880 after more than a decade's absence. Joining her in casts of *La traviata, Il barbiere di*

Siviglia, and *Lucia* were Nicolini and tenors Roberto Stagno and Julián Gayarre. As usual, she was well received by the Spaniards, who, according to her, preferred singers who "always sing loud ... [while] soft singers are always hissed."[37] On the fifteenth, King Alfonso XII and Queen Maria Cristina entertained her at the Royal Palace, an occasion she particularly enjoyed as it was, she said, a time without music. Her fantastic successes in this series inspired an offer of a three-month engagement the following year for 12,000 pounds as well as a house valued at 11,800 pounds, title included, in the most elite section of Madrid. Writing to a business associate on 16 January 1881, she confessed that telling him of her recent professional triumphs had become "rather a difficult thing to do—for it gets very monotonous—to write always the same story over & over again."[38]

From 14 February to 1 May 1880, Patti, absent from the Paris stage for most of the 1870s, gave twenty-two performances in some of her most familiar roles at the Théâtre de la Gaîté, and in 1881 from 5 March to 3 May, eighteen presentations at the Théâtre des Nations. She said the receptions and ovations in Paris at this time had deeply affected her: "I found during these short seasons plaudits that showed to me a sympathy of which I have a right to be proud."[39]

Similar triumphs crowned her efforts in Monte Carlo, where early in 1881 she appeared at an opera house opened just two years before and designed by Charles Garnier, architect of the grandiose Paris Opéra. The *Journal de Monaco* reviewed her in this superb new setting, where her fee was 15,000 francs a performance:

> Time had altered neither her beauty nor her voice by a semitone,
> it had passed without touching either. Was that figure sculpted
> in Paros, was that timbre forged in metal of Corinth? When she
> opened her mouth, pearls and diamonds issued forth in trills that
> would make a nightingale jealous.[40]

At opera-house receptions and at Villa St. Cécile, Patti's Monte Carlo residence during this season, people could not do enough for her, she said. A celebration held at the villa the night before her thirty-eighth birthday included entertainment by a casino orchestra and opera choristers while casino directors presented flowers, onlookers cheered, and fireworks illuminated the scene.

At this time the diva was also planning to tour the United States, where she had been absent for over two decades, and to embark from

82–87 In October 1878, Patti acquired a Welsh estate she named Craig-y-Nos. She originally purchased a square building, but by 1888—the time of these illustrations—two wings and a clock tower had been added. Courtesy General Research Division, The New York Public Library, Astor, Lenox and Tilden Foundations.

A PRIMA DONNA'S HOME

THE BILLIARD ROOM

THE DRAWING ROOM

SKETCHES AT CRAIG-Y-NOS CASTLE — *THE GRAPHIC*, 24 November 1888

THE CONSERVATORY

MADAME PATTI-NICOLINI'S BOUDOIR

88 Patti's elopement with a married man
and father while she too was still married
prompted high society to ostracize her.
Courtesy William R. Moran.

89 Ernest Nicolini was once asked what
opera role he preferred, and he responded
it was the one in which he sang the least.
After he began his affair with Patti,
Nicolini's main focus shifted from women
to hunting, fishing, and everything concerning the dinner table. Courtesy Murry &
Leonie Guggenheim Memorial Library,
Monmouth College.

90 Patti as Semiramide, a role she first performed at Covent Garden on 11 July 1878. A critic wrote that he thought "the audience would bring the roof down." Courtesy Murry & Leonie Guggenheim Memorial Library, Monmouth College.

91 & 92 Patti in 1882. She toured the United States in the fall of 1881 after a two-decade absence and returned for several seasons to help New York Academy of Music manager J. H. Mapleson vie with the newly opened Metropolitan Opera House in the "opera war." Courtesy William R. Moran.

94 Conductor Luigi Arditi, who directed Patti in her many appearances under the aegis of Mapleson, considered her the finest soprano he had ever heard. Author's Collection.

93 Impresario James H. Mapleson ultimately lost the opera war when Patti did not return for his 1885–86 season. Still angry over her exorbitant fees, prima donna airs, and the contractual stipulation that she not be required at rehearsals, he did not always flatter Patti in his 1888 memoirs. Author's Collection.

95 Patti's rival in the 1883–84 U.S. season, Etelka Gerster. Courtesy Murry & Leonie Guggenheim Memorial Library, Monmouth College.

96 Cartoon from the 31 October 1883 issue of *Puck*, depicting the ongoing opera war in New York. Mapleson's arms are around Patti and Gerster, while the Metropolitan's impresario, Henry E. Abbey, rides on the back of Christine Nilsson. Courtesy General Research Division, The New York Public Library, Astor, Lenox and Tilden Foundations.

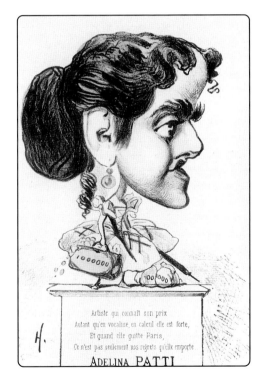

Artiste qui connaît son prix
Autant qu'en vocalise, en calcul elle est forte,
Et quand elle quitte Paris,
Ce n'est pas seulement nos regrets qu'elle emporte

ADELINA PATTI

97 Patti caricature with a French quatrain about her wealth implying that, when she left, she would carry with her not only Paris's regrets, but also a great deal of money. Courtesy Stuart-Liff.

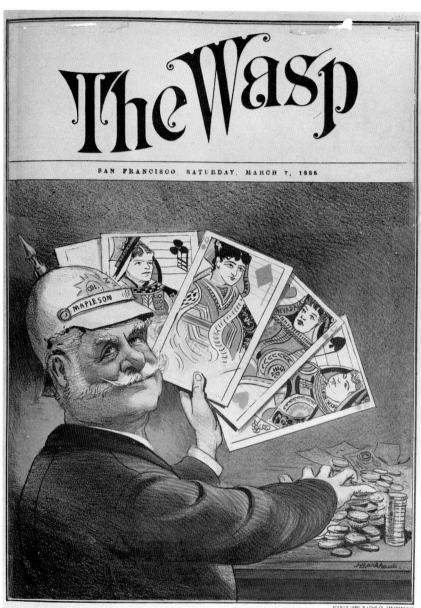

98 Cover of the 7 March 1885 issue of *The Wasp*, with Patti, appropriately, as the Queen of Diamonds in Mapleson's winning hand. Courtesy San Francisco Public Library.

Europe in October 1881. Her representative, Giovanni Franchi, would precede her. Though he had managed her business affairs in Europe, he was unfamiliar with artist management in America. Euphoric, Patti decided to proceed without an American manager, confident her name alone would attract audiences.

For years many in the United States had anticipated this return, which occurred on 3 November 1881. A welcoming party with hordes of press representatives, a brass band, and Signor Franchi waited for the Cunarder *Algeria* to dock at a pier in New York's East River. Neither rain nor fog dampened enthusiasm. Aboard the steamship *Blackbird*—which met Patti's and Nicolini's ship in the bay and which was festooned with flowers over its doors while American and Italian flags waved on high, and a band played American, Italian, and French national anthems—a *World* reporter managed to get Patti's attention. Their brief exchange contained a startling item:

> "And now that you are here, you do not regret having come?"
>
> "How could I? Every one that I find here is so kind. And I have determined to sing only for two years more, so that I must devote some part of that time to America, which seems to me like home."[41]

As the boat neared land, the diva was surprised to hear the band play a waltz she had composed years before, one dedicated to Napoleon's and Eugénie's son.

Upon docking, Patti, Nicolini, and entourage proceeded to the Fifth Avenue Hotel, where hours later a *Herald* journalist plied her with questions about social plans in New York. Perhaps anticipating ostracism by New York society women, Patti evaded the issue: "My first care must be to retain my health and strength. Were I to go out very much I might catch cold or become sick. I have an important season at hand and I must be careful to take needed rest and avoid danger of vocal indisposition."[42]

Several days afterwards Patti became incensed by rumors affecting ticket sales, which had been slow. Her old London acquaintance James Henry Mapleson was in the midst of his New York fall-winter season at the Academy of Music and, aware that Patti's concerts offered serious competition, may have been among those spreading rumors. Since stories had circulated that she intended to sing in opera while in the United States, many people preferred to wait for this kind of entertainment rather than to attend her concerts. There were also rumors about the condition of her voice and the exorbitant admission prices she would command. Patti quickly scotched any talk concerning opera, even when Mapleson proposed she star in his company.

On 9 November, Patti, joined by Nicolini and several other artists, reentered New York's musical life in a concert at Steinway Hall. She sang the aria and cabaletta from act one of *La traviata*— "Ah, fors' è lui" and "Sempre libera"—performing the first part with faultless phrasing and rendering the cabaletta "with a dash and spirit that only such glorious voices are capable of carrying out, and the ascending runs were executed with unparalleled brilliancy, a volume of voice that filled the house."[43] She later sang the aria "Ombra leggiera" from *Dinorah*, joined Nicolini and the bass Augusto Pinto in the *Lombardi* terzetto, and performed several ballads including the inevitable "Home, Sweet Home." Her supporting company, except for a violinist, received only fair or poor comments from critics, who found Nicolini barely acceptable as a vocalist. Most of the adverse comments concerned the high prices, $10 for orchestra seats, which affected the size of the audience. Then, too, some were critical of management, as her concert dates occurred on opera nights at the Academy of Music.

The following day a *Herald* reporter interviewed Patti:

"You saw from the welcome you received, Mme. Patti, that the 'empty benches' were not due to lack of popularity on your own part. Do you not think they were due, however, to the high price charged for seats?"

"Now," said the lady, with some excitement, "I have heard a great deal of that since I came here, and I must say that I feel very badly to think that there are people who believe I am charging an exorbitant price for my concerts. Perhaps $10 may seem a large amount to pay for a seat, but is it really too high when you consider what is charged for entertainments in the great capitals of Europe? . . . Now, when I have returned to America after a long absence, and when I am only going to stay a little while, and when I sing as much at a concert as I do in almost any opera and more than I do in some operas, do you think $10 too high a price for the best seats in the house? And the prices you know are scaled down to $2. I don't wish to be thought grasping nor do I wish people to think I have come here simply to make money, for I assure you I can make just as much or more money abroad. I was inspired by an earnest desire to come back to America and sing while my voice is in its prime and I believe it is admitted by the critics this morning that I have not brought a broken or wrecked voice, as some persons were kind enough to hint beforehand, but that my vocal powers are unimpaired. . . ."

"Is there any truth in the report that you are going to sing in opera here before you return?"

"That report," said Mme. Patti, "has been started, I think, to injure my concert prospects here. Do you know that although everything seems to be plain sailing for me, there are many little disagreeable things being done and many little obstacles being thrown in the way of my success? They do not appear to the public; but they are constantly cropping up before me, and they annoy me greatly."

"But it is said that Mr. Mapleson has made you an offer, and it is reported that you are considering it."

"Now the truth of it is just this," said Mme. Patti. "He has asked me to sing in opera for him, and my answer was this:—That I had no intention of singing in opera, that my time was filled, that I had not the slightest doubt that my concert season would be successful, but, at the same time, if he desired me to sing for him and if I could arrange it so that I could sing with his company I would do so if he would pay me $10,000 a night—in advance," added Mme. Patti, tapping the palm of her hand, "do you understand? In advance! Perhaps you think $10,000 a very high price," she continued. "I think so myself; but do you not consider that the terms were equivalent to saying that I would not sing in opera? They sound that way to me."[44]

The audience at her second concert, the afternoon of 12 November, was smaller than that of the first, high admission prices, again, being the main reason. The following day's reviews lavished praise on Patti's singing with, however, one notable exception in a review written by young music critic Henry T. Finck of the *Evening Post*. An ardent Wagnerite having· recently returned from Germany after seven years there studying music, he scored the program as "a handful of wheat . . . served up in a bushel of chaff" and Patti as a singer interested only in self-display. Years later he apologized for this rash judgment in his autobiographical *My Adventures in the Golden Age of Music*:

> No doubt, everything I said about Patti's shortcomings was true. She was infinitely more interested in showing off her lovely voice than in the music she sang. The composer was for her a mere peg to hang on her trills and frills. . . . But as a singer she was so glorious, so incomparable, that while under the spell of her vocal art the listeners forgot everything else and simply luxuriated in ecstatic bliss. . . . I consider myself fortunate in having been able to listen . . . to the sweetest and most mellow voice the world has ever heard.
>
> It was like the singing of the nightingales I used to be enchanted with in the Tiergarten in Berlin. Patti was a nightingale; why ask more of her? In her way she was absolutely perfect, and perfection of any kind should be honored and extolled, without any of the buts and ifs on which I dwelt too much.
>
> In plain language, I made an ass of myself.[45]

Patti made her third concert appearance, on the 16th, in a benefit for those suffering from Michigan forest fires, with prices lowered to $2 for general admission and $3 more for reserved seats. Audiences at this concert and at the fourth and last one, on 23 November, filled the house to overflowing. Her reception had not been matched since the days of Jenny Lind. Meanwhile, Patti found an American to manage her tour, Henry E. Abbey, who in the past year had served likewise for Sarah Bernhardt in her first American season.

Moments after signing the management contract on 17 November, Abbey outlined his plans to present her in concerts with operatic programs and with such accessories as supporting singers, an orchestra of fifty players, and scenery for scenes from such operas as *La traviata, Faust,* and *Il barbiere.* The public would thus see and hear Patti at her best with general admission at $2, $3 extra for reserved seats. Abbey said he would travel with the company to supervise details.

Abbey first presented her in Brooklyn on 28 November in a concert-opera program that included scenes from *Faust.* The successful venture not only served as a prototype of what followed but garnered Barnum-like publicity, recalling Jenny Lind's receptions. After the affair, young men, who may have been in Abbey's employ, removed the horses from Patti's carriage and dragged it themselves to her hotel. One caustic wit commented that the horses had simply been replaced by asses. Still, the evening illuminated Abbey's methods to ensure her success.

The ensuing tour realized his expectations, professionally and financially, with his star of stars never disappointing him. Patti also knew the value of publicity in attracting audiences and gave a controversial interview in which she expressed her opinions on other contemporary women singers. These statements were not typical of Patti, however, and did not endear her to all subjects while shedding an unfavorable light on her as a professional. Still, they did generate considerable publicity. Patti evaluated Etelka Gerster, a soprano she had first heard at Vienna in 1874; Americans Clara Louise Kellogg, Annie Louise Cary, and Minnie Hauk; and Christine Nilsson:

"You have heard Etelka Gerster sing; what do you think of her?"

"Yes, I heard Gerster once—no, twice. Oh, her voice is very good, but she is merely an instrument—human mechanism, without one particle of expressive animation. She cannot act. She is cold to artistic emotion."

"What of Clara Louise Kellogg!"

"Kellogg is a woman I never admired. She is cold and passionless, and utterly devoid of expression. Kellogg is a much overrated singer."

"And Cary, you certainly have heard her," added the reporter.

"Yes, I have," rejoined Madame Patti, vivaciously. "She is a contralto, and the best one I have ever heard. Miss Cary is the very best contralto America has ever produced and her brilliant success in Europe was richly deserved."

"How do you rate Minnie Hauk?"

"She is a true artist. I regard her as the superior of Gerster in every respect. You see, Miss Hauk not only has the voice and the power and ability to use it, but she is an actress. She acts from the heart. Ah! . . . that's the great point. An opera singer must not only sing, but she must act and portray the character with emotional intensity. All this Miss Hauk does."

"Where is Nilsson now?"

"I think she is in Paris. Poor Nilsson, she had a good voice, though somewhat lacking expression, but she sang night after night until she wore it out. She sings occasionally in concert, but always to poor houses. Nilsson's day has passed. She sang too often to last long. I wouldn't think of singing six nights in succession. Never since my career have I sung oftner [*sic*] than three times in one week."[46]

These remarks did not go unchallenged. Mapleson, for one, expressed his views with another reporter:

Now I am going to talk to you about Patti. She is one of the most aggravatingly capricious young women I have ever known. It takes all your time to listen to her wrongs. . . . Her remarks the other day, about her sister prima donnas were most unjust. I undoubtedly think that Mme. Patti holds an unrivaled rank in her profession, nor do I think a finer *premiere* has ever existed. She is the best *Traviata* that ever sang before any public, and her *Ninetta* in "Gazza Ladra" and her other light soprano parts have seldom, if ever, been equaled. But Patti enjoys one fault in common with most other opera singers, past and present. She will reverse her voice. She is not contented with light soprano. She must try heavy soprano parts like *Aida* and other kindred *roles*, and then becomes savage at severe criticism.[47]

Mapleson may have been resentful over the exorbitant fees Patti extracted from him for performances in February at the Cincinnati Festival, where for two presentations, he paid her 1600 pounds ($8000) each.

At this tour's end and upon returning to New York in late February, Abbey presented Patti in complete opera performances at the Germania Theater, where from 27 February to 3 April 1882, operagoers applauded and cheered her as Violetta, Rosina, Marguerite, Leonora in *Il trovatore,* and Lucia. She particularly shone in her portrayal of Violetta, the brilliance of which was due not only to her voice and acting but also to the fabulous diamonds she wore. New York had never seen a stage personality with such gems: solitaires in her ears sparkled and

a diamond butterfly fluttered and flamed from her shoulder; nine different necklaces rainbowed around her neck and the front of her corsage; rings flashed from her fingers; and on her arms blazed bracelet after bracelet, culminating in one band of selected stones, each of which scintillated like a star.[48]

Four individuals, called Patti's Diamond Men—two professional detectives and two watchmen from her hotel, guarded the stones to and from the theater. The diva refused to have the diamonds with her in a carriage, fearing violence from thieves.

Her associates in this New York series, including Nicolini and her stepbrother Nicolo Barili, merited little critical acclaim while Patti received only superlatives. All told, from 28 November to 3 April, she made thirty-eight appearances under Abbey's aegis and cleared, according to him, $175,000. Her return to the United States thus ended in a professional and financial triumph.

Several hours before leaving for Europe on the afternoon of 4 April, Patti, with Nicolini at her side, seemed exuberant: "I feel as bright and happy as a little girl of sixteen.... What a mistake the newspapers make who say I was born in 1843. Why, I'm only seventeen! Isn't it so, Ernesto?"[49] She continued the conversation with a *Herald* reporter in her rapid, polyglot style (termed by the reporter her Franco-Anglo-Teutonic-Italian chatting) and confessed that this mix of languages occasionally created problems:

> "A very funny incident happened yesterday," the diva presently said, and she related what follows with great gusto and infinite drollery, showing her remarkable powers as a comedienne:— "One of the waiters was dying to hear me, and so we promised him some *entrées*—some admissions—a few days ago for the last night. Yesterday we got a couple of admission tickets for him and I said to him, carelessly, as I suppose, 'We shall have those two *entrées* to-day,' meaning, of course, the admission tickets which I had got for him. I was very much astonished that he never even said 'Thank you,' but presently returned with tears in his eyes. The poor fellow had been crying with disappointment. As we usually take a very light meal before singing he thought we would have certain two little made dishes, *entrées*, which we often have for ourselves, and not the two *entrées*—admission tickets—for him. Oh, it was intensely comical when I explained to him his mistake! How I laughed, and how glad the poor fellow was!"[50]

A later exchange concerned her liaison with Nicolini, with the reporter asking, "Do you find that it aids you in your great love scenes to sing with a person you like?" Whereupon she said, "Oh, of course. . . . Ernesto helps me wonderfully. . . . Last night I could not have sung Lucia but for him!"[51]

In his final question the reporter wanted to know whether she intended to return in the fall. The diva evaded the issue:

> "It is uncertain; the entire matter is in Franchi's hands. You know I'm not a business woman; I can't do figures and all that sort of thing, and so I leave everything to Franchi. . . . He sees all the impresarios who want to engage me, listens to their terms, weighs everything carefully—not only the pecuniary profit, but also the question of artistic success, which always influences him—and then decides. He makes out the contract, puts it before me and says, 'Here, Madame, sign,' and I sign—basta! and done with. And I never regret what he has done for me in this manner. An artist can't be a business woman as well—she must leave her arrangements to some one in whom she has confidence."[52]

To the contrary, however, Patti's business acumen was awe-inspiring.

Weeks passed before an announcement of her return in the fall. For the new engagement, extending six months beginning in November, Mapleson agreed to pay her $4400 a performance for fifty presentations, with the services of Nicolini included. This demand required Mapleson to raise admissions for the operas in which she starred and to charge the Academy of Music's two hundred stockholders, who customarily occupied free seats, in order to pay Patti's $44,000 deposit. This contract was the first of three she made with Mapleson for American seasons from 1882–85. During these years she also fulfilled numerous European engagements; but as commitments to Mapleson extended over approximately half each preceding year, the United States became the focus of her career.

Meanwhile, Patti participated in her twenty-second consecutive Covent Garden season. While appearing in familiar roles, she also created a new part on 4 July 1882: the title role in the world premiere of Charles Lenepveu's *Velleda* with Valleria (Ina), Nicolini (Celio), Cotogni (Teuter), and Édouard de Reszke (Senon). Although this opera was not a critical or popular success because of its unoriginal music, critics admired her portrayal.

Velleda's poor reception was not the only disappointment for Patti during this season as she had no doubt become aware that Nicolini's presence at Covent Garden was deplored, his voice in poor condition. Other problems followed. During the next two Covent Garden seasons, Italian opera no longer attracted audiences, and Gye's management by the close of the 1884 series was in serious financial trouble, a circumstance ending his association with the opera house.

Still, during Gye's final seasons, Patti received her most treasured compliment, from Jenny Lind, who attended a performance in the early 1880s and told Arthur Sullivan, *"There is only one Niagara; and there is only one Patti."*[53]

In the fall of 1882 Mapleson finalized arrangements for Patti's return to the United States. With Barnum-like instincts, he orchestrated a brilliant welcome for her arrival at the end of October, a reception guaranteeing wide press coverage and piquing public curiosity. Mapleson described the ensuing welcome:

> The *Servia* was out in the middle of the stream, and we steamed up alongside, when we saw Patti, who had been up since half-past four in the morning. . . . Our band struck up "God Save the Queen" and everyone bared his head. . . . Hand-shaking and greetings followed. After we got . . . Patti through the Custom House she was placed in a carriage and taken to the Windsor Hotel, the room being piled up with telegrams, cards, and bouquets. There was also a large set piece with the word "Welcome!" embroidered on it in roses. In the evening there was a midnight serenade in front of the Windsor Hotel, and ultimately *la Diva* had to appear at the window, when orchestra and chorus, who were outside, performed the grand prayer from *Lombardi.* After three hearty cheers for Adelina Patti people went home.[54]

The press responded as Mapleson had anticipated, and the publicity continued for months in New York and on tour. It became part of the Patti legend. Rupert Christiansen in his history *Prima Donna* noted this element of publicity, especially in her tours of the United States, labeling it "fabricated razzmatazz, repeated *ad nauseam* in every visited city. . . . It was a phenomenon worthy of Mark Twain's witheringly sceptical eye."[55]

Mapleson scheduled Patti's reentry at the Academy of Music for 6 November 1882, in the role of her opera debut in the same house twenty-three years before: Lucia. Assisting her were Nicolini as Edgardo and baritone Antonio Galassi as Ashton. Operagoers crowded the auditorium, wildly applauding and cheering Patti, who sang "throughout with artistic grace, and this, with the incomparable beauty of her voice,used at all times with rare taste and judgement, made her performance a rich treat."[56] She followed with more great performances, ending on 30 December, as Violetta, Marguerite, Leonora in *Il trovatore*, Rosina, Dinorah, Amina, Semiramide, and Linda di Chamounix. Of these portrayals, Mapleson particularly lauded her singing in *Semiramide* as well as that of contralto Sofia Scalchi, who had made her New York debut on 20 December as Arsace in this Rossini opera.[57]

In early December, a deputation from Kalakaua, King of the Hawaiian Islands, conferred upon Patti the Royal Order of Kapirlani, a jeweled star, and a citation that said, in part, that she was then a "Knight Companion of our Royal Order of Kapirlani, to exercise and enjoy all the rights, pre-eminences and privileges to the same of right appertaining, and to wear the insignia as by decree created."[58]

During this New York season Mapleson made a curious observation: some patrons bought tickets only for those operas in which Patti sang the most notes. He also observed that a few individuals shared a ticket. Some of these observations were probably exaggerated as the impresario regularly hyperbolized.

> Amongst the numberless inquiries at the box-office several were made as to how long Mdme Patti remained on the stage in each of the different operas; and the newspapers busied themselves as to the number of notes she sang in each particular work; larger demands for seats being made on those evenings when she sang more notes. *La Traviata* generally carried off the palm.... A party of amateurs would buy a ticket between them, each one taking 20 minutes of the ticket and returning with the pass-out check to the next. Lots were drawn to decide who was to go in first; and in the event of anyone overstaying his 20 minutes he had to pay for the whole ticket; correctness of time being the essence of the arrangement.[59]

Mapleson also observed calculations published in the press as to monetary values for each note Patti sang. If, for example, one divided the number of her utterances in *Semiramide* by the salary she received per performance, Patti, according to a Washington, D.C., mathematician, merited 42⅗ cents a note, precisely 7 1/10 cents more for each of these than Rossini had earned for the opera's composition. In Boston estimates ranged from 30 cents for every note she sang in *Semiramide* to 40½ cents per utterance in *Lucia*.

Soon after the beginning of 1883, the company began its extended tour. It first visited Baltimore, where a smallpox epidemic had struck, a situation necessitating vaccinations for the troupe, excepting Patti, who, afraid of exposure to this dreaded disease, remained in Philadelphia. She later captivated Philadelphians as Lucia, with the proceeds amounting to over $14,000. Her presence no doubt seemed miraculous to those who had heard of her recent demise—she, according to reports, having been devoured by mice only hours before. In an interview with a reporter from the *Philadelphia Press*, Patti related the circumstances prompting the story:

> "When I went to bed last evening my maid turned the clothes over for me to get in, when out jumped six mice—a complete family, in fact; nice fat little fellows. I was not frightened; at least, I was only astonished. I took my bon-bon box and scattered some sweetmeats on the carpet so that the tiny intruders should have some supper, and I went to sleep without any apprehension. In the middle of the night, however, something disagreeable occurred, and I was awakened by a sharp pain in my ear. I put my hand to my head when a mouse jumped to the floor, and I felt blood trickling on the side of my cheek. I got up and called my maid, and examination showed a bite on my left ear. It bled a good deal, and to-day my ear is much swollen. I shall not put any bon-bons down tonight," continued Mdme Patti, "and when I sleep in the day time I shall place my maid to act as sentry."[60]

Makers and patentees of mousetraps thereafter besieged her to purchase devices guaranteeing the end of such problems. Possibly she settled for a cat or cats. Meanwhile, there was all that publicity!

Performances in Chicago, St. Louis, and Cincinnati followed with Patti's reveling in crowded houses and enthusiastic receptions. No doubt hoping for more of the same in Detroit, her next tour city, she unfortunately found herself unable to perform, suffering from a severe cold. Operagoers became outraged, having experienced her cancellation a year before. Some concluded that this latest episode was another example of a prima-donna caprice or that she had succumbed to the influence of liquor. To counter such stories, Mapleson obtained medical verification that the diva indeed suffered from a cold. Her recovery was so slow that she remained in Detroit several days after the company proceeded to Toronto and Buffalo, rejoining the troupe in Pittsburgh. After performing there and in Washington and Boston, Patti returned to New York, where in March and April she not only repeated some earlier successes of the fall-winter series but added the roles of Gilda in *Rigoletto*, Zerlina in *Don Giovanni*, and Caterina in *L'étoile du Nord*.

Socially, in the 1882–83 season Patti had remained *persona non grata*, this especially so to Gotham's high-society women, who were contemptuous of those transgressing strict moral codes. What may have particularly galled Patti was her exclusion from a social reception given by the William K. Vanderbilts, one more brilliant than New York had possibly ever known. This splendid affair marked the opening, on 26 March 1883, of their Fifth Avenue mansion costing millions, a veritable palace. To celebrate it, the Vanderbilts gave a fancy dress ball to which they had extended invitations to more than a thousand guests. The elite world responded in a frenzy; the questions of what to wear, according to *The New-York Times*, thereafter "disturbed the sleep and occupied the waking hours of social butterflies, both male and female."[61] The names of those attending the affair and descriptions of their sartorial splendors subsequently filled columns in the daily presses. Among the guests that evening was Christine Nilsson. The opera world's greatest star, however, was conspicuously absent.

Professionally, Patti had exceeded all expectations with her superb portrayals, and operagoers looked forward to her next season. For a time, however, plans remained unsettled. Only at the end of the spring series was an announcement made that she would reappear in November for another engagement with Mapleson, who, to make this possible, raised her fee to $5000 a performance with fifty presentations guaranteed. This fiscal increase was the result of startling developments in New York's musical affairs—opera war!

Hostilities primarily began when New York's nouveaux riches— the Roosevelts, Goulds, Whitneys, Morgans, and Vanderbilts— coveted the opera boxes held by the stockholders and other wealthy patrons of the Academy of Music. This group, referred to as the Old Guard or the St. Germain set, included the Belmonts, Lorillards, Van Nests, Van Hoffmans, Schuylers, and Astors. Opera boxes were among this era's most cherished status symbols. Though Academy directors had tried to accommodate the newly wealthy by adding boxes to the existing eighteen, there still were not enough to meet the demand. The parvenus thereupon founded a new house in the spring of 1880: the Metropolitan Opera.

Beginning early in 1883, Abbey, then manager of the newly constructed theater to open in October, challenged Mapleson and his interests, raiding his forces and luring away some principal artists, orchestral players, chorus, wardrobe keepers, scene painters, the call-boy, and even his ballerina daughter-in-law, offering them more money than Mapleson could afford or was willing to pay. Among the outstanding artists under Abbey's aegis were Marcella Sembrich, Sofia Scalchi, Italo Campanini, and Christine Nilsson. Abbey failed, however, to engage Patti, who was willing to remain with Mapleson at a higher fee per performance. She also required some perquisites, one being a private railway car especially built for her use on tours. Costing 12,000 pounds ($60,000), it was, according to Mapleson, a superb coach:

> The curtains were of heavy silk damask, the walls and ceilings covered with gilded tapestry, the lamps of rolled gold, the furniture throughout upholstered with silk damask of the most beautiful material. The drawing-room was of white and gold, and the ceiling displayed several figures painted by Parisian artists of eminence. The woodwork was sandal wood, of which likewise was the casing of a magnificent Steinway piano, which alone had cost 2,000 dollars. There were several panel oil paintings in the drawing-room, the work of Italian artists. The bath, which was fitted for hot and cold water, was made of solid silver. The key of the outer door was of 18-carat gold.[62]

To launch his new season, Mapleson proposed opening with a favorite of theatergoers and an artist Abbey had wanted: Etelka Gerster. In her first appearance at the Academy of Music, on 11 November 1878, she had captivated the audience with her charm, artistry, and singing. When later performances there and elsewhere had confirmed her excellence, she became a valued member of

Mapleson's company. According to Mapleson, Gerster, unlike Patti, was a delight to manage, free of the proverbial prima-donna airs. In a private correspondence he wrote: "She is a most admirable singer, and a charming woman into the bargain, and in addition a most attractive artiste and easy to manage as she has always the interest of the theatre at heart."[63] Later he would regret such sentiments.

Before Patti's reentry at the Academy, Gerster had begun the series to wild acclaim on 22 October as Amina in *La sonnambula*—the same evening Abbey opened the Metropolitan Opera with Nilsson and Campanini in *Faust*—and had followed that triumph with other successes as Gilda, Lucia, and Linda di Chamounix, all brilliantly accomplished. Patti returned on 9 November as Ninetta in *La gazza ladra,* with her presence quickly altering Gerster's position, then relegated to a lesser status. Troubles soon began, but Patti denied these to a reporter:

> I am very happy in the academy. It is like an old home to me. My audiences are splendid, and we get along very well. . . . Mme. Gerster is a very nice lady; she stays in her corner and I stay in mine. There is no trouble of any kind.[64]

Meanwhile, Mapleson was losing money at an alarming rate, though not at all comparable to losses suffered by Abbey, and shortened this series, beginning his annual tour earlier than planned, thereby avoiding his rival on the road whenever possible. Ironically, during the peregrinations Mapleson found that the most difficult problem he faced was due not to his competitor, but, instead, to Patti and Gerster.

One of the first concerned Patti's $5000 fee per performance, an amount she was to receive by two o'clock each day of a representation. In Boston on 18 December, when Franchi attempted to collect this sum before the evening performance of *La traviata,* he found the impresario unable to oblige, with, according to Mapleson, only $4000 in box-office revenue at hand, whereupon the agent declared that Mapleson had breached his contract with Patti and that their association was at an end. When informed of what had transpired, Patti amazed Franchi with her response, which he duly related to the impresario:

> I cannot understand . . . how it is you get on so well with prime donne, and especially with Mdme Patti. You are a marvellous

man, and a fortunate one, too, I may add. Mdme Patti does not wish to break her engagement with you, as she certainly would have done with anyone else under the circumstances. Give me the £800 and she will make every preparation for going on to the stage. She empowers me to tell you that she will be at the theatre in good time for the beginning of the opera, and that she will be ready dressed in the costume of Violetta, with the exception only of the shoes. You can let her have the balance when the doors open and the money comes in from the outside public; and directly she receives it she will put her shoes on and at the proper moment make her appearance on the stage.[65]

Before her appearance on stage that evening, she did receive the full amount.

Then, towards the end of January ill feelings between Patti and Gerster intensified, the two no longer staying in their respective corners. The fury began in Baltimore when Gerster noted a playbill with Patti's name in larger type than hers and prices for admissions to some Patti performances exceeding those to her own. More and more resenting Patti's preeminence, Gerster determined to leave the company and entrained for New York, telling no one of her flight. Fortunately for Mapleson, a chorus member who had seen her going towards the railway station told him of this, whereupon the impresario wired to Wilmington, the first stop after Baltimore, to delay the train and to relay a message to Gerster that all problems would be settled upon her return. Meanwhile, the express from New York was detained at Wilmington by a railroad manager to take Gerster back after her train rolled into the station, about forty-five minutes later. All might have ended well had not the express held Patti, ensconced in her stateroom. When told the reason for the delay, she became outraged, feeling victimized by a lesser's folly. In Baltimore, Nicolini impatiently awaited Patti and found his emotional state complementing hers. A special dinner he had ordered for them would be ruined. Back at Wilmington, Gerster, having discovered Patti was on the express, refused to board it and traveled on to New York. Many hours later, Mapleson arrived in New York and finally persuaded the errant prima donna to return to the fold by acceding to her demands.

Not long thereafter in Chicago, Mapleson defied fate and cast these two stars in the same opera, *Les Huguenots,* on 30 January, with

Patti as Valentine and Gerster as Marguerite. Here, too, a contretemps occurred. Some ushers' errors ended in Patti's declaring she would never again perform in a cast including Gerster. At the end of the first act, the house responded with deafening cheers and torrential applause, seemingly a time for floral presentations. Usually Franchi directed ushers as to when such tributes should be given to Patti; on this occasion, however, he was absent. Galvanized by the cheering and applause, ushers proceeded to hand all floral offerings to the orchestra conductor, who, in turn, gave them to Patti. As Gerster had sung most of the act and Patti's part had been limited, such tributes rightfully belonged to the younger artist. Seeing Patti the recipient of one floral offering after another, the audience became restless; finally, when the conductor handed Gerster a small bouquet, the house went wild, giving her an ovation.

After this performance, back at the hotel, Patti became hysterical recalling this incident, convinced that Mapleson had had his hand in it to lower her in public esteem and to reduce her fee and that its primary origin had been due to Gerster's malevolent powers (she, in Patti's opinion, possessed an evil eye). Nicolini concurred in this view, apparently as superstitious as his beloved. Thereafter whenever any mishap occurred in Patti's presence, she immediately uttered her *bête noire*'s name. In San Francisco, when several minor tremors struck the city, she at once shrieked the ghastly name—Gerster! At another time, passing in a darkened hall before this loathed one's hotel room and wishing to neutralize any malevolent vibrations from within, Patti extended the first and fourth fingers of one hand to avert effects of the evil eye and nearly struck Gerster's husband's forehead as he placed his shoes outside the door.

In St. Louis, where the company gave performances from 18 to 23 February, Patti's antipathy towards her rival increased due to Gerster's comments regarding age.

Originally Mapleson had cast the two in another *Les Huguenots*. True to her vow, Patti refused to be in the cast, whereupon the impresario arranged a performance of scenes from *Rigoletto* starring Gerster as Gilda and excerpts from *Lucia* with Patti in the title role. Patti also sang "Home, Sweet Home" during a presentation that Missouri's Governor Thomas Crittenden attended. In an interview with a local press representative, she recalled what had happened following her rendition of this ballad:

Your Governor-Crittenden, I think his name was—yes, Gov. Crittenden, came to me after that night, and what do you think he did? . . . Well, he kissed me. He said, "Madame Patti, I may never see you again, and I cannot help it," and before I knew it he threw his arms around me and was kissing me. . . . Now it wouldn't do, you know, to have everybody washing my face, but an old gentleman and a nice-looking old gentleman—I think he was nice-looking, but the truth is, he kissed me so quick I didn't have time to see—and especially when they do not give me time to object, what can I do?[66]

The governor's remembrance of the incident hardly resembled Patti's:

I called next day in company with some friends, and as I approached Patti's room, I met in the corridor of the hotel a party of young girls, who said to me that they had just been given that which I should never have—a kiss from Patti. After the introduction to the lady I repeated what those happy young creatures had said, to which she laughingly replied that she did not see why that should never be. No sooner was this said than I had my kiss. I then remarked that this was better than even "Home, Sweet Home." The joke of it all is that in telling on me afterwards the friends with whom I had gone in declared that I said the kiss was . . . better than anything at home.[67]

Gerster seemingly had the last word on what became known as the Patti kiss:

MODEST REPORTER: I suppose, Mdme Gerster, you have heard about that kissing affair between Governor Crittenden and Patti?

MDME GERSTER: I have heard that Governor Crittenden kissed Patti before she had time to resist; but I don't see anything in that to create so much fuss.

REPORTER (interrogatively): You don't?

GERSTER: Certainly not! There is nothing wrong in a man kissing a woman old enough to be his mother.[68]

Before the end of this St. Louis series, a rumor circulated that Patti was not going with the company to the West Coast. Interviewed by a local reporter, she vehemently denied it:

I want to correct a silly story about my going West; I should like to know how it started. It is reported that I am not going West, and there is no truth in it. There are some people in our company who do not want me to go West, and poor Col. Mapleson has been in great trouble, but it is not for me to speak about that. Such people I simply look upon as plagues. Col. Mapleson came to me and told me that I must go West with him or his business would be ruined, and of course I am going. I shall sing in Denver, San Francisco and Salt Lake City. . . . As far as I know we sing in the Mormon temple in Salt Lake. I think Sig. Franchi wants to go there so he can get several wives.[69]

Mapleson maintained that at this juncture, Gerster, still holding dire feelings towards Patti, had agreed to remain with the troupe only if her rival's future appearances occurred infrequently. The impresario agreed to this demand, as he had already planned several weeks without Patti's services. She had by then fulfilled more than half the guaranteed performances in her contract.

Before the beginning of the San Francisco series, Patti had appeared in only one of the nine performances given en route, while Gerster had sung in six. Even so, Mapleson continued to have problems with Gerster.

Arriving in San Francisco early Sunday morning, 9 March, Patti soon granted interviews and expressed wonderment in being there:

According to every physical rule I should be a very tired little woman today, but, *au contraire,* I am so filled with the electricity of novelty and excitement that I really haven't time to grow weary. Everything possible has been arranged for my comfort in travelling, but the weather has been so very naughty that it gave me no rest at all last night. . . . Ah! If you but knew how much has been done to prevent my coming; but I have come, and am consequently in humor to smile on everybody and everything.[70]

Hours later Mapleson announced that Patti would make her San Francisco debut as Violetta on Thursday, 13 March. News of this so fired operagoers that many rushed to buy tickets long before the opening of the box office the following day.

Though Gerster's portrayal of Lucia on opening night, 10 March, and of Adina in *L'elisir d'amore* two evenings later had been thrilling, San Francisco had never seen anything like the demonstrations occurring for Patti's debut. According to a local publication, the city resonated with an endless chant: "Patti, Patti, Patti, Patti! The word rang all day long, all up and down the streets, and within the houses."[71]

Long thereafter, Mapleson recalled the events before that evening's presentation:

> On the day of the performance it took the whole of the police force to protect the theatre from the overwhelming crowds pressing for tickets, although it had been announced that no more were to be had. Long before daylight the would-be purchasers of Patti tickets had collected and formed into line, reaching the length of some three or four streets; and from this time until the close of the engagement . . . that line was never broken at any period of the day or night. . . . Later on it was announced that a limited number of gallery tickets would be sold, when a rush was made, carrying away the whole of the windows, glass, statuary, plants, etc.[72]

Hours later conditions around the opera house worsened. Admission to the theater became difficult, with people nearly fighting to gain entrance. Police found the situation so chaotic, they ordered reinforcements. Inside, patrons struggled through crowded vestibules and aisles to their seats in the auditorium, which was so crowded by curtain time that Chief of Police Crowley informed Mapleson he intended to press charges for violation of the fire ordinance. The house's seating capacity was 2200, but on this evening there were over 4000 auditors. A journalist described the scene thusly:

> They stood upon stools, they sat upon steps, they hung on to balcony rails by their eyelids. They were five deep in the back of each circle of the auditorium, and fifty deep in the vestibule. They were uncomfortable, hot, cross, nervous, weighted with the importance of the occasion.[73]

Throughout the performance, the house cheered Patti as Violetta. They must also have noticed her jewelry: mammoth diamond solitaires, squares of diamonds on a collar, three sparkling bracelets on each arm, diamonds in her hair, and diamond rings flashing to the gallery—all these worn during the party scene of act one. The third act, the ballroom scene, however, eclipsed these marvels. Then all her

famous diamonds came to the fore. The wonderful necklace,

with its long rivières of huge sparklers; the great horse-shoe, shoulder-brooch with its long trail of diamonds running across the breast; a long shoulder-clasp, and another pair of matchless bracelets; diamond pins to stay the draperies of her dress—diamonds, diamonds everywhere![74]

While the next day's reviews lauded Patti's personality, acting, and voice, local publication *The Argonaut* emphasized her more as a spectacle than as a great artist:

> What is there to say of Patti's voice that people have not been saying for twenty-five years? And how many went to hear her voice? She has become a spectacle, like Jumbo or any other freak, and the world goes to see rather than to hear.
>
> I doubt if twenty women in the house heard the music in the ballroom scene. *La diva* treated the house to a view of as many of her diamonds as she could carry without being brought in on trestles.[75]

When the following day's tickets for Patti's second appearance on March 18, as Leonora in *Il trovatore* with Nicolini as Manrico, went on sale, there was such bedlam at the box office, people howling and fighting for tickets, that later the theater's entrance and lobby looked "as if they had been visited by a first-class Kansas cyclone in one of its worst moods."[76]

Critical and popular acclaim followed as Patti later portrayed Annetta in *Crispino e la comare* and Linda di Chamounix. Her farewell as Annetta, on 29 March, brought a cyclonic demonstration.

Meanwhile, the Patti-Gerster rivalry continued. One demonstration of it evolved from a tragedy. After the death of a member of the company, bass Luciano Lombardelli on 17 March, various personnel contributed sums to his widow. Discovering Patti had given $150 in his memory, Gerster contributed $1000, thereby giving proof, according to Mapleson, of her superiority. Newspapers listed the contributions with Patti then looking like a piker. On 27 March, Gerster again attempted to upstage Patti, who sang in a concert that evening at Mechanics' Pavilion for some nine thousand auditors, by simultaneously holding a reception and inviting the press. The following day, Gerster's notices eclipsed Patti's. The night before, however, Patti had anticipated Gerster's move and called journalistic attention to a grand ball given in her honor by the Italian Margherita Club while Gerster was appearing as Lucia.

What, however, may have caused Patti's greatest resentment of Gerster was an article in *The Argonaut*, which stated, in part, that the "women of good society in San Francisco honored themselves when they recognized in one the womanly virtues, and in the other did not condone the practices of a life at war with the proprieties of American civilization."[77]

From San Francisco the troupe entrained for Salt Lake City, where on 1 April, Patti repeated the concert program of 27 March for six or seven thousand enthusiasts. Earlier, en route to San Francisco, the company had presented *Lucia* with Gerster, on 6 March, at Salt Lake City. At that time Mapleson asked Patti to help him persuade the religious leaders to allow a concert in the Mormon Tabernacle when the troupe returned from the Pacific Coast. Patti then invited the dignitaries to a *déjeuner* on her private railway car and convinced them that such an event would not be sacrilegious, as she had recently been inspired by some inner light and might join the Mormon Church.

Patti was back in New York on 7 April, and from the 14th to the 25th, she sang in four presentations at the Academy of Music: Linda di Chamounix, Juliette with Nicolini as Roméo in Gounod's opera, Annetta, and Semiramide. Critics considered the presentation of *Semiramide*, on 25 April, the outstanding event of the entire fall-winter-spring season. Patti as the Assyrian queen outdid herself. Joining her on stage was Sofia Scalchi as Arsace; by then the contralto had terminated her association with the Metropolitan.

Soon thereafter, Patti and Nicolini sailed for Europe, taking some $250,000 in fees from the American season. She departed also with the knowledge that her presence at the Academy of Music and on tour had greatly affected Abbey's season, which even before its end was a financial disaster. In the opera war, Mapleson had prevailed.

To ensure similar success for his next American series, Mapleson needed Patti, who agreed to return for the new season beginning 10 November 1884 and ending six months later.

Meanwhile, the spring publication of a book entitled *Fourteen Years with Adelina Patti*, written by her erstwhile companion Louisa Lauw, ruffled and then infuriated its subject because of references to her unconventional affair with Nicolini. In the literary work, Lauw provided vivid details of Nicolini's promiscuity while married as well

157

as intriguing aspects of his pursuit of the diva. At the same time Lauw portrayed the Marquis de Caux in a sympathetic light. Of this, Patti said:

> That book was doubtless written for the marquis' benefit. His intimacy with [Lauw] caused me to dispense with her and she had been playing a part for him. There was nothing in her book worthy of notice; at any rate I did not propose to assist in giving her the notoriety she sought by my taking notice of it.[78]

The subject further prompted Patti to speak candidly about her marriage and De Caux:

> I was pressed into that ill-considered match and I have suffered enough through it. The attachment of the marquis was purely mercenary. He wanted my earnings and property. His conduct since our separation has been outrageous. Not only did he take half my property in France but he sent experts to London to appraise my carriage horses, furniture and even the jewels that had been presented to me as souvenirs.[79]

The publication of Lauw's book as well as Patti's seemingly unending marriage to De Caux frustrated her, and she more and more rebelled against what she and many others perceived as the subjection of females in Victorian life. The singer longed for a divorce from the marquis; evidence of this is substantiated in letters from Josiah Pittman—pianist, composer and occasionally Patti's accompanist—to Edward Hall at Covent Garden. Since French divorce laws had by then become more lenient, Patti hoped she would soon be granted a divorce.

After the 1884 Covent Garden season, Pittman became her guest at Craig-y-Nos. In a letter dated 8 August he wrote that Patti had had "no end of bother about the Divorce business. . . . I only hope Providence will protect her and keep her from harm. She has no bed of roses."[80] Ten days later in another missive to Hall, Pittman said that Patti was "very much annoyed at the delay about the Divorce. . . . We must be very careful to say nothing to annoy our good friend for she is extremely sensitive."[81] On 31 August Pittman again referred to Patti's frustrations while also explaining her delay in securing passage on the *Oregon* for her return to the United States:

> If you knew the anxiety and pain dear Madame Patti has had to

endure through the Divorce business you would at once understand why she could not "three months ago take places by the *Oregon*." Every day she has been liable to be called to Paris, and is now positively ill from suspense and worry.[82]

Ironically, several months later the First Chamber of the Civil Tribunal of the Seine granted the marquis a divorce while denying one to Patti, reasoning that her demand was not sustained and nonsuited. This judgment required her to pay all expenses.

Before opening his American 1884–85 musical season, Mapleson made a shocking announcement: in the months ahead Patti would make her farewell appearances in the United States. (By then the diva had apparently had enough of Mapleson's brand of opera with his troupe, which he ever proclaimed the best of all possible opera companies, with him, of course, the best of all possible impresarios.) The series would also mark an epoch in her artistic life, as she was to celebrate the twenty-fifth anniversary of her opera debut at New York's Academy of Music, on 24 November 1859, at the age of sixteen. Mapleson proposed memorializing this Silver Jubilee with a gala in her honor.

At the same time the Metropolitan, beginning its second season, determined to challenge the Academy in a repertoire of operas in German under the musical direction of Dr. Leopold Damrosch, who during the past summer had assembled an impressive array of artists. In adopting German opera, directors at the new house were meeting a musical need long felt by various New York critics. Such a series should attract the city's enormous German population.

On 10 November Patti opened Mapleson's seventh season at New York's Academy of Music in one of her greatest roles: Rosina in *Il barbiere di Siviglia*. Four evenings later she so triumphed as Violetta that the *Times* music critic said her assumption of the part as "a combination of voice, lyric execution, and histrionic skill . . . had and has no rival on the operatic stage."[83]

In the following week Patti appeared as Semiramide and Violetta. Some operagoers then divided their allegiance with the Metropolitan Opera, beginning its second season on 1 November with a splendid representation of *Tannhäuser*. Productions of *Fidelio* and *Les Huguenots* followed, attracting large audiences and favorable critical reviews.

For many, however, the most memorable performance at either house occurred on 26 November at the Academy of Music: Patti as Lady Harriet in *Marta*, a gala celebrating the twenty-fifth anniversary of her opera debut. The music critic of the *Tribune*, Henry Edward Krehbiel, struck the right note for this occasion: "Stars of great brilliance have flashed across the firmament and gone out in darkness, but the refulgence of Patti's art remains undimmed, having only grown mellower and deeper and richer with time."[84] To this Krehbiel added:

> It was perpetually amazing how [Patti's] singing made the best efforts of the best of her contemporaries pale, especially those who depended on vocal agility for their triumphs. Each performance of hers made it plainer than it had been before that her genius penetrated the mere outward glitter of the music and looked upon the ornament as so much means to the attainment of an end; that end, a beautiful interpretation of the composer's thought.... Her ideas of art were the highest.[85]

At the conclusion of the performance, Patti, surrounded onstage by members of the company and the Seventh Regiment Band led by Carlo Cappa, responded to her celebrants with a brief speech, her voice shaking with emotion:

> My dear friends, it is twenty-five years ago since I sang here for the first time. The reception you have given me to-night is a tribute I shall never forget. It overcomes me. I am so overwhelmed I can say nothing more.[86]

Later, Krehbiel and another New York music critic, believing such an anniversary merited further tribute, proposed to organize a banquet for the singer and to invite highly prominent New Yorkers. Patti readily acceded to their proposal. Unfortunately, these two men had forgotten an absolute in the Victorian world: good Gotham ladies refused to honor fallen women. Embarrassed, the critics approached the diva anew with a plan to invite only gentlemen, representatives of the city's legal, artistic, and literary worlds. The "Queen of Hearts" (for so Patti fancied herself, at times signing her personal correspondence in this fashion) graciously acquiesced. Perhaps she appreciated the new guest list more than the original one.

The banquet, held at the Hotel Brunswick on 13 December, gave her much pleasure, she the cynosure of all men's eyes, radiant in a magnificent gown and ablaze with diamonds. Highlighting the occasion was a brief speech by Max Maretzek, who, of all those present, probably had known her longest, having been her conductor when she made her concert debut on 22 November 1851 at the age of eight.

The following day the *Times* paraphrased his remarks:

Max Maretzek said he made Patti's acquaintance when she was about 3 years old, (laughter,) in the Astor-Place Opera House, and she then kissed him and called him uncle. Two or three years after Patti's mother sang Norma in the Howard Athenaeum, and the child . . . wanted to sing her mother's part. (Laughter.) When 8 or 9 years old she first appeared as a prima donna, but when about to go on she wanted to know what she was singing for, and would not sing until she had received a hatful of bonbons as her price. She was not yet demanding $5,000 a night. (Laughter. Patti joining in and Nicolini appearing pleased.)[87]

After the end of this New York season, on 27 December, Mapleson began a prolonged national tour with Patti's farewell widely advertised. She first performed in Boston and Philadelphia to enthusiastic houses and without grave problems. A potential catastrophe awaited, however, in the next city: New Orleans. During an intermission of *La traviata* with Patti as Violetta, on 27 January, plaster fell from the front of the dress circle, a situation creating alarm with a number of patrons leaving the theater. Fortunately no one was hurt.

While touring in other cities during February, Patti looked forward to her return to San Francisco, where she arrived a week before the series there began in order to socialize. Meanwhile, she informed Mapleson via telegraph that she refused to make her reentry as Semiramide, unwilling to share the limelight on this occasion with Scalchi. Then, discovering that the soprano Emma Nevada, a member of the troupe and a native Californian, intended to sing "Home, Sweet Home" at her San Francisco debut, Patti decreed the opera for her reentry must be *Linda di Chamounix*, in which she regularly interpolated this ballad. Though angered, Mapleson wisely accepted the inevitable.

The diva duplicated her great successes of the past San Francisco season, triumphing anew in a number of her familiar roles. As before, whenever she sang, operagoers filled the house to suffocation. A performance of *Aida* on 24 March, with Patti as the titular heroine and Nicolini as Radames, enticed operagoers as few events had. Mapleson recalled the onslaught:

> On this day we discovered the "Chinese swing". . . . In the alleyway leading to the theatre is a lodging-house facing a sort of opening into the building used for ventilation. An ingenious fellow had rigged up a swing, and so adjusted it that he could toss people from his house on to the roof of the theatre to the ventilation hole. Once there, the intruder passed downstairs. . . . The police had to cut the ropes and take the swing away. So many devices were resorted to for entering the theatre without payment that I had to put it during this performance in a state of siege, as it were, and to close the iron shutters, as people came in from ladders through the windows of the dress-circle unobserved in many instances.[88]

In Chicago, where Mapleson presented a two-week series from 6 to 18 April, Patti performed as Semiramide, Linda di Chamounix, Lady Harriet in *Marta*, Aida, and Marguerite in *Faust*. Public response to this short season, designated a festival, was such that some 115,000 operagoers attended.

Parenthetically, while there, Nicolini saw a poster on which Patti's and Nevada's names were alike in size. He even used a ruler to ascertain this horror. He knew Patti's contract stipulated that her name on such advertisements be a third larger than that of any other artist. Mapleson duly ordered Nevada's name altered in its dimensions.

Several weeks later in Boston, Patti as Lady Harriet in *Marta* made her "last appearance" on the American stage, thereafter leaving for Europe. Before departing, however, she bade farewell to the United States:

> I felt that America should have only my best, and that the country where I first was received with open arms when a mite of a child should not remember me as a worn-out singer. I shall not sing much longer anywhere. I have all my old friends in Europe to say good-bye to, and when my adieus are all made I shall live, I hope, happy and contented in my dear home among the people who have learned to love me for myself, and not for my voice alone.[89]

After returning to Europe, Patti enjoyed some weeks of respite at Craig-y-Nos, where fresh air and relaxation revitalized her. While there she finalized plans to appear at Covent Garden for a series managed by Mapleson, who had obtained her services despite stiff demands.

His contract with the diva contained twelve particulars, probably like those in former agreements between them. One clause stipulated that she "shall be free to attend Rehearsals, but shall not be required or bound to attend at any." Another related to the size of her name on advertisements. Patti demanded certain roles exclusively: Rosina, Violetta, Lady Harriet in *Marta,* and Zerlina in *Don Giovanni.* The contract further provided that she was at liberty to cancel the engagement if there occurred an epidemic of cholera, small pox, fever, or any other contagious or deadly disease "within the range of the London Bills of Mortality."[90]

The Covent Garden season began on 20 June with Patti as Violetta and ended on 25 July with her portraying Leonora in *Il trovatore.* She also assumed a new role, Bizet's exotic, mercurial gypsy, Carmen, which aroused great interest.

Music critic Herman Klein first met Patti shortly before this appearance as Carmen; his description of her suggests that she had the perfect mien for this part:

> She looked astonishingly young. Though in her forty-third year, she did not appear to be a day more than thirty, and her movements seemed still to retain the impulse and freedom of girlhood. The merry laugh, the rapid turn of the head, the mischievous twinkle in the keen dark eyes when she said something humorous, were as natural to her as that rapid, forward *élan* when she extended her hand to *Alfredo* in the supper scene of *Traviata.* . . . The Patti of the stage and the Patti of real life were, in outward semblance and deportment, one and the same. It followed, therefore, that the woman was as unaffected, as fascinating, as the artist.[91]

In her first impersonation of the Spanish gypsy, on 14 July, Patti's portrayal lacked sufficient color, dash, and diablerie. Also, this role did not display her voice advantageously. Klein, like other critics, noted that point:

> The charm of the incomparable voice and much beautiful singing could not ward off this penalty, for the simple reason that most of the music lay too low for her. A pure soprano is very seldom heard to advantage in a part that has been written for a mezzo-soprano. . . . She elected to raise the *tessitura* of *Carmen*'s music by making numerous changes and introducing "ornaments" which were out of keeping with the design of the composer. This naturally aroused adverse criticism; indeed, the press notices as a whole were frankly unfavorable.[92]

Others in the cast included Pierre Engel as Don José, Giuseppe del Puente as Escamillo, and Louise Dotti as Micaela.

The short season ended with a gala performance of *Il trovatore* with Patti as Leonora, an occasion honoring her twenty-fifth consecutive Covent Garden engagement. At its conclusion Mapleson made a speech laced with compliments to the diva and presented her with a diamond bracelet from various admirers. Later a procession of torch-bearers, a band, and other celebrants accompanied Patti from the theater to her hotel, where the band continued to serenade her while from time to time fireworks lighted the dark sky.

Months later she undertook another lengthy tour, extending from November to mid-April with a geographic range from Eastern Europe to the Atlantic Ocean, under the aegis of impresarios Schürmann and Pollini, of Hamburg. During these peregrinations Patti sang in opera and concerts, at times joined by Nicolini; the tenors Julián Gayarre, Roberto Stagno, and Angelo Masini; and baritone Antonio Cotogni.

In December Patti successfully performed in Amsterdam, Budapest, Prague, and Vienna. Writing from Vienna on the 27th, she referred to a preceding night's presentation of *Il barbiere*: "I thought the house would come down . . .—I received lots of presents and flowers on the stage and Don Bartolo presented me such a *sweet* little Xmas tree—after the lesson scene."[93]

Though scheduled to appear in Bucharest in January, Patti refused to journey to this city, where temperatures had plummeted to record lows. Sensitive to cold, she remained adamant in this decision. Schürmann nonetheless proved to be a manager of fortitude and guile, telegraphing to his secretary already in Bucharest to send him a message stating that a grand reception of many noblemen as well as representatives from the ministry awaited Patti's arrival in the capital. When he received the dictated telegram, the impresario shared its contents with the singer, who at once agreed to go. Upon arrival at the Bucharest railway station, she reveled in the attention of sixty formally dressed gentlemen, flowers thrown at her feet, a band, and a triumphal procession to her hotel with her in a sleigh. Schürmann had to pay this welcoming party, composed neither of nobles nor of diplomats. He had also rented their suits and coats.[94]

Following this comedy, a tragedy occurred during a performance of *Lucia*. To gain a better perspective of Patti, a man in the wings climbed the irons at stage-side. Then becoming dizzy, he slipped and fell on a woman standing below, who shrieked for help, her cries resounding in the auditorium. At this point someone called out "Fire!" Sensing that a stampede for exits might ensue, Patti stated that there was no fire and that the backstage disturbance was nothing. She hardly lost a musical beat and continued singing her cadenza.

Early in February she gave several concerts in Paris. A critic at the first of these especially praised her rendition of an aria from *Linda di Chamounix* and Gounod's "Ave Maria":

> In her second selection, from *Linda*, Patti . . . may well have sung as well, but certainly never better; from low note to high D flat there was not a trace of weakness, fatigue, or use. She played with the embellishments, the stacatti, the runs and trills . . . ; she seemed to revel in new shadings, and evidently aimed at surpassing her own self. In reply to some dozen recalls, amid offerings of lilac trees, monster rose bushes, pulled on the stage in large boxes by liveried lackeys, Patti began again the entire cavatina, and then, the critics wondered if she could twice repeat the same perfect rendering. She did even better. . . . She repeated thrice Gounod's "Ave Maria," . . . to which she gave new life and inspiration without disregard of the composer's intent.[95]

While in Paris, Patti turned down an engagement at the Opéra, citing several reasons:

> At the Opera House I should have to sing in French—which is not the tongue I best manage; and you know how severe the

Parisians are when the pronunciation is not faultless. Also, in the Italian Opera the whole soul may express itself through the throat. Dramatic technique, as well as feeling, is needed at the Grand Opera. I don't set up to be an actress. I am a song-bird, you know. French critics have always been on my side. But I came among them when I was twenty, and I have been sixteen years away. In some respects I may have gained as an artist. But I am no longer a young girl and have no taste for coquetry, which is said in France advantageously to replace youth.[96]

Indeed, it had been sixteen years since Patti had appeared at the Théâtre-Italien.

In Nice Patti received her usual acclaim, but in Barcelona, the next tour city, she experienced the opposite: a virtual fiasco in the opening night's presentation of *La traviata*. Tenor Roberto Stagno had originally been cast as Alfredo; but he, unwilling to be compared to Julián Gayarre, who had earlier enthralled audiences in this part, insisted the opera be changed to *Il barbiere di Siviglia*. Patti did not cooperate and demanded that Nicolini replace Stagno, whose supporters, some no doubt paid for their services, then disrupted the opera until Schürmann came on stage and offered to refund those dissatisfied with the cast change. Though the opera then proceeded fairly well, Patti cried and threatened to break her contract. In time, however, she decided otherwise. Several nights after the opening, some Patti followers made life difficult for Stagno, appearing with her in *Il barbiere di Siviglia*, and booed him while wildly cheering the diva. Stagno, according to his daughter Bianca, thereafter referred to Patti as a difficult woman and partner.

Following a series in Valencia and Madrid, the tour ended on 17 April in Lisbon, where at the Teatro de São Carlos, Patti portrayed Rosina, Lucia, Violetta, and Carmen. Two of her tenors were Angelo Masini and Frenchman Albert Guille. The tour was an artistic and financial success, with large sums realized in all places.

Throughout these months Patti's greatest pleasure may have been the judgment of her divorce from the marquis on 15 July 1885. In the final settlement he was awarded 1,500,000 francs ($300,000). Free at last, Patti looked forward to marriage with Nicolini, this ceremony set for early in June 1886. As for De Caux, he did not long enjoy the fiscal benefits from this settlement. His death occurred on 13 December 1889.

Among those rejoicing with Patti in her marital plans were Welsh neighbors who had learned to respect and to admire her despite her cohabitation with Nicolini. In time it was said that Patti and Nicolini no longer lived in sin, since the Greek Church had blessed their union. Above all else what impressed many living nearby, however, was her generosity.

Since settling in Wales, the diva had responded to various requests for charity; no unfortunate, it was said, appealed for her help in vain. Known as "Lady of the Castle," "Lady Bountiful," and "Queen of Hearts," she gave with an open hand. In the United States she had telegraphed a Swansea firm to distribute three wagon-loads of flannels and blankets for poor cottagers near Craig-y-Nos. She had directed household domestics to feed beggars whenever they appeared on the scene. In time she volunteered her services at what resulted in a nearly annual charity concert for the benefit of local hospitals or charitable institutions, organizing programs that included other artists and paying their fees. Over the years these concerts occasioned the proclamation of local holidays. Dignitaries met Patti at railway stations, addressing her in formal speeches and presenting flowers. Carriages lined up to convey her, Nicolini, their guests, other artists, and local dignitaries to the concert hall, often with a military escort and band leading the way.

Her first Welsh charity concert was given in Swansea on 14 September 1882. According to the 15 September issue of *The Cambrian,* hundreds had crowded into the gaily decorated town to witness Patti's arrival from Craig-y-Nos in her private saloon railway carriage. The paper stated that the concert was "the most remarkable ever witnessed in Swansea."[97] Other artists on this program included solo pianist Tito Mattei, baritone Bonetti, violinist Thérèse Castellan, Nicolini, and accompanist Wilhelm Ganz.

The Cambrian's review read, in part, as follows:

> Madame Patti thus made quite a triumphal visit to our town and the generosity of her conduct to the public charity, coupled with her affability and readiness to respond to the popular manifestations of enthusiasm, have left the most pleasing impression upon

the town and neighbourhood. We are glad to be able to add, what was indeed sufficiently obvious to all who had opportunities of observing, that Madame Patti herself carries away most agreeable remembrances of the real enthusiasm which greeted her on her first public visit to our town. May it not be her last![98]

In the next three years Patti participated in two more charity concerts in Swansea and one in Brecon. Her occasional accompanist and secretary Josiah Pittman wrote of the second Swansea benefit on 14 August 1884 to a colleague:

Such a scene as that of yesterday I never saw. Our Queen was welcomed most heartily in arriving at Swansea. The Ships in the Harbour were gay with flags, the streets also, and the cheering at the Stations along the line was only excelled by the people in the town. The Hall was crammed—I know more than 2100 people were within it.

I need not say how our Queen sang—you know she can only sing in one way and that way is as far from others as Heaven is from Earth.

But we were all successful with our pieces and the concert proceeded to the end to everybody's satisfaction. Then came a supplemental scene that would have done you good to witness.

Sir Hussey Vivian . . . came onto the platform and addressed the audience—He first requested them to stand, he then asked them after a few preliminary compliments and thanks to Madame Patti to give three cheers as a manifestation of their pleasure and gratitude to her for her generosity and kindness on behalf of the Hospital.

No Queen of any country ever received such spontaneous hommage [*sic*] as our Queen.[99]

The proceeds from these concerts in Swansea and Brecon as well as Patti's public and private contributions to the needy had endeared her to many in Wales. Her marriage to Nicolini on Thursday, 10 June 1886, gave neighbors and admirers an opportunity to do something for her. Meanwhile, Patti determined to involve thousands of her neighbors in the marriage. The rector Rev. E. L. Davies-Glanley of Ystradgynlais Church, the setting for the marriage, explained her actions in London's *Pall Mall Gazette* on the wedding day: "I believe Madame Patti wishes her marriage to be as public as possible, for probably she is under the impression that the world condemns her life as it is at present."[100]

On Monday, 7 June, four chefs began preparing the wedding day banquets in the huge Craig-y-Nos kitchens. On Tuesday Patti and Nicolini, both French subjects, entrained for Swansea to sign the marriage contract before the French Consul M. de Trobriand. Later at Craig-y-Nos the mayor and corporation of Brecon addressed Patti with these words:

> We trust that you may long continue to live among us, and honestly hope that there are in store for you many years of prosperity and happiness, which, we feel sure, will be devoted, as in the past, to the furtherance of the welfare and felicity of those amongst whom your lot is cast.

Replying on the diva's behalf, an old friend of hers chose felicitous words:

> All the world is agreed that Madame Patti is a most remarkable woman; but among her splendid talents and noble qualities there is one to which I can especially testify after many years of friendship—the goodness and kindness of her heart, which rise far above all the special gifts with which she has been endowed.[101]

On Wednesday Patti and Nicolini, accompanied by friends serving as witnesses, again left for Swansea, where at the French Consulate they signed the civil contract of marriage. Towards evening in the English billiard room at Craig-y-Nos, committees from Swansea, Ystradgynlais, and Ystelafera offered congratulations in the presence of wedding guests. Representatives of the Swansea Hospital handed her and Nicolini a resolution expressing best wishes for marital happiness and a long life in which they might continue their generous deeds. A spokesman for the hospital reminded Patti that a ward there had been named in her honor and that this ward was at her disposal for the benefit of any of the poor in her neighborhood or others whom she might wish to send. Representatives of the other Welsh communities expressed similar sentiments.

Meanwhile, in the surrounding areas of Craig-y-Nos, neighbors had spent their "small savings in decking their villages and highways with banners, garlands, and gay devices."[102] In turn, she had provided refreshments for three thousand local schoolchildren and new clothes for the three hundred poorest among them.

At about ten o'clock on the nuptial day, under a glorious sun, the wedding party left Craig-y-Nos for religious ceremonies at Ystradgynlais Church, seven miles away. Occupying the first carriage, an open landau drawn by horses with glittering harnesses and adorned with freshly cut flowers, were Patti and several friends; a second landau conveyed Nicolini and two men serving as witnesses at the marriage ceremony while four more landaus and two four-in-hands followed with members of the wedding party staying at Craig-y-Nos.

At the church Patti was greeted by a band, a local presentation committee, some one thousand singing schoolchildren, and eight tiny flower girls from the village. Some seven hundred guests watched her walk down the aisle, "arrayed in a lovely dress . . . of pale blue silk, shrouded in cream-coloured Duchesse lace, and ornamented with tiny bunches of forget-me-nots and lilies-of-the-valley."[103] She carried a bouquet of these flowers and white heather, narcissus, and violets. Music from the organ and a hymn from the choir swelled as she proceeded to the altar, where she and Nicolini were at last united in holy matrimony.

After the ceremony and the signing of the marriage register, Patti, Nicolini, and wedding party drove to Craig-y-Nos

> between long lines of school-children in holiday garb, under triumphal arches, and past brass bands and local choirs, all vociferously musical, without number. What with friendly societies in their full "regalia," villagers, excursionists from Swansea and Brecon, and the "rising generation" of the valley, there was scarcely a hiatus in the double line of congratulants.[104]

At the castle, minute guns fired in celebration and a band played: Craig-y-Nos itself wore colorful bunting, flags of the countries where Patti had sung in opera with the Royal Standard flying above the rest.

The wedding guests, soon enjoying a Lucullan feast, were not the only ones to partake of the newlyweds' hospitality as Patti had arranged food and drink for neighbors at the foot of the Rock of the Night: "tons of fresh meat, waggonloads of white bread and pastry, and huge casks of strong beer."[105] The diva had also made arrangements for the schoolchildren singing at Ystradgynlais Church to have refreshments after the ceremony.

Patti and Nicolini received many costly gifts, among these a diamond arrow pin from the Prince and Princess of Wales. Two items were especially significant because of their local association. Swansea admirers gave them a complete dessert service of eighteenth-century Swansea china, prevailing upon some owners to relinquish these antiques as a sign of gratitude for Patti's and Nicolini's past kindnesses. Ystradgynlais admirers presented an elegant casket of silver and gold with an illustrated address of congratulations inside. There were also some 150 congratulatory messages: among these were greetings from the Prince of Wales, the Queen of the Belgians, the Rothschilds, the Duchess of Newcastle, Christine Nilsson, and Lillie Langtry. A greeting to Patti from Elizabeth, Queen of Romania, was particularly heartening: "In sending you my best felicitations, I entertain the warmest hope that the future has in reserve for you as much pleasure as you yourself have already given to the entire world."[106]

In the evening some fifty guests assembled for a sumptuous dinner party in the winter garden, commanding a magnificent view of Swansea Valley encircled by high elevations and illuminated by a new marvel of the age, electric lights. During this repast, the Band of the 3rd Glamorgan Rifles played opera and dance music, Welsh tunes, and a wedding march written for the occasion. At the same time in a long, vaulted hall of the castle, over a hundred individuals—yeomen, tradesfolk, and servants—prepared a feast for themselves.

Several hours after the winter garden banquet, the newlyweds and guests watched a display of fireworks and heard the firing of cannons from the castle grounds. On a nearby mountaintop some other celebrants saluted this occasion by lighting a huge bonfire, visible for miles. The activities at Craig-y-Nos ended with a ball, which did not conclude until daybreak.

Thereafter, Patti insisted that she be addressed not with her given family and professional name but with her second husband's surname. After all, to merit this appellation, she had endured much.

Madame Patti-Nicolini

Thirteen days after the wedding, Patti gave the first of four concerts during June and July at London's Royal Albert Hall. These 1886 presentations began two decades of annual Patti concerts at the hall and provided Londoners virtually the only opportunities to hear her. Management and conditions at Covent Garden at that time did not inspire confidence, and the contract with her concert manager precluded any London opera engagements. A rare exception occurred on 15 July, when she appeared as Rosina at London's Drury Lane Theatre. The cast included Nicolini as Almaviva and Giuseppe del Puente as Figaro. This performance was a benefit for Mapleson, who was in fiscal straits, and generated a large sum for its beneficiary and glory for Patti. Mapleson had recently returned from the Uni. ed States, where his 1885–86 season had been so financially disastrous that he gave up American engagements for the next decade, thereby leaving the Metropolitan Opera the main operatic force in the States.

Socially during these months, the newlyweds were often invited to London dinner parties and soirées. As a married woman, Patti was once again acceptable to high society. Of these invitations, she especially cherished those from music-lover and patron Alfred de Rothschild, who for years had advised her concerning investments and had sent as wedding presents a ruby and diamond brooch for Patti and a ruby- and diamond-studded leather cigar case for Nicolini. It was said he had been in love with the diva. He extended invitations to his London townhouse at 1 Seamore Place, where eighteenth-century French masterpieces hung on the walls and where a single mantel held objects worth thousands of pounds. Cecil Roth in *The Magnificent Rothschilds* described one of these occasions: "Often the guests included the Heir Apparent to the throne, who was there once at a luncheon party when Patti and Nicolini both sang, and the loveliness assembled to meet him rivalled that of the Gainsboroughs on the walls."[1] For some, however, the London mansion paled next to Rothschild's country estate, Halton House in Buckinghamshire, where he often directed his own symphony orchestra with a white ivory baton encircled by diamonds and maintained a private circus at which he acted as ringmaster and drove a zebra four-in-hand.

At Craig-y-Nos, Patti and Nicolini provided their own hospitality, usually involving many houseguests. One of these, a Viennese journalist, later described his stay: noontime meals prepared by the cordon-bleu and served in the conservatory, these and all meals planned by Patti and the chef; the setting outside the dining area—a panorama of mountains, sky, valley, wood, and water; afternoon drives in landaus and phaetons, led by Patti in her carriage; sumptuous dinners with guests in formal apparel, the diva resplendently garbed and bejeweled, Nicolini imposing in classic attire; music played by the orchestrion, an electrical mechanism with a pipe-organ tone standing in the French billiard room. Here Patti "seated herself on one of the raised leather-cushioned *bancs*, surrounded by her feminine guests, and, while coffee was being served, listened to the orchestrion in its pleasing execution of her and her husband's favorite 'rolls.' "[2] The diva, calling this mechanism the castle's soul, often sang to its accompaniment and, when appropriate, played castanets. Here, too, she sometimes played billiards with Nicolini, who, she said, was occasionally rude enough to win.

For the Viennese journalist, Patti had ordered the flying of his nation's flag from the castle's central turret as was her custom to honor an esteemed guest or guests in residence.

Then Patti and Nicolini prepared for another lengthy tour to the United States, where she had been absent over a year, and to Mexico

City. These plans were instigated by Henry E. Abbey, who with his wife had been a wedding guest at Patti's marriage to Nicolini. While at Craig-y-Nos, he had offered a contract stipulating $5000 a performance with fifty concert-opera presentations.

Arriving in New York on 14 November 1886, Patti amazed some reporters by her appearance, looking years younger. Some of the press attributed this change to her marital bliss. She insisted on being addressed as Madame Patti-Nicolini. To a *Times* reporter, she rhapsodized over the Statue of Liberty, which had been dedicated about three weeks before, perhaps relating its symbolism to her newfound freedom from De Caux. She called it "the greatest statue in the world."[3] Patti anticipated an epochal tour, featuring her and contralto Sofia Scalchi, baritone Antonio Galassi, bass Franco Novara, tenor Albert Guille, and conductor Arditi in concerts with scenes from such operas as *Faust, Marta, La traviata,* and *Semiramide.*

Her first New York program, on 18 November, was typical of those that followed, and the next day the *Times* reported: "Never was the great soprano in better voice. . . . The voice . . . was the same . . . perfectly even and true and of exquisite quality. . . . Between Mme. Patti as an executant and the best singers of the age no comparison whatever can be established."[4] Abbey followed this presentation with three more in New York, the last on 1 December, and then took the company to other major American cities prior to the engagement in Mexico City, from which early in December reports had emerged of a fraud regarding ticket sales.

Some months before, in New York, Harry Benson had ingratiated himself with several of Abbey's business associates and obtained information as to the Mexican engagement. Later in Mexico City, posing as the brother of one of Abbey's representatives, Benson claimed to have the authority to sell tickets for the Patti engagement. Large sums poured in at the box office, and Benson later absconded with $22,000 in bills, but, fearing detection, left behind thousands of silver dollars. A year later, detectives apprehended him in New York. The press called this fraud the greatest swindle in theatrical history.

A welcoming party of twelve Mexican civil leaders, bands, and dense crowds with children waving flags greeted the diva upon her arrival in Mexico City late in December. For weeks the city had anticipated the event, with storekeepers placing her picture in windows and displaying such objects named for her as fans, bon-bons, hats, gloves, and stockings. Though elated by this welcome, Patti was so fatigued from the long journey that she proceeded with little ceremony to the Hotel del Jardín, where people crowded balconies to see her and to throw flowers in her wake. Fortunately by the time this series began, on 30 December, she was in top form for her performances at the Gran Teatro Nacional. Commentators observed that not since the days of Emperor Maximilian and Empress Charlotte had the capital seen such lavish displays of jewels and finery and that at each performance audiences packed the theater.

From Mexico City, Patti, Nicolini, and associates took a train to Los Angeles, where they fulfilled a single engagement, and thence to San Francisco, where from 24 January to 9 February they gave six performances. At the final presentation a man named James Hodges attempted to throw dynamite into a box occupied by millionaire James Flood, but it exploded prematurely and injured only Hodges. Patti carried on as if nothing untoward had occurred and calmly signaled Arditi to lead the orchestra in the opening strains of "Home, Sweet Home."

Years later the diva recalled a similar experience at her New York opera debut in 1859, when "a man had hung his coat carelessly over the front of the gallery and a pistol in the pocket went off in the middle of the performance. For an instant every one stopped still on the stage; then we went ahead again, and the audience, was reassured."[5]

After touring other American cities, Patti and the company returned to New York for opera performances at the Metropolitan Opera House, from 11 to 23 April. Usually appearing only twice weekly in opera, she agreed to six performances during the two weeks, taking the leading roles in *La traviata, Semiramide, Faust, Carmen, Lucia,* and *Marta.* Receipts, according to Krehbiel, totaled approximately $70,000. On 18 April New York operagoers saw her for the first time as Carmen. Local critics commended her singing, but claimed that the vocal part lay at times too low to display "those brilliant and powerful tones" she used so effectively as Lucia, Violetta, and Semiramide. Dramatically, Patti gave some the impression that she was "too refined in her methods of action to give an adequate delineation of the wicked ... gypsy."[6] Her Carmen was "naughty, perhaps, but not downright wicked . . . only mischievous and sometimes a little obstinate . . . nevertheless, an attractive and interesting Carmen."[7]

After performing in several other Eastern cities, Patti returned to the Metropolitan Opera House for a final program, on 13 May, of excerpts from *La traviata*, the second act of *Marta*, and the third act of *Aida*, with Nicolini as Alfredo and Radames. The following day she, Nicolini, and entourage sailed for Europe, along with sixty-five trunks, three dogs, five small parrots, one large parrot, three small birds, and the handsome sum of $250,000—her portion of the tour's box-office receipts.

Also accompanying Patti on this transatlantic passage was her niece Carlina, sixteen-year-old daughter of Carlo Patti, who had died in 1873. For a while the diva took an intense interest in Carlina; indeed, Nicolini's first will named her as an inheritor of Craig-y-Nos should he and Patti precede her in death. But a serious rupture followed. Rumor had it that the young and very probably homesick girl was not sufficiently grateful for her aunt's solicitations, nor did Carlina share Patti's fond wish that she marry one of Nicolini's two sons.

After remaining at Craig-y-Nos for several weeks, Patti entrained for London for three Albert Hall concerts followed by an opera performance, on 1 July, as Violetta at Her Majesty's Theatre with a company under Mapleson's aegis. Herman Klein described this event and its aftermath:

> Mme. Adelina Patti made her first (and only) appearance on the boards of Her Majesty's Theatre in Verdi's "Traviata," on Friday, July 1, 1887. To the vast majority of Mme. Patti's admirers her performance in opera during the present season came as a surprise. At the time of her return from America it was anticipated that she would sing at one or other of the London opera houses; but the negotiations all fell through, and when Mme. Patti went home to Craig-y-Nos after her last concert in town, it was distinctly believed that she intended remaining there for her summer holiday.
>
> However, Mr. Mapleson subsequently arranged matters with Mr. Abbey (who then had the exclusive right to Mme. Patti's services in London), and here was the diva once more exercising her old fascination, in the character of *Violetta*, before an audience that filled every available nook and corner of Her

Majesty's. It is scarcely needful to add that the great artist was enthusiastically received. For herself, indeed, the evening constituted a long series of triumphs. Of her supporters on the stage the less said the better.

Mme. Patti was to have appeared in "Il Barbiere" on the following Tuesday, but an attack of hoarseness was declared to be the cause that prevented her singing. This circumstance compelled Mr. Mapleson to close his theatre once more. He announced that it would reopen on the Saturday with "Faust," Mme. Patti appearing as *Marguerite*. The house opened, truly, but the opera given was "Carmen," with Mme. Trebelli in the title character, and, curious to relate, no charge was made for admission to the performance. . . . This, however, was the "last dying flicker." Thenceforward the doors of Her Majesty's remained closed, so far as Mr. Mapleson was concerned, terminating the most remarkable series of operatic ventures ever conducted by an impresario in course of a single season.[8]

Early that October, in Paris, Maurice Strakosch died, leaving Amalia (his wife of thirty-five years) and his son and daughter deeply bereaved as was Patti, who owed "a great deal to his practical experience and sage counsel at the most critical period of her life."[9] One not in mourning, however, was Nellie Melba, who only several months before had signed a contract with Maurice, giving him exclusive rights to her performances for the next decade. Later, he infuriated Melba by refusing an offer for her opera debut at the Monnaie in Brussels. Her Brussels debut took place four evenings after his death.

At this time, too, Nicolini was planning Patti's first tour of South America, an engagement that would bring her the highest fees she had ever received. On the recent tour of the United States, Nicolini had broached the subject of a South American engagement with Abbey and Marcus Mayer, another New York manager and Abbey's business associate, and when both agreed that the time seemed propitious, negotiations with South American impresarios began. What ultimately transpired was an agreement for Patti to appear in opera in Buenos Aires, Montevideo, and Rio de Janeiro, beginning in April 1888. Not only did Abbey guarantee $5000 a performance, but the diva was to receive a percentage of the gross receipts.

Before venturing to South America, Patti gave a series of presentations in Lisbon from December to mid-January and in

Madrid in February, where she, appropriately enough, celebrated her forty-fifth birthday. In both places she enjoyed her usual successes as Rosina, Linda, Annetta, Violetta, and Gilda, adding Dinorah in Lisbon. Sharing the stage with her in some Madrid performances was a young Italian tenor destined for a distinguished career: Fernando de Lucia.

Finally, accompanied by Nicolini, her niece Carlina, "Karo" Baumeister, Abbey, Mayer, and her English friend Augustus F. M. Spalding, Patti left Lisbon for Buenos Aires and her opening night on 4 April 1888 as Rosina at the Teatro Politeama, revenues for this opening exceeding 4000 pounds ($20,000). Obviously Patti-fever had struck and neared epidemic proportions. This situation prevailed throughout the remaining twenty-three presentations. By the end of this season, box-office receipts totaled 70,000 pounds ($350,000), with her share at 38,400 pounds ($192,000).

The most memorable evening of the season was perhaps on 3 July, when Roberto Stagno was Almaviva to Patti's Rosina. Local critic Antonio Astort considered him incomparable in the role, and the two artists in combination caused such commotion that the evening was "true madness."[10]

Though originally the tour had included Rio de Janeiro, Patti refused to fulfill her engagement in the city because yellow fever had broken out there. Instead, she and her party proceeded to Montevideo, where in July and early August she gave eight performances at the Teatro Solis in familiar roles and one new assumption: the titular heroine in Léo Delibes's *Lakmé*. Here, too, a Patti-epidemic raged while box-office receipts mounted to approximately 20,000 pounds ($100,000). The seasons in Buenos Aires and Montevideo ended as artistic and fiscal triumphs.

The diva wrote a farewell letter, published in the 10 August edition of local newspaper *El Siglo*:

> I have waited until the last moment of my pleasant stay on these hospitable shores to say farewell sadly to Buenos Aires and to Montevideo. I decided to cross the ocean knowing that I was going to visit places knowledgeable in the art that I dedicate myself to, but I had not predicted so much enthusiasm. . . .
>
> A genuine feeling of satisfaction brought tears to my eyes when in Buenos Aires, as well as in Montevideo, I saw the stage covered with flowers that had been thrown by the ladies and I

saw them on their feet applauding me. And so to say, goodbye! to ... the generous public of these two countries. I have cherished hopes of returning ... but now I leave you with my undying gratitude ... for your kindnesses.[11]

From this tour she realized more than 50,000 pounds ($250,000) in just over four months, with an average of $8000 a performance.

After returning to Craig-y-Nos, Patti accepted an engagement in Paris beginning the end of November to recreate the role of Juliette in a revival of Gounod's *Roméo et Juliette,* which from this time forward received critical and popular acclaim. Among the composer's changes was, most notably, a new third act finale, which he composed for Jean de Reszke as Roméo. The State determined to celebrate this revival in a spectacular setting, decreeing that the production with new mise-en-scène and a superb cast should take place at the Paris Opéra or Académie Nationale de Musique. Gounod was to conduct the premiere on 28 November 1888.

At preliminary rehearsals in early October the French soprano Hariclea Darclée assumed the role of Juliette. As time passed, however, she appeared so nervous that Pierre Gailhard, former opera bass and then joint-director of the Opéra, decided the only artist to save the situation was Patti. With Gounod ignorant of his plan, Gailhard sent her a telegram that he intended to visit. During a dinner at Craig-y-Nos, he astonished her with his proposal, as she had surmised that his visit was to engage her for the 1889 Paris Exhibition. Patti immediately responded that to join the new production was impossible: she had always sung Juliette in Italian and there was little time to relearn it in French and to rehearse in Paris before the premiere. Even so, Gailhard persisted, saying that for the sake of Gounod and all involved in this production she should make the attempt, that her presence would confer lustre "upon an occasion to which *tout Paris* is looking forward,"[12] and that, if necessary, the date would be postponed for her convenience. Though flattered, Patti refused to commit herself: "No, it won't do to alter the date, because I must be back in London to sing again at the Albert Hall on December 11. But you must give me time to consider. I will talk it over with Ernest and let you know in two or three days."[13] Two days later, while conferring with Gounod in Paris, Gailhard received Patti's telegraphic response: "I was deeply touched by your visit to me at Craig-y-Nos Castle. You invite me to assist in the performance of an artistic masterpiece conducted by the Maître himself to create Juliette at the Opera. My reply is Yes—Patti Nicolini."[14] Gounod's reaction was to embrace all the company members around him and to despatch a reply to his "*chère Adelina* thanking her with all his heart for the promise of her 'gracious and inestimable help.'"[15] Several days later Gailhard received a letter from Nicolini, stating that his wife agreed to give four performances, while in a later communication from him the number dropped to three, on 28 and 30 November and 3 December; but a fourth was eventually added for 7 December.

News of Patti's engagement created hysterical demands for admissions. Would-be purchasers soon found no tickets available at any price. The premiere promised to be *the* musical event of the decade, with Patti as Juliette, matinee idol Jean de Reszke as Roméo, and Gounod at the podium.[16] Nellie Melba, who just a year before had made her opera debut as Gilda at the Théâtre de la Monnaie in Brussels, declared: "I am going to Paris . . . whatever happens. I do not care if I have to postpone performances. I don't care if I never sing again. To hear Patti and Jean de Reszke would make up for anything, any sacrifice."[17]

Nicolini wrote Gailhard that his wife would arrive in Paris on the 24th, that she would not need an orchestral rehearsal, and that she wanted to confer with Gounod about some small changes she had made in recitatives and the transposition of a few notes. He asked that the composer and Jean de Reszke meet in her suite at the Hotel Meurice on the 25th or 26th. Patti thus allowed herself little time before the premiere on the 28th, but after several rehearsals in Paris under the composer's direction, she amazed everyone with her mastery of the French text, her charming portrayal, and her vocal power. Gounod was ecstatic, declaring Patti and De Reszke his ideal interpreters.

At the premiere, the London *Times* maintained, there had never been an audience "more numerous, more animated."[18] Among the most ebullient was Herman Klein:

> I went over to Paris expressly to attend the new production of *Roméo*. It was one of the most brilliant functions ever witnessed in the imposing *salle* of the Opéra. In my despatches to the *Sunday Times*, the *Manchester Guardian*, and other English papers, superlatives inevitably abounded. I shall never forget the

reception accorded to Gounod and Patti—to the former as he made his way into the orchestra; to the latter when she entered the Hall of the Capulets, led for a few steps by *Juliette's* father, then tripping down the stage with all her accustomed *brio,* radiant with smiles, ... looking positively more youthful than when she had last sung the part at Covent Garden. ... Nervous beyond the common she may have been; the accidental skipping of four bars in the waltz told eloquently of unwonted excitement. (Everybody was nervous, Gounod most of all, although sheer presence of mind enabled him more than once to save the situation.) Still, this was quite another *Juliet*; something more than a picture; a flesh-and-blood Italian girl, in all things redolent of Southern passion at its height; in short, the ideal embodiment, so far as the opera will allow, of the loving and lovable maiden. ... How she sang there is no need to say, but from the dramatic point of view the famous artist that night took the sternest of French critics by surprise.[19]

Melba declared that Patti possessed perhaps the most golden voice she had ever heard, its timbre exquisite, her diction pellucid. H. Moreno, in *Le Ménestrel,* said that her voice was marvelous and that she was a consummate and often stirring artist. According to *Les Annales du Théâtre et de la Musique,* Patti remained faultless, brilliant, and remarkable while the critic of another publication maintained that by eleven o'clock the whole audience was Roméo. Still, a few faulted her for what they considered several labored runs, some veiled high notes, and the transposition of the waltz. Jean de Reszke, on the other hand, received nothing but praise for his delineation. Probably never before, said the London *Times,* had "Patti sung with a Romeo more worthy to share her success."[20] Such acclaim may have annoyed the diva, accustomed to monopolizing the limelight. She later told an American acquaintance that her experiences with this tenor had not always been heartening, that he had struggled for high notes and had stepped on her foot during a performance.

Before embarking for a second South American tour beginning in April 1889, Patti gave a concert at London's Albert Hall, which was reviewed by George Bernard Shaw:

Madame Patti kissed hands last night, in her artless way, to a prodigious audience come to bid her farewell before her trip to South America. The unnecessary unpleasantness of the most useful of Mr. Louis Stevenson's novels makes it impossible to say that there is in Madame Patti an Adelina Jekyll and an Adelina Hyde; but there are certainly two very different sides to her public character. There is Patti the great singer: Patti of the beautiful eloquent voice, so perfectly produced and controlled that its most delicate pianissimo reaches the remotest listener in the Albert Hall: Patti of the unerring ear, with her magical *roulade* soaring to heavenly altitudes: Patti of the pure, strong tone that made God save the Queen sound fresh and noble at Covent Garden: Patti of the hushed, tender notes that reconcile rows of club-loving cynics to Home, Sweet Home. This was the famous artist who last night sang *Bel raggio* and Comin' thro' the Rye incomparably. With Verdure Clad would also have been perfect but that the intonation of the orchestra got wrong and spoiled it. But there is another Patti: a Patti who cleverly sang and sang again some pretty nonsense from Delibes' Lakmé. Great was the applause, even after it had been repeated; and then the comedy began. Mr. Ganz, whilst the house was shouting and clapping uproariously, deliberately took up his *bâton* and started Moszkowski's Serenata in D. The audience took its cue at once, and would not have Moszkowski. After a prolonged struggle, Mr. Ganz gave up in despair; and out tripped the *diva*, bowing her acknowledgments in the character of a petted and delighted child. When she vanished there was more cheering than ever. Mr. Ganz threatened the serenata again; but in vain. He appealed to the sentinels of the greenroom; and these shook their heads, amidst roars of protest from the audience, and at last, with elaborate gesture, conveyed in dumb show that they dare not, could not, would not, must not, venture to approach Patti again. Mr. Ganz, with well-acted desolation, went on with the serenata, not one note of which was heard. Again he appealed to the sentinels; and this time they waved their hands expansively in the direction of South America, to indicate that the prima donna was already on her way thither. On this the audience showed such sudden and unexpected signs of giving in that the diva tripped out again, bowing, wafting kisses, and successfully courting fresh thunders of applause. Will not some sincere friend of Madame Patti's tell her frankly that she is growing too big a girl for this sort of thing.[21]

Her return to the Teatro Politeama at Buenos Aires on 9 April as Violetta demonstrated her sway over Argentinean operagoers, with one critic considering her singing, acting, and attire perfect, an incarnation of the composer's dreams. The critic said that she looked ten years younger than last season and that her voice had regained the freshness of eight years before. Others in the cast did not fare so well, while impresario Cesare Ciacchi received kudos for his enterprise and untiring efforts in organizing the Patti season. Other leading artists included soprano Eva Tetrazzini, tenor Fernando de Lucia, contralto Guerrina Fabbri, baritone Arturo Marescalchi, and basses Giulio Rossi and Victorio Arimondi, with Cleofonte Campanini, Arnaldo Conti, and Romualdo Sapio as conductors.

For many in Buenos Aires, their greatest pleasure was in hearing her Juliette in Italian. After her first performance on 13 June, a critic of the *Standard* wrote that she had accomplished the impossible, singing and acting irreproachably. Her Roméo on this occasion, Fernando de Lucia, supported Juliette fairly well, though at times his singing and acting were disappointing. Her benefit on 6 July, featuring excerpts from *Marta, Dinorah,* and *Lucia,* was another memorable evening at the Politeama. During an intermission she received bouquets, diamonds, and a bombardment of nosegays. After the Mad Scene from *Lucia,* Patti responded to a mad scene in the auditorium by giving three encores; the press declared her the idol of Buenos Aires. At her final performance, on 22 July, as Rosina, with De Lucia as Almaviva, demonstrations bordered on the cyclonic. During the lesson scene her rendition of Arditi's "Il bacio" resulted in twenty-three curtain calls, and at the end of the opera when she shared one of her recalls with impresario Ciacchi, the applause and roars, a reporter noted, were so intense that gas lights sputtered while the theater seemed to rock on its foundation. Though this series had provided Patti with some of her most memorable triumphs and moments of great joy, it was marred by news of her sister Carlotta's death, on 27 June, in Paris.

Nicolini was also received enthusiastically on his three appearances with Patti, twice in *Lucia* and once in *La traviata*. In a letter to Alfred de Rothschild dated 28 June, he expressed pleasure in their successes and displeasure in the expenses they had incurred, spending more than 150,000 francs ($30,000) during the season. Part of that sum was paid to rent a house with a garden at Calle Sante Fe

3681, which they preferred to a suite at the noisy Grand Hotel. Still, their expenditures were insignificant compared to the more than 1,000,000 francs ($200,000) they took away.

Approximately four months later, on 13 November, after a brief sojourn at Craig-y-Nos and a concert tour of the British Isles, Patti left for another tour to the United States beginning in December 1889, to Mexico City from 11 January to 2 February 1890, and then back to the States from 10 February to 25 April. By then her "farewell" tours in the States had become a joke. The *Boston Gazette* commented they should be numbered or qualified as "farewell engagement. Last Farewell engagement. Positively farewell engagement. Positively last farewell engagement—and so on, until she has sung the last note she has left to the public, and drawn from it the last note it is willing to pay for hearing her."[22]

Abbey had again persuaded the diva to accept an engagement under his management, offering her the usual high fees. He intrigued her not only with fiscal matters but also with an appearance at the inauguration of Chicago's multi-million-dollar auditorium; opera performances in Mexico City, which had formerly seen her solely in operatic excerpts; and a return to San Francisco, which of all American cities most idolized her. Two of Abbey's associates in this new venture were Marcus Mayer and Maurice Grau.

Abbey assembled tenor Francesco Tamagno, who possessed stentorian high notes and had created the title role in Verdi's *Otello* at its world premiere only two years before; sopranos Emma Albani, Lillian Nordica, Maria Pettigiani, and Giulia Valda; tenors Luigi Ravelli and Eugenio Vicini; contralto Guerrina Fabbri; baritone Giuseppe del Puente; and bass Franco Novara. Arditi served as music director and principal conductor.

Arriving in New York, on 5 December, Patti with Nicolini, servants, two small dogs, and forty-five trunks remained in the city only overnight, leaving for Chicago on a private coach the following day. Meanwhile, she had generated much publicity with her turn from brunette to blonde, hair coloring then a shocking matter.

The tour opened on 9 December at the dedication of Chicago's new auditorium. Approximately eight thousand spectators filled the auditorium while a thousand more sat in tiers onstage. "In such a place," averred the *Chicago Times,* "the heroes and the triumphs of all ages must come into a new existence for the gratification and

99 Patti by John Singer
Sargent—her favorite portrait.
Courtesy The Billy Rose Theatre
Collection, The New York Public
Library for the Performing Arts,
Astor, Lenox and Tilden
Foundations.

100 Patti in a photo known as
the "Lost Gainsborough."
Courtesy William R. Moran.

101 Jean de Reszke as Roméo in an 1888 Paris performance. Courtesy Murry & Leonie Guggenheim Memorial Library, Monmouth College.

102 Patti as Juliette in the 1888 Paris revival of Gounod's opera. Courtesy Murry & Leonie Guggenheim Memorial Library, Monmouth College.

103 Craig-y-Nos in 1890, with the Patti Theatre addition to the extreme left, next to the clock tower. The winter garden is on the right. In Wales Patti was called "Lady of the Castle," "Lady Bountiful," and "Queen of Hearts." By permission of the National Library of Wales.

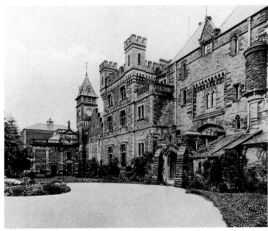

104 The Craig-y-Nos grounds, with the terraces Beatty-Kingston described as "a wide staircase of giant's steps covered with green velvet." Author's Collection.

105 Main entrance of Craig-y-Nos. Author's Collection.

106 The castle's tennis ground. Author's Collection.

107 The auditorium of the Patti Theatre held about 150 people, and the floor could be raised to a level even with the stage, transforming the space into a ball-room. The act-drop portrays Patti as Semiramide. Author's Collection.

108 The gallery at the rear of the Patti Theatre, where Craig-y-Nos domestics gathered for performances. Courtesy Music Division, The New York Public Library for the Performing Arts, Astor, Lenox and Tilden Foundations.

109 Patti near the time of the formal Patti Theatre opening, 1891. The diamond coronet she is wearing may be the one Czar Alexander II of Russia gave her in 1873. Courtesy Carin Cederström Ekelöf.

110 Alfredo Barili, Sr., Patti's nephew and a pianist whose playing writer James Gibbons Huneker claimed could affect him "like catnip on a feline. I rolled over the floor. The music made my nerves naked." Courtesy Mary Barili Goldsmith.

111 Patti in a photo she signed for Alfredo Barili, Sr. Courtesy Mary Barili Goldsmith.

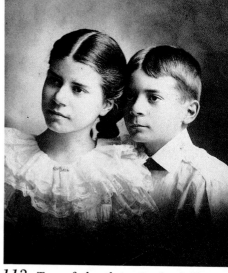

112 Emily Barili, wife of Alfredo. Courtesy Mary Barili Goldsmith.

113 Two of the three Barili children, Patti's grandniece and -nephew, Viola and Alfredo, Jr. Their older sister Louise was especially dear to Patti. Courtesy Mary Barili Goldsmith.

114 Patti in the 1890s—a royal view of her extensive gem collection. Courtesy
William R. Moran.

С.-ПЕТЕРБУРГЪ, 1891.
Паровая Скоропечатня А. В. Пожаровой, Загородный просп., домъ № 8.

115 An 1891 illustration of Patti. Courtesy M. E. Saltykov-Shchedrin State Public Library, St. Petersburg, Russia.

116 Critic Peter G. Davis wrote of Patti that she was "the singer who would seem to have given the term prima donna its definitive meaning." Courtesy John W. Booth.

117 Patti in the title role of Emilio Pizzi's *Gabriella,* an opera composed for her and one of the last new roles of her professional career. The opera premiered in Boston on 25 November 1893. Courtesy William R. Moran.

118 Patti in concert at London's Albert Hall, 1896. Courtesy Music Division, The New York Public Library for the Performing Arts, Astor, Lenox and Tilden Foundations.

119 The interior of the Grand Theatre, Swansea, which Patti dedicated at its opening on 26 July 1897. Courtesy Karisa Krcmar.

120 Patti with her godchild and secretary, Mabel Woodford, boating on a Craig-y-Nos lake. Courtesy William R. Moran.

121 Patti in the 1890s, exhibiting sartorial panache. Courtesy William R. Moran.

122 Ernest Nicolini's grave in Pau, France, in 1898, just after his interment, with a tribute from Craig-y-Nos employees and flowers from Patti and others. This is a copy of a sepia-toned print that was damaged at the top right corner when a protective member of the castle staff sought to destroy all Patti's personal papers in a bonfire on the grounds after her death. Courtesy John W. Booth.

elevation of modern society."[23] Ceremonies reached a climax with the introduction of Benjamin Harrison, then President of the United States, and, in turn, with his introduction of Patti: "Only the voice of the immortal singer can bring from these arches those echoes which will tell us the true purpose of their construction."[24] The house erupted as the diva, dressed in white brocade with black satin stripes and a corsage adorned with pearls and diamonds, made her way to center stage to sing "Home, Sweet Home." The *Herald* reported that "the mellow notes of the flute came with delicious sweetness. A harp, played by a woman's hand, joined in. . . . Then came the song, beginning so faintly yet so clearly that it sounded like the warble of a bird concealed among the flowers on the stage. . . . [Thereafter, there was] only a blushing, bright-eyed woman, bowing with crossed arms."[25] The audience would not let her go without an encore, Eckert's "Echo Song." Her fee for these two selections set a new high: $4000.

The following evening the opera series began with Patti and Ravelli in *Roméo et Juliette,* sung in Italian. Critics found much to praise in her delineation, but her singing, some said, was not so fluent and spontaneous as before. Of this criticism, George Upton wrote:

> At that time, in her forty-sixth year, she displayed the same ease of manner, the same fine method of vocalization which had so long characterized her, but there were clearly apparent the necessity of husbanding her resources and of greater care in singing, a lack of the old strength in the high notes, and a suspicion of wavering intonation.[26]

Her other appearances were as Lucia, Semiramide, Harriet, Violetta, Amina, and Rosina. Of the other principal artists, Tamagno was most impressive, with audiences "half-bewildered at the notes hurled from his deep, prodigious chest like missiles from a catapult."[27] (Parenthetically, Tamagno never appeared with the diva during this 1889–90 tour, as his repertoire was entirely different from hers.) Revenues for this four-week season totaled an astonishing $223,000. This series was "Chicago's most successful, creating more genuine excitement than any in the city's history."[28] There was no doubt that Patti kindled "more popular interest in opera than the rest of the company put together."[29]

Leaving Chicago behind, Abbey's troupe boarded a special train comprised of twelve cars for a long trip to Mexico City. Patti's private car bearing her name brought up the rear. The first days on the road, according to Arditi's wife, Virginia, passed pleasantly, and she and the maestro spent one evening as Patti's dinner guests, with the food prepared by her personal chef and served in her private coach "decorated in the most artistic fashion, her monogram being interspersed here and there on the walls with flowers and musical instruments" and "furnished with lounges and chairs of pale-blue plush, and her bedroom ... made of inlaid satin wood, with a brass bedstead, a plush counterpane bearing her monogram exquisitely embroidered."[30] Other luxuries included a private bath, electric light, and a piano.

In Mexico, on 8 January, a broken bridge caused a delay of hours, and the next day, while crossing on a temporary bridge, the troupe viewed the broken one with a railway engine and cars lying at its base, the wreck having occurred four days before. "Everybody," wrote Mrs. Arditi, "is so thankful for the lucky escape that there has been no grumbling or discontent all day!"[31]

Opening night in Mexico City, on 11 January, with Patti as Semiramide amazed Mrs. Arditi:

> The house for our first performance was magnificent. Such wealth, dresses, and diamonds; such a galaxy of beauty, and such appreciative though exacting audiences one does not often see combined. Money seems to be of no value to some people, and I heard of a lady who positively paid £30 for a box, and £14 for two seats in the gallery for her maid and her husband's valet![32]

Patti donated her fee for the 22 January performance to orphans in the city. Enrique Olavarria y Ferrari in his history of the theater in Mexico noted that four days later the diva gave la Señora Diaz, the President of Mexico's wife, a handsome sum of money. In Mexico, as elsewhere, Patti was known to many as "Queen of Hearts" as well as "Queen of Song."

Her benefit on 29 January as Violetta netted many tokens of admiration including a silver box with precious coins from Señora Diaz. Mrs. Arditi recalled that this occasion was a tremendous success and that by this time box-office receipts totaled more than 40,000 pounds ($200,000).

After five more performances the company headed north for a

San Francisco engagement, beginning on 10 February, with Tamagno in *Guillaume Tell* playing to a less than full house. The next evening was a different story, for it marked Patti's reentry, with the theater packed for her Semiramide. Press notices reported that even "the Philistines got all their money's worth and honestly enjoyed themselves"[33] and that the house "was not only filled, but with the right people."[34] Operagoers continued to flock to her performances as Amina, Lucia, Harriet, and Violetta.

By the time this San Francisco series ended on 22 February, there was no doubt that the tour had set fiscal records. In mid-March Maurice Grau elaborated on this subject:

> The company, to put it roughly, has traveled up to the present time over 10,000 miles, and it has garnered in receipts approximating $700,000. For the season . . . in New-York . . . we have already received orders for seats exceeding $70,000 in cash value; and upon this basis it is not without the boundary of reason to estimate that the entire season will result in a cash receipt of fully $1,000,000. This is unprecedented.[35]

After performances in Denver, Omaha, Louisville, Boston, Philadelphia, and Chicago, Abbey closed the tour in New York, where from 24 March to 25 April at the Metropolitan Opera House his company attracted enormous audiences, particularly for the Patti operas. After her reentry as Semiramide on 26 March, the *Herald* trumpeted that she remained the Queen of Song and that there was only one Patti; a *Times* critic, while detecting a loss of some sweetness in her highest notes, declared the lowest had become more round with the middle register still retaining "that marvelously beautiful flute-like timbre which since November, 1859, has made Mme. Patti's voice unique in all the world."[36] *The World* also rhapsodized over her voice, which had lost "nothing of its beauty," while also noting she had retained "that petite, youthful figure, the same charm of voice and manner that have made her supreme for so long a time."[37] For many the greatest moment of this evening was Patti's singing of "Home, Sweet Home" at the end of the opera. The only new role in which Patti appeared was that of Lakmé, first presented on 2 April. She concluded the series on 25 April in her matchless portrayal of Violetta. The *Herald* expressed a sentiment shared by many: "There are not two Pattis in the world. We cannot spare the supreme singer. It will be time enough for her to bid goodby to America when the golden voice begins to falter, the faultless art to weaken."[38] Of the New York series, Patti operas had brought the highest revenues—$104,109 of the total $154,364.

After a respite at Craig-y-Nos, the diva resumed touring in the fall. At one concert in the provinces on 21 October, she met British statesman and four-time prime minister William Ewart Gladstone, who complimented her for her rendition of a Scotch song and who later began a correspondence with her (now in the British Museum archives) that reveals their mutual admiration. Early in 1891, Patti began another tour that was to include St. Petersburg and Moscow, but she dropped these cities following a disagreement with the Russian impresario. After performing in Berlin, she went to Nice for an opera engagement and remained there until 21 March. Later, on 20 June, she gave a concert at London's Albert Hall, assisted by such artists as tenor Sims Reeves and piano virtuoso Ignaz Jan Paderewski.

Meanwhile, at Craig-y-Nos workers were completing an addition to the north wing of the residence, which Patti referred to as the jewel of her country estate: a private theater and opera house. For months she had planned its formal dedication on Wednesday, 12 August 1891, and had sent invitations. Local publication *The Cambrian* theorized that Patti intended it as a medium for her artistic improvement: "Who shall say that Patti has not some serious and high artistic purpose at heart in the erection of the Theatre at Craig-y Nos?"[39]

The auditorium, accommodating some 150 seated guests, measured 40 feet long, 26 feet wide, and 24 feet high; ten Corinthian columns with gilded capitals and bases supported the ceiling; and the wall panels were pale blue, cream, and gold. At its end was a gallery that domestics generally occupied during a performance. The orchestra pit, separated from an audience by a balustrade and accommodating as many as twenty-four players, was 6 feet below stage level; the proscenium stood at 20 feet wide and 19 feet high; and the stage was 22½ feet deep and 40 feet wide. The auditorium floor and orchestra pit could be raised to stage level, the entire area then a ballroom extending over 60 feet. Every modern appliance for stage productions had been provided, and the 281 lights were controlled by a switchboard. Behind the stage were dressing rooms on the first and second floors. The stage curtains were blue silk plush, and the act-drop depicted Patti as Semiramide in a Roman chariot. Above the gilded proscenium were the names of Verdi, Rossini, and Mozart, surmounted by her monogram in gold.

The Patti Theatre's inauguration intrigued not only the neighborhood but also personalities throughout the world. Swanseaites took special interest, as some chorus members and orchestral players from W. F. Hulley's local opera company had been engaged. Various news agencies planned to cover the event, which had already been widely publicized.

Houseguests began arriving several days before the opening, including the Spanish ambassador; Baron and Baroness Julius de Reuter (he was the founder of the news agency bearing his name); Sir Henry Hussey Vivian, Bart., M.P., and Lady Vivian; the Comte de Lille; Mr. and Mrs. William Beatty-Kingston, he a writer for the *Daily Telegraph*; M. Thomas Johnson of *Le Figaro*; Edward Lawson, later called Sir Edward and Lord Burnham; Augustus Spalding; Percy Harrison; Maestro Arditi and wife; and various opera artists. Two unable to attend were Alfred de Rothschild and the great actor Henry Irving, who was to deliver the inaugural address. Of these guests, perhaps the one Patti most appreciated was her thirty-seven-year-old nephew Alfredo Barili, son of Ettore and a family member of whom she could be proud.

Then living in Atlanta, Georgia, with his wife, Emily, and their three young children, Alfredo was a superb pianist and teacher, having studied in the United States with his father and pianist Carl Wolfsohn and at the Cologne Conservatory under such well-known musicians as Friedrich Gernsheim, James Kwast, and Ferdinand Hiller and, in Paris, with pianist Theodore Ritter. Alfredo's concerts were critically well received. Later, moving to Atlanta, Alfredo was the city's outstanding musician in performing, teaching, conducting, and composing; he also founded his own school of music, where he and his pianist wife taught.

Months before the opening, Patti had assured Alfredo it would be memorable: "We have already sent out invitations for our grand opening night at the theatre for August—it's to be a *splendid* affair and I do believe a thing that you will never forget after you have seen it."[40]

One who never forgot it was music critic and journalist Herman Klein, who first visited Craig-y-Nos four days before the opening ceremony and who wrote about the event at length in his Patti biography. His arrival after some eight hours on a train from London occurred just moments before dinner. After a quick change he joined the group in the conservatory, used as summer dining room, and later described the evening:

> Vividly do I recall the picture of Mme. Patti herself at the head of the table, looking astonishingly youthful and *svelte* in a Parisian gown of blue and white, just received from Worth or Doucet. Her rippling laugh was rarely unheard, her abundant flow of talk in four languages the life and soul of the conversation. Every now and then she would address a remark in French, with well-nigh ventriloquial skill, to the other end of the table.... And back would come the reply, *"Oui, ma mignonne,"* in the resonant tenor notes of Nicolini, busy with some Italian dish or emptying his own particular bottle of his own special brand of champagne. And so the gorgeous Gargantuan meal went on.... This banquet was the beginning of a series of feasts that was to last for days.[41]

What followed these sumptuous meals, according to Klein, was invariably the same:

> Always *en grande toilette* of the latest Parisian model; always wearing some wonderful necklace, with bracelets, rings, and occasionally a dazzling tiara ...; seated upon one of the comfortable lounges that skirted three sides of the billiard-table, she was invariably the centre of a bright, animated group, a veritable queen in the midst of her courtiers. For courtiers they were, most of them, male and female, ready with a flattering speech, ever bidding for the gracious smile that each endeavored to win in turn. There they would drink their coffee and smoke ... while talking over the events of the day, making plans for the morrow, discussing various people, social and artistic, or ... listening to the orchestrion. Gifted with an abundance of ready wit and lively repartee, with an easy command of at least five languages, the Queen of Song, surrounded by her court, made a striking and alluring picture; nor could one ever forget that the personality of the central figure was that of Adelina Patti.[42]

Klein accustomed himself to the daily routine at Craig-y-Nos and found it strenuous and never dull because Patti was incapable of being a bore and likewise avoided anyone or thing tedious:

> It was an inestimable privilege to enjoy the daily society and conversation of Adelina Patti; to hear her ever and anon burst into song; to catch the ring of her sunshiny laugh; to come under the spell of a personal charm such as few women possess. . . . Her memory is extraordinary. She tells a hundred stories of her early life in America . . . how they used to stand her upon the table to sing; how she first rendered "Casta Diva" by ear without a single mistake; and how, when her eldest sister, Amalia, was striving hard to master the shake, the tiny Adelina stopped her and asked, "Why don't you do it like this?" therewith executing a natural and absolutely irreproachable trill.[43]

A correspondent of the *Boston Herald,* also a guest at this time, maintained that life at Craig-y-Nos was like perpetual opera.

When the final stage rehearsals for the opening were under way, Patti agreed to participate in one at the behest of Arditi. Klein recalled their dialogue:

> Now was the moment when plans for the following day were to be talked over, when arrangements for final stage rehearsals were discussed. Maestro Arditi was called to the front.
> "*Caro Luigi,*" cried the gracious Adelina, "do you want me to-morrow?"
> "I t'ink is better," smiled Arditi. "*Veramente* I like you rehearse twice, if is possible. I want *Traviata* before lunch, *Faust* after lunch. E-e-eh?" The sly old conductor was laughing inwardly. He knew he could make her do here something that in an ordinary opera house she would not have done for a thousand pounds. She pretended to hesitate.
> ". . . And with piano only?"
> "You know my orchestra he not come from Swansea till nex' day; Mr. Hulley he bring 'eem with the chorus. *Domani* is principals; *e senza di te non va!* [and without you it does not go!]" This with an indescribable imploring grimace.
> "Very well; I suppose I must."[44]

The following day, Klein briefly attended the piano rehearsal and found all the principals onstage extremely serious, Arditi solemn, and Patti performing as for the first time roles she had portrayed on innumerable occasions. On her own stage, rehearsing was a labor of love. The other principals in *La traviata* were Durward Lely as Alfredo, Ellen Flynn as Flora, Reginald Brophy as Gastone, Edwin Ball as Marchese, and E. Jones as Barone.

On the inaugural day, Craig-y-Nos housed continuous festivity. Patti was everywhere and beaming. In the early afternoon the chorus and orchestra had a last rehearsal under Arditi's direction, and hours later a special train from Swansea, chartered by Patti, conveyed friends to the estate just before the big event. Though scheduled to begin at eight, the program began a half hour later. Meanwhile, the audience had entered the sumptuous auditorium under the electric lights and had picked up their satin programs.

Moments before the performance began, actor William Terriss, deputizing for an indisposed Henry Irving, stepped before the footlights to deliver the inaugural address written by Beatty-Kingston:

> Ladies and Gentlemen: I stand here as the humble and inadequate representative of the first of living English actors. It had been the intention of Mr. Henry Irving to signalize his appreciation of Mme. Adelina Patti's transcendent talent as singer and actress, and to mark his strong sense of the close alliance connecting the musical and dramatic arts, by speaking a few inaugural words on this occasion—one that is unique in operatic and theatrical annals alike. For we are met here to be present at an initial performance held in a theatre which, at the generous behest of the Queen of Song, has been erected and provided with every mechanical appliance perfected by modern science in the very heart of a wild Welsh valley, teeming with the beauties of nature, but remote from the busy haunts of men.
>
> As far as Mr. Irving is concerned, circumstances have intervened rendering his personal participation in to-night's celebration impracticable. He has, however, empowered me to act as his envoy, and I have been accepted in that character for the performance of this agreeable and sympathetic duty by our gracious and gifted hostess, the châtelaine of Craig-y-Nos—the good fairy who haunts the "Rock of the Night"—the true friend of the poor, whose benefactions have for a dozen years past ripened unnumbered throughout the length and breadth of this picturesque region.
>
> In this beautiful theatre, dedicated to the allied arts and

adorned with the counterfeit presentments of great musicians
and dramatists, you will this evening be privileged to listen to
that incomparable voice which ever binds its hearers in a spell of
wonder and delight. I will not retard your supreme enjoyment by
further dilating on the attractions of that which you have eyes to
see and ears to hear, but will conclude my grateful task by
declaring the Patti Theatre open for the late summer season of
1891.[45]

After the audience applauded, Arditi raised his baton to begin
the prelude to act one of *La traviata*. At its end, the house again burst
into applause for the scenery and chorus, numbering about fifteen;
the applause then redoubled when Patti, ablaze with diamonds,
tripped onto the stage in a pink satin gown trimmed with white
embroidery and roses. Bowing acknowledgments, she received a
standing ovation with many waving handkerchiefs. In time the performance began. Klein said he had never heard her execute "Ah! fors'
è lui" and its cabaletta with "more dazzling brilliancy or greater
aplomb. The long-sustained trill on the G-A flat during the exit at the
end was as birdlike as ever."[46] In the second part of the program, the
Garden Scene from *Faust*, Patti was supported by Nicolini in the title
role, Franco Novara as Méphistophélès, and Giulia Valda doubling as
Siébel and Marthe. This scene, according to Klein,

> went even better. . . . But the miracle that overshadowed all else
> was the sweet, virginal *Marguerite* of the singer of forty-eight
> summers, who could cheat us into the belief that she was still the
> girl depicted by Goethe. . . . More than once one had the impres-
> sion that the whole thing was a dream. Could this truly be Patti,—
> the inimitable and adorable songstress worshipped in two
> hemispheres,—still looking and singing like a maid in her teens
> and striving her hardest to please on her own twenty-five-by-
> twenty-five-foot stage down in this remote corner of Wales?[47]

When the performance ended and the applause subsided, the
audience adjourned to the conservatory for a buffet supper. Patti in
elaborate new array, with Nicolini at her side, soon joined her guests.
Many toasts were given while champagne was poured from some 450
bottles. Several hours later all but the houseguests departed.

The diva hosted a ball the following evening in the theater with
its floor raised to meet stage level. Once again many in the valley,

despite rain and mist, journeyed to Craig-y-Nos. During this evening, indefatigable Patti showed herself a superb waltzer, dancing with one partner after another. When Klein marveled at this ability, she said:

> I never had a lesson in ball-room dancing in my life, but I waltz so easily that it never seems to make me out of breath. I must have a good partner, though; otherwise I stop after a few turns. I suppose that when I waltz it comes naturally to me to manage my breathing, as I do when I sing. Take good deep breaths, glide lightly without exertion, don't "reverse" much, and you can waltz a long while before feeling tired.[48]

That Saturday the diva held a matinee to which she had extended more invitations than the theater could accommodate. The program consisted of the third act of *Marta* with Patti as Harriet, Valda as Nancy, Lely as Lionel, and Novara as Plunkett and the Balcony Scene from *Roméo et Juliette* with Patti and Nicolini as the lovers. In the former opera, some who had heard her in London confessed that her voice never sounded lovelier. As Roméo, Nicolini proved worthy of his Juliette, whose portrayal, Klein declared, was rendered beyond the reach of any other artist; he maintained she sang with "more passion and grandeur"[49] than when he had heard her in this part at the Paris Opéra three years before. The matinee concluded with an encore, Arditi's "Il bacio," conducted by the composer and sung by Patti.

Though by now several houseguests had departed, Klein, among others, accepted an invitation to remain. On Monday Patti announced that Queen Victoria's son-in-law Prince Henry of Battenberg intended to visit soon. He was staying at nearby Clyne Castle, the residence of Graham Vivian, and had anchored his yacht at the Mumbles off Swansea. Patti arranged a performance in her theater to honor him on Saturday, 22 August, when Prince Henry and entourage would join her and Nicolini for lunch, attend the matinee, and return to Clyne Castle after tea.

Meanwhile, to keep herself and guests amused, Patti proposed they prepare either a comic or tragic pantomime. According to Klein, the former type of wordless play, often based upon a tale from *Arabian Nights*, allowed considerable individual interpretation and humor, whereas the latter pantomime, requiring more preparation time, was "definite and dramatic in action, and performed to a regular descriptive musical setting."[50] Participants selected both types, and the subject for their comic play was the story of Bluebeard, while that for their serious mime was based on Sardou's drama *La Tosca*, one of Sarah Bernhardt's great vehicles and not yet the subject of Puccini's opera. Patti asked Klein to prepare a scenario for this melodrama.

Augustus Spalding proved a skillful director, teaching cast members how to infuse comedy into the absurd situations concerning Bluebeard. They performed a clever burlesque without making a sound, and Patti provided costumes, wigs, make-up, and scenery from the new theater. By the time the group performed it on Wednesday evening, with music supplied by Hulley, they amused not only themselves but also their audience. Patti, Klein wrote, amazed everyone with her contributions, particularly "the lightning rapidity with which she seized a comic point and elaborated it, . . . her memory for detail, her agility and grace of movement."[51]

Already she had used the Patti Theatre to improve her acting, developing her skill in mime. She said to Klein:

> I love the stage. I love to act and to portray every species, every shade of human emotion. Only I want freedom—more freedom than opera, with its restricted movements and its wear and tear on the voice, can possibly allow the actress. I care not whether it be comedy or tragedy, so long as I feel that I can devote my whole energy, my whole being, to realizing the character that I have to delineate. Even words trouble me; they take time to commit to memory, and their utterance fatigues a singer too much. Yet I want to act, to feel myself upon the boards. . . . What does there remain for me to do? What but to enact scenes and plays in "pantomime"; to utilize the ancient art of the Italian mime and express every sentiment by means of gesture, action, and facial expression. I must have music . . . ; I cannot do entirely without my own art and all its wealth of suggestive force.[52]

Of course what then primarily concerned the diva was Saturday's reception for Prince Henry, with the main attraction being a reprise of the Garden Scene from *Faust* with the cast from the Patti Theatre opening. She arranged for a twenty-one gun salute to mark the arrival of His Highness and entourage at the Penwyllt station, and afterwards, at Craig-y-Nos, Patti intended to do all in her power to make this occasion memorable.

On that Saturday, Spalding and Klein drove at midday to the little railway station. Upon the prince's arrival, the two men quickly explained why they had been deputized to do the honors: Patti and Nicolini were busy with preparations for the afternoon's performance. His Highness said that he had hardly expected them to meet the train with a program in the offing and that he was delighted it would consist of the Garden Scene from *Faust*, as he had never seen Patti in this opera. Klein described the prince's reception at Craig-y-Nos, where the diva,

> in her latest Paris gown, . . . an elegant creation in some soft silken material of bluish grey that showed off to perfection her *svelte* figure, . . . looked extraordinarily juvenile as she made her graceful courtesy and, shaking hands with Prince Henry, bade him welcome to *"notre petit château de Craig-y-Nos."* Then, after presenting her husband, she led her royal guest to the little drawing-room in the old wing, and showed him her highly interesting collection of curios, bric-à-brac, and gifts of various kinds that had been offered to her in course of her long career.[53]

Moments thereafter, Patti led the way to the conservatory, where her twenty-five or thirty guests enjoyed a luncheon. With Prince Henry on her right and Graham Vivian on her left, she kept up such an animated conversation that Nicolini, concerned she might strain her voice, cautioned her several times to be careful. Needless to say, his warning went unheeded.

The performance under Arditi's direction pleased Prince Henry and the other guests immensely. At its end, Patti sang two of the conductor's compositions for encores. During tea, music continued from the orchestrion. The prince's parting words were "I bid you *au revoir*, madame, not good-bye, and again I thank you a thousand times for your delightful entertainment. It has been a great privilege to hear you sing in your beautiful theatre. I shall never forget it."[54] At Penwyllt, Prince Henry entrained to a twenty-one-gun salute, which was protocol (Patti had adopted Royal traditions with alacrity).

Then, while some departed, other guests began arriving. Among these were various artists who were to participate on Friday, 28 August, in another of Patti's charity concerts at Swansea and Sir Augustus and Lady Harris, he at that time Sheriff of London and impresario of the Royal Opera at Covent Garden and manager of Drury Lane Theatre. Sir Augustus apparently never suggested the possibility of her performing at Covent Garden during this visit, probably because of the high fees she commanded. He was also, no doubt, aware of her contract with Percy Harrison, who managed her tours in Great Britain.

Several days before the Swansea charity concert, the diva and some guests rehearsed another wordless play, this one based on Sardou's *La Tosca*, with Patti as Tosca, Klein as the villainous Chief of Police Baron Scarpia, and Nicolini's son Richard, a young French actor, as Tosca's inamorato. Patti urged Sir Augustus to assist as stage manager; but he declined, saying he needed a respite from theatrical matters. Still, he did view a rehearsal and was particularly impressed with her acting. He said had she not become an opera star, she would have been one of the world's greatest actresses.

Her reception at Swansea also impressed Sir Augustus: the extraordinary enthusiasm of crowds along the way to and from the concert hall, the tumultuous demonstrations in the auditorium, and a full house giving ovations.

The next evening, 29 August, guests in the Patti Theatre enjoyed *La Tosca* not as a mime play, requiring too much preparatory time, but as a series of *tableaux vivants* or pictorial illustrations. This performance concluded the inaugural festivities. In gratitude to the artists who had assisted during this time, Patti presented all with handsome gifts. Accepting his, Maestro Arditi, having often received similar largesse from her, responded with his usual remark on such occasions: *"Mille grazie; spero che non sarà l'ultimo!* [Thousand thanks; I hope this will not be the last!]"[55]

In September Patti enjoyed some leisure hours at Craig-y-Nos, but weeks later began her annual fall series of some fifteen concerts throughout Great Britain, receiving 500 pounds ($2500) for each. Upon their completion she prepared for another lengthy tour in the United States beginning in January 1892 and ending in May, with Abbey and Maurice Grau as managers. At this time these two men together with John B. Schoeffel presented opera in Italian and French with all-star casts at New York's Metropolitan Opera. After seven seasons of opera in German, the house directors had decreed a change in artistic management.

Her American tour programs consisted of an opera excerpt, all principals in costume, and miscellaneous contributions from Patti, Fabbri, Guille, Del Puente, and Novara with Arditi conducting. The series evolved as a tremendous artistic and financial success, with Arditi maintaining that receipts for each engagement never fell below $8000. In March, Abbey, Grau, and Schoeffel, wishing to end the Metropolitan Opera 1891–92 season in glory, engaged the diva for performances in Boston, New York, and Philadelphia. Of these cities, New York saw Patti most often: as Violetta, Harriet, Lucia, and Rosina. Excluded from the presentations in these cities was contralto Sofia Scalchi, a member of the Metropolitan Opera in the 1891–92 season. Patti refused to appear with her because of a past disagreement.

The 3 April *Herald* greeted Patti's return to New York's opera world with a tribute:

> The voice never grows old and the woman never grows old and, strange to say, the audience never grows old. Its personnel must have changed largely, practically, wholly in the last—we won't say how many—years, but its method is immutable. On other singers it bestows approval. To Patti it renders homage.... Why is it? Largely because of the way the homage is received. To be Patti is not only to have the most wonderful singing voice in the world. To be Patti is—is to be Patti. It is to be *en rapport* with every one of some 3500 or 4000 people. It is to kiss your finger tips to these thousands but once, and yet to kiss them to each individual of the thousands in that once. It is to divide a smile, a bow, a show of white teeth, among those thousands so that each of them has the smile, the bow, the flash all to him or herself. It is to be able to seem to glow with a new thrill of delight at each manifestation of homage, to appear to be surprised when the huge standard of roses looms up at the lower left entrance of the stage. It is to protest poutingly at the wicked tenor, who will not bear his proper burden of the applause, but runs off into the wings, adding his own palm plaudits to the embarrassment of riches bestowed by the house upon the diva. It is to form the lips about the syllables "Home, Sweet Home" that every one knows as soon as Arditi does that the loyal subjects of Adelina Imperatrix have received the great favor for which they have prayed.... To be Patti, in short, is to be queen and to wear the crown with the perfect grace born of absolute confidence.[56]

Her final performance, on 9 April, at the Metropolitan Opera House
as Rosina occasioned scenes and demonstrations prompting Krehbiel in the *Tribune* to write that all incidents "showed in a most
forcible way how genuine is the regard in which this great singer is
held by her admirers"[57] and that Patti had "every reason to feel glad
.and grateful at the admiring esteem . . . awarded to her by the public
of New York."[58] This public must also have appreciated the portrayal
of Almaviva by Italo Campanini, for years one of New York's favorite
tenors, though he was no longer vocally at his best.

J. H. Duval, who may have heard the diva at this time, later
recalled the quality of her voice:

> She was a high soprano with the notes in the very high register
> necessary to sing *Lucia*, *Il Barbiere*, etc., but with a voice the size
> of a lyric, a very rich lyric, with a lower range of a little mezzo-
> soprano. In fact when she sang some of her very low phrases her
> companions-in-art called her "Il contraltino."
>
> Her voice was gorgeous, of a lovely rich colorful ring that
> carried so well she could be heard in the vast auditoriums better
> than some of the strong voiced dramatic singers who were her
> companions.[59]

In May Patti gave three concerts at greatly reduced admission
prices in New York's Madison Square Garden. She wanted those who
could not usually afford an opera ticket to hear her. Public response
was as she had anticipated: the Garden was filled for her concerts on
10, 12, and 14 May. At the last of these, a matinee, some twelve
thousand crowded into the huge auditorium where Patti captivated
them "by. her winning personality, her seeming to sing to every
auditor personally."[60] On this occasion, she sang the aria "Bel raggio"
from *Semiramide*, the Gounod "Ave Maria," "Il bacio," "Robin Adair,"
and "Comin' thro' the Rye." Responding to great applause, she
repeated the Gounod.

Before sailing for Europe on 18 May, Patti announced another
tour of the United States, beginning in November 1893, under the
management of Marcus Mayer, who agreed to a fee of $4500 a per-
formance. One press representative wondered whether it was to be
her final American farewell, as there had been quite a few to date.
Patti replied:

> It is suggestive of horrible possibilities which I absolutely refuse

to contemplate until they are forced upon me, and I hope that will be a long time from now. I shall sing just as long as I am able to do myself justice, and I have never authorized anybody to announce a "farewell" tour for me. To drop personal feeling for a moment and regard the subject purely from a business standpoint, I don't believe that word "farewell," with its gloomy sound, ever drew a dollar from the public. If people want to hear me sing they will come, without regard to whether it is to be my last tour or not. I certainly hope my visit to America next year will not be my last, either professionally or otherwise. Please don't call it a farewell tour. Circumstances over which I can have no control will determine that.[61]

At a final press conference held hours before her departure, Patti divulged other future plans:

I shall go from Liverpool direct to London, where I am to give my first Albert Hall concert June 11. I am to give another in July, but the exact date of that has not yet been fixed. Then I am to give my annual series of fifteen concerts in the English provinces, beginning in October, under the direction of Percy Harrison, the nephew of the man with whom I have given them for fifteen years.... You hear a good deal of talk about my salary in this country; would you like to know what I receive for those concerts in England? I get £800 ($4000) for my London concerts and £500 ($2500) for those in the provinces, and at each I only sing a cavatina and two ballads. Considering the hard work I do in America, and the voyage to and from, do you think there is such a discrepancy between my salary in England and my salary here?

No, I don't mean to do any other professional work than that I have mentioned from now until I return for the next tour of America. I need a good rest and I am going to take it.... Of course I shall spend a good deal of time at ... Craig-y-Nos, and I must be there about Christmas or the children would think that evil days had fallen upon them.[62]

For a number of years at Christmas, Patti had provided refreshments to hundreds of children living near her. Holiday season 1892 was no exception. In a letter dated 21 December 1892, to her nephew Alfredo Barili, she referred to a tea she had provided for over three thousand children. The old and needy in the neighborhood had not been forgotten either: "Yesterday I gave my annual distribution of money to all the poor old people of the district—it was a most touching sight and everyone, myself included, cried."[63]

Early in the new year 1893, the diva gave a series of performances in Nice and Milan. On 20 January she began an engagement at La Scala, first appearing there as Violetta. Among those in the audience that evening was eighty-year-old Verdi, in Milan for rehearsals of his last opera, *Falstaff,* its world premiere due on 9 February. In a letter to Klein, Patti described not only her reception but also Verdi's reaction as he shared the box of Milanese publishers Giulio and Tito Ricordi:

> The Scala was crowded—crammed from floor to ceiling; numbers of people were turned away, unable to obtain seats. My reception was simply grand, everybody standing up to greet me. The enthusiasm was so great throughout the performance that Verdi . . . actually wept tears of joy and delight. It appears that he said . . . that my phrasing was too touching for words and that I sang divinely![64]

Two days later the *Gazzetta Musicale di Milano* reported that Patti was

> *tuttora quella sublime artista che meritamente affascina e commuove;—il canto meraviglioso, l'atteggiamento della elegante persona, i dettagli finissimi dell'azione scenica, non possono essere superati: si admira, e si resta commossi* [still the sublime artist who fascinates and moves;—the marvelous singing, the pose of the elegant person, the very refined details of the motions, cannot be surpassed: one admires and remains moved].[65]

Though daily engaged in piano and stage rehearsals, Verdi took time to visit Patti and Nicolini in their hotel suite. On the 25th she wrote:

> Verdi is coming to pay us a visit at 5 o'clock, after his rehearsal of Falstaff—his rehearsals begin at 1—and last until 5 o'clock daily—he is a *wonderful* man—80 years of age and only looks 60, he is *much* younger looking than Gladstone, and is as jolly and gay as a lad.[66]

Before Patti left Milan on the 31st, Verdi gave her his photograph on which he wrote in Italian "to the marvelous artiste." Leave-taking, Patti said, saddened everyone.

From Milan, the diva had planned to fulfill an engagement in

Florence but decided against it when a local manager failed to send money in advance as stated in the contract. Instead, she and Nicolini proceeded to Nice and remained there until 23 February, thereafter returning to London, where Alfred de Rothschild had invited them to a party in honor of the Prince of Wales and Prime Minister William Ewart Gladstone.

Months later Patti and Nicolini attended another party at Alfred de Rothschild's London residence in honor of the Prince of Wales's son and his fiancée, Princess Mary (later known as the Duke and Duchess of York, the future King George V and Queen Mary). At the dinner, Princess Mary sat to the right of the host and Patti sat on his left. The Prince of Wales surprised Patti, she wrote, by toasting her:

> There were many Royalties and distinguished persons present, and I was chatting away gaily, when the Prince . . . proposed the health of his "old and valued friend, Mme. Patti." He then went on to tell the company that he had first heard me in [Philadelphia], as long ago as 1860, in "Martha," and ever since then his own attendance at what he called my 'victories in the realm of song' were his pleasantest memories.[67]

Then the Prince and Princess of Wales extended Patti an invitation to the garden party at Marlborough House on 5 July in honor of their son and Princess Mary, whose marriage was to occur the next day. Though many Royalties—including Czarevitch Nicholas, later Czar Nicholas II, and King Christian IX and Queen Louise of Denmark—were present, all eyes were on Queen Victoria and her Court. Such moments, Patti said, were great fun.

She then spent time at Craig-y-Nos, interrupted only when she took the train to London for two concerts at Albert Hall. After one of these, George Bernard Shaw commented that though she had sung as gloriously as ever, time had transposed her down a minor third, rendering her "the most accomplished of mezzo-sopranos."[68] Fall saw her engaged in another provincial tour under Percy Harrison's management. Upon its completion little time remained before she had to prepare for the 1893–94 American tour.

After an unpleasant voyage Patti disembarked in New York on 3 November still ill with grippe, which worsened in the days ahead. Though advertised to appear in concerts on 9 and 11 November at Carnegie Hall, she canceled these. Throughout this ordeal, her manager Marcus Mayer was always, in her words, "a *perfect gentleman*."[69] Incidentally, perhaps it was at this time that Nicolini made a cylinder recording at the Fifth Avenue studio of pioneer recordist Gianni Bettini. By 1896, a publication reported that the cylinder had been overplayed by those wanting to hear Patti's husband and was excessively worn.

On the eighteenth, the diva offered a concert/opera program at Carnegie Hall. On this occasion the opera excerpt was the third act of *Faust,* and joining her were Fabbri, Louise Engel, Durward Lely, Galassi, and Novara with Arditi conducting. The following day the *Herald* reported that Patti remained "in the plentitude of her powers and were she at her worst . . . she would still sing better than many . . . at their very best."[70]

In Boston on 25 November 1893, she undertook a new role in an opera written for her, creating the titular heroine in *Gabriella,* with words by Charles Byrne and music by Emilio Pizzi, who, in Patti's opinion, was "decidedly a very clever man, his music . . . charming, and his *orchestration perfect*."[71] Critics confirmed some of this evaluation, particularly citing a beautiful duet for soprano and tenor, an impressive scene for baritone and bass, and Patti's triumphant assumption of Gabriella. She then featured this short opera in other American cities with tolerable success.

Throughout this tour, the diva drew large houses, at this time apparently the only performer able to do so. The United States was in such deep financial crisis that the public evinced little interest in other box-office attractions. Also during this tour, she received one notably poor review by a Chicago critic concerning (of all selections in her repertoire) her singing of "Home, Sweet Home." William Armstrong, meeting Patti only hours after her having seen this unfavorable review, found her still indignant about it.

> On her arrival in Chicago, Mr. Mayer took me to call upon the diva. It happened to be the afternoon of a day in which she had read that she did not know how to sing the words of *Home, Sweet Home*. She was excited. Carolina Bauermeister [*sic*], . . . the singer's companion for untold years, had used her eminent talent for promoting a disturbance. Arriving at Madame Patti's bed-side, she had broken the news by saying, "Good morning, Madame. You do not know how to sing *Home, Sweet Home*." Then she produced the newspaper. That had taken place at nine

o'clock in the morning. When I arrived at five P.M., Carolina's kindness was still actively working.

After the situation had been rehearsed in all its phases, Madame Patti said, "I am going to sing *Home, Sweet Home.* Tell me what is wrong with it?" Standing in the middle of the floor she gave the song from start to finish, making me stand beside her and follow the newspaper's account of her sung words. She held the music. I was expected to follow on that too. If my attention strayed, she would stop, reprove me, and begin afresh. When at last she had finished, she asked with a child's eagerness, "How else could I do it?" There was no assumption of arrogance or injured dignity, only desire to discover if she sang the words correctly.[72]

Like many others before and afterwards, Armstrong found her singing of this ballad unusual:

In that song I have never heard any approach the beauty of Patti's *mezza voce,* gentle as a breath; the entrancing sweetness and the varied tone color of her voice carried clearly to the farthest limits of a vast hall. People, held spellbound, would bend forward in breathless stillness as if fearful of losing a single note, and when she ended a long sigh preceded the frantic outburst of applause.[73]

The tour ended in March. In New York, Patti appeared in only the first of two advertised farewell concerts, on 16 March, which featured a miscellaneous program as well as a performance of *Gabriella.* She canceled the second one of 22 March, pleading illness. Two days later she, Nicolini, and party sailed for Europe.

Towards the end of April 1894, the diva gave a performance in the Patti Theatre for friends and admirers, one of her selections being Wagner's "Träume," in German. The song was among his studies for *Tristan und Isolde.* Though admiring Wagner's music, she had refrained from singing it publicly. This number, however, suited her voice to perfection, and, pleased by the audience's reception of it, Patti decided to include it in her London Albert Hall concert on 19 May. Not long before this event, she conferred with Herman Klein as to her pronunciation of German, which he found flawless, his only suggestions relating to breathing places in extended passages. Klein said she had one complaint:

> It is a beautiful song, and I shall love to sing it; but there is not a single resting-place where I can stop *to swallow*. From first to last, the voice goes on without interruption. It is that which fatigues; and it is one of the things that make Wagner hard to sing. Still, I shall do my best.[74]

Critics concurred that Patti had done her best in the delivery of this Wagnerian song. George Bernard Shaw was impressed by the "wonderful even soundness of the middle of her voice, its beauty and delicacy of surface, and her exquisite touch and diction,"[75] adding he wished she would sing more expressive music like "Träume" rather than florid show pieces. Success with this number inspired Patti to attempt more Wagner, and at her London Albert Hall concert of 7 July she sang an excerpt from one of his earlier operas, Elisabeth's "Prayer" from *Tannhäuser*. George Bernard Shaw maintained that she sang it "with the single aim of making it sound as beautiful as possible" and that in her interpretation she went "straight to the right phrasing, the right vocal touch, and the right turn of every musical figure, thus making her German rivals not only appear in comparison clumsy as singers, but actually obtuse as to Wagner's meaning."[76]

After returning to Craig-y-Nos, Patti sang at another Swansea charity concert on 12 July, this the sixth benefit there since her initial 1882 program. She must have laughed when, *en route* to the music hall, a gentleman in one of the carriages conveying Patti and her guests doffed his hat to the cheering crowd and raised his wig as well, which then blew off into the elements.

Among the Patti Theatre presentations given during this summer were *Kathleen Mavourneen, Sonnambula, Fidelity,* and *Black Eye'd Susan.* There were also *tableaux vivants,* musicals, and garden parties. Among distinguished guests was the eminent violinist August Wilhelmj, who, though retired, still played brilliantly in private whenever he chose to do so. On at least one occasion at Patti's, he played the violin obbligato to her rendition of Gounod's "Ave Maria" with Clara Eissler at the harp and Herman Klein at the harmonium. Patti sang this number, according to Klein, with "electrifying fervor, *élan,* and gorgeous beauty of voice."[77] Her recording of this composition made years later attests to the accuracy of his description.

Apparently this 1894 summer was like many previous ones with Craig-y-Nos the scene of lavish hospitality. In mid-August Patti wrote that she was busy attending to guests and that there were programs in the Patti Theatre virtually every night. Of these guests and programs, a Monsieur de Saxe, relating his experiences to the eminent vocal teacher Mme. Matilde Marchesi's daughter Blanche, said he had found his visit unsettling. Both Patti and Nicolini impressed him as supreme egotists, concerned only about themselves, with her ever in need of the guests' undivided attention and adulation and Nicolini always in bad humor. De Saxe said guests were "really invited as spectators to the most curious existence ever witnessed."[78]

Upon his arrival at Craig-y-Nos, De Saxe found not his hostess and host receiving him, but a footman who escorted him to a suite by way of the conservatory. Here parrots and cockatoos shrieked, flew towards De Saxe and terrorized him. Moments later in his bedroom he was startled anew by the entrance of a lady's maid carrying a large tray containing jewel boxes. As a special favor, Madame Patti, so this domestic said, requested monsieur to select the jewels she would wear at dinner, whereupon this lady's maid opened all the boxes, "spreading out before him complete sets of rubies, emeralds, sapphires, diamonds and pearls, each set containing a tiara, necklaces, brooches, rings, earrings, bracelets, etc."[79] Embarrassed, De Saxe selected the ruby set. Mission accomplished, this domestic, curtsying, returned to her mistress with the desired information.

Hearing the dinner bell, De Saxe hastened to the drawing room, where he discovered other formally attired guests standing in two rows as if awaiting royalty. Soon thereafter, Patti, dressed in a magnificent gown and wearing the ruby set, with Nicolini at her side, swept regally into the room and walked down the line to greet one guest after another, kissing some female intimates on the cheek and occasionally presenting her hand to a man.

At dinner constant references to and exchanges with Patti precluded any other topic of conversation with, in De Saxe's opinion, some guests seemingly there only for the purpose of fawning. Other features of the meal also dismayed De Saxe:

> Nicolini drank his own special wine; quite another one was served to the guests—needless to say of an inferior mark. He tasted the food put on the plate destined for Patti and, after having tasted, declared solemnly every time: "You can eat it."

The cigars that were offered at the end of the meal were also, like the wine, different in quality for the host and for the guests.[80]

After dinner all adjourned to the Patti Theatre, where De Saxe noted the gallery occupants were tradesmen, gardeners, servants, and farmers, obliged, he said, to be there in turns. When the curtain opened on a scene from *La traviata,* De Saxe saw on stage not only Patti as Violetta but also, to his amazement, the butler playing opposite her as Alfredo, miming his part and stoically reacting to her smiles and tears. Perhaps what amazed De Saxe even more occurred at the end of this scene when "frantic applause and torrents of bravas poured from the gallery, the noise apparently having been perfectly rehearsed and organised, and suddenly, after many curtain calls, a shower of artificial flowers and garlands were sent flying from the gallery and fell at the feet of the diva, who, smiling and sending out kisses from her finger-tips, bowed and pressed the flowers to her heart."[81] At the end of the performance footmen retrieved all the artificial flowers from the stage floor and saved them for future curtain calls.

De Saxe found an experience the following day also distasteful. Accompanying Nicolini on a fishing expedition, De Saxe and other guests were not invited to participate but served only as spectators. Had Patti joined her husband on this occasion, De Saxe may have been further displeased by her typical fishing apparel, bloomers she had designed for this activity.

Following Patti's annual fall provincial tour, during which she had sung Wagner's "Träume" and Elisabeth's "Prayer," she further broadened her concert repertoire by introducing, on 28 November at London's Albert Hall, Mozart's aria "Voi che sapete" from the part of the young page in *Le nozze di Figaro.* Previously she had sung in concert only arias from roles she had assumed in an opera house. Klein said her rendition combined tonal loveliness, piquant charm, and faultless purity.

On 6 December Patti received a telegram "commanding" her to sing for Queen Victoria and guests on 11 December at Windsor Castle. She wired back that she could not possibly travel without a saloon carriage, which was duly supplied. Though honored by the monarch's command, Patti apparently had ambivalent feelings toward Queen Victoria, who had snubbed her for twenty-two years,

Patti's last appearance before her being in 1872. Concerts at Buckingham Palace, at which she had often performed, were not generally attended by Her Majesty, who was represented by the Prince of Wales.

Concerning the monarch's air of moral propriety, Patti often told a story about Queen Victoria (mimicking her) and two morally wayward prima donnas. It seems that when the first artist sang before Her Majesty, the ladies in attendance were silent concerning the singer's private life. Silence regarding the other woman did not prevail, however, and the gossip reached such a fervor, with the queen so gloriously aghast, that the ladies started in on the first singer and so excited Queen Victoria that her false teeth slipped out.

While at Windsor Castle, Patti stayed overnight as a guest of Sir Henry and Lady Ponsonby in the Norman Tower. Writing to Alfredo Barili, she said that her host and hostess had been most gracious; that Queen Victoria had especially enjoyed the singing of Elisabeth's "Prayer," complimenting her German pronunciation; and that the queen had given her a ruby ornament with the initials V. R. in diamonds as well as a diamond and sapphire brooch.

That Christmas at Craig-y-Nos Patti told Klein, a guest during this holiday, of her command performance:

> The Queen was gracious beyond measure. She paid me the unusual honor of directing that I should remain at the castle for the night, so as to spare me the fatigue of the late journey back to town. Ganz went with me and of course played my accompaniments. Her Majesty received me with the utmost amiability, and expressed great pleasure at hearing me again after many years. She conversed with me in the sweetest manner between each of my pieces. Naturally, at the end I sang "Home, Sweet Home," and I could see that it brought tears to the dear Queen's eyes. She was really deeply moved.[82]

While enjoying such holiday festivities at Craig y-Nos as dances, elaborate dinner parties, teas, and musical and theatrical entertainments in the Patti Theatre, Klein waited for the right moment to broach a subject he had long cherished: Patti's return to Covent Garden. Several months before, Klein had suggested the possibility to Sir Augustus Harris, Covent Garden impresario, and to her manager Percy Harrison. Both men had said they would gladly cooperate in such a venture. Sir Augustus wondered, however, whether she would accept 300 pounds ($1500) a performance, which would be the highest fee paid to a singer at that opera house but which was not even half the amount Patti received for a concert at London's Albert Hall. Sir Augustus said he needed her decision before the new year 1895.

One morning, while accompanying Patti on a stroll in the winter garden, Klein began his inquiry in judicious fashion by asking about her season at Nice in February:

> "In what operas will you sing at Nice?"
> "In *Traviata, Roméo et Juliette, Barbiere,* and *Lucia.*"
> "Lucky Nice!"
> She laughed. "Why do you say that?"
> "Because the Riviera is so much more fortunate than London, where everybody is pining to hear you in opera just once again."
> "Everybody! The old subscribers, the *vieille garde,* perhaps. But there is a new generation at Covent Garden now; are they equally interested?"
> "Can there be any doubt? They go to hear you at the Albert Hall, and go away wishing for more."
> "But Harris—"
> "Say rather Harrison!" And then I unfolded my mission with all the necessary diplomacy and care. She listened attentively and nodded her head very graciously.
> "I will talk it over with Ernest and Percy, and to-morrow you shall know. I am not altogether sure whether I want to; but we will see."[83]

The next day, as promised, Patti told Klein she would meet with Sir Augustus early in the new year to discuss a summer season at Covent Garden. Several weeks later Patti and Sir Augustus agreed that she would reappear at Covent Garden for six performances beginning in mid-June. What followed thereafter is revealed in a letter dated 21 February 1895 that Patti, in Nice, wrote to William Armstrong:

> The success of my concerts was unparalleled, and in Berlin, Vienna, and Dresden the enthusiasm of the audiences was so great that I was in danger of being torn to pieces in their frantic endeavors to get on the platform to kiss my hands and my dress! It was exceedingly flattering to me and a little overpowering.

In Dresden the Crown Princess of Saxony was present, and expressed a wish to be presented to me, so amidst a scene of the wildest excitement on the part of the audience, who stood up and cheered without ceasing, I had to go to the Princess in the hall among the people, where she spoke to me for a long time and complimented me very warmly on my singing.

Since we came to Nice, about three weeks ago, our time has been almost entirely taken up in accepting invitations to lunch and dinners, invitations which pour in daily like the visitors, who come from early in the morning until late at night!

Last week I sang *Traviata,* when I had the most brilliant success imaginable. All my pieces were encored, and I had a perfect ovation at the end of the first act. The house was crammed from ceiling to floor, and the enthusiasm and delight of the audience increased from the beginning till the end until it knew no bounds, and in answer to innumerable recalls I was obliged to appear again and again. My entrée in the *Barber* was another succés fou. This week I sang *Lucia* and after that *Romeo.*[84]

Though asked for additional performances at Nice, Patti refused, looking forward to a brief respite from singing before departing on 25 March for a London gala in her honor.

On 3 April, during a concert at Queen's Hall, directors of the Philharmonic Society presented Patti with a gold medal in recognition of her illustrious career. She sang two arias and the inevitable "Home, Sweet Home," and she confessed that the ceremony had given her great pleasure. What the event revealed, above all, was the superb condition of her voice, presaging a triumphant return to opera in London.

Meanwhile, people fought for admissions to Patti's Covent Garden performances. Klein noted that the "rush for places . . . was a vivid reminder of old times," that prices for tickets "recalled the extravagant figures recorded in connection with the famous bygone Patti nights," and that high society was "fairly agog in anticipation of an experience now regarded almost as a tradition—an experience whereof the most brilliant Melba and de Reszke nights never furnished more than a faint replica."[85] *The Sketch* maintained that "it was considered *the thing* to hear Patti, and many went for the sake of their reputation as fashionable folk."[86]

On 11 June 1895, Patti as Violetta astounded the audience with her voice, artistry, and youthful appearance. That she had made her

European debut in this opera house thirty-four years before hardly seemed possible. Patti began the performance overexcited and later confided in Klein:

> When I made my entry, when I looked across the footlights at the familiar picture, as I went on bowing again and again, while the storm of applause seemed as if it would never cease, I felt more like breaking down and crying than singing. But after we had sat down to the supper-table and De Lucia [the Alfredo] had begun the "Libiamo," I suddenly regained my confidence and courage. I never lost them again.[87]

Of all her roles, Patti then preferred Violetta:

> Violetta seems to me to be the very ideal of what a part ought to be. I love singing and I love acting, and where is one given more room for the practice of both arts than in the part of Violetta? The first part affords one a chance of proving one's mettle as a *fioiture* singer, the second part must be really lived.[88]

What probably most astounded operagoers this particular evening, however, occurred in the third act, the ballroom scene, when Patti wore over a white gown a cuirass she had had made of some thirty-seven hundred of her diamonds dismounted from their regular settings. According to Nicolini, their value amounted to 200,000 pounds ($1,000,000). The *Standard* made much of this display and its worth but failed to mention that the setting and unsetting alone cost her 800 pounds ($4000), a small fortune then. To guard Patti and her gems, officers of the law lingered backstage and numbered among those onstage in this scene. Several days later a London publication commented on the subject:

> To-morrow night another opportunity will be afforded at the opera of seeing the Patti costumes and the Patti diamonds, which in *La Traviata* last Tuesday shared the honours even with Mme. Patti's singing. The value of these gems . . . has rendered necessary certain precautions at the opera house . . . where a couple of individuals not wholly unknown at the Bow Street establishment opposite, silently figure among *Violetta's* guests. In the Banquet Scene Mme. Patti wears some wonderful sapphires; but in the Ball Scene, altogether apart from coronet, necklace, and bracelets, the front of her dress is a perfect blaze of gems. At night . . . the Patti diamonds are in perfectly secure custody.[89]

Sir Augustus was overjoyed, going about the opera house in a "veritable seventh heaven of delight."[90] The conductor, Luigi Mancinelli, was also pleased, and the cast members, including Fernando de Lucia as Alfredo and Mario Ancona as Germont, were named "worthy of the event."[91] The next day the *Times* maintained the performance should be considered "as an unqualified triumph for Mme. Patti and as a testimony to the perfection of her method of vocalization."[92] *The Sketch* stressed that hyperbole became "infectious when one writes of the exquisite notes of this great singer."[93] She was, according to *Punch*, "in her 'best tra-la-la-viata.'" The knowing ones observed high keys politely transposed to suit Adelina, but what manager could refuse to *put down the notes* when Adelina agrees to sing."[94] The *Pall Mall Gazette* declared the evening "a wild, whirling, triumphant affair."[95] Of her voice, this paper said:

> Her voice has been, and probably still is, the most purely exquisite thing of its kind, when it is at its best, among the voices of the world. It is true that brilliance has somewhat forsaken it, that the high notes, having lost the smoothness of the strength of youth, are often harsh and untameable, that there are occasional gaps and weaknesses; but if you throw all these things into the scale, there still remains a wonderful beauty of tone, a magical and quite individual smoothness, roundness, sweetness of expression, a magnificent style.[96]

At the end of the third act, critics noted that the house went practically insane in its enthusiasm and excitement. It "rose at the diva, called her forward again and again, and, from the front row of the stalls to the hindmost ranks in the gallery and slips, substantially acknowledged that there was only one Patti in the world."[97]

Three evenings after this return to Covent Garden, Patti sang at a Buckingham Palace State Concert at Queen Victoria's request. The following evening, she repeated her portrayal of Violetta at Covent Garden before a demonstrative audience.

In the next several weeks, only four Patti presentations remained: two Rosinas and two Zerlinas in *Don Giovanni*. She first essayed the role of Rosina on 19 June, retaining "in fullest measure the qualities of vivacity, piquancy, grace, and charm that had so long rendered it an inexhaustible source of delight."[98] In the lesson scene, she sang "Bel raggio" from *Semiramide*, introducing new ornaments and bringing the house down with a final cadenza. Among her associates were Charles Bonnard (Almaviva), Ancona (Figaro), Antonio Pini-Corsi (Bartolo), and Arimondi (Basilio). During the next week, Patti appeared twice as Zerlina, initially on 24 June, and at this and a later performance, Victor Maurel assumed the role of the dissolute Don. Klein maintained that her Zerlina,

> if finer now than ever, was so only because Mozart's music fell easily within the compass of her medium and lower head tones, the timbre of which had grown more round and beautiful with the gradual elimination of the acuter notes in the head register,[99]

and that her delineation and singing were a revelation to operagoers who heard her for the first time. Patti ended her engagement on 4 July as a vivacious, piquant Rosina.

Many wondered about the secret of her voice that had been so beautifully preserved. In response she said:

> If I gave lessons I should cultivate the middle tones and the voice of the singer would be good at the age of a hundred.... My success is founded on those notes, and there can be no enduring success without them. How many can sing very high and yet cannot sing "Home, Sweet Home"! Some pooh-pooh the idea of the difficulty of that simple melody. But it is more difficult to sing "Home, Sweet Home" than the waltz song from *Romeo and Juliet*, because of its demands upon the development of the voice. Without the beautiful middle notes there is no cantabile, and upon the proper development of these, and the avoidance of strain by forcing high and low notes, the enduring powers of the singer depend ... but, lose the middle notes, and you lose all. The very high and the very low notes are the ornaments, but what good are Gobelins and pictures if you have no house to hang them in?[100]

Later she shared any would-be secrets regarding her youthful appearance:

> Up to 40 I stinted myself in nothing, and ate and lived as I chose. After 40, however, I took to a comparatively strict way of living. Since then I have eaten no red meat and have drunk only white

wine and soda. When I feel weak a glass of champagne picks me
up. I never touch spirits or liquors. My diet consists of light food
and white meat, chiefly sweetbreads, sheeps' brains, fowl and
vegetables. I always sleep with the window wide open in
Summer and partly open in Winter so as not to get cold air
straight in my face. I never get to bed early, hardly ever before
12:30 or 1 o'clock. A severe hygiene and elaborate toilet before
bed are absolutely necessary to any woman who does not want to
get fat. That is my only secret of health.[101]

Not long after returning to Craig-y-Nos, Patti, writing to William
Armstrong, highlighted some of her recent London experiences:

Now that I am back once more at dear Craig-y-Nos, and am able
to find time to breathe again after the unceasing whirl of success
and gaieties of the past four weeks in London, I devote some of
my first spare moments to write and tell you about my season of
triumphs. For it has indeed been one of the most gratifying
triumphs of my career, to have returned to Covent Garden after
an absence of ten years, and to have met with a reception, which
I believe has never been equalled for enthusiasm, and to have
repeated my successes of thirty years ago!

The house was a wonderful sight—it is said that not even on
Gala Nights has such a display of royalties, notabilities, and
diamonds been seen. Seats were at a premium, the stalls fetching
ten pounds each.

The Prince and Princess of Wales with their daughter were
present, also the Duke and Duchess of York, the Duchess of Fife,
and the Duke and Duchess of Mecklenburg-Strelitz, and I was
most warmly congratulated by the Prince of Wales on my
success, and also on my return to Covent Garden. After the first
act I had showers of bouquets, and the most beautiful baskets of
flowers presented to me. Altogether it was a most memorable
night.

The following Saturday I repeated *Traviata* with similar
success—the Duchess of Coburg, the Crown Prince and
Princess of Roumania, and the Grand Duke and Duchess of
Hesse, etc., being present.

The *Barbier* was my next opera, and again the same story of a
crowded house, masses of flowers, and another enormous
success. I enclose you some articles which will give you a better
description than I can of my performances, and will show you
what the critics thought of me.

Don Giovanni drew a crowded house each time. In fact it was packed from ceiling to floor, the prices always being enormously raised. I finished my season last Friday in the *Barbier*, when I again received an unparalleled ovation. All the royalties were present. The Princess of Wales has been present on the occasions when I sang *Traviata*, the *Barbier* and *Don Giovanni*. Sir Augustus Harris was anxious that I should prolong my engagement, and sign again for next year, "*Mais, nous verrons!*"

Besides the opera I was invited to sing at the State concert at Buckingham Palace, the date of which was altered to suit my convenience. Last Wednesday I was present at a garden party at Clarence House, given by the Duke and Duchess of Coburg, when I was congratulated by all the royalties present on my recent success at Covent Garden.[102]

Parenthetically, a rumor soon mushroomed that Patti would appear at Covent Garden the following season as Elsa in Wagner's *Lohengrin*. Years before she had been keenly interested in performing this part; but, it was said, the Marquis de Caux persuaded her against it, being, after the Franco-Prussian War, anti-German in his sentiments. Patti denied this rumor and asked Klein to correct it in his *Sunday Times* column; she said she found the role too fatiguing at this time in her life.

As usual, in succeeding weeks, Craig-y-Nos swarmed with guests, often entertained in the Patti Theatre. One of the presentations was a mime play entitled *Mirka l'Enchanteresse*, inspired by Georges Boyer, Paris Opéra secretary general and a *Le Figaro* journalist, with music by André Pollonnais. This pantomime involved some houseguests, while serving as a vehicle to entertain others, and was performed twice, on 22 July and 3 August. The production of another mime play followed: a work based on Mrs. Henry Wood's novel *East Lynne* with a cast including Patti as Lady Isabel and Mme. Vine, Augustus Spalding as Captain Levison, Herman Klein as Richard Hare, and little Cecilia Hulley, nine-year-old daughter of W. F. Hulley, as the dying child. Pollonnais composed music for this version as well as for a lullaby with words written by Klein that Patti sang to her dying child. Its performance, on 17 August, in Klein's opinion, was artistically outstanding. Nicolini, however, loathed it and expressed horror at seeing his wife in "widow's weeds," which he considered bad luck. Perhaps he was haunted by a premonition.

By October, Patti was once more concertizing in various cities in the British Isles during the annual autumn tour, which, according to her secretary Mabel Woodford, was financially and artistically most successful. In a letter dated 24 October 1895, she wrote:

> Last night in Manchester the audience would not be satisfied till Madame had given them four encores ... & when she finished with "Comin' thro' the rye," all the people in the stalls stood up & waved their handkerchiefs, ... & on Saturday we sail ... for Queenstown, & after the 2 concerts in Dublin, & one in Belfast, we return to the Castle passing through London on the morning of November 6th.

Woodford then wrote of their discomfort:

> We have been living the whole time in draughts—Hotels, & the concert hall too have been terrible ... in Haddonsfield, Madame was obliged to sing the whole evening in a cloak!—The concerts at Birmingham & Glasgow at which Madame was unable to sing, owing to the cold she contracted in Wolverhampton, have been postponed till the second week in April.[103]

In Belfast, where this 1895 autumn tour ended, Patti said enthusiasm bordered on madness, with hundreds of people unable to gain admission and with some breaking down several doors. Apparently she was in a generous mood that evening and added five encores to the program. Her London Albert Hall concert, on 26 November, also inspired enthusiasm.

In 1896 Patti continued to entertain many guests at Craig-y-Nos and to fulfill professional engagements. The only novelty in which she appeared took place in Monte Carlo on 3 February, when she gave a private matinee of the mime play *Mirka l'Enchanteresse* for Czarevitch George, ailing brother of Czar Nicholas II, and two public presentations of this work on 4 and 20 February. The following year saw few professional engagements and a lessening of activities at Craig-y-Nos due to Nicolini's poor health. In her brief series on the Riviera, Patti, on 22 February 1897 in Nice, created for the first time the title role of André Pollonnais's opera *Dolores*, a work not meriting much critical praise.

What in these two years Patti may have found especially memorable took place closer to home. In September 1896, she gave a charity concert at Cardiff. Originally she had planned to give it in Swansea; but when word reached her that admissions had been lower than in previous years, Patti refused to appear there. The 23 July edition of the *South Wales Daily Post* reported that she regarded the reduction "as a gratuitous, though, of course, unintentional insult to herself."[104] Several weeks later a member of the Swansea Hospital Committee declared he regretted "far more than the loss of the money that a kind and charitable lady should have her feelings hurt."[105] Actually the hospital and poor of that town did not lose money, for Patti sent some proceeds from the Cardiff concert to Swansea. When the charity concert benefiting the Cardiff Infirmary was given, on 16 September, it attracted an enormous house. Joining the diva were Marianne and Clara Eissler, the former lady playing violin and the latter the harp; Wilhelm Ganz as accompanist; and two Welsh singers. After the concert, Patti asked Herman Klein to represent her in a vote of thanks. In his remarks he noted she had already given over ten Welsh charity concerts with Swansea having had the most, Neath two, and Brecon three. Klein later commented that in the near future, "with the aid of the two Welsh singers they had heard that day . . . she would endeavor to accomplish an authentic rendering of 'Land of My Fathers' in their native tongue."[106] In response to this announcement the house became pandemonium.

In Wales, on 24 May 1897, Brecon's mayor and corporation made her an honorary burgess of the town, the first woman to be so named, and the ceremonies for this affair equalled those reserved for Royal honors. Authorities first met Patti and her party, traveling via private saloon carriage, at the railway station where the mayor and mayoress extended a warm welcome, the mayoress presenting the diva a beautiful bouquet. The mayor then led her and her guests to numerous carriages in line for a procession to the new Market Hall, where the municipal ceremony was to take place. Immense crowds lined the streets, applauding and cheering Patti and the mayor in his carriage. At one point this procession slowed before passing under a castellated arch, where the deputy-mayor proclaimed: "Admit Mme. Patti-Nicolini into the confines of the borough of Brecon!"[107] The procession thereafter proceeded with more bugle blares and drumbeats. At the hall, Patti received not only the honorary title but also a casket containing the scroll of freedom carved of oak originally part of a beam from Brecon Priory Church, an edifice said to be a thousand years old. At the conclusion of ceremonies the procession reassembled to escort her and her guests to the railway station, once again amid applause, cheers, and hails to Brecon's honorary burgess.

Patti subsequently said this tribute was one of the greatest she had ever received: "Amongst the gifts I am proudest of is the splendid casket containing the freedom of the city of Brecon. I love Wales and I love the Welsh people, and this is the tangible reminder that this love I have borne them for so many years is returned."[108]

Two months later, on 26 July 1897, the diva participated at the opening of Swansea's new Grand Theatre on Singleton Street. After a reception committee at the railway station welcomed Patti, her god-child and secretary Mabel Woodford, "Karo," and her stepsons Richard and Robert Nicolini, a procession of carriages, escorted by mounted policemen, passed through streets full of cheering spectators. At the theater, a band, the Swansea Choral Society, and several orators comprised the formal program, of which Patti's part was to christen a memorial stone. She anticipated doing this with despatch and aplomb. However, when the time came for her to break a bottle of champagne on the marble block, a man behind her had become entangled in the cord releasing the bottle, which then came out of its hammock. The *Western Mail* described what ensued: "Fortunately, it hung and swung high and dry, and did not touch anything harder than the gentleman's—well, say head! The bottle was put back into its cradle above, and Patti, having got to the right spot further on, pulled the trigger, and the bottle went to execution most bravely. Sure, never a bottle was cracked with greater eclat."[109] Moments later one of the theater's builders presented Patti with a gift and gave a brief speech:

> Madame, I beg of you to accept a small souvenir of your visit to our theatre to-day. . . . I beg of you to accept a small key, and to accept it as a token that you will be always welcome to the building. (Hear, hear, and cheers.) I am told that it is an exact model of the key used to lock up Newgate debtors in the old days. (Laughter.) I wish, Madame, that it enabled us to keep you a prisoner in this theatre (Madame winsomely shook her head and there was a burst of laughter) for then I am sure that it would make our theatre the most popular in the world. . . . Perhaps I

shall not be assuming too much when I say that the door of all doors which it will most readily open will be the stage door—(hear, hear)—for I am sure you will be able to open that door as easily and readily as you have opened the hearts of your adopted countrymen in South Wales.[110]

Before this occasion, in 1875, Patti had laid the foundation stone of the Central London Throat and Ear Hospital, and in 1887 she had presided at the formal opening of the Severn Tunnel on a new railway between London and the Welsh town of Neath.

Nicolini was unable to join Patti in Brecon and Swansea. For several years his health had declined, primarily because of kidney and liver disorders. William Armstrong, visiting Craig-y-Nos early in the summer of 1897, recalled her concern:

One night... she came hurrying into the billiard-room nervously unstrung. "Something awful has happened!" she exclaimed. "Just now Nicolini staggered into my room holding onto the furniture. I started to catch him, for I feared he would fall. 'It is death! It is death!' he gasped. 'I know it is death!' I tried to soothe him. But I, too, thought it death. I tell you, these scenes are frightful."[111]

In a letter dated 21 August, Patti wrote of their travails:

I have been passing through a terrible time of anxiety and worry on account of Mr. Nicolini, who, about two months ago, had a very serious relapse.

As soon as he became a little stronger, the Doctors ordered him to Langland Bay, near Swansea, in hopes that he would derive benefit from the sea air. Unfortunately it makes me ill to stay near the sea, so for the last seven weeks I have been going backwards and forwards from the castle to Langland Bay to see him, leaving here at eight-thirty in the morning, and arriving at nine in the evening.

Mr. Nicolini, I am glad to say, is decidedly better for his stay near the sea, but last week he fancied the air was too relaxing and expressed a great wish to go to Brighton. We therefore arranged to have a comfortable invalid carriage for him, and he went to London on Tuesday last and is now at Brighton. ... Of course my plans are very uncertain for the winter, as they must depend entirely upon the state of Mr. Nicolini's health.[112]

In September Nicolini and his son Richard traveled to Paris to consult a specialist for his liver complaints. The doctor advised a strict regimen and recuperation in the Riviera. Nicolini soon thereafter went to Cannes, where by mid-November his health seemingly improved. Though Patti had planned to visit him by then, her Paris doctors declared that to go to the Riviera, "where the heat was *intense,* and to return to England for [her concert] in December, would be a very great risk."[113] Two and a half weeks after the new year, she finally joined her husband in Pau, where he had gone to take the waters. She arrived there only a short time before his death on 18 January 1898.

Klein, in his biography of Patti, maintained that her life with Nicolini had generally been happy. He added that whatever "his faults (and they were neither few nor negligible), he knew how to take care of her, to shield her from annoyance, to look after her health, to prevent her from over-taxing her strength, above all, to ward off monotony or *ennui*."[114] What Klein did not mention, however, was Nicolini's last will.

In this document, dated 29 June 1897, Nicolini left his entire estate—valued at more than $200,000—to his sons, Richard and Robert. It contained not a single reference to Patti, while in two earlier wills dated 18 October 1886 and 26 January 1889, Nicolini had bequeathed to her "absolutely everything which the law allows."[115] If she predeceased him, all was to be divided equally between his two sons. Nicolini's wishes as stated in his final will, however, were not fulfilled. According to a letter written by notary A. Labouret, on 8 February 1898, to the London Rothschild Bank, French law decreed that his assets be divided among his five children and Patti (Nicolini's first wife had died on 27 January 1889).

This might lead one to wonder what part the sons, visiting Craig-y-Nos during the 1897 summer, played in their father's changing the will; why his daughters Marie, Caroline, and Jeanne were not mentioned; and what had occurred domestically in Nicolini's final year that prompted him to exclude Patti.

A possible answer to the last question appears in William Armstrong's chapter on Patti in his book *The Romantic World of Music*. Though not giving any specific reasons, Armstrong, visiting Craig-y-Nos during the 1897 summer, speculated that all was not well between husband and wife:

I scarcely think ... he held her love at that time; a situation which made her constancy all the more creditable. When I went in the early summer of that year to say good-bye to her, I spoke of her biography, which she had expressed the wish to do with me. "Come back next summer," was the reply, "and we will write it. Then *this* will be over, one way or the other." "This" meant Mr. Nicolini's illness, and her tone was quite serene in saying it.[116]

After Nicolini's funeral, Patti spent several weeks in the Grand Hotel Royal at San Remo in deep mourning—prostrated, she said, by troubles and worries; however, by 24 March she was in Paris for a few days, seeing no one and going nowhere. In mid-April she returned to Craig-y-Nos, where she enjoyed "long walks and drives every day" and where she had some improvements made, "the principal one being the laying of a magnificent rose garden."[117]

Patti reappeared in public at a concert, on 26 May, in London's Albert Hall, still wearing "widow's weeds." Two months later at another concert in Albert Hall she was no longer dressed in such attire. Between these two affairs she sang on 7 June at Wilhelm Ganz's Jubilee Concert and on 25 June at the Crystal Palace before some twenty-three thousand spectators. Also on that program were Clara Butt, Edward Lloyd, and Charles Santley with August Manns as conductor and Wilhelm Ganz as piano accompanist.

During that autumn Patti resumed her annual tour of the provinces, ending at Nottingham in late October. Then, after a brief stay at Craig-y-Nos, she returned to London for a concert at Albert Hall on 14 November 1898, where during an intermission, she surprised friends with intriguing news: she intended to remarry. By her side stood her fiancé, the Swedish Baron Rolf Cederström. Klein, with her permission, made the announcement public in an article he wrote for the *Manchester Guardian* and the *Scotsman*. The news account stated, in part, that the engagement would not be "formally announced for some time, for scarcely a full year has yet elapsed since the death of M. Nicolini," that her fiancé had been "a visitor at Craig-y-Nos Castle during the recent summer holidays," and that the wedding would take place in February.[118]

Thus the marriage would occur shortly before Patti's fifty-sixth birthday, while Cederstrom would be twenty-eight. He was the son of noblewoman Märta Leijonhufvud and Claës Edvard Cederström, whose familial nobility extended back to the seventeenth century and who was himself a former officer in the Swedish Royal Horse Guards at Stockholm. Patti's fiancé had served in the Swedish military before coming to London as the director of a Health Gymnastic Institute that followed the principles of physical therapy as developed by the Swede Jonas Henrik Kellgren. Some gossiped that the baron had been Patti's masseur and that "English society thought it rather *infra dig* for a lady who was a great prima donna and had once been the wife of a nobleman . . . to marry a man whom they considered, on account of his profession, beneath her."[119] According to one source, Patti first met him at a party where he had asked to be introduced to her. News accounts said that they had been introduced at Cannes in 1897 and that he had spent a month with her at Craig-y-Nos in the summer of 1898. Still another version was that she had first met her fiancé in London while consulting him for relief from physical ailments. Baron Cederström's niece Carin Ekelöf maintains that they became acquainted at the London Health Gymnastic Institute. Shortly before the marriage Cederström became a naturalized Englishman, "thus leaving his wife complete control of her large fortune, which under Swedish law she could not have had."[120] Some months earlier, on 16 July 1898, Patti had also become a British citizen, with her references provided by Dr. Edward Hamilton, Percy Harrison, Sir Edward Lawson, Alfred de Rothschild, and Marianne Elizabeth Woodford (Mabel Woodford's mother).

Writing to Alfredo Barili, Patti expressed joy in anticipation of this marriage:

> And now, my dear Alfredo, I know you will be pleased to hear that I am engaged to be married to a very charming man, Baron Rolf Cederström, you met him here, and I believe you liked him very much. He is a Swede, and he belongs to one of the first families in Stockholm—Everybody that knows him thinks him most charming . . . I am *very, very* happy—The wedding is going to take place at Brecon, after which we are going to Florence.[121]

Though originally scheduled for February, the wedding took place on 25 January 1899, in St. Michael's Roman Catholic Church at Brecon, where the borough celebrated it as a municipal holiday. A local paper expressed the sentiments of many people who esteemed her "not only for the incomparable songstress that she is, but for the many kindnesses she has showered upon them."[122]

Rarely before had Brecon been "stirred to its foundations"[123] as on this wedding day with decorations consisting of shields, banners, flags, arches, streamers, and bunting. Thousands had poured into the town to witness the procession from the train station to the church. It began shortly after 10:30 on a sunny morning, Patti and her fiancé and wedding guests having arrived on a special train only moments before.

At the church, Patti, carrying a bouquet of white orchids, "looked a perfect picture of health and beauty in her lovely costume of pale blue grey satin de Lyon."[124] The wedding ceremony was short, after which the newlyweds drove off in a carriage with thousands cheering and showering them with confetti. As their train left Brecon, it moved off to more cheering "in hearty style."[125]

Returning to Penwyllt, the wedding party entered another special train and departed for London, the wedding feast being served en route in a saloon car formerly occupied by the Prince of Wales. After several days in London, Patti and Cederström—hereafter, said the *Pall Mall Gazette,* to "be known ... as Mme. Patti's husband"[126]—left for the Riviera and Italy, remaining on the continent until Easter. On this honeymoon, Patti took two hundred pieces of luggage, which a Welsh publication said formed but a little lot.

CHAPTER VII

Baroness Cederström

The first years of Patti's marriage to Cederström saw marked changes in her professional and private life. She made just one public appearance in opera, limited concert engagements, and participated in few charity benefits. At Craig-y-Nos, Patti Theatre events, parties, and houseguests generally ceased. While Baron Cederström was primarily responsible for these and other changes, the baroness's health and vocal concerns were also factors in this new way of life.

Her one public performance in opera, which was also her last, occurred at Covent Garden on 22 February 1900 (thirty-nine years after her debut there), when she and French tenor Albert Alvarez appeared in the Chamber Scene from Gounod's *Roméo et Juliette*. Earlier that evening, she sang two arias and two encores at a benefit for the Marchioness of Lansdowne's War Fund for Officers' Wives and Families. According to Cecil Roth in *The Magnificent Rothschilds*, her participation in this affair was due to Alfred de Rothschild:

> During the Boer War, it was Alfred de Rothschild who arranged the famous Gala Night at Covent Garden on behalf of war charities-and only he could have arranged it. For no one else would Patti have . . . come to sing with Alvarez—brought over specially from New York. . . . There were few other persons who, even for such a cause as this, could have obtained the services of the massed bands of the Household Cavalry and the Brigade of

Guards.... It was a great success. The Prince and Princess of Wales graced the Royal box.[1]

Backstage, according to singer Lucette Korsoff as quoted by Charles Neilson Gattey in his *Queens of Song*, Patti had presented a picture quite different from the one onstage:

> At last, after two long intervals, Korsoff, standing back-stage, saw a tiny woman appear. Her wrinkled face seemed even older because it was "transfigured by fear," her eyes were bleary and she kept trembling under her shawl. Lucette claims that she overheard her murmuring: "I am afraid, I am afraid!" This was the great Patti. The stage-hands crowded near her, muttering enviously: "Look at her corsage—those are real diamonds!"
>
> When the diva sang, Lucette found her notes "still pretty and pure," but she breathed after every word. In the ensemble Alvarez's voice covered hers involuntarily.[2]

Several days later the *Sunday Times* celebrated the performance:

> To say that Mme. Patti worked hard is to give a poor notion of the extent to which the great prima donna interested herself in and contributed to the success and *éclat* of this noteworthy event. She came to London expressly for it, and she sent specially to Paris for the three new gowns which she wore in course of the evening. She sang encores after each of her operatic airs, and lavished the full measure of her genius upon a delighted and astonished crowd. I say "astonished" because the word fitly expressed the feelings with which old opera habitués gazed upon the still young-looking face of the diva and listened to the ever-fresh tones of her incomparable voice.... Although it had ended all too soon, the *duo* left behind the exquisite fragrance of an enchantment long past and yet again renewed.[3]

While thereafter abandoning public opera performances, Patti did continue to give concerts, almost exclusively at London's Albert Hall and on autumn tours of the provinces. Pianist Helen Farewell Hutter participated in one of these as a member of a musical group managed by Percy Harrison that included several vocalists, a violinist, and veteran baritone Sir Charles Santley. She first met Patti moments prior to the opening concert. Before introducing her, Harrison advised the artists: "Now I want you to be very nice to her ... because she likes attention."[4] Hutter described what then transpired:

> In a moment he reappeared with Patti on his arm. I never shall forget the apparition. She came in like a flame—with diamonds from head to foot, diamonds shimmering and trembling from her hair, gleaming from her neck, glittering from her gown and arms and hands. When she walked she blazed.
>
> She was a tiny slip of a woman, her face enameled and painted and on her head an artificial chignon of some sort, built very high. This was something that she always wore, regardless of fashion. She was extremely gracious in her manner, smiling and charming. She quickly shook hands with each of us, one after the other down the line. ... Then, in this line of soloists, a supposedly new company to which she was being introduced for the first time, she came to her old friend Santley, whom she had seen around all her life. ...
>
> She stopped and cocked her piquant little head on one side with a droll expression, and then, as if overwhelmed with a great emotion, she threw her arms around his neck in exaggerated devotion and kissed him, saying: "Oh, my dear Mr. Santley, I am so glad to see you again after this long, long separation!"
>
> And everybody roared with laughter.[5]

Hutter said Patti's singing "outdazzled the diamonds."[6] As usual at such concerts, she sang several arias and ballads, ending her part of the program with "Home, Sweet Home." Throughout the tour, Hutter said, Patti repeated this order, saving that song for the last encore. She resisted singing it, however, until the audience's sweet compulsion brought it forth. "They would clap and stamp and cheer," Hutter wrote, "until she sang that."[7] It would be the evening's great event:

> The audience knew it, and Patti knew it—and fed upon it. Yet she would pretend that it was a surprise to her, and that she was obliged reluctantly to do it only to appease the great clamoring. She would come back into the wings, go out front again, come back, repeat this many times, and then she would say to Mr. Harrison, as if she were annoyed by the great demands for her singing: "Oh, dear, there is no use in my attempting to come back before I have sung 'Home, Sweet Home'; you *know* I always have to sing it"—as if she were aggrieved, when all the time we knew it was her greatest triumph of the evening and she would not have missed it for anything![8]

Always she sang it with such intense feeling that her eyes were full of tears.

This group traveled in four private railway cars with Patti, her husband, maids, and numerous trunks and boxes occupying two of these, the women of the company in a third car, the men in the fourth. The diva and Cederström made an attractive couple. The American singer and diplomat's wife Mme. Hegermann-Lindencrone, who had known Patti when she was the Marquise de Caux, marveled that she looked amazingly young, scarcely older than her third husband.

Hutter said of Cederström: "That was evidently his job—furnishing devotion and flattery for Madame Patti, who could not live without it any more than the earth can live without heat."[9] Patti especially impressed Hutter with her self-discipline, endurance, cheerfulness, abstemiousness, and charm.

Of the few charity benefits in which Patti participated at this time, there were several memorable affairs: one in Rome (only weeks after her third marriage), a concert at which she met the Queen of Italy; one in Stockholm in September 1900, when the King of Sweden conferred upon her the Swedish order Literis et Artibus; another in Paris in April 1901 in aid of the Caisse des Secours Immédiats; and two in Brecon in 1900 and 1902, when she sang for the borough's poor and needy. Of the charity concert at Brecon on 2 August 1900, Patti wrote:

> The town was gaily decorated with flags and banners in honour of the occasion, and I had a most enthusiastic reception and ovation—The Mayor came to meet us at the station, and I had some beautiful bouquets presented to me—I am very happy to think that a good sum of money was realized by the concert, all of which will be distributed among the poor of the surrounding districts.[10]

As for Patti's curtailing engagements at this time, Klein understood the main reason:

> The watchful and expert observer could alone perceive the significance of the modifications that were now taking place. So slow, so gradual, were they as to be almost imperceptible. . . . An extra breath here and there; a transposition of a semitone down or maybe two, fewer excursions—and those very "carefully" managed—above the top line of the treble staff; some diminution of resonant power or of sustained vigor in the higher

medium notes—what were these, after all, but trifles when one could still derive so much pleasure from the superlative qualities that Patti, and Patti alone, possessed?[11]

Klein then wrote: "The critics, of course, observed these things; but, showing creditable delicacy and consideration, either passed them by or touched upon them so lightly that little reservations almost escaped attention. They emphasized only what could still be admired."[12] British music-lovers were notoriously reluctant to let their favorites retire.

Among the rare presentations at the Patti Theatre were a performance of *La traviata*, on 16 October 1899, in honor of the baron, who had never seen his wife in opera; a memorial service for Queen Victoria after her death in 1901; and a program on 31 July 1903 for members of the British Medical Association for whom the diva had arranged a reception.

Then for a time Patti proposed to sell Craig-y-Nos. On 7 January 1901, she wrote to Alfredo Barili: "We intend to sell the Castle—not on account of health . . . but as we wish to spend a great part of each year in Sweden with my husband's parents."[13] Another plan was to live closer to London. No one, however, offered a sufficient amount for the estate at the sale on 18 June 1901, and the option was withdrawn.

Primarily responsible for these changes was Patti's young husband, whose influence gradually extended over every facet of her life, even affecting her views on people she had known for years. Apparently he did not care for many of her friends or sycophants, who were then no longer welcome at Craig-y-Nos. Houseguests were generally only family members, hers and his. He soon instituted economic measures at the estate, reducing, for example, the number of staff inside the castle until it numbered a mere eighteen. He liked to be on the continent and arranged for their winter months in Italy, the Riviera, or Biarritz (after Christmas at Craig-y-Nos) and summer and early fall months in Sweden, Switzerland, France, or Germany to attend music festivals.

In a letter to Alfredo Barili, written on 4 August 1901 from the Fahrens Villa near Saltsjöbaden, Sweden, Patti described some experiences she had recently enjoyed:

After a 3 weeks stay at Schinznach, we went to Lucerne, where we had a most delightful time, taking long excursions every day—Can you imagine *me* going up the Rigi, Mont Pilatus, and the Bürgenstock, and other similar places? We were well rewarded for our courage in going up those perpendicular heights, for the view from the top is simply beyond description— I never could have imagined the magnificence and immensity of it all, unless I had seen it with my own eyes—From Lucerne we went to Bayreuth for the "Ring" performances—We also heard "Der fliegender Hollander" [*sic*] and "Parsifal." I must confess I was *greatly* impressed by "Parsifal," in fact, I think it was the most perfect thing I ever saw—The scenery was grand, and the staging beyond reproach, and I cannot find words to express the beauty of the last act.[14]

Patti ended this letter delineating plans for the near future: "We are now here comfortably installed in our Villa since the last three days, and we expect to remain here until the beginning of September, when we shall return to England, as my concert tour commences the first week in October."[15]

Their trips to Sweden, a country Patti had not visited before, gave her opportunities to become acquainted with her husband's mother, father, two brothers, and three sisters. Of these she particularly enjoyed the company of Gustaf Cederström, the baron's brother who, when twenty-four, had served as best man at her wedding. She often extended him invitations to visit and to remain with them for lengthy periods. In time, an affectionate relationship evolved with Patti's becoming increasingly protective of him and his interests. When in the spring of 1902 he announced plans for marriage, she responded with this advice:

Your letter bringing the news of your engagement, has, as you can well imagine, been a great surprise to me—I need scarcely point out to you that it is a *very* serious step for you to contemplate marrying without any money on either side, and entering into an engagement which may last a great many years before you could make a home for your fiancée—I only hope and *pray* that later on you may not regret what you are doing, and feel that you acted rashly in taking a step without more consideration—At the same time, I must assure you that, whichever way you decide the matter, it will not affect my feelings of friendship and affection towards you, only I want you

229

to do what will bring you happiness and not to hastily rush into an engagement which might prove disastrous to you and the lady you wish to marry.[16]

Later she again advised Gustaf not to marry without sufficient funds: "Do not marry in poverty, for that is *real* condemnation and misery."[17] By the fall of 1903, his engagement had ended because of personal and financial matters. On 14 October 1903, Patti assured him he had made a wise decision:

> I write at once to tell you how happy I am to hear that after serious consideration, you have ... come to the very wise decision of breaking off your engagement—I know quite well that it required courage and determination to do this—and I feel very proud of you—In years to come I know that you will be thankful that you have acted in the right way—God bless you—dear Gustaf, and I ... pray that this shadow on your life will soon pass away, and that many years of joy and happiness await you.[18]

Soon after Patti wrote those lines, she and her husband embarked for a tour of the United States.

On 24 February 1903, Patti's new American manager, Robert Grau (younger brother of impresario Maurice Grau), announced her return to the United States in October for a tour of sixty concerts lasting six months. He had obtained that agreement only after protracted and difficult negotiations.

When Grau first proposed this undertaking at Craig-y-Nos, Patti was wholly averse to it. The baron's reaction, however, differed from hers as he was intrigued by the United States, where he had never traveled, and by the large sums she would derive from such a tour. She resisted, however, until Grau raised the ante and played, in his words, a trump card:

> Not only will I pay you $5,000 a night, but I will give you 25 per cent of the gross receipts at each concert in excess of $7,500; also I will pay transportation for your entire party to and from America and will give you a private palace car in America throughout the tour![19]

Grau also said he would deposit 8000 pounds ($40,000) at a London bank as guaranty. (While not personally possessing this sum, he soon amassed it by forming a corporation with various individuals investing money as speculation. A Dr. William E. Woodend invested $70,000. Later there were various court cases concerning incompetent management.) As for her contributions in the arrangement, the diva needed to sing but one aria and one encore in each program's two sections.

Patti agreed to make this tour in part because of a desire to show Cederström around the United States. Later, while there, she wrote to her brother-in-law Gustaf: "Rolf is in the seventh heaven of delight visiting and seeing all that there is to be seen everywhere he goes."[20] Parenthetically, Nellie Melba, according to William Armstrong, said that Patti intended to give her young husband all the proceeds from this venture.

American publicity mills soon churned with news of Patti: her early struggles; incomparable voice; triumphs in concert and opera; associations with the world's elite; life at Craig-y-Nos; her favorite parrots (one of which, named Cooky, customarily fell from his perch in the dark, so Patti had ordered a night-light with which he might see his way back); her wardrobe requiring at least five hundred trunks and evaluated as the largest in the world; her friendship with the Prince of Wales, then King Edward VII, a relationship said not to have been completely platonic; her fabulous jewels; the three marriages; the song "Sweet Adeline," supposedly inspired by her; her endorsements of such commercial items as Pears' Soap, throat remedies, beauty aids, pianos, and Flor de Adelina Patti cigars; her appearance at sixty years of age; the enormous fees she still commanded (one published report was that American theatrical managers Weber & Fields agreed to pay her $13,500 for a single performance in Harlem in November). It was also reported that Patti intended to tour with twenty-one dogs, a goat, and sixty birds and that at each concert she would wear a different gown created by one of France's greatest couturiers. Excerpts from critics' reviews of a program she had given at London's Albert Hall, on 28 May 1903, also appeared in the American press. Mixed with these and other items were such apocryphal old tales as her first having received vocal training from a blind girl and her having sung for and cheered President and Mrs. Lincoln at the White House during the Civil War.

Meanwhile, demands for admissions to the first two New York concerts were so great that Grau arranged for a third one. Many of those clamoring for admissions had never heard or seen Patti, whose last New York appearance had occurred nine years before. They may have anticipated more vocally than she at sixty could deliver.

After arriving in New York on 31 October, the diva granted interviews to reporters. Mme. Adelina Patti-Caux-Nicolini-Cederström, as she was dubbed in one New York daily, insisted that this was indeed her farewell tour: "This is the first and only farewell tour which I have ever made. On my last tour here the notices read that it was my farewell, but I did not authorize any such notice. This tour, however, is my authorized farewell to the American public."[21]

Patti allowed little time before her first New York concert on 2 November. Its critical reception would thereafter affect box-office revenues. Never a good sailor, she had spent most of the trip in her stateroom, as the weather was unusually rough. The baron, too, had rarely gone on deck. Years later, Grau recalled that the afternoon of the first concert, Patti seemed tired, highly strung, and somewhat hoarse and that despite his advice to cancel, she resolved to appear that evening. He felt that she had cast away old precautions and that she was then in the United States only for cash.

Hours later the audience filled Carnegie Hall, an assemblage, wrote Klein, that was "a new public—and essentially a critical one" and that "could enjoy brilliant *coloratur* and elegant *nuances,* but raved far more loudly over opulence of vocal tone and strenuous (Wagnerian) declamation."[22] To such an audience the evening's old-fashioned miscellaneous program offered little appeal except for one overriding factor: Patti's presence on stage. Assisting her at this concert were vocalists Wilfred Virgo, Kathleen Howard, and Claude A. Cunningham; instrumentalists Vera Margolies, Roza Zamels, and Anton Hegner; and Romualdo Sapio as conductor. These participants hardly mattered, however. The audience awaited Patti.

When she finally appeared onstage, the house exploded in a fusillade of welcome. After the tumult subsided, Patti, apparently quite nervous, launched into one of her old warhorses: "O luce di quest'anima" from *Linda di Chamounix.* As an encore, she sang "The Last Rose of Summer." Later in the program she offered "Il bacio" and, after several recalls, "Home, Sweet Home" and a song written for her: "The Last Farewell." Though she received sufficient

123 Patti months before her third marriage, 1898. Courtesy Stuart-Liff.

124 Baron Rolf Cederström—Patti's third husband—was twenty-eight and she almost fifty-six when they married in 1899. Courtesy Stuart-Liff.

125 Patti, an animal lover, with a favorite dog. She taught one of her parrots to shriek "Cash! Cash!" whenever impresario J. H. Mapleson entered the room, and she counseled grandniece Louise Barili: "Never marry a man who hates animals—he must be a brute!" Courtesy Stuart-Liff.

126 Karin Cederström (left), sister of the baron; Baron Rolf Cederström; Patti; and Karoline Baumeister in Sweden in 1901. Courtesy Carin Cederström Ekelöf.

127 Patti, Baron Cederström, and chauffeur in a new motorcar that Patti said flew up the hills. Courtesy Carin Cederström Ekelöf.

128 Craig-y-Nos domestics, who in Nicolini's day numbered over forty. Giacomo Longo stands at the left; Patro, whom Patti acquired before the Civil War and in angry moods would threaten to sell, sits in the second row at left; and Karoline Baumeister is the woman with the hat in the third row. The photograph was taken in the early 1900s. Courtesy Brecknock Museum/David Brinn.

129 Patti and Jean de Reszke at Mont Dore, July 1903. Courtesy Carin Cederström Ekelöf.

130 Patti in a 1903 publicity photo for her American concert tour of that year.
Courtesy Carin Cederström Ekelöf.

131 Patti and Baron Cederström standing on her private railway car, Los Angeles, January 1904. Giacomo Longo and Karoline Baumeister stand in front of the car. Courtesy Carin Cederström Ekelöf.

132 Alfredo Barili, Jr. Courtesy Mary Barili Goldsmith.

133 Viola Barili, second daughter of Alfredo Barili, Sr. As a young woman, she taught at the Barili School of Music and was, like her aunt, a superb mimic. Courtesy Mary Barili Goldsmith.

134 Louise Barili, Patti's favorite niece. It was said that Patti wished to adopt her. Courtesy Mary Barili Goldsmith.

135 Patti (extreme left) greeted by the Mayor and Mayoress of Swansea, Mr. and Mrs. David Harris, at the railway station before her last charity concert in Swansea on 19 September 1907. Courtesy Georgia Department of Archives and History.

136 Patti and Mayor Harris driving through Swansea, 19 September 1907. Courtesy Mary Barili Goldsmith.

applause after each of her offerings, enthusiasm was noticeably lacking.

The following day's critical reviews gave the reason: her singing was disappointing with her voice lacking sweetness, the highest notes reached with effort, occasional false intonation, and a gasping for breath. At the second New York concert, on 4 November, however, she was in better voice: "Her tones sounded fresher and appeared to be more surely under control, fuller in volume, and the voice in its middle portions better in quality than on Monday evening."[23] After a third concert, on 7 November, Richard Aldrich wrote a lengthy article in *The New York Times* about the condition of her voice. He thought it amazing that for a woman nearly sixty-one she sang as well as she did; few singers had ever known such a long career. Still, Aldrich regretted that Patti had determined to undertake this tour, preferring to remember her past greatness:

> The laws of nature are inexorable. Mme. Patti, thanks to the perfection of her art, has been able to postpone their operation longer than most singers have done; but even she cannot defy them. There was certainly cause for wonder at her appearances in New York in the week just past that she could retain and utilize in public even so much of her voice as she did.[24]

Another eminent New York critic William J. Henderson wrote: "Of course, Patti is only a wreck of what she was once; but what a wreck! She has half a dozen tones in her voice that are simply marvellous for a woman of her age. They are full, rich, powerful and entirely youthful in quality."[25] In other comments Henderson was less gracious:

> Her audiences are curious collections of persons who never or very rarely go to hear music of a high order. She occupies much the same position in the world of art as Sousa's band.... All of which is a pity, for Patti was in her time the greatest singer that ever lived. She ... deliberately pandered to low tastes and cultivated cheap sensationalism. Her singing of parlor ballads, which genuine artists avoid, is a piece of cheap clap-trap which puts her outside the pale of serious criticism. She sings them well, to be sure.... Let it be added in conclusion of these remarks that the lady's demeanor on the concert stage was extremely undignified. To see a woman of sixty in a blonde wig trying to ogle an audience and play kittenish tricks is far from edifying.[26]

Despite these critical reviews the Patti name still attracted large audiences. Box-office receipts for the three Carnegie Hall concerts totaled $25,000. Philadelphia, on 9 November, gave Patti a $13,800 house, with her share being $7200. Concerts in Boston and Baltimore later that month also drew well.

A return to New York for a fourth concert, on 27 November in Harlem, provided quite a different financial story. It occurred at the West End Theater on 125th Street and Eighth Avenue, a playhouse managed by Joseph Weber and Lew Fields. A man representing her interests discovered a short time before the afternoon concert that there was only $3200 in box-office receipts. According to her contract, the diva needed not sing at any engagement until she had $5000 in hand. Hearing of the Harlem situation by telephone, she made clear there would be no program without this guaranteed sum. When the concert had been delayed for over a half hour, Weber authorized payment of the $5000; he and Fields made up the difference. Patti then proceeded to Harlem in an automobile that may have set a speed record, arriving at the playhouse an hour after the originally announced time. Despite the long delay, the audience received her enthusiastically. This concert marked the last time she sang in New York.

Soon the transcontinental tour began, with Patti traveling in a seventy-two-foot-long Pullman car named Craig-y-Nos, formerly used by Prince Henry of Prussia and President Theodore Roosevelt but then remodeled and refurbished for her. It consisted of a drawing room, also serving as a dining place; separate bedrooms for Patti and her husband; a music room—with a Steinway piano specially constructed for limited space—opening to an observation area almost entirely of glass. Patti also required a private baggage car for her fifty-one trunks. Elsewhere there were accommodations for a Mrs. George Baird, one of Patti's friends; "Karo"; Patti's maid; and her husband's valet, Giacomo Longo. Also attending to her and the baron's needs were a steward, chef, and waiter supplied by the Pullman Company. Such luxurious arrangements epitomized the elegance and comfort of early twentieth-century American travel.

Throughout much of this tour the average box-office total was approximately $7000. Grau later recalled some exceptions: "Patti on tour was still the magnet.... Toronto gave $8,000, Detroit a little more than that sum. Chicago gave $25,000 for two concerts; San

Francisco $35,000. . . . In other cities the receipts averaged close to $7,000."[27] She thus made a great deal of money, but Grau's expenses were considerable.

In letters to her husband's brother Gustaf, the diva expressed pleasure in her successes during December and January. From St. Louis, on 19 December, she wrote:

> You will be pleased to hear that grand success is following me everywhere we go—and that the Americans are *exceedingly* enthusiastic—Money is flowing in rapidly and if all goes well until the end, I shall have had a most brilliant season. I sang here last night to a nine thousand dollar house, which is considered enormous in St. Louis.[28]

In another letter to Gustaf, from Seattle on 22 January, Patti wrote:

> I sang here last night to an immense house—The enthusiasm was enormous—and at the end, after having sung several encores, and bowed my thanks over 7 times, I was obliged to come out again in my fur cloak. . . . It is always the same enthusiasm everywhere we go.[29]

Not long before this Seattle engagement the diva had enjoyed similar success in San Francisco, the scene of many of her past opera triumphs. Just prior to the first program there, Patti, interviewed by a *Chronicle* reporter, commented on critics of her voice:

> I do not read unpleasant things. The papers I do not read. In a general way, I know that many of the critics have been very severe. They contend that because I have been singing for fifty years the volume is closed. The people who say this do not understand me. Mark this—when you hear me to-morrow evening you will not hear a vibration in my voice; you will understand every word I say—a detail not observed by the later singers, and you will hear that the quality of my tones remains unchanged. I would like to know who also at 60 can do that; surely not any of the unfriendly critics.[30]

The second subject she commented on related to her age and that of her husband: "The public concerns itself with my age and his—quite naturally. Well, we are not absurd together. . . . He is 33, but truth to tell, I am younger than he is. For a fact, I can outwalk him now."[31] Receipts for the two San Francisco concerts amounted to $35,000 with the house full on both occasions. The local press observed the extreme enthusiasm of her auditors.

A later concert in Atlanta may have given her the greatest pleasure, since her nephew Alfredo Barili and his wife, Emily, lived there. As for their children in 1904, Louise was 24, Viola 21, and Alfredo, Jr., 17. Over the years Patti had materially assisted these relatives and sent, for example, a check for 100 pounds ($500) each Christmas. She was soon helping to defray college expenses for Alfredo, Jr., studying architecture at Columbia University. She also paid for the elder Alfredo's seven trips to and from Craig-y-Nos and for Louise on the five occasions she visited there. Letters from Patti to these relatives—there are many—reflect her interest in their activities and her devotion. She called Alfredo, Sr., "the only *real, good boy*" in her family.

While she experienced many pleasurable moments during these peregrinations, there were times affording few or none at all. "The work," Patti admitted, "was enough to kill anyone—as we seemed to be always en route—Sometimes travelling for three days and nights without stopping, then arriving to give a concert, and start again immediately afterwards."[32] Occasionally because of insufficient box-office receipts, concerts were canceled. One painful incident occurred in Philadelphia on 24 February at a return engagement there. William Armstrong recalled it with indignation and regret:

> During the tour I had occasion to go to Philadelphia, where the day previous a disgraceful scene had transpired at the Academy of Music. Not enough tickets being sold for the Patti concert, it was postponed; failing to get their money back at the box-office, some started a riot.
>
> Going to Madame Patti's hotel, I learned that she was ill in bed, but saw Baron Cederström. When I expressed deep regret at the Academy of Music incident, he answered smilingly, "But *we* did not lose anything." That was his point of view; there was another.[33]

After a concert at Hot Springs, Arkansas, on 8 March, the diva abruptly decided to cancel all remaining dates, ostensibly because of fatigue. She returned the $40,000 guaranty for her final eight appearances. From Hot Springs Patti went directly to New York, where she and the baron boarded, on 12 March 1904, the Cunard Line steamship *Lucania* for Europe. Some estimated that she had realized more than $200,000 from this final American tour.

William Armstrong, visiting Patti the previous day, heard her constantly say she was happy to be going home. This effusiveness and forced gaiety masked, in his opinion, hurt feelings. "She was," he wrote, "as a queen who had returned to her own country, where once all had worshipped her, only to find pitifully few subjects loyal."[34] She must have realized that her career as a singer was ebbing away.

For weeks Patti rested at Craig-y-Nos, occasionally remaining there without the baron. In late spring, he went to Sweden to visit relatives and to comfort his mother, whose physical condition constantly concerned him. Late in June, Patti and the baron journeyed abroad to take the waters at Mont Dore, and in August, they attended performances at Bayreuth, where she especially enjoyed *Tristan und Isolde*, "all *too* lovely and poetic for anything." Not all, however, had pleased her; she said that "one must get accustomed to the *wonderful* lot of screaming," which had made her "jump a little" off her seat.[35] In Bayreuth, Wagner's widow, the formidable Cosima, entertained the baron and baroness at Villa Wahnfried.

Returning to Wales early in September, Patti made arrangements for her annual provincial fall tour. This time the baron drove from city to city in a new and luxurious automobile, while she traveled by private saloon car so that she might rest between programs. Patti concluded her tour with a concert at London's Albert Hall on 17 November, an affair for Father Bernard Vaughan's charity benefiting poor children. By this date, she had agreed to return to St. Petersburg, after an absence of twenty-seven years, for a concert on 14 December 1904 to aid wounded Russian soldiers fighting in the war with Japan. Though the trip there was daunting, Patti resolved to go: "The journey seems so awfully long—but as it is for the poor wounded soldiers, it is best not to complain."[36]

Grand Duke and Duchess Vladimir, uncle and aunt of Czar Nicholas II, had invited the baron and baroness to be their guests from 12 to 17 December in their St. Petersburg palace. Son of Czar Alexander II, Grand Duke Vladimir had first heard Patti during her initial seasons at St. Petersburg, beginning in 1869. He never forgot those performances, and as President of the Academy of Fine Arts, he eagerly awaited her return to the city that had seen some of her greatest triumphs.

On the day of arrival in St. Petersburg, Grand Duke André and several ladies-in-waiting were among others receiving Patti and her husband at the railway station. Moments later the Grand Duke and Duchess Vladimir welcomed them at their palace, having come from Tsarskoe Selo for the occasion. Magnificent receptions followed, all in honor of the diva, who said she had never known such excitement.

Two evenings after her return to Russia, Patti sang in concert before an assemblage consisting of the diplomatic corps, the capital's aristocrats, the Imperial Family, Czar Nicholas II, and Czarina Alexandra. Years later, Russian Princess Bariatinsky recalled the diva as she appeared that December evening:

> She was a little woman, with refined and delicate features, but with very dark eyes that shone with great brilliancy out of her thin face, which was so well enamelled that it looked quite natural. Her dress was of the fashion of 1870, and she resembled nothing so much as a dainty piece of Dresden china.[37]

Of this concert, Patti wrote:

> It would take me days to write about the ovation the Russian people gave me when I sang for the poor wounded soldiers and about the reception given in our honor and all the beautiful presents and photos given me by all the Imperial family— During the Concert the G. D. presented me a magnificent solid gold laurel wreath . . . and the Duchess gave me her portrait in a lovely gold and red enamel frame with her initials in diamonds on the top. By a clever contrivance these initials can be removed and worn as a brooch.[38]

This concert realized $37,000, all of which benefited Russia's wounded soldiers. After this affair, Patti received the Russian Croix Rouge Order.

A few days later Patti and Cederström left St. Petersburg. At the railway station several grand dukes saw them off, assisting the diva in entering her private saloon car. As the train started, thousands shouted good-bye and waved handkerchiefs while heavy guns thundered a final salute.

Soon after new year 1905, she and the baron traveled to Paris and then to Rome, where they stayed for a considerable time at the Grand Hôtel du Quirinal. At some social gatherings there, Patti likely shocked those in attendance by smoking little cigarettes. Once while so indulging, she carelessly set alight a veil she was wearing; fortunately the baron quickly extinguished the flame. After a short stay at Craig-y-Nos in April, they rented a house in London for the season, on Wednesdays and Fridays attending performances at Covent Garden. Later they again went abroad, taking the cure at Mont Dore and Carlsbad, and remained on the continent until the end of August. While abroad, Patti wrote of a great recent tribute: the French Legion of Honor. In a letter from Mont Dore, written on 10 July, her husband's thirty-fifth birthday, she acknowledged his brother Gustaf's congratulations:

> Let me thank you ever so much for congratulating me "pour la Légion d'Honneur" conferred upon me by the President of the Republic—an honor which I feel *exceedingly* proud of—I am at present the only woman possessing it—& I can assure you nothing could have given me greater pleasure than this proof of esteem & consideration from the . . . French nation.[39]

Also at Mont Dore, Patti met Jean de Reszke, for several years retired from opera and then serving as a vocal teacher whose pedagogical skills had impressed her when she had listened to lessons from an adjoining room in his Paris home. Patti confessed to De Reszke that she was having trouble producing upper notes, and he assured her that his method of singing would alleviate the problem. De Reszke recommended one of his advanced pupils, a Miss Florence Stevens, who was well-versed in his teachings and who, he thought, would be willing to travel to Craig-y-Nos for lessons. Early in August, his wife wrote this young woman a letter explaining the situation. At first, Stevens was incredulous that she was being asked to teach Patti but, reassured by a second letter from Mme. de Reszke, accepted the challenge. Stevens subsequently gave her impressions of the diva in a letter to her mother:

> Patti is a darling. She looks and acts like a girl. . . . Her voice, of course, is wonderful, but some of the muscles are weak and it is for that, I suppose, that de Reszke sent me here. He is sure his method will help her and I think it will. . . . She is so impatient about her work. It is so funny, yet she does try so hard. She

doesn't believe in getting up in the morning and says I should stay in bed until 9 and then dress very quietly. She doesn't approve of any violent exercise . . . nothing . . . but a good walk every day which lasts an hour. Then to bed at 10, eat lots of oysters, but don't let anything ruffle or disturb you. Keep everything unpleasant far from you.[40]

Stevens also confided to her mother that Patti possessed two sets of eyeteeth, which probably provided the basis of a story that her smile was Dracula-like and the reason she never showed her teeth in photographs. Later, on a short provincial tour, Patti wrote to Stevens, saying that her singing had benefited immensely from the lessons. Word subsequently got out about this coaching, much to the diva's chagrin.

After this tour Patti went to Paris, having agreed to sing there at a charity concert on 14 November. Appearing on the same program was young American violinist Albert Spalding, who years later recalled this occasion organized by the famous actor Renolt Constant Coquelin and featuring various celebrities as well as Édouard Colonne's orchestra.

At the affair Patti, aware that Spalding's piano accompanist was missing, interceded on his behalf, summoning the young violinist to her dressing room. Here he found the diva, her face heavily enameled, looking like "an animated wax figure lent by Madame Tussaud for the afternoon."[41] She immediately wanted to know whether he would be willing to perform without rehearsal. That Spalding assured her would be no problem. Patti then kindly offered him the assistance of her own accompanist. His pieces subsequently went exceedingly well, followed by enthusiastic recalls.

As for Patti's presentations, Spalding said he would never forget them. Her singing of "Voi che sapete," an aria that lay in the middle range of her voice, deeply affected him; but the later rendition of another favorite of hers, "Il bacio," with its extensive range, scales, roulades, amazed him more for what he saw than for what he and the audience heard. Spalding described an unusual performance:

> When she approached a passage where she apprehended difficulty, or perhaps disaster, she employed her fan with telling results. She would start the scale or arpeggio with aplomb, the fan in her outstretched arm slowly unfolding. This would continue to the register beyond which lay danger. Then, with a

sudden gesture, the arm would fly up, the fan snapped shut with a click, the audience would burst into a tumult of applause drowning out both orchestra and voice, and triumph greeted a *fioritura* or a high note that was never heard.[42]

In early December, Patti returned to Craig-y-Nos, where she faced one of the greatest challenges in her career. Employees of the Gramophone Company were coming to record her voice.

Although in past years representatives of various talking machine companies had tried to persuade Patti to record, she had resisted all advances, considering the gramophone a toy. Despite the fact that by 1905 such artists as Caruso, Tamagno, Calvé, and Melba had made records, Patti still declined. The Gramophone Company's English manager, Sydney Dixon, nonetheless persisted. He arranged for her to listen to several recordings while she was in London for an Albert Hall concert on 10 November. What Dixon played at her hotel then included records by De Lucia and Caruso. He finally enticed Patti to agree to a contract provided that the records she made satisfied her. Arrangements for recording were left to her solicitor, Sir George Lewis, who stipulated that the recordists were to go to Craig-y-Nos with all the necessary machinery and to have the apparatus in readiness for the precise moment she deemed appropriate.

Back at Craig-y-Nos, Patti feared the inevitable. Waiting with her were the baron and his brother Gustaf, who, on leave from the Swedish military, had joined them for the Christmas holiday. In early December Fred Gaisberg and his brother Will were dispatched to record Patti, and upon their arrival, they displayed admirable patience:

> When my brother and I went to Craig-y-Nos Castle we travelled by a narrow gauge railway to Penwylt [*sic*]. . . . Here a bus met us and we drove to the sombre and imposing edifice where the singer lived. There we were greeted at the door by her agent, Mr. Alcock, and his wife. . . . I heard later that when my brother and I arrived Madame instructed her friend, Mrs. Alcock, to take a peep at these two suspicious characters and report to her what they were really like. When Mrs. Alcock returned and said we

looked like harmless young men, she said, "Well, look after them well." . . .

We soon discovered that every provision had been made for receiving us: two large bedrooms had been cleared and were placed at our disposal. Here we assembled our recording machine. We had a curtain over one of the doors, and through a hole projected the recording-horn. The piano was placed on wooden boxes and when Madame Patti entered the room she was terribly intrigued as to what was behind that long horn. She had the curiosity of a girl, and peeped under the curtain to see what was on the other side. . . .

Do not imagine for a moment, however, that when we set up the recording machine Madame rushed into the room to sing. Not a bit of it. She needed two full days to get used to the idea, during which she simply looked in every now and again and saw the ominous preparations for immortalising her voice. She did not know whether to be glad or sorry. To reward us for this long wait she would say: "Those two nice gentlemen—let them have champagne for dinner tonight to make up for their disappointment."[43]

Patti selected as her piano accompanist young Landon Ronald, who, though retained by the Gramophone Company to persuade eminent artists to record, had not had a hand in negotiations with her. After his arrival at Craig-y-Nos, Ronald, like the Gaisbergs, awaited her decision to record, a circumstance he related in his memoirs:

Those few days will ever remain impressed on my memory as amongst the happiest I have spent. She was a delightful hostess, and her husband (Baron Cederström) one of the kindest and gentlest of men. She was just a few weeks off sixty-[three], and her voice in a room was still amazing. After dinner she would get me to play her some of *Tristan*, which she had gradually learned to love, and would then, after a little persuasion, just see if she "was in voice." And it was then that she sang divinely—for her husband, her brother-in-law, and myself. We were all quite overcome by her great artistry, and agreed that the records must be made the next morning. She assented, and accordingly at [eleven] o'clock everything was made in readiness for the event. Her first selection was Mozart's famous "Voi che sapete." She was very nervous, but made no fuss, and was gracious and charming to everyone. When she had finished her first record she begged to be allowed to hear it at once. This meant that the record would be unable to be used afterwards, but as she promised to sing it again, her wish was immediately granted.

I shall never forget the scene. She had never heard her own voice, and when the little trumpet gave forth the beautiful tones, she went into ecstasies! She threw kisses into the trumpet and kept on saying, "*Ah! mon Dieu! maintenant je comprends pourquoi je suis Patti! Oh, oui! Quelle voix! Quelle artiste! Je comprends tout!* [Ah! my Lord! now I understand why I am Patti! Oh, yes! What a voice! What an artist! I understand all!]" Her enthusiasm was so naïve and genuine, that the fact that she was praising her own voice seemed to us all to be right and proper. She soon settled down and got to work in real earnest, and the records, now known all the world over, were duly made.[44]

Will Gaisberg's part in those recordings was to supervise the equipment preparing the wax blanks; Fred's part, to direct Patti's movements:

It was an ordeal for her to sing into this small funnel, while standing still in one position. With her natural Italian temperament she was given to flashing movements and to acting her parts. It was my job to pull her back when she made those beautiful attacks on the high notes. At first she did not like this and was most indignant, but later when she heard the lovely records she showed her joy just like a child and forgave me my impertinence....

She had a large and noble heart, but was decidedly temperamental; she would be calling everyone "darling" one minute and "devil" the next. But perhaps a woman who had sacrificed so much for her art and for her friends and relatives could be forgiven all these outbursts of temper....

I have always instinctively felt that Patti was the only real diva I have ever met—the only singer who had no flaws for which to apologise. No doubt she had so mastered the art of living and protecting herself from the public gaze that she could plan her appearances for just those moments when she was at her freshest and brightest.[45] ... I noticed that she never overtaxed herself, and her appearances were only for short periods of an hour, two or three times a day.... She was very devout, and I was told she offered prayers in her beautiful private chapel to her patron Saint for the success of the records. From 11 to 12 o'clock in the morning for four days in succession we made the records.[46]

Among songs Patti recorded were "The Last Rose of Summer," "Comin' thro' the Rye," "Kathleen Mavourneen," and "Home, Sweet Home" and from opera the arias "Voi che sapete" (*Le nozze di Figaro*), "Batti, batti" (*Don Giovanni*), and "Air des bijoux" (*Faust*). In all she recorded some twenty sides while also including a message to the baron, intending it only for his ears.

In a letter to Alfredo Barili, Patti expressed pleasure in this new experience:

> You will be pleased to hear that I have been singing in a Gramophone & that it all has turned out satisfactorily—my voice & phrasing come easy & simply perfect out of the instrument & I think the company will make a fortune.... I have received a splendid deposit.[47]

Test-pressings of these records bear the rubber-stamped date 18 December 1905. According to Dixon, Patti heard some or perhaps all of them at Craig-y-Nos the following day; but it was probably eleven days later that she chose fourteen discs for publication. After having been processed and pressed in Hanover, the records were ready for sale on 8 February and were greatly publicized. They featured an endorsement by Patti from a letter she had written to the directors of the Gramophone Company, in which she said that the records had faithfully reproduced the sound of her voice. Sales soon boomed on discs carrying the "Patti label" in pink, her favorite color, and priced at a high twenty-one shillings. The sales warranted another recording session, to take place in June 1906, with Alfredo Barili as piano accompanist.

Barili and his daughter Louise arrived at Craig-y-Nos on 7 April. Before then, Patti had written to Louise of her longing to see them:

> Though I have *so* many dear friends, nothing can make up for one's own relations--I sometimes feel quite lonesome for something belonging to me! Uncle often says, when I express that sort of feeling to him—"Well! What am I? . . . Am I not everything to you?" Yes, but that is *not* the same thing—Of course, my darling Rolf is a dear, & there is *no one* like him—but what the Italians call "*I legami di sangue* [bonds of blood]" is *quite* a different thing, & I feel that owing to my mother's side, if ever so little, there must be something of that kind between you & me![48]

Patti proposed that Alfredo and family should move to London, so that they would be "near one another & never part until our Father above calls us." She hoped that event would be "as late as possible."[49]

Soon after the Barilis' arrival, Louise wrote a lengthy letter to her mother, stating that their reunion was overpowering, Patti being the most excitable person imaginable. Louise thought the diva had aged, not in appearance but in her ways. That evening after dinner Louise heard her aunt's records:

> I must say I was bitterly disappointed with all the numbers except "Voi che sapete." How unsatisfactory it is that when you want a thing in a high key it alters the tempo so that things go at a terrific speed; and to lower it everything must drag. Still it is very wonderful, though not artistic.[50]

Louise subsequently commented that these and later records were but faint shadows of her aunt's singing, though they did show "the marvelous agility and execution of her voice."[51]

Louise also noted changes at Craig-y-Nos. Several concerned individuals long associated with the estate. Karoline Baumeister had departed the past November after having been in Patti's service for some forty years. Apparently the baron had urged Patti to let her go. Another old retainer, Patro, had become so weak-minded that the diva contemplated the possibility of a nursing home for her. Louise observed such other changes as improvements both inside and outside the estate. Uncle Rolf's new library, she said, was most attractive while the grounds seemed more beautiful than ever.

As for the proposed move to London, Louise believed it not possible, confiding this in a letter to her mother: "I am sorry to tell you there is nothing definite as to the London proposition and must say both Uncle Rolf and Aunt Adelina act like a couple of infants in regard to this question."[52] Ultimately Alfredo decided against any relocation despite his aunt's pleas to the contrary.

The following weeks passed pleasantly enough except for a period in early May when the baron's mother's health took him to Sweden and when both Barilis were quite ill, all of which depressed Patti.

In June, Fred Gaisberg with an assistant traveled to Craig-y-Nos for the second recording session. At this time the diva, accompanied by Alfredo, made nine records, with some titles she had previously recorded. The new titles included the song "La calesera" and the arias "Casta diva" (*Norma*), "Connais-tu le pays?" (*Mignon*), and "Ah, non credea mirarti" (*La sonnambula*). Of this recording session, Louise said:

> The facilities for making the records were crude.... Aunt Adelina stood on a small movable platform which, for shading, was moved toward or away from the recording machine. As this was done while my aunt was singing, it made her very nervous. Father, too, was agitated, because he had to play with the piano elevated, high up, on boxes. Papa was told not to do any shading, as it would not record, but he could never play mechanically.[53]

Later Gaisberg made some observations about Patti and his second Craig-y-Nos experience:

> To see her, one was amazed that such a slight wisp of a woman could have exerted such tremendous influence over a vast audience, simply by her singing. She was always *belle soignée* and so carefully groomed that one could see no trace of any grey in her hair. . . .
>
> I and my assistant, Charlie Scheuplein, had meals with Mr. and Mrs. Alcock, and their conversation was mostly about the lively entertainments and gaiety of Craig-y-Nos when Signor Nicolini was alive. Operas and concerts were staged in the small private theatre and the two often appeared in the famous love-scenes from the operas. It seems that altogether Nicolini was keenly alive and kept the diva continually amused and entertained. The Alcocks contrasted those days with the sober and slow tempo of the Cederström régime.
>
> I can imagine that at the time of my visit life tucked away in the Welsh hills must have been somewhat dull for the little lady. She quite obviously welcomed the diversion of having her voice recorded and she was determined to enjoy it to the limit, although it must have entailed a lot of extra work to her establishment. She frequently looked in on us and seemed happy in exchanging conversation and watching us at our work.
>
> She was always sending us grapes from the big green-houses, and when we left she loaded us with a basket of choice fruit for our return journey to London.[54]

Shortly before this second session, Fernando de Lucia had expressed a desire to record some opera duets with Patti. Nothing, however, evolved in this respect. De Lucia's biographer, Michael

Henstock, theorized that insufficient time had precluded such an arrangement.

J. B. Steane in his *The Grand Tradition: Seventy Years of Singing on Record* evaluates Patti's recordings, observing her vocal limitations at the age of sixty-two and sixty-three while at the same time lauding what remained of her voice.

In noting faults, Steane refers to four selections: "Comin' thro' the Rye," "Batti, batti," "Casta diva," and "The Last Rose of Summer." He cites such shortcomings as snatched breaths, scrambled or missing notes, broken phrases, simplified fioriture, light aspirates, scooping, and overly loud assaults on some notes. Steane maintains that what spoils these records is not the condition of her voice nor the primitive recording techniques; instead, he finds "certain features of Patti's style at this date simply ... not musical."[55] Still, there is, according to this critic, much to be valued and enjoyed, such as a "brightly energetic voice ... a most beautiful and distinctive tone to be heard in the middle register ... the trill ... of unrivalled grace and delicacy."[56] Of her singing of the aria "Connais-tu le pays?" from *Mignon*, he writes:

> Some exquisite phrases in this bring us close to the sound that charmed so many audiences for so many years. At the line *"Où la brise est plus douce et l'oiseau plus léger"* she uses the lightest of tones that still has the glow of a gentle warmth. In the last phrase—*"C'est là que je voudrais vivre"*--this soft, perfectly supported sound is allowed freedom to linger; one can, for a few bars, hear the famous voice without flaw.[57]

In comparing her rendition of "Ah, non credea mirarti" from *La sonnambula* to that of five other eminent singers—including Tetrazzini, Callas, and Freni—Steane considers hers the most richly varied performance, with swift turns and a flawless trill—"perhaps the most finely grained of all, and it came naturally as a part of the main flow of tone, not as a specially added ornament."[58] Perhaps the recording of Antonio Lotti's song "Pur dicesti" best displays the Patti trill. It is "a triumph of interpretation ... perfectly and flawlessly recorded."[59] Steane also praises her singing of "Air des bijoux" from *Faust* and the Spanish song "La calesera." The recording of this Spanish number, according to Sackville-West and Shawe-Taylor, is

> sensationally brilliant; the singer might be in the room, so powerfully does her voice ring out—not to mention the excitable

Spanish screams which irritated her husband . . . and perhaps led to the cancellation of this famous record a few months after its issue in 1907 (a subsidiary cause may have been that the powerful recording was found to cause blast and wear, as indeed it still can).[60]

Other recordings worthy of praise are "Voi che sapete," "On Parting," Bach-Gounod's "Ave Maria," "La serenata," "Kathleen Mavourneen," "The Banks of Allan Water," and "Robin Adair." These as well as her other recordings are also noteworthy for the clear enunciation of the text whether sung in Italian, French, Latin, Spanish, or English. Numerous singers have been exceedingly careless in this respect, emphasizing tone rather than text. Patti, by contrast, did not sacrifice one for the other.

Michael Scott in *The Record of Singing to 1914* gives a concise summary of the recordings enshrining Patti's art:

Her variety of expression was the result of infinitely refined vocal colouring, the vitality of her interpretations produced by a voice alive to every rhythmic subtlety. Unfortunately much of the brilliance . . . was a thing of the past by the time she came to make recordings. Still her singing remains more affecting in itself than anyone else's on records. In her recordings, we can hear so many of the ancient graces of singing; here are the real portamento style, the elegant turns and mordents, the trill free of any suggestion of mechanical contrivance. . . . Patti's operatic recordings, notwithstanding the all-too-obvious depredations of age, contain many wonderful things; the trill and flourish at the beginning of the Jewel Song has never been executed by any other singer with such elegance and finesse. How perfectly she captures the mood in Thomas's beautiful setting of Mignon's song. Perhaps best of all is the subtle variety of graces and rubato in that most exquisite interpretation of Amina's sleepwalking aria. In the songs we have a recollection of all that was eloquent in the music of the salon.[61]

Not long after the second recording session, Alfredo Barili and Louise left Craig-y-Nos to return to the United States. Patti then intended to end her annual fall provincial tour in the near future and

137 Patti in retirement, 1908. Courtesy Carin Cederström Ekelöf.

138 Patti and Baron Cederström at Carlsbad, where they often went for the waters. Courtesy John W. Booth.

139 Craig-y-Nos, with a view of the limestone outcrops from which the gray stone for the original castle was taken. Courtesy Carin Cederström Ekelöf.

140 An iron bridge below the terraces crossed the Tawe River. Courtesy Carin Cederström Ekelöf.

141 A view from outside the conservatory, with an ornamental fountain at right. Courtesy Georgia Department of Archives and History.

142 The fountain inside the winter garden. Lights of various colors illuminated the jets of water. Courtesy Georgia Department of Archives and History.

143 Craig-y-Nos reception room. Among other works of art it held a favorite painting of Patti's by Manet. Courtesy Carin Cederström Ekelöf.

144 The conservatory overlooked the river, valley, and hills; its long back wall (right) was covered with frescos. It was used as a dining area and for grand receptions. Courtesy Georgia Department of Archives and History.

145 The castle's drawing room, circa 1910. A Winterhalter portrait of Patti (reproduced on the present book's jacket) is on the left wall; Patti's bust stands nearby. On the circular table at rear in front of the wide window sits the casket containing the Freedom of the Borough of Brecon scroll. Courtesy Carin Cederström Ekelöf.

146 The library under Baron Cederström. The Winterhalter portrait of Patti as Rosina hangs over the fireplace. Courtesy Carin Cederström Ekelöf.

147 Patti's chapel, where all members of the Craig-y-Nos household were welcome to worship. Fresh flowers were placed there daily. Courtesy Georgia Department of Archives and History.

148 On occasion, Patti would take up a cue in this French billiard room. She called the electric orchestrion at the back the soul of Craig-y-Nos. Courtesy Georgia Department of Archives and History.

149 Patti and a Mr. Gilbertson at the opening of the Pontardawe Institute and Hall on 6 May 1909. Courtesy John Vivian Hughes.

150 Eleonore and Gustaf Cederström with their children, two-year-old Carin and infant Rolf. Courtesy Carin Cederström Ekelöf.

151 Patti with umbrella standing behind Baron Cederström; Eleonore
Cederström, Gustaf's wife; and Märtha de Geer, the baron's niece, 1912.
Courtesy Carin Cederström Ekelöf.

152 Patti with Märtha de Geer in 1912 at Craig-y-Nos. Courtesy Carin Cederström Ekelöf.

153 One of the last photos of Patti, 1914, with Alfredo Barili, Sr. (left), Louise, and Baron Cederström. Patti's face may be enameled. Courtesy Georgia Department of Archives and History.

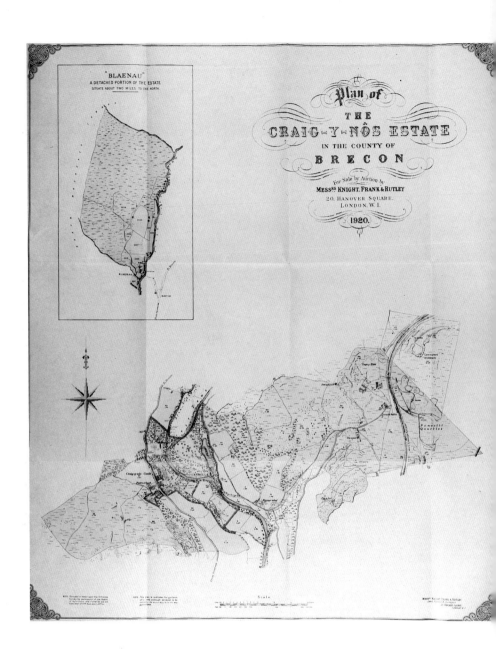

154 A plan of Craig-y-Nos from an advertisement offering the castle for sale after Patti's death on 27 September 1919. Author's Collection.

to let her Albert Hall concert in December be her final professional one in London. The time had come for formal leave-takings, which, of course, saddened her; still, she determined to make the best of this situation, as revealed in a letter to Louise a few days before the London concert:

> When I see, or even write the word farewell it always gives me a sort of grip at my heart. I really ought not to be so sad over it all— ... retirement should be a blessing. *Mais tout-de-même le mot "Adieu" est terrible* [But all the same the word "farewell" is terrible]—However, ... my farewell will after all only be to strangers, & not to my friends—so there is somewhat of a consolation in that![62]

Patti had found her annual concert tour more and more onerous. The one in the fall of 1906 was no exception:

> If you only knew how I *hate* this knocking about from place to place just like Barnum's menagerie, only I must confess that the immense success which awaits me everywhere I go is a very great recompense & shall remain engraved in my heart as long as I live.[63]

Soon after the end of this tour, Patti went to London to give her final professional concert at Albert Hall on 1 December 1906, an event that caused her exceptional emotional distress. In an interview published in the 24 November 1906 issue of *The Graphic,* she said:

> Professionally ... I am retiring, and my decision is irrevocable. After December there will be no more Patti concerts in London, and after next autumn there will be no more provincial tours. Am I sorry? Of course I am. My friends are so kind, and I love singing to them. The *tournée* which is just over was a brilliant success. The halls were always crowded, the audiences were always enthusiastic, and I think that I sang better than I have sung for years. But I am getting a little tired of it all.[64]

Patti added that she would continue to sing for charity:

> I shall sing for the poor. There is so much that one ought to do for the poor, and though I have always done what I can, I want to do more. Then, too, there are a hundred other things for which I have never had time hitherto.[65]

The musical program was similar to past Albert Hall Patti

249

concerts—a miscellaneous affair with the diva contributing three pieces: "Voi che sapete," "La serenata," and "Il bacio." To these she added several encores, the final one being "Home, Sweet Home." Wilhelm Ganz accompanied her at the piano. Other featured artists included organists H. L. Balfour and H. C. Tonking, vocalists Ben Davies and Ada Crossley, pianist Elsie Horne, and violinist Pablo de Sarasate.

Many of the auditors were hysterical, and floral tributes filled the stage. Patti, always the professional, appeared to mask painful emotions during the farewell performance. Joseph Bennett of the *Daily Telegraph* best summarized her historic importance and this London farewell:

> Will any deny her right to be described as historic? Certainly none who have heard her, year in, year out, for nearly two generations, during which the art that she has so long adorned has undergone something like a complete change, and with it public opinion of it. Yet, in spite of this, the diva has gone on her way, looking neither to the right hand nor to the left, untouched by the transitions of music or musical life, singing largely the music of a by-gone day, yet singing it as she only could sing it. And none, surely, would have it otherwise.
>
> To praise her singing is almost an impertinence, yet not a soul in that vast crowd on Saturday but must have asked himself where, as song after song was delivered, the equal of that singing, the rarest beauty of phrasing, the perfection of the technical command, and the grace and elegance of the style were again to be heard.
>
> One little instance. Will any forget that literally marvellous trill—not in the least like that of the proverbial bird, but a lovely human thing—which Mme. Patti uttered at the close of "Pur dicesti," given as an encore after Tosti's "Serenata"? Whether as the result of the Wagnerisation of the singing art, and the advent of the modern declamatory style, need not be argued; certain it is that to Mme. Patti one had to go—and, alas, can go no longer—to find its possibility.[66]

The day after this concert, Patti and Cederström went to Paris, a change for which she was grateful according to her letter to Louise Barili dated 21 December:

> I cannot begin to tell you how touched I was at the reception I

had at that concert—in fact it was almost more than I could bear—& had Uncle Rolf not taken me away for a complete change I hardly can realize how I should have got through all the fearful emotion.[67]

Perhaps while in Paris, she made plans for an operatic farewell in one of her favorite roles: Rosina. The affair was private, occurring on Saturday, 25 May 1907, at Jean de Reszke's little theater in his Paris residence. Her associates were Giuseppe Anselmi (Almaviva), Mario Ancona (Figaro), Édouard de Reszke (Don Basilio), and Antonio Pini-Corsi (Don Bartolo). The small chorus composed of Jean de Reszke's students included a soprano destined for greatness: Maggie Teyte. Maestro A. Catherine conducted the small orchestra.

During the lesson scene, Patti sang "Voi che sapete" and Tosti's "La serenata." At the end of the opera, festivities went on for hours, she and the baron returning to their hotel at five in the morning. In a letter to Louise Barili dated 27 May, Patti maintained that she had never thought she "could be so full of fun & brightness" as during this performance and that it had been a *"tremendous success."*[68]

On the farewell fall provincial tour, the diva gave seventeen concerts and received grand receptions and ovations that she said were heartening.[69] On 20 October, however, Patti wrote of sad news she had received while in Newcastle-on-Tyne:

> Our tour so far has been a tremendous success—crowded houses & great enthusiasm everywhere we have been—... unfortunately joy seems never to be able to continue for long without some ray of sadness—on Thursday morning the day of my concert here, we received a telegram ... announcing the death of poor Patro! ... Poor old soul, she was such a good faithful creature & servant—We shall certainly miss her very much when we go back home.[70]

These travels culminated in a benefit on 29 November 1907 at London's Albert Hall for her longtime manager Percy Harrison. Though other artists contributed their services at this benefit and were well received, the audience reserved its greatest welcome for Patti. Klein noted that familiar scenes were revivified with the audience wildly acclaiming her and that she retained her art and exquisite voice.

With her professional career ending, some thought this a propitious time for Patti to write the autobiography long promised; but she quickly expressed her reservations:

> For many years past my friends all over the world have been urging me to write my reminiscences. In truth, to them it must seem a very simple thing to sit down at leisure with a pen in one's hand and write of the people one has seen and known, and the experiences one has enjoyed. But to me it is not at all so simple. I fear I should not be content with a mere chronicle of what has happened to me, and how kind the great musical public all over the world has been to me. That would not be enough; I fear I should not stop there. I should want to express my opinions on art—the art that is as dear to me as life itself—to reveal to the world what the experience of sixty years has taught me of the value of our modern musical culture, of critics and criticism, of this or that school of singing. And then what would happen? Some of my friends would be offended at my plain-speaking, and perhaps rebuke me for my temerity. And the critics—ah, what would the critics say?
>
> Supposing I thought that the prevailing fault in musical criticism in the present day is ignorance—that most of the critics cannot discriminate a good singing style from a bad one, how could I tell the world so? How could I say that critics are influenced by what pleases them at the moment, perhaps by a good dinner or by pleasant surroundings? It may be that they do not always stop to reflect that the style of singing they encourage may exert a very evil effect on young vocalists and establish generally a false standard of excellence; and, if so, how could I write and not speak of all this? Whenever I go to hear one of the new school who is so full of *acrobati* and vocal fireworks I really almost feel tempted to say to him or her, "My dear, you have beautiful furniture, you have pretty curtains at the windows, and charming pictures, but, *ma foi,* you have no house to put them all in!" One goes nowadays so often to the opera to be fed on sweets, sweets, sweets! How one longs for something more substantial, for, believe me, in music as in life man cannot live by sweets alone.
>
> I always say to my young friends, not Can you shake? Can you trill? Can you imitate a lark or a mocking bird? but—Can you sing a simple ballad in honest, straightforward fashion, such a ballad, for example, as "Home, Sweet Home"? That is the real test. A great many people think so much rests with the words, the senti-

ment of that song, no matter how it is sung. Of course, association counts for a great deal. But I shall never forget that at
Buenos Ayres [sic] I sang "Home, Sweet Home" to an audience
which did not understand a word of English, yet an audience
with, as I was told afterwards, the tears running down their faces,
and which demanded it again and again.

But, there, you see now some of the difficulties I should have
to surmount in writing my autobiography.[71]

William Armstrong thought of another reason for Patti's deciding
against a full-length memoir: "Her explanation was that too many
people's feelings would be hurt should it be written. Perhaps the real
reason, though, was one on which she had remained silent. Her
memory extended very far back indeed; Cederström was many years
her junior."[72]

From 1908 to 1914, Patti and the baron followed a fixed routine like
the one established early in their marriage: winters after Christmas at
Craig-y-Nos in Italy, Biarritz, or the Riviera; springs in Wales; summers abroad at music festivals and at such watering places as Mont
Dore and Carlsbad; and autumns in Wales. Of course, Craig-y-Nos
remained the anchor of her life, and she stayed there for approximately six months each year. The estate seemed lovelier than ever
with attractive changes both inside and out. Among those she
particularly liked were a new drawing room and, outside, new rose
and rock gardens. The baron, always fond of hunting, took up golf
with a gusto; in July 1909 at Carlsbad he won a prize in this game, and
Patti wrote of it to her brother-in-law Gustaf: "Rolf is as happy as a
child over his first golf prize—I must confess that I also felt proud, for
I know what awful trouble & pain it takes to be able to succeed in that
game."[73]

A domestic at Craig-y-Nos during this period named Ethel
Rosate-Lunn remembered her tenure there as a happy time, extending from 1909 to 1914. The inside staff in those years numbered
eighteen, quite a reduction from former days, and in addition to the
house domestics there were four gardeners in residence and other
day-workers. Rosate-Lunn especially recalled Patti's amicability, her
singing, and Christmases.

The diva's joie de vivre infected those around her. Each day, she took two walks around the grounds or adjoining areas, stopping to greet anyone in her employ or strangers on the road near the estate. Encountering a vagabond on her walks, she invariably offered food from the Craig-y-Nos kitchen. Patti, according to Rosate-Lunn, liked visiting at the cottage of her head gardener and his wife and five children, the Con Hibberts. She also found pleasure chatting and joking with gamekeeper Dai Price.

The baron's occasional absences prompted Patti to arrange evening entertainments involving the staff, which were sometimes fancy-dress affairs with the domestics clothed as they wished and Patti donning one of her opera gowns. Then, to the staff's delight, she would entertain them by singing, dancing, and playing castanets. Rosate-Lunn especially treasured her singing of such ballads as "Comin' thro' the Rye," "The Last Rose of Summer," and "Home, Sweet Home." On these occasions, the baroness would order the butler Giacomo Longo to pop corks, so that they all might imbibe in a glass of champagne or port.

Rosate-Lunn said Christmas at Craig-y-Nos was always joyful. During the day, Patti customarily went to the servants' dining hall to drink a glass of champagne with them, to join in holiday songs, and to extend season's greetings. Other features of this day also impressed Rosate-Lunn:

> There was always a large Christmas tree in the theatre, laden with presents, cheques and jewellery. . . . There was a staff dance on Christmas evening and Madame Patti always danced with the chef, butler and footman, while her husband . . . danced with the head girls.[74]

A special occasion at Craig-y-Nos that Rosate-Lunn did not mention was the visit of Prince Eugène of Sweden and his suite on 28 October 1910. Anticipating it, Patti said that "all the household is excited at the event, & everything is being made ready, pleasant & comfortable for His Highness's arrival."[75] Afterwards she wrote that Prince Eugène and his entourage had seemingly enjoyed their visit, that at His Highness's request she had sung for them, and that everyone at Craig-y-Nos had done everything possible "to make his stay . . . agreeable."[76]

Some months before Prince Eugène's visit, there had been a

period of mourning at Craig-y-Nos following King Edward VII's death on 6 May. Several weeks later, Patti wrote of it to brother-in-law Gustaf:

> We have not yet got over the terrible shock of the King's death! We are all going to the service . . . which is held in the church . . . where poor Patro was buried—The Queen Alexandra sent me a most touching telegram last week in answer to one I sent her of sympathy in her terrible loss.[77]

What increasingly occupied her during this period was family. She drew closer to her only remaining sister, Amalia Strakosch, living in Paris, and to Amalia's son Robert Strakosch; to her nephew Alfredo Barili and family; and, of the Cederströms, to her husband's brother Gustaf.

Patti always looked forward to visiting Amalia and reminiscing about their early lives in the United States—Amalia's memory going back further, of course, than Patti's. What saddened Patti was the state of her sister's health, which gradually weakened. Still, in her late seventies and early eighties, this lady remained a delightful personality. William Armstrong, meeting her in Paris years after Patti's last American tour, enjoyed their conversation and recalled that the

> history of little Adelina was still very fresh in her mind; her varying moods; her constant presence in her mother's dressing-room, for she was too small to be left at home, and her singing even then of the big arias from the old repertory.[78]

In a correspondence dated 22 November 1910, Patti made clear her love of and devotion to her nephew Alfredo and family in a letter to his wife, Emily:

> Nothing gives me greater pleasure than to hear about all his doings, & besides—he is *my* boy! & the only *real*, good boy I have in my family—also, his wife & children are, I can assure you, very dear to me, & my love, very great for them![79]

By then the Barilis owned their first home in Atlanta. Alfredo, Sr., Emily, Louise, and Viola were teaching music in a school under his aegis at the Atlanta YMCA building; Alfredo, Jr., was an aspiring architect, had married, and in August 1913 fathered a son, Alfredo Barili III. These relatives' activities and accomplishments always interested the diva, though Alfredo, Sr., received most of her attention.

At times his commitment to education and composition worried Patti, who, aware of problems with his nerves, counseled him not to work too hard: "*Do, darling* Alfredo, take things in, peacefully & quietly. I am *so* much older than you are, & have found out that this is the only way to get on well in this world." In a similar vein, she advised him not to get himself "too much worked up over those wonderfully clever Americans" and not to "worry too much . . . & only think that all the worry & excitement cannot possibly remediate matters."[80]

The other Barili receiving much of her attention was Louise, apparently at times uncertain as to her aunt's affections though Patti reassured her on that matter:

> I have tried to persuade you of my true & sincere devotion—I am quite sure, you believe me when I say, that I love my dear, sweet darling Louise "*avec toute la force de mon coeur*" . . . I write it in French, as it expresses much more deeply the meaning of the phrase than in old flat English![81]

As in years past, Patti confessed to Louise that she felt increasingly lonely. "*Oh*! how I wish," she wrote to Louise, "you were mine! & how I would thank God for having given you to me!"[82] In another letter, she referred to Louise and her sister Viola, expressing the need to fill a void in her own emotional life:

> I always seem to envy you both, having your Mother, Father, brother—Something belonging to you—& I, besides my husband, only have numerous of strangers [*sic*], people about me, but *nothing* which I could call my own. . . . Sometimes it is *very* sad—especially I, who *cannot* love everybody & pick up strangers—However, I must not complain—many offer sincere friendship & devotion to me, *mais avec tout cela,* it is *never* the same.[83]

Such feelings were momentarily assuaged the spring of 1911, when Alfredo, Sr., and Louise again visited Craig-y-Nos for two months, this his sixth visit and her fourth. Their reunion was joyous, but they found Patti more and more dependent on the baron and extremely emotional whenever he left her to attend to matters in London or to visit relatives in Sweden. At times she complained about physical ailments, complaints which prompted Louise to remark, somewhat facetiously, "Poor thing, she has neuralgia, lumbago, and every known ache."[84] Still, what usually prevailed was her joie de vivre, which Alfredo and Louise enjoyed.

During this period, the diva also lavished attention on her husband's relatives, commiserating with them when the baron's mother died in 1908 and rejoicing with them over Gustaf's marriage in 1911.

She followed Gustaf's military career, vicariously sharing his travels and providing moral support, especially in affairs of the heart. When he finally found the woman of his dreams and announced their engagement, Patti dashed off a note of congratulations on 26 May 1911:

> I am *so* delighted to think you are at last completely happy, & that you have found such a charming sweet companion for your future wife—& you know, how my heart wishes you everything of the *very very* best—God bless you both, & may you thoroughly understand each other, which is the chief thing in married life.— My thoughts & prayers are with you both.[85]

In August, Patti and the baron attended Gustaf's wedding in Stockholm. Among other guests were the Crown Prince and Princess of Sweden. Patti found the ceremony beautiful with all the flowers, toilettes, and jewels.

Early the morning of 10 January 1913, Patti and her husband received a telegram stating that Gustaf's wife, Eleonore, had just given birth to a girl, Carin Eleonore Jeanna Adelina. When they asked the diva to be the baby's godmother, she acquiesced with pleasure and later sent a silver christening cup that Carin throughout her life treasured.

From 1908 to the beginning of 1914, the diva continued to attend opera performances at Covent Garden or abroad and occasionally participated in a charity concert in London or Wales.

Though some leading artists at Covent Garden may have been unsettled by Patti's presence in the audience, one new star was not: Luisa Tetrazzini, who had made a sensational debut there in November 1907. In her autobiography, Tetrazzini wrote that whenever she caught her gaze, the diva "always answered with her sweet and appreciative smile."[86] Tetrazzini referred to the day she was introduced to Patti as "the greatest day"[87] of her life, as she had always worshiped her from afar. Tetrazzini so treasured a letter written by her idol after a performance of *La traviata* on 30 April 1908 that she quoted it verbatim in her memoirs:

Carlton Hotel, London
May 1st, 1908.
My Dear Madame Tetrazzini,
Bravo! Bravo! and again *Bravo!* I cannot tell you how much
pleasure it gave me to hear you last night, and what a joy it was to
me to hear your beautiful Italian phrasing, and how immensely
touched I was by the wonderful feeling and pathos of your voice.
You made me cry in the last act. I should like also to add that in
addition to the phenomenal brilliancy and purity of your high
notes, your beautiful method, your phrasing, the ease and
flexibility of your voice and your acting, all gave me the very
greatest pleasure, and I shall take the first opportunity of going
to hear you again.
I *heartily* rejoice in your well-deserved triumph—Bravo!
Bravo! And again Bravo![88]

Tetrazzini's admiration of Patti was unbounded. Patti's admiration for Tetrazzini, however, was not at such a high level. She
tempered her remarks a month after having written the preceding
letter:

I heard Tetrazzini several times whilst I was in London—I
enjoyed her singing in some things very much & her acting is
charming but . . . I must frankly confess . . . I would not change
my voice today for *any* of the voices I have heard at the present
time.[89]

Patti also attended performances of Wagner's music dramas at
Covent Garden and abroad and shared her impressions with Alfredo
Barili: "What a blessing to be able to love & understand & appreciate
Wagner! . . . Now that I have given up singing in Opera, I find the
greatest of pleasure & happiness in listening to Wagner's music."[90]
Her husband, she said, shared this view: "The Baron and I are both
devoted to Wagner. We never miss a Bayreuth Festival, and Covent
Garden during Wagner-time is one of the joys of our lives."[91]
Eminent contralto Ernestine Schumann-Heink, encountering Patti
at a Bayreuth festival, marveled that even with advancing years she
retained much, if not all, of her old verve and dash and that an aura of
greatness clung to her.
Occasionally during these years, the diva sang at a charity affair
or made an appearance at a public function honoring her. Of these,
perhaps the most memorable were a benefit concert at the opening

of the Pontardawe Institute and Hall on 6 May 1909; a Wilhelm Ganz benefit in London on 1 June 1911; and Swansea's enrolling her as an honorary freewoman of the borough on 20 June. 1912.

Patti's participation at Pontardawe inspired another grand reception by the Welsh, residents celebrating the occasion with colorful decorations, bands, and cheers. "Almost every house," according to the local press,

> flew its flag... and streamers were hung at frequent intervals.... Near the Institute there was an arch of welcome, built in imitation of a castellated Roman gate way.... Over it a Welsh harp glittered in the bright sunshine.[92]

What made the Ganz benefit especially memorable was not only that it honored the musician who for decades had been Patti's accompanist but also that it marked the fiftieth anniversary of her London debut. Another outstanding feature of this affair was her accompanist: nephew Alfredo Barili. Several months before, she had asked him to assist in this undertaking: "Would you care to do so? I feel it would do you a *great* deal of good in your profession & I shall be *so* proud to show you off & make a fuss over my own darling boy."[93] Alfredo had no reason to regret accepting the invitation, for his playing at the benefit was favorably noted. Tetrazzini was in the audience, and mounted the stage after Patti's last song to embrace her. A critic later commented on the diva's appearance, writing that with her many medals and decorations she looked like a field marshal.

Swansea's tribute created tremendous interest, as Patti was the only woman in Great Britain honored by two boroughs. She said that this honor had elated her. In a letter to Gustaf Cederström's wife, Eleonore, on 25 June 1912, Patti wrote:

> I know that you & darling Gustaf will be very pleased to hear that everything went off splendidly—Rolf made a most lovely speech which pleased everybody *immensely*;—I must say that I never saw such enthusiasm in Swansea before—You will see by enclosed . . . what a beautiful Casket I have received. How I wish you could see it, . . . so wonderfully well worked & modelled—I hope that ere this you will have received the paper I sent you & that you will have enjoyed reading all about the great event.[94]

As Swansea's first honorary freewoman, she joined such past

recipients as former Prime Minister William Ewart Gladstone, explorer Henry Morton Stanley, Field-marshall Lord Grenfell, and orator Lord Rosebery.

Patti's plans for the first months of new year 1914 resembled those of the recent past: weeks abroad, this time she and the baron remaining at Cannes. After returning to Wales in early spring, Patti rejoiced in the company of Gustaf and Eleonore Cederström for a brief time. Then in May Alfredo Barili and his daughter Louise arrived from the United States, but their return to Atlanta in mid-July occurred all too soon. When it came, Patti, then seventy-one years old, seemed more emotional than ever, virtually begging Louise to remain. Shortly thereafter she and the baron again went abroad with the destination Carlsbad, where they stayed longer than planned, detained at the spa by forces beyond their control. They finally made their way back to Craig-y-Nos with considerable difficulty. European nations had declared war, fated to be one of the bloodiest in the history of the world; still, it was, many hoped, a war to end wars.

In the following months, Patti did what she could to aid the cause, making a rare appearance at a London concert on 24 October benefiting the war fund, an occasion marking the last time she ever sang in public. She also visited the wounded in hospital wards near Craig-y-Nos; knitted mufflers and working comforts for soldiers and sailors; and gave money to help those in need whose loved ones were at the front. At times her health and the baron's created concern while the death of his father in late 1914 deeply affected her as did her sister Amalia's demise in Paris the following year. Still, Patti redoubled her efforts in the cause of war relief. In a letter dated 14 November 1915, she told Louise Barili her duties were "*so* numerous that days ought to be made double as long, if it were possible for [her] to be able to fulfil all [there is] to do—especially now in the war time . . . busy working for our dear brave soldiers & sailors."[95]

Life at Craig-y-Nos ultimately changed dramatically, with virtually all able-bodied men called to the front and few male workers remaining at the estate. The baron assumed more of the manual and administrative duties. Potatoes and vegetables were being raised where once flower gardens had flourished; and inside, to save light, Patti and the baron breakfasted at eight, lunched at twelve, and dined at seven. They rarely entertained, and only once during these war years were they visited by a family member, Gustaf Cederström, who, in the Swedish military, had been invited by the British government in 1917 to observe war movements of the Allies in France and who thereafter was able to travel to Wales.

Only occasionally did Patti and her husband leave Craig-y-Nos for short stays in London or Brighton. On one of these, she made her final will, signing it in London on 17 March 1917. She left virtually everything to the baron—large sums of money (later estimated at $580,000), stocks and bonds, Craig-y-Nos with its hundreds of acres, household goods, art objects, and jewelry. She bequeathed 4000 pounds to Alfredo Barili, 2000 pounds to Robert Strakosch, 500 pounds to the widow Ellen Burgess, 100 pounds to her butler Giacomo Longo, 600 pounds to her maid Odile Peslier, 200 pounds annually to "Karo" for the rest of her life, and one year's wages to each domestic who had been in service at Craig-y-Nos two years before her death. She also left various items of jewelry, some to Alfred de Rothschild, the Eissler sisters, "Karo," and Mabel Woodford. Finally, she bequeathed a stole worn by Pope Leo XIII to the nephew of the priest Reverend Bernard Vaughan, who had given it to her years before.

Correspondence with the Barilis and Cederströms increasingly contained passages of despair. Death, said Patti, seemed everywhere: "How full the world is of sadness. In every paper one takes up one reads of death of people one knew—It really is the most wicked & terrible war the world has ever seen."[96] In time she wrote that life was "no more the same,"[97] that she and the baron lived in *"complete darkness & misery,"*[98] that they talked of "nothing else the *whole* day long—no more music, no more laughing, nothing but *war,"* and that she more and more felt "sinking & *terribly* tired out."[99] She longed for news from relatives, making this point clear to Gustaf: "At last I get news from Sweden. Eleonore & yourself are the only ones who write—not too often, but you do write to me now & then . . .—In these times of trouble one always likes to hear from those one loves!"[100] On 25 January 1918, her nineteenth wedding anniversary, Patti wrote to Louise: "We shall try & feel happy if possible which I doubt—as this war is *absolutely* finishing me slowly up."[101]

Approximately three months later, Patti's health caused grave concern; she was extremely depressed and nervous, tired easily, and suffered from poor digestion and a weak heart. In another letter to Louise, written on 9 April, Patti confessed that the war and her health had so affected her she wondered whether she would be able to carry on. More and more Patti relied on Cederström while he, she realized, did everything possible to be of help. To Emily Barili, she wrote: "All I can say is that my dear husband has behaved like an angel, & has done all in his power to make the remaining part of my existence as agreeable & peaceful as possible in this infernal time."[102] When doctors advised that his wife needed a change, the baron arranged a short trip to London in early June to get her away from the monotony of Craig-y-Nos and to visit friends who would try to cheer her.

Apparently time in London did little to console Patti, who back at Craig-y-Nos wrote that she felt not only nervous but also enervated and that her past seemed "like a dream now, when we live so quietly & monotonously."[103] Still, when needing reassurance as to glories in that past, she had but to look about her in the drawing room, library, and her boudoir where myriad souvenirs evoked memories of extraordinary experiences. "To see them," William Armstrong said, "was to feel the wonderful romance of her career. And the length of it! Kingdoms had changed to republics and wars wiped out boundaries, but the whole civilized world had continued to give her unswerving allegiance."[104] Armstrong especially recalled some treasures in the drawing room:

> On the floor . . . piled in one corner were silver laurel wreaths, so many in number that no place else could be found to put them; in cabinets were bon-bon boxes of every material, from simple mother-of-pearl to elaborately carved ones of gold, and out of every country; there were engraved gold invitation cards to dinners and banquets; a crown presented to her on the stage in South America; a wreath of laurel in gold, with the name of a rôle on each leaf, given her in Naples; there were caskets, one inlaid with silver and made of wood a thousand years old, part of a beam from the Priory at Brecon, and in which the freedom of the borough had been presented to her; there were lamps and other objects which had been buried under the dust of Pompeii until the day when she was carried through its ruins in a sedan chair and by special order all that was exhumed during her visit became her property.[105]

In November the war finally ended, but by then Patti's health had seriously worsened. However, she occasionally rallied enough to give cause for hope as revealed in a letter dated 18 November to Eleonore Cederström:

> *Enfin, Dieu Merci*; now that peace has been declared—Rolf has made up his mind to arrange, if possible, to take me, abroad, to France for a couple of months & see what that can do for me—I have been so bad that even writing has not been allowed— nothing but rest, & remaining quite quiet.[106]

In a last letter to Alfredo Barili, dated 2 March 1919, she seemed optimistic: "The papers must have written very serious things about my health, for everybody has been writing for news of me to Rolf! *Dieu Merci* I feel much better but not yet completely well."[107]

In months that followed, seventy-six-year-old Patti became weaker and weaker, her heart deteriorating. Then the morning of 27 September 1919, she lost consciousness. She lingered thus for several hours and died peacefully, her husband holding her hand to the last.

In a letter to Louise Barili, Mabel Woodford, who had been at Craig-y-Nos before and after the death, wrote of Patti's final days and the immediate aftermath:

> I can imagine how the news . . . must have come upon you as a thunderbolt. Even *now,* I *cannot* realize it—nor do I feel that she is really gone—Her personality was so vivid & so *alive*—& since I first knew her in 1890, she was so much in my thoughts—that a world without her, does not seem possible. I think you know that I had gone down to Craig-y-Nos to stay with her on Sept. 10th— with Mrs. Baird—& on our arrival we found her *far from well.* However for some days she rallied & went out on the terrace with us—& lunched & dined with us—& then suddenly one day her heart troubled her more than usual—& in a few hours the doctors—3 of them—gave us practically no hope—Poor darling, she was brave & patient all the time—& thank God—we do not think she had any actual suffering. What we went through that week—or how the Baron suffered I cannot tell you—She knew me 4 days before she passed away—put her little arms round my neck—& said a few words to me in Italian. . . . I had known for many months that her heart & health were failing fast—but we always hoped against hope—& she had rallied so

well in the summer months—that the sudden collapse was very unexpected—I know what her loss must be to you—Dear Louise—She *always* loved you—& always talked to me about you & yours—She wrote very few letters during the last year—but she always liked getting letters—& was very pleased to get your letter (it must have been about Sept. 15th) & she read it through to me—& asked me to give you her fond love when I wrote to you—which I think I did that night. The Baron is brokenhearted about her—Poor man—his devotion to her was wonderfully touching—& his loneliness without her must be terrible.[108]

The body, as the diva had wished, was placed in Père Lachaise cemetery in Paris. Here a tomb was erected on which, as in life, the name PATTI dominated all else.

Years before, Henry Edward Krehbiel wrote an appreciation of her art that serves as this Queen of Song's true epitaph:

For the generation of opera-goers who grew up in the period which ought to be referred to for all time in the annals of music as The Reign of Patti, she set a standard by which all aspirants for public favor were judged except those whose activities were in a widely divergent field. . . . Her talent was so many sided and so astonishing, no matter from which side it was viewed, that rhapsody seems to be the only language left one who attempts analysis or description of it.[109]

Epilogue

In 1920 Baron Cederström put up for sale virtually all inside furnishings at Craig-y-Nos. Also during this year, the winter garden was dismantled and removed to Swansea, where it remains as the Patti Pavilion, an entertainment center for the town. In 1923 Baron Cederström married Hermione Frances Fellowes, the daughter of the second Lord de Ramsey. They subsequently became parents of a girl, who, as of this writing, lives in England and is a devoted wife and mother. On 26 February 1947, Baron Cederström died.

As for Craig-y-Nos Castle, in 1921 the Welsh National Memorial Association purchased it together with some adjoining forty-eight acres for 19,000 pounds to be used as a tuberculosis sanatorium, which was named The Adelina Patti Hospital. In the 1950s it became an institution for the practice of geriatrics as well as the treatment of the chronically ill and continued as such until 1986, when all patients were transferred to a new hospital at Ystradgynlais. In recent years the grounds around Craig-y-Nos have been opened to the public as a Country Park by the Brecon Beacons National Park Authority.

Today, though some rooms at Craig-y-Nos have been converted for dining, banquets, and conferences, the castle primarily functions in the summer and autumn as a center for artistic events in the music room and Patti Theatre. A highlight has been the annual series provided by the Neath Opera Group, which in August 1991 as part of the Adelina Patti Theatre Centenary reenacted the inaugural 1891 performance. The elegant auditorium thus remains functional and vital.

This temple of art, once the jewel of the diva's private domain, has been transformed as a rare gem of the Welsh public domain. No doubt Patti would be pleased.

Adelina Patti's Baptismal Register

From Baltasar Saldoni's *Diccionario Biográfico*, vol. I, pages 285–286.

Libro XLII de bautizos, folio 153 vuelto. En la villa de Madrid, correspondiente á la provincia y partido del mismo nombre, á 8 de abril de 1843: Yo D. José Losada, teniente cura de la iglesia parroquial de San Luis, bauticé solemnemente á una niña que nació á las cuarto de la tarde del dia 19 de febrero próximo pasado de dicho año, hija legítima de D. Salvador Patti, professor de música, natural de Catania, en Sicilia, y de doña Catalina [sic] Chiesa, natural de la ciudad de Roma, siendo abuelos paternos D. Pedro y doña Concepcion Marino, naturales de dicho Cantania; y maternos D. Juan [Chiesa], natural de la ciudad de Venecia, y doña Luisa Caselli, natural de Marino, en los Estados-Pontificios. Se la puso por nombres Adela, Juana, María. Fueron sus padrinos D. José Sínico, natural de Venecia, professor de música, y su esposa doña Rosa Manara Sínico, natural de Cremma, en Normandía, á quienes advertí el parentesco espiritual y obligaciones que por él contrarian: fueron testigos Julian Huezas y Casiano García, naturales de Madrid, sacristanes de esta iglesia. Y para que conste estendí y autoricé la presente partida en el espresado dia 8 de abril—José Losada.

Book of Baptisms, No. 42, page 153. In the city of Madrid, province of the same name, on 8 April 1843: I, Don José Losada, Vicar of the Parish of St. Louis, solemnly baptized a girl born at four o'clock in the afternoon of 19 February of the current year, the legitimate daughter of Salvatore Patti, professor of music, born in Catania, in Sicily, and of Catalina [*sic*] Chiesa, born in Rome, the paternal grandparents were Pedro Patti and Concepcion Marino, born in Catania; and the maternal were Juan [Chiesa], born in Venice, and Louisa Caselli, born in Marino, in the Pontifical States. The child was given the names Adela, Juana, María. Her godparents were José Sínico, born in

Venice, professor of music, and his wife Rosa Manara Sínico, born in Cremona, in Lombardy, whom I have warned of the spiritual duties they have contracted to fulfill by this act: the witnesses were Julian Huezas and Casiano García, born in Madrid, sacristans of this parish. And as the witness whereof I have signed and delivered the present certificate on the day 8 April— José Losada.

Notes

Prologue

1. Calvé 1922, 161.
2. Calvé 1922, 161.
3. Tetrazzini 1921; U.S. edition, 2.
4. Melba 1925, 49.
5. Eames 1927, 36.
6. Klein 1920, 381.

CHAPTER I   *Postlude/Prelude*

1. Wood 1938, 295–296.
2. King George V of England, October 1914.
3. Ashbrook 1982, 34–35.
4. Ashbrook 1982, 112–113.
5. Lauw 1884, 41.
6. Dickens 1884, 276–277.
7. Poe 1988, 25.
8. Nevins and Hakey Thomas, eds., 1952, I, 287–288.
9. *Morning Courier and New-York Enquirer,* 5 January 1847.
10. Haswell 1896, 438.
11. *Morning Courier and New-York Enquirer,* 27 February 1847.
12. *The New York Herald,* 23 March 1847.
13. White, June 1882, 206.
14. Brasher 1970, 208.
15. White, April 1882, 880.
16. Nevins, ed., 1927, II, 836.
17. *The* [New York] *Albion,* 11 December 1847.
18. *New-York Daily Tribune,* 29 January 1848.
19. New York *Spirit of the Times,* 6 May 1848.
20. White, June 1882, 205.
21. Klein 1920, 17.
22. Shultz 1962, 200.
23. Patti 1904, 606.
24. Klein 1920, 23.
25. Arditi 1896; reprint ed., 70–72.
26. Schermerhorn 1982, 33–34.
27. Foot 1894, 4.
28. Foot 1894, 4.
29. Foot 1894, 4.

30. Arditi 1896; reprint ed., 73.
31. Foot 1894, 4.
32. Arditi 1896; reprint ed., 69.
33. Arditi 1896; reprint ed., 70.
34. Arditi 1896; reprint ed., 70.
35. Arditi 1896; reprint ed., 70.
36. Maretzek 1968, 49.
37. *The New York Times,* 12 October 1919.
38. *New-York Daily Tribune,* 24 November 1851.
39. Foot 1894, 4.
40. James 1967, 79.
41. *Illustrated Sporting and Dramatic News,* 8 August 1874, 558.
42. Philadelphia *North American and United States Gazette,* 23 September 1852.
43. Philadelphia *North American and United States Gazette,* 23 September 1852.
44. *The* [Baltimore] *Sun,* 13 October 1852.
45. Bubna 1902, 347.
46. Upton 1908, 37–38.
47. Browne, ed., 1898, 86–87.
48. Bubna 1881, 397.
49. Bubna 1881, 397.
50. Armstrong, W., 1903c, 550.
51. *The New York Herald,* 5 April 1882.
52. Armstrong, W., 1903c, 549.
53. Patti 1906, 658–659.
54. Patti 1906, 659.
55. *The New-York Times,* 20 February 1855.
56. Patti 1904, 606–607.
57. Klein 1920, 21.
58. Kuhe 1896, 158.
59. Foot 1894, 4.
60. Gottschalk 1964, 19–20.
61. Patti 1899.
62. Jackson, L. H., 1927, 7.
63. Klein 1920, 44.
64. Klein 1920, 44.
65. Armstrong, W., 1903b, 3.
66. Klein 1920, 387.
67. Klein 1920, 43.

CHAPTER II *Superstar*

1. "Musical and Theatrical" 1860, 243.
2. *New-York Daily Tribune,* 25 November 1859.
3. *The New York Herald,* 25 November 1859.

4. *The New York Herald*, 26 November 1859.
5. *The New-York Times*, 25 November 1859.
6. *New-York Daily Tribune*, 25 November 1859.
7. *The New York Herald*, 3 December 1859.
8. *The New York Herald*, 23 December 1859.
9. Klein 1920, 49.
10. Foot 1894, 4.
11. *The New York Herald*, 2 December 1859.
12. *Musical World and New York Musical Times*, 10 December 1859, 2.
13. *The New-York Times*, 5 December 1859.
14. *The New-York Times*, 28 December 1859.
15. *Boston Daily Evening Transcript*, 23 January 1860.
16. *The New York Herald*, 7 February 1860.
17. *New-York Daily Tribune*, 9 February 1860.
18. *The New-York Times*, 9 February 1860.
19. *The New-York Times*, 12 April 1860.
20. *The New York Herald*, 8 May 1860.
21. *The New-York Times*, 4 October 1860.
22. *The New-York Times*, 4 October 1860.
23. *The New-York Times*, 6 October 1860.
24. Mudd n.d.; Winterstein 1863, 774.
25. Kellogg 1913, 148.
26. Leslie 1954, 63.
27. *The* [New Orleans] *Daily Picayune*, 3 January 1861.
28. *The* [New Orleans] *Daily Picayune*, 3 January 1861.
29. *The* [New Orleans] *Daily Picayune*, 9 February 1861.
30. *The* [New Orleans] *Daily Picayune*, 1 March 1861.
31. *The* [New Orleans] *Daily Picayune*, 5 March 1861.
32. *The* [New Orleans] *Daily Picayune*, 23 March 1861.
33. Maretzek 1968, 51.
34. Arditi 1896; reprint ed., 77.
35. Beale 1890, 352–353.
36. Mapleson, J. H., 1966, 30.
37. Kuhe 1896, 153.
38. Kuhe 1896, 153–154.
39. *The* [London] *Times*, 15 May 1861.
40. *The* [London] *Times*, 15 May 1861.
41. *The Illustrated London News*, 18 May 1861, 465.
42. Patti 1906, 661.
43. Klein 1920, 414.
44. *The Athenæum*, 18 May 1861, 669.
45. *The* [London] *Times*, 15 May 1861.
46. Patti to Costa, 24 August 1862.
47. "Royal Italian Opera" 1861, 348.
48. *The Athenæum*, 1 June 1861, 734.
49. *Musical World*, 29 June 1861, 409.

50. *The* [London] *Times,* 5 July 1861.
51. *The* [London] *Times,* 5 July 1861.
52. *The* [London] *Times,* 5 July 1861.
53. *Musical World,* 13 July 1861, 442.
54. Sutherland Edwards 1888, II, 78–79.
55. Klein 1920, 99.
56. R. S. 1862, 119.
57. *The* [London] *Times,* 6 August 1862.
58. London *Standard,* 6 August 1862.
59. Busch 1978, 407.
60. C. L., 22 November 1862, 747.
61. "Auber and Adelina Patti" 1862, 811.
62. *The Athenæum,* 29 November 1862, 704.
63. Bernard 1862, 410.
64. Lauw 1884, 3.
65. Weinstock 1968, 272.
66. Weinstock 1968, 276.
67. Weinstock 1968, 277.
68. Weinstock 1968, 277.
69. Jackson, L. H., 1927, 7.
70. Jackson, L. H., 1927, 7.
71. Jackson, L. H., 1927, 7.
72. Jackson, L. H., 1927, 7.
73. Jackson, L. H., 1927, 8.
74. Jackson, L. H., 1927, 7–8.
75. Jackson, L. H., 1927, 8.
76. Jackson, L. H., 1927, 8.
77. C. L., 29 November 1862, 762.
78. P. 1862, 811.
79. *Musical World,* 17 January 1863, 43; Klein 1920, 117–118.
80. Klein 1920, 117–118.
81. Lauw 1884, 5.
82. Lauw 1884, 5.
83. Hanslick 1950, 194–195.
84. Sutherland Edwards 1888, II, 85.
85. Hanslick 1950, 191–192.
86. Hanslick 1950, 192.
87. Hanslick 1950, 193.
88. Sutherland Edwards 1888, II, 87.
89. *The Athenæum,* 18 April 1863, 529.
90. *Musical World,* 1 August 1863, 493.
91. *Musical World,* 1 August 1863, 484.
92. *Musical World,* 1 August 1863, 493.
93. *The* [London] *Morning Star,* 3 June 1863.
94. Klein 1920, 430–431.
95. Armstrong, W., 1903b, 3.

CHAPTER III   *Celebrity of Celebrities*

1. *Le Temps,* 26 January 1864.
2. *The Musical Record,* September 1886, 1.
3. *The Athenæum,* 11 June 1864, 813.
4. Lauw 1884, 20.
5. Peltz 1964, 14.
6. Patti to Max Strakosch, 5 March 1864.
7. Patti to Max Strakosch, 16 September 1864.
8. Berlioz 1960, 516.
9. Berlioz 1960, 518.
10. Berlioz 1960, 518.
11. Peltz 1964, 14.
12. Patti to Max Strakosch, 2 October 1864.
13. Peltz 1964, 14–15.
14. Patti to Max Strakosch, 12 October 1864.
15. Patti to Max Strakosch, 12 October 1864.
16. Peltz 1964, 15.
17. Peltz 1964, 15.
18. Searle, ed., trans., 1966, 193.
19. *The New York Herald,* 25 February 1877.
20. *The New York Herald,* 25 February 1877.
21. Lauw 1884, 19.
22. "Fragments from Patti's Album" 1903, 286.
23. Dalmazzo 1877, 23.
24. North-Peat 1903, 150.
25. *The Athenæum,* 20 July 1867, 91.
26. London *Pall Mall Gazette,* 29 July 1868.
27. Klein 1920, 169–170.
28. Dumay 1901.
29. Kellogg 1913, 130.
30. Patti 1884, 5.
31. Gosling 1973, 20.
32. Conati, ed., 1984, 53.
33. Hanslick 1950, 198.
34. Lauw 1884, 27.
35. Lauw 1884, 27.
36. Lauw 1884, 28.
37. Lauw 1884, 28.
38. Soissons 1920, 108.
39. Loliée 1909, 159.
40. *The Illustrated London News,* 26 December 1868, 638.
41. Lauw 1884, 32–33.
42. Lauw 1884, 34.
43. Engel 1886, II, 276.
44. *The Illustrated London News,* 16 May 1868, 490.

CHAPTER IV   *The Famous Marquise*

1. *The New York Herald,* 25 February 1877.
2. Lauw 1884, 42.
3. Sutherland Edwards 1888, II, 87.
4. Knepler, ed., trans., 1970, 284.
5. Lauw 1884, 43.
6. New York *Spirit of the Times,* 29 July 1868.
7. Loliée 1909, 161.
8. "Adelina Patti" 1874, 558.
9. Klein 1920, 174.
10. Weinstock 1968, 349.
11. Lauw 1884, 49.
12. Klein 1920, 176–177.
13. San Francisco *Morning Call,* 10 March 1884.
14. Patti 1904, 608.
15. Patti 1904, 608.
16. "Fragments from Patti's Album" 1903, 286.
17. Engel 1886, II, 286.
18. Unidentified clipping.
19. Klein 1920, 181.
20. Bernhardt 1923, 152–153.
21. Lauw 1884, 52.
22. Conati, ed., 1984, 51.
23. Lauw 1884, 52.
24. *The Illustrated London News,* 31 July 1869, 122.
25. *Musical World,* 4 June 1870, 383.
26. *The Illustrated London News,* 18 June 1870, 631.
27. *Musical World,* 4 June 1870, 409.
28. *The Illustrated London News,* 9 July 1870, 43.
29. Lauw 1884, 52.
30. *The Athenæum,* 12 October 1872, 475.
31. *The Athenæum,* 16 November 1872, 641.
32. *Musical World,* 2 March 1872, 141.
33. *The Musical Record,* 1 September 1899, 389.
34. Stanislavsky 1924, 32–33.
35. Leyda and Bertensson 1947, 141.
36. *Musical World,* 9 March 1872, 159.
37. Armstrong, W., 1903c, 554.
38. London *Pall Mall Gazette,* 11 March 1873.
39. *Musical World,* 6 December 1873, 814.
40. *The Light of Other Days* 1924, 160–161.
41. Loftus 1894, II, 87–89.
42. Arditi 1896; reprint ed., 176.
43. Hanslick 1950, 188.
44. Hanslick 1950, 189–190.

45. Hanslick 1950, 202.
46. Hanslick 1950, 200.
47. Hanslick 1950, 206–207.
48. Rosenthal 1958, 181.
49. Patti to Marie Bevignani, 14 September 1888.
50. *Orchestra and the Choir,* January 1875, 187.
51. *The Athenæum,* 20 May 1871, 631.
52. "Fragments from Patti's Album" 1903, 286.
53. *The Athenæum,* 1 July 1876, 26.
54. Klein 1920, 188.
55. *The Illustrated London News,* 20 July 1878, 66.
56. *The Athenæum,* 20 July 1878, 90.
57. Klein 1920, 194.
58. *The Athenæum,* 19 May 1877, 650.
59. Prince Arthur to Queen Victoria, 16 April 1871.
60. Prince Arthur to Queen Victoria, 23 July 1871.
61. Prince Leopold to Princess Louise, 15 May 1871.
62. Queen Victoria of England, 4 July 1872.
63. Lauw 1884, 63.
64. Hanslick 1950, 199.
65. Hegermann-Lindencrone 1912, 240.
66. Knepler 1970, 285.
67. Liszt 1979, 127.
68. Knepler 1970, 285.
69. Kuhe 1896, 159.
70. Lauw 1884, 65.
71. *The New-York Times,* 9 March 1877.
72. *The New-York Times,* 9 March 1877.
73. Tolstoy 1988, 583.
74. Tolstoy 1988, 585.

CHAPTER V   *The Infamous Marquise*

1. *The New-York Times,* 1 March 1877.
2. *The New York Herald,* 25 February 1877.
3. Gipson 1940, 172.
4. Kellogg 1913, 184.
5. *Le Figaro,* 22 February 1877.
6. *The New-York Times,* 9 March 1877.
7. *Musical and Dramatic Times and Music Trade Review,* 18 April 1877, 211.
8. "Echoes from Abroad" 1877, 299.
9. *The* [San Francisco] *Wasp,* 14 March 1885, 4.
10. Kellogg 1913, 130.
11. London *Daily Telegraph,* 6 August 1877.
12. London *Daily Telegraph,* 6 August 1877.

13. London *Daily Telegraph,* 6 August 1877.
14. Vienna *Morgen Post,* 1 October 1876.
15. London *Daily Telegraph,* 6 August 1877.
16. London *Daily News,* 6 August 1877.
17. *Musical and Dramatic Times and Music Trade Review,* 18 August 1877, 133.
18. *The* [New York] *World,* 21 April 1884.
19. Knepler, ed., trans., 1970, 285–286.
20. London *Pall Mall Gazette,* 16 May 1877.
21. Dalmazzo 1877, 40.
22. Klein 1920, 202.
23. Busch 1978, 407.
24. *Gazzetta Musicale di Milano,* 4 November 1877, 364.
25. Werfel and Stefan 1942, 340–341.
26. Busch 1978, 409.
27. Busch 1978, 409.
28. *Musical and Dramatic Times and Music Trade Review,* 23 November 1878, 13.
29. *Musical and Dramatic Times and Music Trade Review,* 28 December 1878, 4.
30. Hersee 1878, 27–28.
31. Shaw 1937, 371.
32. Jones-Davies, November 1971.
33. "Patti in Paris" 1886, 9.
34. "Patti at Home," 1885, 8.
35. Beatty-Kingston 1883, 108.
36. *Illustrated Sporting and Dramatic News,* 8 September 1883, 643.
37. Patti to Edward Hall, 24 December 1880.
38. Patti to Edward Hall, 16 January 1881.
39. Patti 1884, 5.
40. Walsh 1975, 20.
41. *The* [New York] *World,* 4 November 1881.
42. *The New York Herald,* 4 November 1881.
43. *The New York Herald,* 10 November 1881.
44. *The New York Herald,* 11 November 1881.
45. Finck 1926, 184.
46. "Patti as a Critic" 1882, 259.
47. "A Chat with Mapleson" 1882, 308.
48. *Music and Drama,* 4 March 1882, 2.
49. *The New York Herald,* 15 April 1882.
50. *The New York Herald,* 15 April 1882.
51. *The New York Herald,* 15 April 1882.
52. *The New York Herald,* 15 April 1882.
53. Klein 1920, 381.
54. Mapleson, J. H., 1966, 157.
55. Christiansen 1986, 115–116.

56. *The New York Herald,* 7 November 1882.
57. Mapleson, J. H., 1966, 160.
58. Mapleson, J. H., 1966, 159.
59. Mapleson, J. H., 1966, 157–158.
60. Mapleson, J. H., 1966, 162–163.
61. *The New-York Times,* 27 March 1883.
62. Mapleson, J. H., 1966, 208.
63. *The New York Herald,* 4 December 1883.
64. Mapleson, J. H., 1966, 182.
65. *The New York Herald,* 24 April 1883.
66. *St. Louis Post-Dispatch,* 25 February 1884.
67. *The* [San Francisco] *Morning Call,* 30 March 1884.
68. Mapleson, J. H., 1966, 205.
69. *St. Louis Post-Dispatch,* 25 February 1884.
70. *The* [San Francisco] *Morning Call,* 10 March 1884.
71. Betsy B. 1884, 14.
72. Mapleson, J. H., 1966, 197–198.
73. Betsy B. 1884, 14.
74. Betsy B. 1884, 14.
75. Betsy B. 1884, 14.
76. *The* [San Francisco] *Morning Call,* 15 March 1884.
77. *The* [San Francisco] *Argonaut,* 15 April 1884, 1.
78. *Omaha Daily Bee,* 15 December 1884.
79. *Omaha Daily Bee,* 15 December 1884.
80. Josiah Pittman to Edward Hall, 8 August 1884.
81. Josiah Pittman to Edward Hall, 18 August 1884.
82. Josiah Pittman to Edward Hall, 31 August 1884.
83. *The New-York Times,* 15 November 1884.
84. *New-York Daily Tribune,* 27 November 1884.
85. Krehbiel 1908, 126–127.
86. *The* [New York] *World,* 27 November 1884.
87. *The New-York Times,* 14 December 1884.
88. Mapleson, J. H., 1966, 228.
89. *New-York Daily Tribune,* 3 May 1885.
90. Mapleson, J. H., 1966, 236–237.
91. Klein 1920, 224.
92. Klein 1920, 227.
93. Patti to unidentified individual, 27 December 1885.
94. Schürmann 1893, 45–50.
95. *The New-York Times,* 27 February 1886.
96. "Patti in Paris" 1886, 9.
97. *The Cambrian,* 15 September 1882.
98. *The Cambrian,* 15 September 1882.
99. Josiah Pittman to Edward Hall, 15 August 1884.
100. London *Pall Mall Gazette,* 10 June 1886.
101. Beatty-Kingston 1886, 38–39.

102. Beatty-Kingston 1886, 38.
103. Beatty-Kingston 1886, 40.
104. Beatty-Kingston 1886, 40.
105. Beatty-Kingston 1886, 38.
106. Beatty-Kingston 1886, 41.

CHAPTER VI   *Madame Patti-Nicolini*

1. Roth 1939, 100.
2. Klein 1920, 280.
3. *The New-York Times*, 15 November 1886.
4. *The New-York Times*, 19 November 1886.
5. Armstrong, W., 1903b, 3.
6. *The New-York Times*, 19 April 1887.
7. *The New-York Times*, 19 April 1887.
8. Klein 1920, 241–242.
9. Klein 1920, 243.
10. Montevideo *La Tribuna Popular*, 5 July 1888.
11. Montevideo *El Siglo*, 10 August 1888.
12. Klein 1920, 250.
13. Klein 1920, 250.
14. Patti to Pierre Gailhard, 23 October 1888.
15. Klein 1920, 251.
16. Klein 1920, 251.
17. Melba 1925, 52.
18. *The* [London] *Times*, 29 November 1888.
19. Klein 1920, 251–252.
20. *The* [London] *Times*, 29 November 1888.
21. Shaw 1937, 54–55.
22. *The Musical Record*, December 1886, 2.
23. Eaton 1957, 43.
24. *The Chicago Tribune*, 10 December 1889.
25. *The Chicago Herald*, 10 December 1889.
26. Upton 1908, 43.
27. Eaton 1957, 43–44.
28. Davis, R., 1966, 52.
29. Davis, R., 1966, 52.
30. Arditi 1896; reprint ed., 244.
31. Arditi 1896; reprint ed., 244.
32. Arditi 1896; reprint ed., 244.
33. Eaton 1957, 45.
34. Eaton 1957, 45.
35. *The New-York Times*, 14 March 1890.
36. *The New-York Times*, 27 March 1890.
37. *The* [New York] *World*, 27 March 1890.
38. *The New York Herald*, 26 August 1890.

39. *The Cambrian,* 14 August 1891.
40. Patti to Alfredo Barili, 12 January 1891.
41. Klein 1920, 280.
42. Klein 1920, 232–233.
43. Klein 1903b, 320–321.
44. Klein 1920, 281.
45. Klein 1920, 284–285.
46. Klein 1920, 287.
47. Klein 1920, 287–288.
48. Klein 1920, 289.
49. Klein 1920, 291.
50. Klein 1920, 296.
51. Klein 1920, 298.
52. Klein 1903b, 313–314.
53. Klein 1920, 299.
54. Klein 1920, 300.
55. Arditi 1896; reprint ed., 264.
56. *The New York Herald,* 3 April 1892.
57. *New-York Daily Tribune,* 10 April 1892.
58. *New-York Daily Tribune,* 10 April 1892.
59. Duval 1958, 34.
60. Odell, 1927–49, XV, 180.
61. *The New-York Times,* 19 May 1892.
62. *The New-York Times,* 19 May 1892.
63. Patti to Alfredo Barili, 21 December 1892.
64. Klein 1920, 313.
65. *Gazzetta Musicale di Milano,* 22 January 1893, 50.
66. Patti to Edward Hall, 25 January 1893.
67. Patti 1908, 714.
68. Shaw 1977, III, 3.
69. Patti to Edward Hall, 16 November 1893.
70. *The New York Herald,* 19 November 1893.
71. Patti to Edward Hall, 26 November 1893.
72. Armstrong, W., 1922, 6–7.
73. Armstrong, W., 1922, 7.
74. Klein 1920, 315.
75. Shaw 1977, III, 225.
76. Shaw 1977, III, 268.
77. Klein 1920, 318.
78. Marchesi, B., 1923, 138.
79. Marchesi, B., 1923, 139.
80. Marchesi, B., 1923, 140.
81. Marchesi, B., 1923, 141.
82. Klein 1920, 320–321.
83. Klein 1920, 323–324.
84. Armstrong, W., 1922, 2.

85. Klein 1920, 327.
86. "Notes from the Opera" 1895, 408.
87. Klein 1920, 328.
88. Hoare 1906, 680.
89. Klein 1920, 329.
90. Klein 1920, 329.
91. Klein 1920, 329.
92. *The* [London] *Times,* 12 June 1895.
93. "Notes from the Opera" 1895, 408.
94. *Punch,* 22 June 1895.
95. London *Pall Mall Gazette,* 12 June 1895.
96. London *Pall Mall Gazette,* 12 June 1895.
97. Klein 1920, 449.
98. Klein 1920, 330
99. Klein 1920, 331.
100. Armstrong, W., 1903b, 3.
101. "Patti Interviewed" 1907, 8.
102. Armstrong, W., 1922, 33–35.
103. Mabel Woodford to Edward Hall, 24 October 1895.
104. *South Wales Daily Post,* 23 July 1896.
105. *South Wales Daily Post,* 6 August 1896.
106. Klein 1920, 339.
107. Klein 1920, 451.
108. Patti 1908, 715.
109. *Western Mail,* 27 July 1897.
110. *Western Mail,* 27 July 1897.
111. Armstrong, W., 1922, 11.
112. Armstrong, W., 1922, 13.
113. Patti to Alfredo Barili, 7 November 1897.
114. Klein 1920, 343.
115. Nicolini's wills dated 18 October 1886 and 26 January 1889.
116. Armstrong, W., 1922, 12.
117. Patti to Alfredo Barili, 25 April 1898.
118. Klein 1920, 347.
119. "Mephisto's Musings" 1919, 7.
120. Harbord 1899, 2.
121. Patti to Alfredo Barili, 12 December 1898.
122. *The Brecon County Times,* 27 January 1899.
123. *South Wales Daily Post,* 25 January 1899.
124. *South Wales Daily Post,* 25 January 1899.
125. *South Wales Daily Post,* 25 January 1899.
126. London *Pall Mall Gazette,* 25 January 1899.

CHAPTER VII   *Baroness Cederström*

1. Roth 1939, 99.
2. Gattey 1979, 146.
3. Klein 1920, 350.
4. Hutter 1920, 59.
5. Hutter 1920, 59.
6. Hutter 1920, 59.
7. Hutter 1920, 59.
8. Hutter 1920, 59.
9. Hutter 1920, 60.
10. Patti to Gustaf Cederström, 16 August 1900.
11. Klein 1920, 354–355.
12. Klein 1920, 355.
13. Patti to Alfredo Barili, 7 January 1901.
14. Patti to Alfredo Barili, 4 August 1901.
15. Patti to Alfredo Barili, 4 August 1901.
16. Patti to Gustaf Cederström, 22 April 1902.
17. Patti to Gustaf Cederström, 3 January 1904.
18. Patti to Gustaf Cederström, 14 October 1903.
19. Grau 1912, 22.
20. Patti to Gustaf Cederström, 3 January 1904.
21. *The New York Times*, 1 November 1903.
22. Klein 1920, 359.
23. *The New York Times*, 5 November 1903.
24. *The New York Times*, 8 November 1903.
25. Henderson 1903, 321.
26. Henderson 1903, 321–322.
27. Grau 1912, 22.
28. Patti to Gustaf Cederström, 19 December 1903.
29. Patti to Gustaf Cederström, 22 January 1904.
30. *San Francisco Chronicle*, 7 January 1904.
31. *San Francisco Chronicle*, 7 January 1904.
32. Patti to Gustaf Cederström, 24 March 1904.
33. Armstrong, W., 1922, 31–32.
34. Armstrong, W., 1922, 32.
35. Patti to Louise Barili, 26 August 1904.
36. Patti to Gustaf Cederström, 27 November 1904.
37. Bariatinsky 1923, 43.
38. Patti to Alfredo Barili, 25 December 1904.
39. Patti to Gustaf Cederström, 10 July 1905.
40. Leiser 1933, 300.
41. Spalding 1943, 47.
42. Spalding 1943, 48.
43. Gaisberg 1942, 91–93.
44. Ronald 1922, 103–104.

45. Gaisberg 1942, 91–92.
46. Gaisberg 1943, 123.
47. Patti to Alfredo Barili, 8 December 1905.
48. Patti to Louise Barili, 26 November 1905.
49. Patti to Louise Barili, 26 November 1905.
50. Louise Barili to Barilis, 8 April 1906.
51. Ruskin 1943, 4.
52. Louise Barili to Barilis, 8 April 1906.
53. Ruskin 1943, 4.
54. Gaisberg 1943, 123–124.
55. Steane 1974, 15.
56. Steane 1974, 15–17.
57. Steane 1974, 15–16.
58. Steane 1974, 17.
59. Hurst, P. G., 1963, 84.
60. Sackville-West and Shawe-Taylor 1952, 362.
61. Scott 1977, I, 22–23.
62. Patti to Louise Barili, 25 November 1906.
63. Patti to Louise Barili, 31 October 1906.
64. Hoare 1906, 680.
65. Hoare 1906, 680.
66. Klein 1920, 368.
67. Patti to Louise Barili, 21 December 1906.
68. Patti to Louise Barili, 27 May 1907.
69. Patti to Gustaf Cederström, 20 October 1907.
70. Patti to Gustaf Cederström, 20 October 1907.
71. Patti 1908, 706–707.
72. Armstrong, W., 1922, 14.
73. Patti to Gustaf Cederström, 28 July 1909.
74. Rosate-Lunn 1961, 182.
75. Patti to Gustaf Cederström, 27 October 1910.
76. Patti to Gustaf Cederström, 28 November 1910.
77. Patti to Gustaf Cederström, 19 May 1910.
78. Armstrong, W., 1922, 28.
79. Patti to Emily Barili, 22 November 1910.
80. Patti to Alfredo Barili, 9 June 1908, 21 April 1909, and 14 October 1909.
81. Patti to Louise Barili, 17 March 1909.
82. Patti to Louise Barili, 22 June 1910.
83. Patti to Louise Barili, 2 July 1910.
84. Louise Barili to Barilis, 15 May 1911.
85. Patti to Gustaf Cederström, 26 May 1911.
86. Tetrazzini 1921; U.S. edition, 233.
87. Tetrazzini 1921; U.S. edition, 232.
88. Tetrazzini 1921; U.S. edition, 233–234.
89. Patti to Emily Barili, 29 June 1908.

90. Patti to Alfredo Barili, 20 April 1910.
91. Hoare 1906, 680.
92. *The Cambrian Daily Leader,* 7 May 1909.
93. Patti to Alfredo Barili, 14 March 1911.
94. Patti to Eleonore Cederström, 25 June 1912.
95. Patti to Louise Barili, 14 November 1915.
96. Patti to Louise Barili, 6 November 1914.
97. Patti to Louise Barili, February 1915.
98. Patti to Louise Barili, February 1915.
99. Patti to Gustaf Cederström, 16 August 1915.
100. Patti to Gustaf Cederström, 25 June 1916.
101. Patti to Louise Barili, 25 January 1918.
102. Patti to Emily Barili, 27 May 1918.
103. Patti to Louise Barili, 18 June 1918.
104. Armstrong, W., 1922, 21.
105. Armstrong, W., 1922, 21.
106. Patti to Eleonore Cederström, 18 November 1918.
107. Patti to Alfredo Barili, 2 March 1919.
108. Mabel Woodford to Louise Barili, 16 March 1920.
109. Krehbiel 1908, 126.

References

Books and Articles

A. A. 1862. "Mlle. Adelina Patti at Berlin." *Musical World* (11 January): 26.

Abbiati, Franco. 1959. *Giuseppe Verdi*. 4 vols. Milan: Ricordi.

"A Chat with Mapleson." 1882. *The Musical Record* (11 February): 308.

"Adelina Patti." 1874. *Illustrated Sporting and Dramatic News* (8 August): 558.

"Adelina Patti." 1903. *Gazzetta Musicale di Milano* (15 March), vol. 1, no. 3.

"Adelina Patti." N.d. Robinson Locke Collection. Scrapbooks 379–380. Drama Division, New York Public Library.

Albani, Emma. [1911.] *Forty Years of Song*. London: Mills & Boon.

Alda, Frances. 1937. *Men, Women and Tenors*. Boston: Houghton Mifflin.

Aldrich, Richard. [1928.] "Adelina Patti in America." *Musical Discourse from the* New York Times: 242–265. London: Oxford University Press. Reprinted in 1967. Freeport, Ill.: Books for Libraries Press.

Almedingen, E. M. 1962. *The Emperor Alexander II*. London: The Bodley Head.

Altrocchi, Julia Cooley. 1949. *The Spectacular San Franciscans*. New York: Dutton.

Andrews, Wayne. 1941. *The Vanderbilt Legend*. New York: Harcourt Brace.

Apel, Willi. 1944. *Harvard Dictionary of Music*. Second edition, 1969; third edition, 1986. Cambridge, Mass.: Harvard University Press.

Arditi, Luigi. 1896. *My Reminiscences*. New York: Dodd, Mead. Reprinted in 1977. New York: Da Capo Press.

Armstrong, W. G. 1884. *A Record of the Opera in Philadelphia*. Philadelphia: Porter & Coates.

Armstrong, William. 1903a. "Madame Patti To-Day." *The Saturday Evening Post* (11 July): 8–9.

———. 1903b. "Mme. Patti's Advice to Singers." *The Saturday Evening Post* (8 August): 3.

———. 1903c. "Adelina Patti's Achievement." *Success* (October): 549–554.

———. 1912. "When Opera Stars Keep House." *Pictorial Review* (December): 16–62.

———. 1922. *The Romantic World of Music*. New York: Dutton.

Arnam, Ralph N. van. 1948a. "The Patti-Tamagno Operatic Tour of 1890." *Opera News* (5 April): 19–22.

———. 1948b. "Patti & Tamagno at the Metropolitan Opera in 1890." *Opera News* (19 April): 21–24.

Aronson, Rudolph. 1913. *Theatrical and Musical Memoirs*. New York: McBride, Nast.

Artieri, Giovanni. 1963. "Lettere a una Cantante." Rome: Enit.

Ashbrook, William. 1982. *Donizetti and His Operas*. Cambridge, U.K.: Cambridge University Press.

Astort, Antonio. 1888. "Adelina Patti." *Montevideo Musical* (16 June): 1–3.

"Auber and Adelina Patti." 1862. *Musical World* (20 December): 811.

Bariatinsky, Anatole Marie. 1923. *My Russian Life*. London: Hutchinson.

Barthez, Ernest. 1912. *The Empress Eugénie and Her Circle*. London: Fisher & Unwin.

Barzun, Jacques. 1968. *Berlioz and His Century*. New York: World Publishing.

Basso, Alberto, ed. 1988. *Storia del Teatro Regio di Torino*. Turin: Cassa di Risparmio.

Beale, Willert. 1890. *The Light of Other Days*. 2 vols. London: Richard Bentley and Son.

Beatty-Kingston, William. 1883. "Our Omnibus Box." *The* [London] *Theatre* (1 August): 107–108.

———. 1886. "A Nightingale's Wedding." *The* [London] *Theatre* (1 July): 37–42.

———. 1887. *Music and Manners*. 2 vols. London: Chapman and Hall.

Beebe, Lucius. 1959. *Mansions on Rails*. Berkeley, Ca.: Howell-North.

Beecham, Sir Thomas. 1943. *A Mingled Chime*. New York: G. P. Putnam's Sons. British edition in 1944. London: Hutchinson.

Belmont, Eleanor. [1957.] *The Fabric of Memory*. New York: Farrar, Straus and Cudahy.

Bennett, Joseph. [1908.] *Forty Years of Music, 1865–1905*. London: Methuen.

Benson, E. F. 1930. *As We Were*. London: Longmans, Green.

Berlioz, Hector. 1960. *Memoirs*. Annotated and revised by Ernest Newman. New York: Dover.

Bernard, Paul. 1862. "Mlle Adelina Patti au Théâtre-Italien de Paris." *Le Ménestrel* (23 November): 410–411.

Bernhardt, Sarah. 1923. *Memories of My Life*. New York: Appleton.

Betsy B. 1884. "Drama." San Francisco *Argonaut* (15 March): 14.

Bicknell, Anna L. 1895. *Life in the Tuileries under the Second Empire*. New York: Century.

Bierman, John. 1988. *Napoleon III and His Carnival Empire*. New York: St. Martin's Press.

Bird, John. 1976. *Percy Grainger*. London: Paul Elek.

Bispham, David. 1920. *A Quaker Singer's Recollections*. New York: Macmillan.

Black, David. 1981. *King of Fifth Avenue: The Fortunes of August Belmont*. New York: Dial.

Blanchard, Roger, and Roland de Candé. 1986. *Dieux et Divas de l'Opéra*. 2 vols. Paris: Plon.

Blom, Eric, ed. 1954. *Grove's Dictionary of Music and Musicians*. 5th ed. 9 vols. London: Macmillan.

Blumenberg, Marc A. 1903. "Patti and Jean De Reszke at Mont Dore." *Musical Courier* (5 August): 5–9.

Blyth, Alan, ed. 1979. *Opera on Record*. London: Hutchinson.

––––––. 1983. *Opera on Record 2*. London: Hutchinson.

––––––. 1984. *Opera on Record 3*. London: Hutchinson.

Borovsky, Victor. 1988. *Chaliapin*. New York: Alfred A. Knopf and London: Hamish Hamilton.

Brasher, Thomas L. 1970. *Whitman as Editor of the Brooklyn Daily Eagle*. Detroit, Mich.: Wayne State University Press.

Brewer, H. C. 1888. "Craig-y-Nos Castle." *The Graphic* (24 November): 558.

Brinn, David. 1986. *Adelina Patti: A Brief Account of Her Life*. Brecon Beacons National Park.

Brockway, Wallace, and Herbert Weinstock. 1941. *The Opera*. New York: Simon and Schuster.

Brook-Shepherd, Gordon. 1975. *Uncle of Europe*. New York: Harcourt Brace Jovanovich.

Brotman, Ruth C. 1975. *Pauline Donalda*. Montreal: Eagle.

Browne, Charles Farrar. 1898. *The Complete Works of Artemus Ward*. New York: G. W. Gillingham.

Bubna, Augusta de. 1881. "Recollections of a Little Prima Donna." *St. Nicholas* (March): 393–397.

––––––. 1902. "A Playmate of Patti." *Lippincott's Monthly Magazine* (March): 344–348.

Bull, Sara C. 1882. *Ole Bull: A Memoir*. Boston: Houghton Mifflin.

Burchell, S. C. 1971. *Imperial Masquerade*. New York: Athenæum.

Burgess, Harry. 1911. *My Musical Pilgrimage*. London: Simpkin, Marshall, Hamilton, Kent & Co.

Busch, Hans. 1978. *Verdi's Aida: The History of an Opera*. Minneapolis: University of Minnesota Press.

Cabezas, Juan Antonio. [1956.] *Adelina Patti*. Madrid: Bureba.

Calvé, Emma. 1922. *My Life*. Trans. Rosamond Gilder. New York: Appleton.

Cambiasi, Pompeo. [1889.] *La Scala 1778–1889*. Milan: G. Ricordi & Co.

Carette, A. 1890. *Recollections of the Court of the Tuileries*. New York: Appleton.

Carmena y Millan, Don Luis. 1878. *Cronica de la Opera Italiana en Madrid*. Madrid: Minuesa de los Rios.

Carré, Albert. 1950. *Souvenirs de Théâtre*. Paris: Plon.

Castán Palomar, Fernando. 1947. *Adelina Patti*. Madrid: Cibeles.

Celletti, Rodolfo, ed. 1964. *Le Grandi Voci*. Rome: Istituto per la Collaborazione Culturale.

Charnacé, Guy de. 1868. *Les Étoiles du Chant*. Paris: Plon.

Chorley, Henry F. 1862. *Thirty Years' Musical Recollections*. London: Hurst and Blackett. New edition with an introduction by Ernest Newman in 1926. New York: Alfred A. Knopf.

Christiansen, Rupert. 1986. *Prima Donna: A History.* New York: Penguin.

Chusid, Martin. 1978. "Verdi's Early U.S. Premieres." *Opera News* (7 January): 32–33 and (4 February): 12–13.

C. L. 1862. "[Mlle.] Patti in Paris." *Musical World* (22 November): 746–747 and (29 November): 762–763.

Clapp, William W. 1969. *A Record of the Boston Stage.* New York: Greenwood Press.

Clark, Ronald W. 1958. *The Royal Albert Hall.* London: Hamish Hamilton.

Colson, Percy. 1932. *Melba.* London: Grayson & Grayson.

Conati, Marcello, ed. 1984. *Encounters with Verdi.* Trans. Richard Stokes. Ithaca, N.Y.: Cornell University Press.

Cone, John Frederick. 1983. *First Rival of the Metropolitan Opera.* New York: Columbia University Press.

Corsi, Mario. 1937. *Tamagno.* Milan: Ceschina. Reprinted in 1977 with discography by W. R. Moran. New York: Arno Press.

Cox, John Edmund. 1872. *Musical Reflections of the Last Half-Century.* 2 vols. London: Tinsley.

"Craig-y-Nos Castle." 1882. *The Gardeners' Chronicle* (8 April): 464–469.

Da Fonseca Benvenides, Francisco. 1902. *O Real Teatro de S. Carlos de Lisboa, Memorias 1883–1902.* Lisbon: Souza & Salles.

Dalmazzo, G. M. 1877. *Adelina Patti's Life.* London: Cooper Bros. and Atwood.

Damrosch, Walter. 1923. *My Musical Life.* New York: Charles Scribner's Sons.

Dansette, Adrien. 1938. *Les Amours de Napoleon III.* Paris: Fayard.

Davies, Leonora. 1963. "The Day Patti Was Wed a Second Time." *South Wales Evening Post* (10 August).

Davis, Peter G. 1974. "When Patti Wowed Her Fans ...." *The New York Times,* Arts and Leisure Section (1 September): 1–11.

Davis, Ronald L. 1965. *A History of Opera in the American West.* Englewood Cliffs, N.J.: Prentice-Hall.

―――. 1966. *Opera in Chicago.* New York: Appleton-Century.

Davison, James W. 1912. *Music During the Victorian Era.* London: Reeves.

Dawson, Peter. 1951. *Fifty Years of Song.* London: Hutchinson.

Dickens, Charles. 1884. *Pictures from Italy and American Notes.* Boston: Perry Mason & Co.

Dixon, Sydney W. 1921. "How Great Artists First Made Records: The Late Adelina Patti." *The Voice* (June): 6–7.

Doggett, Jr., John. 1851. *Doggett's New York City Street Directory for 1851.* New York: Doggett.

Dorman, Jr., James H. 1967. *Theater in the Ante Bellum South.* Chapel Hill: University of North Carolina Press.

Duey, Philip A. 1951. *Bel Canto in Its Golden Age.* New York: King's Crown Press.

Dumay, Henri. 1901. "Patti's Secret of Youth." *The* [New York] *World* (9 June) Sunday Magazine.

Duval, J. H. 1958. *Svengali's Secrets and Memoirs of the Golden Age.* New York: Speller & Sons.

Eames, Emma. 1927. *Some Memories and Reflections.* New York: Appleton.

Eaton, Quaintance. 1957. *Opera Caravan.* New York: Farrar, Straus and Cudahy.

Echeverría, Francisco. 1988. "El Debut de la Patti en la Habana." *Clave* (November): 50–57.

"Echoes from Abroad." 1877. London *Truth* (8 March): 299–300.

Edwards, Anne. 1984. *Matriarch.* New York: William Morrow.

Engel, Louis. 1886. *From Mozart to Mario.* 2 vols. London: Bentley.

Esperanza y Sola, José. 1906. *Treinta Años de Crítica Musical.* 3 vols. Madrid: Viuda.

Evans, Lindsay. 1976. "Adelina Patti and Craig-y-Nos." *Welsh Music* (Spring): 41–51.

"Fabulous Adelina Patti." 1948. *Opera News* (12 January): 26–30.

Faris, Alex. 1980. *Jacques Offenbach.* New York: Scribners.

Farmer, Konrad. N.d. *Gustave Doré.* 2 vols. Dresden: Haus der Kunst.

Farrar, Geraldine. 1938. *Such Sweet Compulsion.* New York: Greystone Press.

Ferris, George T. 1897. *Great Singers.* New York: Appleton.

Filippis, F. de, and R. Arnese. 1961–63. *Cronache del Teatro di San Carlo.* 2 vols. Naples: Edizione Politica Popolare.

Filon, Pierre Augustin. 1929. *Souvenirs sur l'Impératrice Eugénie.* Paris: Calmann-Lévy.

Finck, Henry T. 1884. "Collapse of Italian Opera." *The Nation* (14 August): 129–130.

————. 1913. *Success in Music and How It Is Won.* New York: Scribners.

————. 1926. *My Adventures in the Golden Age of Music.* New York: Funk & Wagnalls.

Fitzdale, Robert, and Arthur Gold. 1991. *The Divine Sarah.* New York: Knopf.

Fitzlyon, April. 1964. *The Price of Genius.* London: John Calder.

Fleury, Comte. 1920. *Memoirs of the Empress Eugénie.* 2 vols. New York: Appleton.

Foot, Katherine B. 1894. "My Tabooed Playmate, Adelina Patti." *The Ladies' Home Journal* (February): 4.

Forbes, Elizabeth. 1985. *Mario and Grisi.* London: Victor Gollancz.

Foresi, Mario. 1919. "Adelina Patti." *Nuova Antologia* (November-December): 109–115.

Formes, Karl. 1891. *My Memoirs.* San Francisco: Jas. H. Barry.

Fouque, Octave. 1881. *Histoire du Théâtre Ventadour.* Paris: Fischbacher.

"Fragments from Patti's Album." 1903. *The* [New York] *Theatre* (November): 286.

Gagey, Edmond M. 1950. *The San Francisco Stage.* New York: Columbia University Press.

Gaisberg, F. W. 1942. *The Music Goes Round.* New York: Macmillan. (Published as *Music on Record* in 1947. London: Robert Hale.) Reprinted in 1977. Salem, N.H.: Ayer Company Publishers.

———. 1943. "Adelina Patti." *The Gramophone* (February): 123–124.

Ganz, Wilhelm. 1913. *Memories of a Musician.* London: John Murray.

Gattey, Charles Neilson. 1979. *Queens of Song.* London: Barris & Jenkens.

Gatti, Carlo. 1955. *Verdi.* New York: Putnam.

———. 1964. *Il Teatro alla Scala.* 2 vols. Milan: Ricordi.

Gatti-Casazza, Giulio. 1941. *Memories of the Opera.* New York: Scribners.

Gelatt, Roland. 1977. *The Fabulous Phonograph 1877–1977.* New York: Macmillan. First edition in 1954. Philadelphia: J. B. Lippincott. British edition in 1956. London: Cassell.

Gerson, Robert A. 1940. *Music in Philadelphia.* Philadelphia: Presser.

Gipson, Richard McCandless. 1940. *The Life of Emma Thursby.* New York: New-York Historical Society.

Girbal, F. Hernández. 1955. *Julián Gayarre.* Barcelona: Ediciones Lira. Reprinted in 1977. New York: Arno Press.

———. 1979. *Adelina Patti.* Madrid: Lira.

Girouard, Mark. 1979. *The Victorian Country House.* New Haven, Conn.: Yale University Press.

Glackens, Ira. 1963. *Yankee Diva.* New York: Coleridge Press.

Glover, James. 1911. *Jimmy Glover: His Book.* London: Methuen.

Gooch, G. P. 1960. *The Second Empire.* London: Longmans.

Gosling, Nigel. 1973. *Gustave Doré.* New York: Praeger.

Gottschalk, Louis Moreau. 1964. *Notes of a Pianist.* Ed. Jeanne Behrend. New York: Knopf.

Grau, Robert. 1909. *Forty Years' Observation of Music and the Drama.* New York: Broadway Publishing.

———. 1912. "Patti's Last American 'Farewell.'" *Musical America* (25 May): 22.

———. 1913. "Will Patti Return at 71—Why Not?" *Musical America* (24 May): 18.

Grave, Théodore de. 1865. *Biographie d'Adelina Patti.* Paris: Librairie de Castel.

Gronow, Rees Howell. 1900. *Reminiscences and Recollections.* 2 vols. New York: Scribners.

Grout, Donald Jay. 1947. *A Short History of Opera.* 2 vols. New York: Columbia University Press.

Guedalla, Phillip. 1922. *The Second Empire.* London: Constable.

Guérard, Albert. 1943. *Napoleon III.* Cambridge, Mass.: Harvard University Press.

Gutiérrez Nájera, Manuel. 1983. *Espectaculos.* Mexico: Unam.

Hanslick, Eduard. 1885. *Musikalische Stationen.* Berlin: Allgemeiner Verein.

———. 1894. *Aus Meinem Leben.* Berlin: Allgemeiner Verein.

———. 1950. *Vienna's Golden Years of Music 1850–1900.* Trans., ed. Henry Pleasants. New York: Simon and Schuster.

Harbord, Eleanor. 1899. "The Marriage of Madame Patti." *The Sketch* (25 January): 2.

Harding, James. 1980. *Jacques Offenbach.* London: John Calder.

Harrison, Bertha. 1907. "Madame Patti's Farewell to London." *African Monthly* (February): 325–332.

Harvey, H. Hugh. 1953. "Patti's First London Faust." *Opera News* (30 November): 14–15.

Haswell, Charles H. 1896. *Reminiscences of an Octogenarian of the City of New York.* New York: Harper & Brothers.

Hauk, Minnie. 1925. *Memoirs of a Singer.* London: A. M. Philpot.

Havens, Catherine Elizabeth. 1920. *Diary of a Little Girl in Old New York.* New York: Henry Collins Brown.

Hegermann-Lindencrone, Lillie de. 1912. *In the Courts of Memory.* New York: Harper.

———. 1914. *The Sunny Side of Diplomatic Life.* New York: Harper.

Henderson, W. J. 1903. "In the World of Music." *The* [New York] *Theatre* (December): 320–322.

———. 1938. *The Art of Singing.* New York: Dial.

Henschel, George. 1919. *Musings and Memories of a Musician.* New York: Macmillan.

Hensel, Octavia. 1870. *Life and Letters of Louis Moreau Gottschalk.* Boston: Ditson.

Henstock, Michael. 1990. *Fernando de Lucia.* Portland, Ore.: Amadeus Press.

Hersee, Henry. 1878. "Madame Patti as an Actress." *The* [London] *Theatre* (August): 26–29.

Herz, Henri. 1866. *Mes Voyages en Amérique.* Paris: Achille Faure.

Hills, Lucius Perry. 1903. *A Memory of Song.* Atlanta: Franklin Publishing.

Hoare, J. Douglas. 1906. "A Chat with Madame Patti." *The* [London] *Graphic* (24 November): 680–681.

Hodgetts, E. A. 1908. *The Court of Russia in the Nineteenth Century.* 2 vols. New York: Scribners.

Hoffman, Richard. 1910. *Some Musical Reflections of Fifty Years.* New York: Scribners.

Hopper, Striker Matt. 1908. *The New York of Yesterday.* New York: Putnam.

Hufeland, Otto. 1940. "Early Mount Vernon." Mount Vernon, N.Y., Public Library.

Huneker, James Gibbons. 1917. *Unicorns.* New York: Scribners.

———. 1920. *Steeplejack.* 2 vols. New York: Scribners.

Huneker, Josephine. 1922. *Letters of James Gibbons Huneker.* New York: Scribners.

Hurst, Julia. 1962. "The Fairy Godmother of the Swansea Valley." *Country Quest* (Spring): 15–17.

Hurst, P. G. 1958. *The Age of Jean de Reszke.* London: Christopher Johnson.

———. 1963. *The Golden Age Recorded.* Lingfield, Surrey: Oakwood Press.

Hutter, Helen Farewell. 1920. "On Tour with Patti." *The Ladies' Home Journal* (March): 59–60.

Hyde, Adolphus. 1943. "The Centenary of Adelina Patti." *Opera News* (8 February): 10–12.

Ibbeken, Ida. 1961. *The Listener Speaks: The Letters from the Audience to*

Bronislaw Huberman. Ramoth Hashawin, Israel.

"Illustrated Interviews. XII—Madame Adelina Patti." 1892. *The Strand Magazine* (June): 563–570.

Ireland, Joseph N. 1960. *Records of the New York Stage from 1750 to 1860.* N. p. Reprinted in 1966. 2 vols. New York: Benjamin Blom.

Ivanovskaya, S. 1889. "Past of Our Italian Opera 1862–1885." *Kolos'ja:* 177–227.

Jackson, Louise Hull. 1927. "Adelina Patti Love Letters." *Musical Courier* (22 December): 6–9.

Jackson, Richard. 1989. "More Notes of a Pianist: A Gottschalk Collection Surveyed and a Scandal Revisited." *Notes* (December): 352–375.

James, Henry. 1956. *Autobiography.* London: W. H. Allen.

———. 1967. *The American Scene.* New York: Horizon Press.

Jenkins, Stephen. 1912. *The Story of the Bronx.* New York: Putnam.

Jerrold, Blanchard. 1891. *Life of Gustave Doré.* London: W. H. Allen.

John, J. R. 1958. "The Swansea Patti Knew." *South Wales Daily Post* (14 March).

Jones, Alan. 1983. *The Story of the Grand.* Llandybïe, Wales: Christopher Davies.

Jones-Davies, J. 1971. "Adelina Patti and Craig-y-Nos." Brecknock *Museum News* (25 November and 2 and 30 December).

Kallmann, Helmut. 1960. *A History of Music in Canada 1534–1914.* Toronto: University of Toronto Press.

Keefer, Lubov. 1962. *Baltimore's Music.* Baltimore: J. H. Furst.

Kellogg, Clara Louise. 1913. *Memoirs of an American Prima Donna.* New York: Putnam.

Kendall, John S. 1930–31. "Patti in New Orleans." *Southwest Review:* 460–468.

Klein, Herman. 1903a. "Modern Musical Celebrities—Adelina Patti." *The Century Magazine* (May): 44–57.

———. 1903b. *Thirty Years of Musical Life in London: 1870–1900.* New York: Century.

———. 1910. *Unmusical New York.* London: John Lane.

———. 1920. *The Reign of Patti.* New York: Century.

———. 1925. *Musicians and Mummers.* London: Cassell.

———. 1931. *Great Women-Singers of My Time.* New York: Dutton.

———. 1933. *The Golden Age of Opera.* London: G. Routledge & Sons.

Knepler, Henry, ed., trans. 1970. *Man About Paris: The Confessions of Arsène Houssaye.* New York: William Morrow.

Kobbé, Gustav. 1904. *Opera Singers.* Boston: Ditson.

———. 1954. *Kobbé's Complete Opera Book.* Ed. the Earl of Harewood. New York: Putnam.

Kolodin, Irving. 1936. *The Metropolitan Opera: 1883–1935.* New York: Oxford University Press.

———. 1953. *The Story of the Metropolitan Opera: 1883–1950.* New York: Knopf.

_____. 1967. *The Metropolitan Opera: 1883–1966.* New York: Knopf.

Kraus, René. 1943. *Young Lady Randolph.* New York: Putnam.

Krehbiel, Henry Edward. 1887. *Review of the New York Musical Scene, 1886–7.* New York: Novello, Ewer.

_____. 1889. *Review of the New York Musical Scene, 1888–89.* New York: Novello, Ewer.

_____. 1908. *Chapters of Opera.* New York: Henry Holt.

Kuhe, Wilhelm. 1896. *My Musical Recollections.* London: Richard Bentley and Son.

Kurtz, Harold. 1964. *The Empress Eugénie.* Boston: Houghton Mifflin.

Lahee, Henry C. 1898. *Famous Singers of To-day and Yesterday.* Boston: Page.

_____. 1902. *Grand Opera in America.* Boston: Page.

_____. 1912. *The Grand Opera Singers of To-day.* Boston: Page.

Lamaza, Luis Reyes de. 1968. *El Teatro en México Durante El Porfirismo.* Mexico: Universidad Nacional.

Lancellotti, Arturo. 1953. *Le Voci d'Oro.* Rome: Fratelli Palombi.

Laurence, Dan H., ed. 1981. *Shaw's Music.* 3 vols. New York: Dodd, Mead.

Lauw, Louisa. 1884. *Fourteen Years with Adelina Patti.* Trans. Jeremiah Loder. New York: Norman L. Munro. (La Scala Autographs, 1977.)

_____. 1884. *Fourteen Years with Adelina Patti.* Trans. Clare Brune. London: Remington & Co.

Lawrence, Vera Brodsky. 1988. *Strong on Music.* New York: Oxford University Press.

Lawton, Mary. 1928. *Schumann-Heink: The Last of the Titans.* New York: Macmillan.

Lee, Sidney. 1925. *King Edward VII.* 2 vols. London: Macmillan.

Lehmann, Lilli. 1909. *How to Sing.* New York: Macmillan.

_____. 1914. *My Path Through Life.* Trans. Alice Benedict Seligman. New York: Putnam.

Lehr, Elizabeth Drexel. 1935. *"King Lehr" and the Gilded Age.* Philadelphia: Lippincott.

Leiser, Clara. 1933. *Jean de Reszke and the Great Days of Opera.* London: Gerald Howe. United States edition in 1934. New York: Minton, Balch.

Lemmone, John, and E. W. Garside. 1926. "Memoirs of John Lemmone—Flute Virtuoso." *The Flutist* (December): 315–318.

Le Petit Homme Rouge. 1912. *The Court of the Tuileries.* London: Chatto & Windus.

Leslie, Anita. 1954. *The Remarkable Mr. Jerome.* New York: Henry Holt.

Leyda, Jay, and Sergei Bertensson, eds., trans. 1947. *The Musorgsky Reader.* New York: W. W. Norton.

The Light of Other Days. [1924.] London: Nash & Grayson.

Liszt, Franz. 1979. *The Letters of Franz Liszt to Olga von Meyendorff 1871–1886.* Trans. William R. Tyler. Cambridge, Mass.: Harvard University Press.

Litvinne, Félia. 1933. *Ma Vie et mon art.* Paris: Librairie Plon. Reprinted in

1977. New York: Arno Press.

Livanova, T. N. 1960–79. *Musical Bibliography of Russian Periodicals of XIX Century.* 6 vols. Moscow: Sovetski.

Lobe, J. C. 1869. *Consonanzen und Dissonanzen.* Leipzig: Baumgärtner's Buchhandlung.

Loewenberg, Alfred. 1955. *Annals of Opera, 1597–1940.* 2nd ed. 2 vols. Geneva: Societas Bibliographica.

Loftus, Augustus. 1894. *The Diplomatic Reminiscences of Lord Augustus Loftus.* 2 vols. London: Cassell.

Loggins, Vernon. 1958. *Where the Word Ends.* Baton Rouge: Louisiana State University Press.

Loliée, Frédéric. 1909. *The Gilded Beauties of the Second Empire.* London: John Long.

——. 1912. *La Fête Impériale.* Paris: Jules Tallandier.

Long, George. 1951. "Craig-y-Nos in the Patti Heyday." *South Wales Evening Post* (10 March).

Lucas, Clarence. 1918. "Patti's School Days." *Musical Courier* (29 August): 7.

Lumley, Benjamin. 1864. *Reminiscences of the Opera.* London: Hurst and Blackett.

Macchetta, Blanche Roosevelt. 1884. *Stage-Struck.* New York: Fords, Howard & Hurlbert.

MacDonald, Cheryl. 1984. *Emma Albani: Victorian Diva.* Toronto: Dundurn Press.

"Madame Adelina Patti." 1877. *The* [London] *Theatre* (14 August): 42–44.

Magnus, Philip. 1964. *King Edward the Seventh.* New York: Dutton.

Mapleson, J. H. 1888. *The Mapleson Memoirs, 1848–1888.* 2 vols. Chicago: Belford, Clarke & Co. and London: Remington.

——. 1966. *The Mapleson Memoirs.* Ed. Harold Rosenthal. New York: Appleton-Century.

Mapleson, Lionel S. 1895. "An American Opera Tour with Madame Patti." *The Strand Magazine* (May): 330–335.

Marchesi, Blanche. 1923. *A Singer's Pilgrimage.* London: Grant Richards.

Marchesi, Mathilde. 1897. *Marchesi and Music.* London and New York: Harper.

Maretzek, Max. 1968. *Revelations of an Opera Manager in Nineteenth-Century America.* New York: Dover. Originally published in two volumes: *Crotchets and Quavers or Revelations of an Opera Manager in America,* 1855, New York: S. French, and *Sharps and Flats,* 1890, New York: American Musician Publishing Company.

Marks, Edward B. 1944. *They All Had Glamour.* New York: Messner.

Martin, Ralph D. 1969. *Jennie.* 2 vols. Englewood Cliffs, N.J.: Prentice-Hall.

Martin, Sadie E. (Mrs. John B.). 1891. *The Life and Professional Career of Emma Abbott.* Minneapolis, Minn.: L. Kimball Printing Co.

Mason, William. 1901. *Memories of a Musical Life.* New York: Century.

Massie, Robert K. 1968. *Nicholas and Alexandra.* London: Gollancz.

Maxwell, Elsa. 1954. *R.S.V.P.* Boston: Little, Brown.

Mayer, Martin. 1983. *The Met.* New York: Simon and Schuster.

Melba, Nellie. 1925. *Melodies and Memories.* London: Thornton Butterworth. United States edition in 1926. New York: George H. Doran. Reset in 1980 with notes and introduction by John Cargher. Melbourne: Thomas Nelson Australia.

Melnikov, Ivan Alexandrovich. 1909. "Excerpts from Memoirs." *Russkaia Starina:* 349–364.

"Mephisto's Musings." 1919. *Musical America* (11 October): 7.

Merkling, Frank, John W. Freeman, and Gerald Fitzgerald with Arthur Solin. 1965. *The Golden Horseshoe: The Life and Times of the Metropolitan Opera House.* New York: Viking and London: Secker & Warburg.

Meyer, Michael. 1967. *Henrik Ibsen.* London: Rupert Hart-Davis.

"Miss Adelina Patti, the New Prima Donna." 1860. *Harper's Weekly* (24 March): 185.

Moncey, Jannot de (Duc de Conegliano). 1897. *Le Second Empire: La Maison de l'Empereur.* Paris: Calmann Lévy.

Moore, Edward C. 1930. *Forty Years of Opera in Chicago.* New York: Horace Liveright.

Moore, Jerrold Northrop. 1973. "Adelina Patti Makes Records." *The Gramophone* (September): 464–465.

_____. 1976a. *A Matter of Records.* New York: Taplinger.

_____. 1976b. *A Voice in Time: The Gramophone of Fred Gaisberg 1873–1951.* London: Hamish Hamilton.

Moran, William R. 1985. *Nellie Melba: A Contemporary Review.* Westport, Conn.: Greenwood.

_____, ed. 1990. *Herman Klein and The Gramophone.* Portland, Ore.: Amadeus Press.

Morris, Lloyd. 1951. *Incredible New York.* New York: Random.

Mortier, Michel. [1881.] "Biographical Sketch: Madame Adelina Patti." [New York: H. A. Rosi.]

Morton, Frederic. 1963. *The Rothschilds.* New York: Fawcett.

Mott, Hopper Striker. 1908. *The New York of Yesterday.* New York: Putnam.

Mudd, A. I. N.d. "Adelina Patti." Paper on Washington, D.C., Early Appearances. New York Public Library Drama Division.

Muir, J. 1882. "Craig-y-Nos Castle." *The Gardeners' Chronicle* (22 April): 538.

"Musical and Theatrical." 1860. *New-York Illustrated News* (3 March): 243.

Musin, Ovide. 1920. *My Memories.* New York: Musin.

Nectoux, Jean-Michel. 1986. *Stars et Monstres Sacrés.* Paris: Ministère de la Culture . . . .

Nevill, Ralph, ed. 1910. *The Reminiscences of Lady Dorothy Nevill.* London: Nelson.

Neville, Amelia Ransome. 1932. *The Fantastic City.* New York: Houghton Mifflin.

Nevins, Allan, ed. 1927. *The Diary of Philip Hone 1828–1852.* 2 vols. New York: Dodd, Mead.

_____ and Milton Hakey Thomas, eds. 1952. *The Diary of George Templeton Strong.* 4 vols. New York: Macmillan.

Nice, L'Opéra de. 1985. *D'Un Siècle à l'autre—L'Opéra de Nice 1885–1985.* Nice: L'Opéra de Nice.

North-Peat, Anthony B. 1903. *Gossip from Paris During the Second Empire.* New York: Appleton.

"Notes from the Opera." 1895. *The Sketch* (19 June): 408.

"Notes from Paris." 1899. London *Truth* (26 January): 211–212.

O'Connor, Harvey. 1941. *The Astors.* New York: Knopf.

O'Connor, T. P. 1901. *In the Days of My Youth.* London: C. A. Pearson.

Odell, George C. D. 1927–49. *Annals of the New York Stage.* 15 vols. New York: Columbia University Press.

Olavarria y Ferrari, Enrique. 1961. *Resena Histórica del Teatro en México.* Mexico City: Biblioteca Porrua.

Olivier, Henry. 1887. "Souvenirs sur la Patti." *Revue d'Art Dramatique:* 351–354.

Onnore, I. I. 1910. "Eleven Years in the Theater." *Russkaia Starina:* 95–108.

"Orígenes y Desarrollo de la Afición Teatral en Puerto Rico." 1970. Estado Libre Asociado de Puerto Rico.

Orr, N. Lee. 1984. "Alfredo Barili: Atlanta Musician, 1880–1935." *American Music* (Spring): 43–60.

Osborne, Charles. 1971. *Letters of Giuseppe Verdi.* New York: Holt, Rinehart and Winston.

_____ . 1987. *Verdi.* New York: Fromm.

P. 1862. "Patti in Paris." *Musical World* (20 December): 811.

Page, Cecilia. 1958. "I Remember Patti." *South Wales Daily Post* (12 and 13 March).

Pasarell, Emilio J. 1959. "El Centenario de los Conciertos de Adelina Patti y Luis Moreau Gottschalk en Puerto Rico." *Revista del Instituto de Cultura Puertorriqueño* (January-March): 52–55.

Patti, Adelina. 1884. "Adelina Patti." *The Keynote* (12 January): 4–5.

_____ . 1899. "Adelina Patti, on the Eve of Her Third Marriage, Writes the Story of Her Early Life." *The* [New York] *World* (15 January).

_____ . 1904. "The Art of Song, Yesterday and To-day." *The Independent* (17 March): 605–609.

_____ . 1906. "My Operatic Heroines." *The Strand Magazine* (December): 657–662.

_____ . 1908. "My Reminiscences." *The Strand Magazine* (December): 706–715.

"Patti as a Critic." 1882. *Musical Record* (21 January): 259.

"Patti at Home." 1885. *Musical Record* (July): 8.

"Patti in Paris." 1886. *Musical Record* (January): 9.

"Patti Interviewed." 1907. *Musical America* (6 July): 8.

"Patti Scandal." 1877. London *Truth* (9 August): 172–174.

"Patti's Childhood." 1877. *Dwight's Journal of Music* (24 November): 136.

"Patti's Debut." 1899. *Musical America* (27 May): 6.

"Patti v. Patti." 1863. *Musical World* (6 June): 356–357.

"Patti Wedding Souvenir." 1899. *Brecon County Times* (25 January).

Payne, Albert. [1896.] *Berühmte Sängerinnen der Vergangenheit und Gegenwart.* Leipzig: A. H. Payne.

Pearce, Charles E. [1924.] *Sims Reeves.* London: Stanley Paul.

Pearce, Godfrey, Mrs. 1910. *The Romance of a Great Singer.* London: Smith, Elder.

Peltz, Mary Ellis. 1964. "Romance a Hundred Years Ago." *Opera News* (22 February): 12–15.

Peterson, Otto Petrovich. 1946. "Memories of Adelina Patti." *Opera News* (4 March): 13–15.

Pleasants, Henry. 1966. *The Great Singers.* New York: Simon and Schuster.

———, ed., trans. 1978. *The Music Criticism of Hugo Wolf.* New York: Holmes & Meier Publishers.

Poe, Edgar Allan. 1988. "A Certain Portion of the Doings of Gotham." *The New York Times* (27 August): 25.

Ponder, Winifred. 1928. *Clara Butt.* London: George G. Harrap. Reprinted in 1978. New York: Da Capo Press.

Pougin, Arthur. 1912. *Marietta Alboni.* Paris: Librairie Plon.

Radic, Thérèse. 1986. *Melba: The Voice of Australia.* Melbourne: Macmillan.

Rasponi, Lanfranco. 1982. *The Last Prima Donnas.* New York: Knopf.

Reeves, Sims. 1888. *His Life and Recollections.* London: Simpkin Marshall.

———. [1889.] *My Jubilee.* London: London Music Publishing Company.

Reid, Charles. 1965. "Patti at Craig-y-Nos." *High Fidelity* (July): 43–87.

"The Return of Madame Patti." 1895. *The Sketch* (5 June): 294–296.

Ronald, Landon. 1922. *Variations on a Personal Theme.* London: Hodder and Stoughton.

———. 1931. *Myself and Others.* London: Sampson Low Marston & Co.

Root, George F. [1891.] *The Story of a Musical Life.* Cincinnati, Ohio: John Church.

Rosate-Lunn, Ethel. 1961. "My Recollections of Madame Patti." *Brycheiniog:* 179–186.

Roscioni, Carlo Marinelli. 1987. *Il Teatro di San Carlo: La Cronologia 1737–1987.* Naples: Guida Editori.

Rosenthal, Harold. 1958. *Two Centuries of Opera at Covent Garden.* London: Putnam.

Rosselli, John. 1991. *Singers of Italian Opera.* Cambridge: Cambridge University Press.

Roth, Cecil. 1939. *The Magnificent Rothschilds.* New York: Pyramid Books.

"Royal Italian Opera." 1861. *Musical World* (1 June): 348.

R. S. 1862. "Adelina Patti at Brussels." *Musical World* (22 February): 119.

Ruskin, Gertrude. 1943. "Queen of Song." *The Atlanta Journal* (2 May) Magazine Section: 4.

Ryan, Thomas. 1899. *Recollections of an Old Musician.* New York: Dutton.

Sackville-West, Edward, and Desmond Shawe-Taylor. 1952. *The Record Year I.* London: Collins.

Saint-Amand, Imbert de. 1900. *Napoleon III at the Height of His Power*. New York: Scribners.

Saint-Léger, A. 1874. *Nos Actrices*. Paris: Chez Disdéri.

Saint-Saëns, Camille. 1919. *Musical Memoirs*. Trans. Edwin Gile Rich. Boston: Small, Maynard.

Saldoni, Baltasar. 1868–81. *Diccionario Biográfico*. 4 vols. Madrid: D. Antonio Perez Dubrull.

Salès, Jules. 1971. *Théâtre Royal de la Monnaie*. Nivelles: Éditions Havaux.

Santley, Charles. 1892. *Student and Singer*. London: Edward Arnold.

Scharf, J. Thomas. 1886. *History of Westchester County*. 2 vols. Philadelphia: L. E. Preston.

Schermerhorn, Gene. 1982. *Letters to Phil: Memories of a New York Boyhood, 1848–1856*. New York: Leslie-Dwinell.

Scholes, Percy A. 1955. *The Oxford Companion to Music*. 9th ed. London: Oxford University Press.

Schonberg, Harold. 1963. *The Great Pianists*. New York: Simon and Schuster.

———. 1967. *The Great Conductors*. New York: Simon and Schuster.

Schürmann, J. 1893. *Les Étoiles en Voyage*. Paris: Phospho-Cacao.

Schwab, Arnold T. 1963. *James Gibbons Huneker*. Stanford, Ca.: Stanford University Press.

Scott, Michael. 1977. *The Record of Singing to 1914*. 2 vols. London: Duckworth.

Scudo, P. 1863. *La Musique en l'Année 1862*. Paris: J. Hetzel.

Searle, Humphrey, ed., trans. 1966. *Hector Berlioz: A Selection from His Letters*. New York: Harcourt, Brace & World.

Seltsam, William H. 1947. *Metropolitan Opera Annals*. New York: Wilson.

Shaw, Bernard. 1937. *London Music in 1888–89*. New York: Dodd, Mead.

———. 1961. *How to Become a Musical Critic*. New York: Hill and Wang.

———. 1977. *Music in London 1890–94*. 3 vols. London: Constable.

Sheean, Vincent. 1958. *Orpheus at Eighty*. New York: Random House.

Shultz, Gladys Denny. 1962. *Jenny Lind*. Philadelphia: Lippincott.

Smith, Mortimer. 1943. *The Life of Ole Bull*. Princeton, N.J.: Princeton University Press.

Soissons, Comte de. 1920. *The True Story of the Empress Eugénie*. London: Bodley Head.

Soldene, Emily. 1897. *My Theatrical and Musical Recollections*. London: Downey & Co.

Soubies, Albert. 1913. *Le Théâtre-Italien de 1801–1913*. Paris: Fischbacher.

Spalding, Albert. 1943. *Rise to Follow*. New York: Henry Holt.

Stagno Bellincioni, Bianca. 1943. *Roberto Stagno e Gemma Bellincioni Intimi*. Florence: Casa Editrice Monsalvato. Reprinted in 1977 with discography by W. R. Moran. New York: Arno Press.

Stanislavsky, Constantin. 1924. *My Life in Art*. New York: Little, Brown. (Theatre Arts Book, 1948.)

Steane, J. B. 1974. *The Grand Tradition: Seventy Years of Singing on Record*. London: Duckworth.

Steinitzer, Max. 1920. *Meister des Gesangs*. Berlin: Schuster & Loeffler.

Stokes, I. N. Phelps. 1928. *The Iconography of Manhattan Island 1498–1909*. 6 vols. New York: Robert H. Dodd.

Stoullig, Edmond. 1876–1918. *Les Annales du Théâtre et de la Musique*. 41 vols. Paris: Charpentier, 1876–96, and Ollendorf, 1897–1918.

"Strakosch and Patti." 1900. *Musical Courier* (24 October): 26–36.

Strakosch, Maurice. 1887. *Souvenirs d'un Impresario*. Paris: Ollendorf.

Stranger's Guide Around New York and Its Vicinity. 1853. New York: Graham.

Subira, José. 1948. *Historia y Anecdotario del Teatro Real*. Madrid: Editorial Plus-Ultra.

Sutherland Edwards, H. 1888. *The Prima Donna*. 2 vols. London: Remington.

Tetrazzini, Luisa. 1921. *My Life of Song*. London: Cassell. United States edition in 1922. Philadelphia: Dorrance.

Thomas, Theodore. 1905. *Theodore Thomas: A Musical Autobiography*. Ed. George P. Upton. Chicago: A. C. McClurg.

Thompson, Donald. 1970. "Gottschalk in the Virgin Islands." *Yearbook for Inter-American Musical Research:* 95–103.

Thompson, Oscar. 1937. *The American Singer*. New York: Dial Press.

———, ed. 1956. *The International Cyclopedia of Music and Musicians*. 7th ed. New York: Dodd, Mead.

Thurner, A. 1883. *Les Reines de Chant*. Paris: A. Hennuyer.

Tolstoy, Leo. 1988. *Anna Karenina*. Trans. Joel Carmichael. New York: Bantam.

Trevelyan, Raleigh. 1973. *Princes under the Volcano*. New York: William Morrow.

Tuggle, Robert. 1983. *The Golden Age of Opera*. New York: Holt, Rinehart and Winston.

Tully, Andrew. 1947. *Era of Elegance*. New York: Funk & Wagnalls.

Turnbull, Patrick. 1974. *Eugénie of the French*. London: Michael Joseph.

Tyler, Froom. 1967. "Patti, the Lady of Craig-y-Nos." *Glamorgan Historian:* 56–62.

Upton, George P. 1908. *Musical Memories*. Chicago: A. C. McClurg.

Vacano, Emil. 1875. *Der Roman der Adelina Patti*. Vienna: Klie & Spitzer.

Valentine, D. T. 1852. *Manual of the Corporation of the City of New York for 1852*. New York: McSpedon & Baker.

Vanderbilt II, Arthur T. 1989. *Fortune's Children*. New York: William Morrow.

Viel Castel, Comte Horace de. 1888. *Memoirs*. London: Remington.

Vizentini, Albert. 1868. *Derrière la toile*. Paris: Achille Faure.

Vizetelly, Ernest Alfred. 1907. *Court Life of the Second French Empire*. New York: Scribners.

Wagenknecht, Edward. 1964. *Seven Daughters of the Theater*. Norman: University of Oklahoma Press.

Wagnalls, Mabel. 1907. *Stars of the Opera*. New York: Funk & Wagnalls.

Wallace, Irving, et al. 1981. *The Intimate Sex Lives of Famous People*. New York: Dell.

Walsh, T. J. 1981. *Second Empire Opera*. New York: Riverrun Press.

_____. 1975. *Monte Carlo Opera 1879–1909*. Dublin: Gill and Macmillan.
Ward, Artemus. 1860. "Artemus Ward on Patti." *Musical World and New-York Musical Times* (30 June): 7.
Weinstock, Herbert. 1963. *Donizetti*. New York: Pantheon Books.
_____. 1968. *Rossini*. New York: Knopf.
Wenzel, Joseph E. 1978. *Geschichte der Hamburger Oper 1678–1978*. Hamburg: Hamburgische Staatsoper.
Werfel, Franz, and Paul Stefan. 1942. *Verdi*. New York: L. B. Fischer.
White, Richard Grant. 1882. "Opera in New York." *The Century Magazine* (April): 865–882 and (June) 193–210.
Wilder, Marshall P. 1892. "Adelina Patti-Nicolini." *Frank Leslie's Illustrated Weekly* (22 December): 454.
Williams, Clifford, and W. R. Moran. 1956. "Adelina Patti." *The Record Collector* (July-August): 169–195.
Williams, Roger L. 1967. *The World of Napoleon III*. New York: Free Press.
Williams, Stewart, ed. 1963–71. *Glamorgan Historian*. 7 vols. Cambridge-Glamorgan: D. Brown and Sons.
Wilson, Florence. 1892. "A Day in Patti's Castle." *The Ladies' Home Journal* (May): 1–2.
Winterstein, Carl. 1863. "Adelina Patti's First Triumph." *Musical World* (5 December): 774.
Wolff, Stéphane. 1983. *L'Opéra au Palais Garnier*. Paris: Slatkine.
Wood, Henry J. 1938. *My Life of Music*. London: Gollancz.
Wyndham, Henry Saxe. 1906. *The Annals of Covent Garden Theater, 1732–1897*. London: Chatto and Windus.
Z. 1889a. "The Birthday of Patti." *Pall Mall Budget* (28 February): 265–266.
_____. 1889b. "Patti's Castle in Wales." *Pall Mall Budget* (7 March): 304.

Letters and Manuscripts

Prince Arthur of England to Queen Victoria, 16 April and 23 July 1871. Windsor Castle Archives.
Barili, Louise, to Barili family in Atlanta, Georgia, 8 April 1906 and 15 May 1911. Georgia Department of Archives and History.
_____ to Rolf Cederström, 31 January 1920. Georgia Department of Archives and History.
August Belmont, Sr. Papers. Rare Books and Manuscripts Division, New York Public Library, Astor, Lenox and Tilden Foundations.
Cederström, Rolf, to Alfredo Barili, 11 February 1904. Mary Barili Goldsmith Collection.
_____ to Louise Barili, 22 October 1919 and 8 April 1920. Georgia Department of Archives and History.
_____ to Gustaf Cederström, 14 November and 23 December 1904. Carin Cederström Ekelöf Collection.
_____ to Robert Grau, 4 February 1903. Robinson Locke Collection, Drama Division, New York Public Library.

Curtis, John. N.d. "One Hundred Years of Grand Opera in Philadelphia." 7 vols. Unpublished ms. The Historical Society of Pennsylvania, Philadelphia.

Ekelöf, Carin Cederström, to the author, 1978–91. John F. Cone Collection.

Estavan, Lawrence, ed. 1938. "The History of Opera in San Francisco." 2 vols. Monograph 17 from Theatre Research, W. P. A. Project 8386, San Francisco.

King George V of England's Diary, October 1914. Windsor Castle Archives.

Goldsmith, Mary Barili, to the author, 1986–92. John F. Cone Collection.

Grote, Frederick, to Caterina Patti. Deed in Bronx Liber 307. 151.

Prince Leopold of England to Princess Louise, 15 May 1871. Windsor Castle Archives.

Queen Mary of England's Diary, October 1914. Windsor Castle Archives.

New York Academy of Music Papers. Theatre Collection, Museum of the City of New York.

Nicolini, Ernest, to Pierre Gailhard, 22 and 27 October 1888 and 14 November 1888. Bibliothèque Nationale: Paris.

———— to James H. Mapleson, 16 September 1892. Stuart-Liff Collection.

———— to Alfred de Rothschild, 1889–95. Rothschild Archives: London.

————. Wills dated 18 October 1886, 26 January 1889, and 29 June 1897. Somerset House: London.

Patti, Adelina, to Alfredo, Emily, and Louise Barili, 1891–1919. Georgia Department of Archives and History and Mary Barili Goldsmith Collection.

———— to Marie Bevignani, 14 September 1888. Royal Opera Covent Garden Archives.

———— to Mrs. Theodore Brooks, 1896–1907. Music Division, New York Public Library.

———— to Eleonore and Gustaf Cederström, 1899–1918. Carin Cederström Ekelöf Collection.

———— to Michael Costa, 24 August 1862. Harvard Theatre Collection. Harvard College.

———— to Pierre Gailhard, 23 October 1888. Bibliothèque Nationale: Paris.

———— to William Ewart Gladstone, 1890–91. British Museum Manuscript Room.

———— to Mrs. Gwynne, 1900–15. John Vivian Hughes Collection.

———— to Frederick Gye, 8 December 1866, Royal Opera Covent Garden Archives.

———— to Edward Hall, 1880–1905. Music Division, New York Public Library.

———— to Beatty-Kingston, 29 August 1895. Stuart-Liff Collection.

———— to Louisa Lauw, 16 May 1870. Österreichische Nationalbibliothek.

———— to Ada Lloyd, 1891–1918. Glamorgan County Record Office.

———— to Richard Nicolini, 26 February 1898. Stiftelsen Musikkulturens: Stockholm.

———— to Mrs. W. H. P. Robbins, 30 August 1903. National Library of Wales.

_____ to Max Strakosch, 5 March, 16 September, and 2 and 12 October 1864. Metropolitan Opera Archives.

_____ to Robert Strakosch, 21 July and 20 December 1917. Stiftelsen Musikkulturens: Stockholm.

_____ to unidentified individual, 27 December 1885. Cardiff Library.

_____ to unidentified individual, 25 September 1884. Mary Flagler Cary Music Collection. The Pierpont Morgan Library.

_____ to Giulia Valda, 1889–91. Louisiana State University.

_____. Scrapbooks 379–380. Robinson Locke Collection. Drama Division, New York Public Library.

_____. Will dated 17 March 1917. Somerset House: London.

Pittman, Josiah. N.d. "Adelina Patti." Unpublished ms. Cardiff Library.

_____ to Edward Hall, 1878–84. National Library of Wales.

Rubin, Libby Antarsh. 1974. *Gottschalk in Cuba*. Ph.D. Thesis, Columbia University, New York.

Stevens, Roger. N.d. "Adelina Patti, Nicolini and Craig-y-Nos." Brecon Beacons National Park.

Tribble, Edwin. 1972. "The Prima Donna as Goddess: A Life of Adelina Patti." Unpublished ms. La Cañada Memorial Library, La Cañada, California. (Revised 1976.)

Queen Victoria of England's Journal, 4 July 1872. Windsor Castle Archives.

Woodford, Mabel, to Louise Barili, 16 March 1920. Georgia Department of Archives and History.

_____ to Edward Hall, 1895–96. National Library of Wales.

_____. Scrapbook and Letter Copy Book. William R. Moran Collection, microfilm 7838, The Library of Congress. Originals: La Cañada Memorial Library, La Cañada, California.

Newspapers and Magazines

American Art Journal, 1864–1905.

American Musician, 1884–90.

American Queen, October 1883–December 1885.

American Queen and Town Topics, January–February 1885.

Athenæum, 1861–85.

Bad Homburg *Der Taunusbote,* 1865–72.

Ballou's Pictorial Drawing-Room Companion, 1851–59.

Baltimore American, January 1884.

Baltimore *Sun,* January–February 1852.

Boston Daily Advertiser, December 1883, December 1884, and December– May 1885.

Boston Daily Evening Transcript, January–February 1860.

Boston Daily Globe, December 1883–May 1885.

Boston Herald, January 1884–86.

Boston Morning Journal, December 1883.

Boston Post, December 1883–87.
Brecon and Radnor Express, 1897–1986.
Brecon County Times, 1899.
Brooklyn Daily Eagle, November 1883–85.
Buenos Aires *Standard,* 1888–90.
Cambrian, 1878–93.
Cambrian Daily Leader, 1897–1909.
Cheyenne Daily Leader, March 1884–February 1885.
Chicago *Daily Inter Ocean,* January 1884–89.
Chicago Daily Tribune, January 1884–89.
Chicago Herald, January–December 1889.
Critic, October–December 1883.
Denver Republican, February–March 1884.
Denver *Rocky Mountain Daily News,* February–March 1884.
Dwight's Journal of Music, 1852–81.
Educational Herald and Musical Monthly, 1857–62.
Era Almanack, 1879–85.
Etude, 1896–1920.
Freund's Music and Drama, October 1883–July 1886.
Gazette: Burlington, Iowa, April 1885.
Gazzetta Musicale di Milano, 1877–93.
Gil Blas, 1891–1902.
Graphic, 1888–1906.
Harper's Bazaar, 8 December 1888.
Harper's New Monthly Magazine, December 1883–April 1886.
Hartford Courant, 11 September 1852.
Illustrated London News, 1861–1920.
Illustrated Sporting and Dramatic News, 1874–83.
Journal de St. Pétersbourg, 1869–77.
Journal des Débats, 1887–96.
Kansas City *Evening Star,* February 1884–February 1885.
Kansas City Journal, February 1884–February 1885.
Kansas City Times, February 1884–February 1885.
Keynote, 1883–94.
La Chronique Musicale, 1865–70.
L'Art Musical, 1861–90.
La France Musicale, 1862–69.
Le Figaro, 1862–1920.
Le Ménestrel, 1860–90.
Le Temps, 1862–70.
Le Théâtre, 1889–1914.
London *Daily News,* 1861.
London *Daily Telegraph,* 1861–1908.
London *Morning Post,* 1861.
London *Morning Star,* 1863.
London *Pall Mall Gazette,* 1865–1920.

London *Standard*, 1862.
London *Theatre*, 1878–86.
London *Times*, 1861–1920.
London *Truth*, 1877–99.
L'Orchestre, 1862–90.
Madrid *Epoca*, 1870–90.
Madrid *Gaceta*, 1863–90.
Madrid *Revista de Teatros*, 1843.
Minneapolis *Daily Minnesota Tribune*, February 1884.
Minneapolis Tribune, February 1884.
Montevideo *El Siglo*, 1888.
Montevideo Musical, 1888.
Montevideo *La Tribuna Popular*, 1888.
Montreal *Gazette*, December 1883.
Montreal *La Minerve*, December 1883–January 1884.
Montreal *Le Monde*, December 1883–January 1884.
Morning Courier and New-York Enquirer, 1847–56.
Music and Drama, January 1882–December 1883.
Musical America, 1898–1930.
Musical and Dramatic Times and Music Trade Review, 1875–79.
Musical Courier, 1886–1930.
Musical Record, 1882–1904.
Musical Review and Gazette, 1849–62.
Musical Times, 1861–1903.
Musical World, 1859–91.
Musical World and New-York Musical Times, 1852–60.
New Haven *Daily Palladium*, September 1852.
New Orleans *Daily Picayune*, 1860–85.
New Orleans *Times-Democrat*, January–February 1885.
New York *Albion*, 1847–60.
New York Clipper, 1853–1920.
New York Commercial Advertiser, 1852–94.
New York *Daily Graphic*, January 1883–June 1885.
New York *Daily News*, August 1877.
New York *Daily Telegraph*, 1877–99.
New-York Daily Tribune, 1848–1904.
New York Evening Post, 1847–1920
New York *Evening Telegram*, 1867–1920.
New York Herald, 1847–1920.
New-York Illustrated News, 1859–60.
New York *Spirit of the Times*, 1848–68.
New York *Sun*, 1847–1920.
New York *Theatre*, 1903–05.
New York Times, 1851–1988.
New York *Weekly Review of Music*, 1850–73.
New York *World*, 1863–1920.

Omaha *Daily Bee*, 15 December 1884.
Omaha Daily Herald, April 1884.
Omaha Daily Republican, April 1884.
Orchestra and the Choir, 1875.
Philadelphia *North American*, 1882–1904.
Philadelphia *North American and United States Gazette*, 1852.
Philadelphia Press, December 1883–January 1905.
Philadelphia *Public Ledger*, 1852–1904.
Puck, December 1878–June 1886.
Puerto Rico *El Fénix*, 1857.
Punch, 1861–95.
Revue d'Art Dramatique, 1886–89.
Revue et Gazette Musicale de Paris, 1862–89.
Salt Lake City *Deseret Evening News*, March 1884–January 1885.
San Francisco *Argonaut*, March 1884–March 1885.
San Francisco Chronicle, March 1884–February 1904.
San Francisco *Daily Alta California*, March 1884–March 1885.
San Francisco *Daily Examiner*, March 1884–March 1885.
San Francisco *Morning Call*, March 1884–March 1885.
San Francisco *Wasp*, January 1884–June 1885.
Sketch, 1895–99.
South Wales Daily News, 23 October 1905.
South Wales Daily Post, 1893–1920.
South Wales Evening Post, 1935–58.
Springfield Daily Republican, 11 September 1852.
St. Joseph Daily Herald, February 1884–March 1885.
St. Joseph Evening News, February 1884–March 1885.
St. Louis Globe-Democrat, February 1884–February 1885.
St. Louis Missouri Republican, February 1884–February 1885.
St. Louis Post-Dispatch, February 1884–February 1885.
St. Petersburg *Neue Dörptsche Zeitung*, 1869–77.
St. Petersburg *Zeitung*, 1869–77.
Swansea *Daily Industrial World*, 25 May 1897.
Topeka *Kansas Daily State Journal*, February 1885.
Topeka Sunday Capital, February 1885.
Town Topics, March 1885–June 1886.
Vienna *Morgen Post*, 1 October 1876.
Vienna *Recensionen und Mittheilungen über Theater und Musik*, February–
    April 1863.
Western Mail, 1881–1920.
Wiener Zeitung, 1863–80.

The Recorded Legacy of Adelina Patti

by William R. Moran

When Edison's invention of the phonograph came to the attention of the public in 1877, wild speculation about the uses to which the new invention would be applied proved to be premature by a factor of many years. Early attempts to use the machine as a dictating device brought the advance of the use of wax cylinders as a recording medium. The year 1887 saw the introduction of Berliner's disc Gramophone, which employed a lateral-cut groove in a coating of grease on a zinc disk. By 1900, Eldridge Johnson, founder of the Victor Talking Machine Company, was able to improve the Berliner process by cutting the master discs on wax blanks. When late in 1901 he solved the problem of infinite duplication from one original master recording, the infant industry had the tools it needed to take off. What had become an entertainment toy was well on its way to becoming a serious musical instrument and became of interest to serious artists as a mechanical threshold to immortality.

The process of convincing major artists to take the Talking Machine seriously advanced slowly at first, but by September 1902, the Gramophone Company was able to issue a celebrity catalog entitled *"Red Label" Gramophone Records of International Operatic Artists* which included the names of Caruso, Plançon, Renaud, Sammarco, Scotti, Calvé, Chaliapin, and others. Fred Gaisberg of the Gramophone Company made this statement: "Our recording scoop of the year 1903 was Francesco Tamagno." Tamagno's December 1902 contract stipulated for the first time that the artist was to be paid on a royalty basis, receiving 4 shillings per record sold at a price of one pound each. Emma Albani, Sir Charles Santley, Victor Maurel, Mattia Battistini, Édouard de Reszke, Marcella Sembrich, Ernestine Schumann-Heink, and Ben Davies were but a few of the "serious artists" who by the end of the year had consented to make recordings. In March 1904 a major coup was scored by the Gramophone Company when Nellie Melba was added as an "exclusive artist" to their catalogs. On 21 June 1904 Melba wrote the Gramophone Company asking that a set of her records be sent to Jean de Reszke in Paris, so she must have been pleased with them.

Melba had obviously been "converted" at an earlier date. On 4 September 1903, Sidney Dixon, manager of the London office of the Gramophone Company, wrote to the firm's representative in Sydney: "As you know, we have always wanted to make a record of Mme. Melba, but this artiste has always refused to sing for us. She was here at the office a few days ago, and spent some hours listening to Gramophone records. She finally became so interested in them that she wants one of our very best machines and a number [58] of our best records sent as a surprise to her niece . . . in Melbourne." (Melba's selection included recordings by Caruso, De Lucia, Santley, Renaud, and Plançon.) By the end of 1904, two names were conspicuously missing from record company catalogs: those of Jean de Reszke and Adelina Patti. Both singers were certainly well aware of the existence of the gramophone. When Victor introuced the first "Red Seal" Records in the United States with a double-page spread in the *Saturday Evening Post* for 25 April 1903, in addition to photographs of the artists whose records were listed, the advertisement carried a photograph of Adelina Patti with the following quotation: "In listening to the records of Caruso, Plançon etc., it seemed as if those artists were actually singing in my salons."

As the "respectability" of the phonograph began to grow and be recognized by musicians, the decision to record by artists in mid-career or those whose careers were in their ascendency became just a matter of time. For older artists who had retired or were near the ends of distingished careers, it was a different and no doubt very difficult decision. Competition between the recording companies was intense, and artists like De Reszke and Patti were continually besieged by their agents with tempting offers. In a letter to Dixon in London dated 19 May 1904, Alfred Clark of the Paris branch of the Gramophone Company said:

> As to tying up the Reszkes it may be possible to do something with Édouard, who has very little reputation and is practically unknown in France, but Jean de Reszke I feel sure would never do anything with Pathé as long as Pathé sticks to cylinders. Last Sunday Madame Emma Eames said that Jean de Reszke had shown her the Gramophone and that he had told her that he was really anxious to sing, but never would do so until some speed regulator and indicator was put upon the machine, thus confirming what he had already told me several times. There cer-

tainly does not seem to be any possibility of Jean de Reszke making records on a phonograph when he is so jealous of his reputation that he will not put his voice on. a gramophone without this change.

For years, there has been a persistent rumor that Jean de Reszke did record two selections for the Fonotipia Company in Paris on 22 April 1905, the specific date making the story somewhat credible. If the records were indeed made, they must have been destroyed, as they have never been found. Be that as it may, we do know that in the year 1905, Patti was in Paris during the month of February and again towards the end of March, and there is little doubt that she would have seen De Reszke. She had experienced "a little difficulty with her upper tones" during her farewell tour of America, and she and De Reszke were together at Mont Dore from the fifth to the tenth of July 1905, during which time Patti sought help from De Reszke with her vocal problems. This discussion resulted in the visit of De Reszke pupil Florence Stevens to Craig-y-Nos for two weeks at the end of September 1905 (see page 239). In October 1905, Patti had expressed great satisfaction with the results of her coaching in the De Reszke method (Leiser 1933; U.S. ed., 275). At the time of her Albert Hall concert on 10 November, Patti informed Dixon that she would sign a contract with the Gramophone Company (see page 241). If indeed De Reszke had made some recordings in April, it would not seem unreasonable that the matter of recording had come up when he and Patti were together, possibly more than once. With the improvement attributed to the work of Miss Stevens, Patti no doubt decided that as far as recordings were concerned, it was "now or never."

The contract between "the Gramophone Company of the first part" and "the Baroness Adele Maria Juana Patti Cederström (Madame Adelina Patti) . . . of the second part" and "the said Baron Olof Rudolf Cederström of the third part" was dated 23 November 1905 and witnessed by George C. Lewis. The contract stipulated that within a period of six months Patti would record no more than ten selections from her repertoire, and allowed for "additional records of all such other songs sung by her as the Company and Madame Patti may from time to time agree." The financial terms of the Patti contract were the same as those set for the Tamagno recordings in December 1902: the price per record was set at 20 shillings ("or such higher or lower price as shall from time to time be fixed by the Company with the consent in writing of Madame Patti during her life and after her death of the said Baron Olof Rudolf Cederström or his heirs"). Price for sales by the Victor Talking Machine Company was to be $5, with the same provision for adjustment. Royalty was set at 4 shillings per record, to be adjusted in the event of a price change. Patti received a 2000-pound deposit against first royalties. "Madame Patti will not sing or recite for the purposes of reproduction in or by any sound voice reproducing machine or do or consent to any act whereby any person or company other than the Company may be enabled to make records for use in any sound reproducing machine." (Note that there is no prohibition of producing Patti recordings in double-sided form.) Under the date of 7 November 1919, Baron Cederström authorized the Gramophone Company "to catalogue the records of the late Adelina Patti at the same price as Com. Caruso, Dame Nellie Melba and Madame Tetrazzini have agreed to, and I further agree that the royalty payable shall be at the same rate as that paid by the Company to the above-mentioned artistes, namely 10% of the retail selling price of each record sold." One last revision of the contract has been found. On 20 September 1946, Cederström wrote to the company:

> Referring to the contract of the 23rd November, 1905 relative to recordings by the late Adelina Patti, I agree that in lieu of the provisions of the said contract relative to the sale of records reproducing these recordings, the following terms and conditions shall apply:
> 1. that the recordings may be issued throughout the world on double-sided records, both sides of which reproduce recordings by the late Adelina Patti.
> 2. that the royalty on sales of such double-sided records by The Gramophone Co. Ltd. and any person, firm or corporation authorised by it shall be calculated at 10% of the English retail selling price. . . . [For those sold by] The Victor Talking Machine Co. . . . the royalty shall be calculated at the rate of 10% of the retail selling price . . . in the country of manufacture.

On 6 July 1961, the Baroness Cederström authorized EMI (successors to the Gramophone Company) to release Patti recordings on long-playing records, even if coupled with recordings of other artists.

The first recording session took place at Craig-y-Nos on 4, 5, 6, and 7 December 1905. Recording technician Fred Gaisberg's account of the event begins on page 241, and that of Landon Ronald, who played the accompaniments for this first session, on page 242. Ronald's version of Patti's first reaction at hearing her own voice from records was apparently told at a Press Club dinner in 1930 and reported in the *Daily Telegraph*. Herman Klein, writing in *The Gramophone* for March 1930, took umbrage at Sir Landon's story: it differed considerably from his own (Klein 1920, 365), which he again retold. Ronald replied in *The Gramophone* for May 1930, prompting Klein to suggest that both versions of the story are no doubt correct, reporting two different incidents which took place at different times. Ronald's version applies to an immediate playback from a wax plate (which was thus destroyed) made at the time of recording at Patti's urgent request. Klein's story is found under the title "When Patti Heard Herself" in *The Voice of the Victor* for August 1914. The editor of that publication says that the story was reprinted from *The Voice* (which had reprinted it from *Pearson's Magazine*) and seems to refer to a later date in December when the finished recordings were brought to Patti for approval. The conflicting stories and the referenced correspondence are brought together in one place in Moran (1990, 589).

In a letter dated 5 January 1906, Dixon advised the head office of the Gramophone Company of the matrix numbers and titles of the fourteen recordings which Patti had officially approved for release. He further stated: "We have given our word that the Record of Gounod's 'Ave Maria' serial 547 shall be at once destroyed, but others which she has not passed are to be held for the present, but on no account are they to be used, nor are the seconds of 'Home Sweet Home' and 'The Last Rose of Summer.'" (We will come back to the matter of matrix 547f, "Ave Maria," below.)

On 22 March 1906, W. W. Green of the Gramophone Company advised the head office: "We have gone through the Patti Records as requested ... and consider that it would be advisable, if possible, to have 'Home Sweet Home', 'Within a mile of Edinboro' town', 'Kathleen Mavourneen' and 'La Serenata' remade, principally on account of the loud scratching. The last mentioned record has, however, a flat note at the finish." On 1 May, Alfred Clark wrote: "I note that you are arranging for a further series of records by Madame Patti." He specifically requested that she be asked to record the Waltz Song from *Roméo et Juliette*: "It was undoubtedly her greatest success in Paris, and if she can sing this the sale will be large." In reply, the London office noted on 18 June, "As you will doubtless have heard from Scheuplein, the Baroness is to sing some further records this week, and Mr. Birnbaum has arranged to go down to Craig-y-Nos castle when these records are made. ... We have made a special request that Madame Patti should sing the Waltz Song." Apparently such a record was never made.

For the June recording session, Alfredo Barili assisted at the piano, and the recording technicians were Fred Gaisberg and Charles Scheuplein. The eyewitness account of the session given by Louise Barili (see page 246) reveals an interesting detail of the recording process—the moving platform for the singer, an innovation apparently introduced between the two Patti recording sessions—which is seldom found in the literature. At least nine new records were cut, four of them remakes as suggested in the March letter from Green quoted above. The remake of "Home, Sweet Home" has not survived, and the earlier version of "'Twas Within a Mile o' Edinboro' Town" (557f) was apparently more satisfactory than that remade in 1906 (678c). No title is known for one matrix (680c). Three new operatic arias were added, and the final recording of a Spanish ditty by Yradier ("La calesera") completed the session and the recording career of Adelina Patti. The last-mentioned number was initially passed and prepared for publication, but it was quickly withdrawn: rumor has it that Baron Cederström thought it too frivolous. The recording first became generally available when the International Record Collector's Club (IRCC) of Bridgeport, Connecticut, arranged for a special edition to be pressed in April 1933 (coupled with an unpublished Melba recording from "Elaine," about which there will be further comment).

On 12 July 1933, E. C. Forman of RCA Victor in Camden wrote to the Gramophone Company asking if the Patti matrix 547f ("Ave Maria") were still available, and also asking for the date and place of recording. The company replied that the shell was available and that the date was approximately April 1906, but no one could trace where the recording was made! RCA thereupon ordered a copy of the shell, which was used for a special pressing for the International Record Collector's Club and subsequently issued in April 1934 as IRCC No. 33, coupled with 538f (03052, "Pur dicesti"). Someone must have alerted the Gramophone Company that the "Ave Maria" had never been issued and further complained that the IRCC had also issued unpublished Gramophone recordings of Melba. On 20 September 1934, Forman wrote:

> In connection with the shell of the Patti record 547f "Ave Maria" we naturally assumed that your having shipped this shell was an indication that it was perfectly all right for us to use it for pressing purposes. Accordingly the record was supplied to the IRCC, as you will see by the attached list. However, we shall take steps to guard against supplying any more of this particular number. If, after examining the enclosed list, you find other recordings

which come under a similar category, we shall appreciate your notifying us at once providing we should refrain from supplying further records to the club. In one or two instances we have supplied the club with our own recordings of unpublished numbers by living artists, and in these cases Mr. Seltsam [founder of the IRCC] has obtained and submitted to us the artists' personal approval.

In further correspondence, the Gramophone Company apparently objected to the fact that RCA had pressed the "Ave Maria" and other Patti recordings in doubled-sided form. On 24 October 1934, Forman wrote:

With regard to the Patti records which we have issued to the IRCC, we take this opportunity to apologize for any embarrassment we may possibly cause you with double-sided pressings. If we were ever notified by you that this artist's records must be issued in single-faced form only, it was undoubtedly many years ago and unfortunately the fact was entirely overlooked at the time of issuing the records in question. You have our assurance that there will be no recurrence of this kind.

As to artist's royalties on Patti records, we can assure you that this was also an oversight, apparently due to our failure to recognize these as Patti records when passing through our routine. However, we can assure you that the sales have been small.

On 9 November, the International Artistes' Department of the Gramophone Company replied:

We have come to the conclusion that the best arrangement would be for you not to supply any further double-sided Patti records.... On the question of the artiste's royalty on Patti records, no doubt your Royalties Department will check up the sales and make the necessary report, so that full royalties can be accounted for to the artiste's executors. We have already explained to you in previous correspondence the difficulties encountered with Madame Patti's husband, and we are afraid it would be impossible to obtain any concessions from him.

In a bulletin dated 25 February 1936, IRCC 33 (Patti's "Ave Maria") is listed as "withdrawn," as is IRCC 17 (Patti's "La calesera" coupled with the unpublished Melba "Elaine"). In August 1939 Seltsam announced the reissue of "La calesera" as a single-faced record, and at a price which would allow for the payment of the royalty. When the shipment of pressings was received from Camden, it was found that the original double-faced IRCC 17 (Patti/Melba) order had been duplicated in error. Subscribers were overjoyed, and the edition quickly sold out!

On 27 March 1936, Forman wrote to the Gramophone Company asking if it were prepared to furnish parts for Patti's "Il bacio" (544f). On 9 April, Rex Palmer of the International Artistes' Department replied: "Although we have a shell of the recording 544f 'Il Bacio' sung by Adelina Patti, we are unable to furnish you with a pressing or shell, as the recording was never passed and has, therefore at no time appeared in our catalogues."

In 1973, EMI Records published a special limited edition of Adelina Patti recordings on four twelve-inch long-playing sides (set RLS 711) which presented well-engineered transcriptions of twenty-eight Adelina Patti recordings, all that were known, even including the brief personal "New Year's Greeting to Baron Cederström" and all the duplicated and unpublished titles known to exist. Included with the set was a well-produced and informative booklet. In 1988, Pavilion Records issued a collection on compact disc (Pearl GEMM CD 9312) which contained twenty-two of the twenty-eight Patti records (omitted were 539f, 543f, 545f, 548f, 553f, and 678c).

Evaluations of the merit of Patti's recorded legacy have already been given (see pages 247–248). In listening to these recordings, one should keep in mind the remarks of Hugo Wolf, who wrote about a Patti farewell to Vienna on 3 January 1886, some *twenty years* before the recording sessions took place:

> *Adieu à Vienne!* Ten years ago, this sentimental heading to the announcement of a concert by Patti would have left the heart of fashionable society unmoved. . . . Someday it will indeed be an *Adieu à Vienne.* In this farewell greeting there is a suggestion of self-criticism on the part of the famous singer. Unfortunately, we must add our voice to hers, much as we would have liked to contradict her. True, the tones pour silvery clear from the diva throat, but only on the level terrain of the middle voice. She can no longer climb the precipitous heights of the high E and above, nor roam those perilous paths from which trill upon trill once poured down on the delighted ears of enraptured listeners in a fine golden shower. That's all a thing of the past. The fastidious taste of her singing, however, the agility and refinement in the execution of fioritura and mordents, excite admiration now as before. (Pleasants 1978, 177–178).

The Adelina Patti Recordings

Matrix numbers 537f through 557f were recorded in December 1905, with piano accompaniment by Landon Ronald. Matrix numbers 676c through 684c were recorded in June 1906, with piano accompaniment by Alfredo Barili. Pressings from the original 1905 plates show the signature "Adelina Patti Cederström" across the face of the record; the 1906 plates were not so signed. Any 1905 pressings without the signature are mechanical dubbings with inferior sound.

A Note on Recording Speeds   The question of correct playing speeds for early "78 rpm" records has been a vexatious one for many years. No written record of the turntable speeds used when a recording was made appears to have been maintained in early recording sessions. A deviation in speed of four revolutions per minute (rpm) changes the pitch (and thus the key) by one halftone. Not only is the pitch incorrect when a record is played at a speed at which it was not recorded, but more important, the tone quality of the sound is distorted. Many musicians who made early recordings recognized this problem. It was apparently the principal reason Jean de Reszke refused to make recordings: he did not want the general public to be able to tinker with a machine and alter the quality of the famous voice. Early Melba and Eames recordings had the key in which selections were sung printed on the label. The problem was noted by Sembrich when she listened to test pressings of her recordings. Clara Butt must have had this in her contract with the Gramophone Company, as the key of each selection was even printed in the catalogs. It is interesting that the matter was noted in reference to the Patti recordings by her niece, Louise Barili (see page 245). Giving the key of a selection is of little help to the non-musician, so it has become customary to assist the general user by suggesting the turntable speeds at which a record should be played in order to reproduce it correctly. A discussion of various suggestions by a number of experts for the correct playing speeds of the Patti recordings can be found in Williams and Moran (1956) and Aspinall (1992).

The author has in his collection three of Mme. Patti's personal test pressings, on the original sleeves of which are penciled notations. On 542f (No. 7 in the table to follow) is the note: "Not passed [illegible word] last note. L. R." I think we can accept this as a comment from Landon Ronald. There is no speed indicated. On 545f (No. 9), in the same hand, is written: "73. New plate preferred." On 553f (No. 10), again in the same hand, is found: "Psed [i.e., passed] 76½." Here it would seem that we have the final authority for the playing speeds of at least two of the Patti recordings. There has been much discussion about the key in which Patti sang the "Mignon" aria (No. 11), the music for which was published in a soprano and contralto key. In the 1956 article, Favia-Artsay stated she believed it was sung in the soprano key which calls for a playing speed of 78.26; Aspinall (1992) suggests Patti lowered the soprano key by a half-tone, calling for a playing speed of 76.00. Others (including EMI, Pearl, and the present author) prefer to play the recording in the contralto key at 73.47.

The suggested playing speeds of the original Patti recordings shown in the righthand column in the table at right are the result of painstaking study on the part of the author, *but they remain opinions.* They are close to the speeds used by EMI in the preparation of their long-playing album (RLS 711) and Pearl's CD (GEMM 9312) in all cases except the following:

No. 4: EMI and Pearl apparently transcribed this recording at 73.47. Favia-Artsay (in Williams and Moran, 1956) suggested 80.00. The present author favors 77.43.

No. 9: So many copies of 03078 are found with the December 1905 matrix (545f) that it was at one time thought the June 1906 version had never been issued. It was available for a time, however, with Barili correctly identified on its label. EMI used 72.00 for 545f and 73.47 for 676c.

No. 13: Pearl used 74.23; EMI used 76.60, which is also preferred by the present author.

No. 15: EMI used a speed of 75.00; Pearl 73.47. The present author suggests 74.23.

No. 21: Pearl used 74.00; EMI used 76.60, which is also preferred by the present author.

The columns in the discography are headed as follows:

Discography Number   Reference number assigned for this discography.

Matrix Number   The number assigned to each wax at the time of recording, which became the factory reference number for that wax.

Catalog Numbers   The catalog or order number assigned to those recordings which were approved for publication: first the numbers used by the Gramophone and Typewriter Company, or G&T (later "His Master's Voice," HMV); then the catalog numbers used by the Victor Talking Machine Company in North and South America.

Reissue 78 rpm Catalog Nos.   Special issue catalog numbers: IRCC = International Record Collector's Club (United States); HMB = Historic Masters (England); VB = Archive Series (England).

Playing Speed   Suggested playing speeds for original recordings (see discussion above).

Discog. No.	Matrix No.	G&T/HMV Single-face Catalog No.	Victor Single-face Catalog No.	Reissue 78 rpm Catalog Nos.	Playing Speed
1. Ave Maria (Bach-Gounod) (Latin) (pf. Ronald; vln. Marianne Eissler)					
547f	-----	-----	IRCC 33; HMB 78	73.47
2. Il bacio (Luigi Arditi) (Italian) (pf. Ronald)					
544f	-----	-----	-----	73.47
3. The Banks of Allan Water (Old Scottish Song, arr. Charles Horn) (pf. Ronald)					
555f	-----	-----	-----	73.47
4. La calesera (Sebastian Yradier) (Spanish) (pf. Barili)					
684½c	03085	-----	IRCC 17; VB 40	77.43
5. Comin' thro' the Rye (Robert Burns; Old Scottish Air) (pf. Ronald)					
552f	03061	95032	-----	73.47
6. DON GIOVANNI: Batti, batti, o bel Masetto (Mozart) (Italian) (pf. Ronald)					
541f	03055	95039	IRCC 10	74.23
7. FAUST: Ah! Je ris de me voir (Air des bijoux) (Gounod) (French) (pf. Ronald)					
542f	-----	-----	-----	73.47
543f	03056	95037	-----	73.47
8. Home, Sweet Home (from *Clari, the Maid of Milan*) (John Howard Payne; Henry R. Bishop)					
539f	03053	95029	-----	73.47
550f	-----	-----	-----	72.73
679c	(03081)	-----	-----	-----
9. Kathleen Mavourneen (Mrs. Julia Crawford; Frederick N. Crouch)					
545f	03057 & 03078	95035	-----	73.00
676c	03078	-----	-----	73.00
10. The Last Rose of Summer (Thomas Moore; Irish Air, introduced into Flotow's *Martha*)					
546f	-----	-----	HMB 78	73.47
553f	03062	95030	-----	76.60
11. MIGNON: Connais-tu le pays? (A. Thomas) (French) (pf. Barili)					
682c	03083	-----	-----	73.47
12. New Year's Greeting to Baron Cederström (spoken in English)					
-----	-----	-----	-----	-----
13. NORMA: Casta diva! (Bellini) (Italian) (pf. Barili)					
681c	03082	-----	-----	76.60
14. LE NOZZE DI FIGARO: Voi che sapete (Mozart) (Italian) (pf. Ronald)					
537f	03051	95041	IRCC 10	73.47
15. Old Folks at Home (Stephen C. Foster) (pf. Ronald)					
540f	03054	95033	-----	74.23
16. On Parting (Lord Byron; Adelina Patti) (pf. Ronald)					
556f	03063	95042	-----	73.47
17. Pur dicesti (from the pasticcio *Arminio*) (Antonio Lotti) (Italian) (pf. Ronald)					
538f	03052	95040	IRCC 33	73.47
18. Robin Adair (Caroline Keppel; Old Scottish Air) (pf. Ronald)					
549f	03059	95031	-----	74.23
19. La serenata (G. A. Cesareo; F. Paolo Tosti) (Italian)					
548f	03058	95038	-----	73.47
677c	03079	-----	-----	73.47
20. Si vous n'avez rien à me dire (Baroness Willy de Rothschild) (French) (pf. Ronald)					
551f	03060	95036	-----	73.47
21. LA SONNAMBULA: Ah! non credea mirarti (Bellini) (Italian) (pf. Barili)					
683c	03084	-----	-----	76.60
22. 'Twas Within a Mile o' Edinboro' Town (James Hook)					
557f	03064	95034	-----	73.47
678c	(03080)	-----	-----	72.00

Patti Recordings on Cylinders?

Early cylinder phonographs could be used for recording as well as for playback. Such recordings were usually identified by introductory spoken announcements, and spurious recordings with fraudulent announcements are not unknown. It is perfectly possible that Patti's voice was recorded on noncommercial cylinders. It was thought that one such cylinder had indeed been found when William H. Seltsam of the IRCC issued a disc copy of a cylinder on IRCC 219 and again on IRCC 3100, first in November 1942. The cylinder does contain a spoken announcement which identifies it as being by Patti and made in London on 15 June 1895, a date when Patti was indeed in the city. Careful study has shown this record to be spurious, however; the voice is that of Lucette Korsoff, and the cylinder which Seltsam transcribed had been fraudulently copied from a commercial Edison disc (No. 82009). The music is the "Éclat de rire" from Auber's *Manon Lescaut*.

References

Aspinall, Michael. 1973. "Adelina Patti." In accompanying notes (pages 3–7) to *Adelina Patti*. EMI Records RLS 711.

———. 1992. "Adelina Patti—Speeds and Keys." *The Record Collector* (October–December): 268–273.

Crimp, Brian, and Jerrold Northrop Moore. 1973. "Re-Recording Patti." In accompanying notes (page 15) to *Adelina Patti*. EMI Records RLS 711.

Jerrold Northrop Moore. 1973. "Recording Patti." In accompanying notes (pages 8–14) to *Adelina Patti*. EMI Records RLS 711.

Klein, Herman. 1920. *The Reign of Patti*. New York: Century.

Leiser, Clara. 1933. *Jean de .Reszke and the Great Days of Opera*. London: Gerald Howe. United States edition in 1934. New York: Minton, Balch.

Moran, William R., ed. 1990. *Herman Klein and The Gramophone*. Portland, Ore.: Amadeus Press.

Pleasants, Henry, ed., trans. 1978. *The Music Criticism of Hugo Wolf*. New York: Holmes & Meier Publishers.

Williams, Clifford, and W. R. Moran. 1956. "Adelina Patti." *The Record Collector* (July–August): 169–195.

A Chronology
of Patti's Appearances

by Thomas G. Kaufman

The preparation of this chronology has presented a number of problems that were not present when the Caruso chronology (published in 1990 by Amadeus Press) was written. The most important of these are the facts that

- Patti's career started forty years before Caruso's.
- Most of it took place in opera houses and theaters for which there is no published documentation.
- Concert tours (involving many more and smaller cities) played a much larger role in Patti's career than in Caruso's.

Thus, a greater number of compromises have been necessary here, chief among these that, while the listing of Patti's opera performances is probably 95 percent complete, only a much smaller number of the concerts (perhaps 50–75 percent) could be identified in time for publication. It has to be recognized that a chronology of this type can never be 100 percent complete—there will always be another book on a city where she sang or on someone she toured with, another library to visit, or another theatrical journal which just might have some missing information to offer.

This chronology is arranged by season rather than by calendar year, because the usual engagement in many of the capitals of Europe (where Patti spent the greatest portion of her singing career) spanned the autumn of one year and the winter/early spring of the next. All seasons are listed as if they had been in the Northern Hemisphere. Thus a period from May to August in Buenos Aires uses the heading "spring and summer," even though it was actually autumn and winter in the Southern Hemisphere. The operas are listed in chronological order except for side trips, which are indicated as having taken place concurrently with the main season. Principal singers are given when verified. To list full casts, which would

317

frequently have been impossible, would have made this chronology unwieldy and overlong. The same applies to indicating the roles sung by each cast member. Every singer is identified as to vocal register, but this is intended to serve only as a guide, as in many cases it was impossible to determine whether a singer was a baritone or a bass, or, for that matter, a soprano or mezzo-soprano. The symbols used are as follows:

s.	soprano
ms.	mezzo-soprano or contralto
t.	tenor
b.	baritone
bs.	bass
cond.	conductor

It would have been ideal to have made these annals a complete, day-by-day listing. Again, this would have been both impossible because of the many gaps, and unwieldy because the chronology would have been excessively long. Therefore only the dates of the first performance of a work during a season are provided. Since Patti created a number of roles and took part in the local premieres of a somewhat larger number of works, these are shown as follows:

°° world premiere

° confirmed local premiere

No attempt has been made to mark country premieres, as in many instances it would have been impossible to do so with any degree of accuracy. In addition, the absence of an asterisk should not be construed to signify that a given production was not a local premiere— these also could not always be ascertained.

Since concerts played such a large role in Patti's career, a few words of explanation about the various types of concerts are in order.

- "Concert" indicates just that—a performance in which Patti and possibly other soloists sang or played arias, instrumental solos, and ensembles. The accompaniment could be either orchestra or piano. This is not necessarily specified. The chronology does not list the purpose of the concert, that is, whether private, for royalty, for the general public, or for charity; however, these are sometimes discussed in the text.
- "Gala Concert" signals that individual acts or extended scenes of one or more operas were given, almost always in costume.
- "Special Appearance" indicates that Patti appeared at another singer's benefit.

318

As the end of each season approached, it was customary for each star singer, the conductor, and sometimes others who played key roles to have benefit performances. The singer usually selected the opera (if the program consisted primarily of a single work) and sang one or more other selections; other principals might also take part. On other occasions, such a benefit might consist of individual acts of several operas, again selected by the beneficiary. This would be listed as a gala concert. When the benefit was for another singer and comprised an opera Patti did not sing in, but Patti is known to have participated by singing a selection or two, this is indicated as a special appearance. Most such instances are beyond the scope of this chronology, as are most instances where Patti sang additional selections at a benefit concert for herself.

Another interesting consideration is the language that was used for the performances. This is an important piece of information when, for instance, a French opera such as *Faust* was sung in Italian translation. There are many situations, however, where the Italian "translation" of a French or German work is really more than that, and simply stating, for example, *"Martha* in Italian" would not be quite satisfactory. This is because the Italian versions were sanctioned by the composer, with new recitatives or even arias added, as was the case with *Martha, La figlia del reggimento, Dinorah,* and *La stella del Nord. I diamanti della corona* presents a slightly different situation in that Auber was already dead when it was translated into Italian for London. Here, it was the conductor, Augusto Vianesi, who composed the recitatives, added some music from other Auber operas, and rewrote one of the two tenor roles for baritone. For these operas the Italian title will be used.

Finally, a question mark indicates that some doubt exists about the preceding item of information. Thus "Jan.?" means that the month is in doubt, not that the date is unknown. (The latter would be expressed simply as "Jan.") If the 12th of the month is the most likely date, but not absolutely certain, it would be expressed as "Jan. 12?"

Acknowledgments

This chronology would not have been possible without the assistance of many persons. Of these, John Cone deserves special thanks for sharing information that he himself had accumulated over the years; Lim Lai for looking up dates and casts in his fabulous collection of books and programs; and Charles Mintzer, whose profound knowledge of singers and their careers was always of invaluable help. Thanks are due also to Mr. Jordan Massey, whose enthusiasm for Patti inspired this project many years ago; to Dr. S. Frederick Starr of Oberlin College, Oberlin, Ohio, for his help with the 1857–58 Caribbean tour with L. M. Gottschalk; to Mr. Robert Tuggle, Director of Archives of the Metropolitan Opera; to Mrs. Vera Brodsky-Lawrence for providing key details on Patti's early tours; to Mr. Jack Belsom of New Orleans for some key dates in that city; and to Dr. Susana Salgado, who provided dates on Patti's appearances in Uruguay. Dr. Mario Moreau of Lisbon, Mr. Antonio Massissimo of Barcelona, Dr. Eduardo Arnosi of Buenos Aires, and Dr. Antonino Defraia of Cagliari, as well as Mr. Andrew Farkas of Jacksonville, Florida, were also particularly helpful. I am just as indebted to Ms. Karen Kirtley and Ms. Frances Bertolino Farrell of Amadeus for their constant encouragement and many suggestions.

Equally important are the invaluable contributions made by several librarians. Ms. Janet Bone, Mrs. Ruth Schultz, and Mrs. Susan Rowe of the Morris County Free Library, Mrs. Josepha Cooke of the Drew University Library, and Ms. Linda Naru of the Center for Research Libraries, helped me locate and borrow many of the books, newspapers, and periodicals which were essential to compiling this list. Messrs. Donald Wisdom and Frank Carroll of the Newspapers and Periodicals Division of the Library of Congress and their staff were extremely kind in giving me access to countless old newspapers.

I also want to express my sincere thanks to the following individuals and institutions and, at the same time, to apologize to anyone who was inadvertently omitted: Mr. Michael Bott, Mr. Bruno Cagnoli, Mr. Charles Gattey, Mr. Lewis Hall, Dr. Carlo Marinelli-Roscioni, Mr. Francois Nouvion, Mr. William Seward, Mr. Gaspare Nello Vetro, the staffs of the Princeton University Library, the University of Illinois Library, the University of Missouri Library, the University of Minnesota Library, the University of North Carolina Library, the Music Division of the Library of Performing Arts, the Rutgers University Library, the Ball State University Library, and the Music Division of the Library of Congress. I am also grateful to countless other research libraries all over the United States, as well as to the national newspaper libraries of France, the Netherlands, and the United Kingdom.

And finally, I am indebted to my wife, Marion, without whose patience and encouragement this listing would have been equally impossible.

Bibliography

Beetz, Wilhelm. 1952. *Das Wiener Opernhaus 1869–1945.* Vienna: Amaltea Verlag.

Bing, Anton. 1896. *Rückblicke auf die Geschichte des Frankfurter Stadttheaters von dessen Selbständigkeit (1792) bis zur Gegenwart,* vol. 2. Frankfurt am Main.

Caamaño, Roberto. 1969. *La historia del Teatro Colón, 1908–1968.* Buenos Aires: Editorial Cinetea.

Carmena y Millan, Luis. 1878. *Cronica de la Opera Italiana en Madrid desde el ano 1738 hasta nuestros dias.* Madrid.

Cosma, Octavian Lazar. 1976. *Hronicul Muzicii Romanesti,* vol. 4. Bucharest: Editura Muzicala.

Davis, Ronald. 1966. *Opera in Chicago.* New York: Appleton-Century.

Eaton, Quaintance. 1957. *Opera Caravan.* New York: Farrar, Strauss and Cudahy.

Fonseca y Benevides. 1902. *O Real Teatro di S. Carlos de Lisboa-Memorias, 1883–1902.* Lisbon.

Frassoni, Edilio. 1980. *Due secoli di lirica a Genova.* Genoa: Cassa di Risparmia di Genova e Imperia.

Gatti, Carlo. 1964. *Il Teatro alla Scala.* Milan: Ricordi.

González Maestre, Francesco. 1991. *Teatro Real: Historia viva, 1878–1901.* Madrid: Mundimusica, S. A.

Isnardon, Jacques. 1890. *Le théâtre de la Monnaie.* Brussels.

Levy, Richard N., and J. O'Rourke. 1880. *Annals of the Theatre Royal, Dublin.* Dublin.

Marinelli-Roscioni, Carlo. 1987. *Il teatro di San Carlo, cronologie.* Naples.

Noël, Édouard, and Edmond Stoullig. 1875–81. *Les annales du théâtre et de la musique.* Paris.

Odell, George C. 1927–31. *Annals of the New York Stage.* New York.

Olavarria y Ferrari, Enrique. 1961. *Reseña historica del teatro en México.* Mexico City: Biblioteca Porrua.

Opéra de Nice. 1985. *D'un siècle à l'autre: l'Opéra de Nice, 1885–1985.* Nice: L'Opéra de Nice.

Rosenthal, Harold. 1958. *Two Centuries of Opera at Covent Garden.* London: Putnam.

Schürmann, J. 1893. *Les Étoiles en Voyage.* Paris: Phospho-Cacao.

Subira, José. 1949. *Historia y anecdotaria del teatro Real.* Madrid.

Virella y Cassanes. 1985. *La opera en Barcelona: estudio historico-critico.* Barcelona.

Walsh, Thomas J. 1975. *Monte Carlo Opera, 1879–1909.* Dublin: Gill and Macmillan.

Political Newspapers

Baltimore Sun, Baltimore
Boston Evening Transcript, Boston
Chicago Tribune, Chicago
Cincinnati Enquirer, Cincinnati, Ohio
Cleveland Plain Dealer, Cleveland, Ohio
Daily Picayune, New Orleans
Denver Post, Denver
Detroit Free Press, Detroit
El Dia, Montevideo
Evening Star, Washington, D.C.
Frankfurter Zeitung, Frankfurt
Freeman's Journal, Dublin
Glasgow Herald, Glasgow
Golos, St. Petersburg
L'Indépendance Belge, Brussels
Journal de Débats, Paris
Kansas City Times, Kansas City, Mo.
Manchester Guardian, Manchester
Milwaukee Journal, Milwaukee, Wis.
Montreal Daily Star, Montreal
Nashville Banner, Nashville, Tenn.
Neue Freie Presse, Vienna
Neue Preussische Zeitung, Berlin
New York Times, New York
New York Tribune, New York
Nieuwe Amsterdamsche Courant, Amsterdam
Omaha World-Herald, Omaha, Nebr.
Philadelphia Inquirer, Philadelphia
Pittsburgh Daily Dispatch, Pittsburgh
La Prensa, Buenos Aires
Russkaia Vedomosti, Moscow
St. Louis Globe Democrat, St. Louis, Mo.
St. Paul Pioneer Press, St. Paul, Minn.
Scotsman, Edinburgh
Times, London
Times-Picayune, New Orleans
Toronto Globe, Toronto
Wiener Zeitung, Vienna

Theatrical, Literary, and Musical Newspapers and Periodicals

Cosmorama Pittorico, Milan
Dwight's Journal of Music, Boston
Era, London
La Fama, Milan

La France Musicale, Paris
Gazzetta dei Teatri, Milan
Gazzetta Musicale di Milano, Milan
Le Guide Musicale, Brussels
Il Mondo Artistico, Milan
Musical America, New York
Musical Courier, New York
Musical World, London
Neue Berliner Musikalische Zeitung, Berlin
Revue et Gazette Musicale, Paris
Rivista Teatrale Melodrammatica, Milan
Signale für die Musikalische Welt, Leipzig
Il Sistro, Florence
Il Trovatore, Milan

Adelina Patti's Appearances

AUTUMN 1851 NEW YORK CITY—TRIPLER HALL
  Nov. 22   Concert

AUTUMN 1851 NEW YORK CITY—ASTOR PLACE OPERA HOUSE
  Dec. 2   Special Appearance

AUTUMN 1851 NEW YORK CITY—NIBLO'S GARDEN
  Dec. 3   Concert

SPRING 1852 NEW YORK CITY—METROPOLITAN HALL
  May 5   Concert   C. Barili-Patti s.

SPRING 1852 NEW YORK CITY—LYCEUM
  May 12   Concert
  May 14   Concert
  June 7   Concert

SPRING 1852 NEW YORK CITY—METROPOLITAN HALL
  June 17   Concert

AUTUMN 1852 CONCERT TOUR
Tour with M. Strakosch piano and M. Hauser violin. Cities visited include New
Haven (Sep. 7), Hartford (Sep. 9), Springfield (Sep. 10), Montreal (Sep.),
Philadelphia (Sep. 21–30), and Baltimore (Oct. 5, 12–16).

AUTUMN, WINTER, AND SPRING 1852–53 CONCERT TOUR
Tour with A. Patti-Strakosch ms., M. Strakosch piano, and O. Bull violin. Cities
visited include Baltimore (Oct. 28–29), Syracuse (Nov. 11), Cleveland, Lexington,
Ky. (Nov. 22), Cincinnati (Nov. 23–27), Louisville (Nov. 29–30), St. Louis (Dec.

4), Philadelphia (Dec. 16), Providence, Washington, Fredericksburg, Richmond (Jan. 17), Petersburg, Norfolk, Wilmington, N.C., Augusta, Columbia, Charleston (Feb. 8), Savannah (Feb. 10), Macon (Feb. 12), Columbus (Feb. 16), Montgomery, New Orleans (Feb. 26–Mar. 11), Mobile (Mar. 15), Natchez, New Orleans (Mar. 22), Memphis, St. Louis (Apr. 16), Louisville, Cincinnati, Chicago (Apr. 21–May 2), Milwaukee, Detroit, Buffalo, Toronto, Montreal, Rochester, Utica, and Albany.

SUMMER 1853 NEW YORK CITY—NIBLO'S SALOON
Sep. 1	Concert
Sep. 15	Concert

SUMMER 1853 BROOKLYN
Sep. 1	Concert

AUTUMN AND WINTER 1853–54 CONCERT TOUR
Tour with A. Patti-Strakosch ms., M. Strakosch piano, and O. Bull violin. Cities visited include Boston (Oct. 4–15), Philadelphia (Nov. 2 and 4), Washington (Nov 7), Baltimore (Nov. 10), Springfield (Nov. 18), Toronto (Nov. 23), Buffalo, Cleveland (Nov. 28), Cincinnati (Dec. 2), Louisville (Dec. 8), Cincinnati (Dec. 12), Chicago (Dec. 14), Pittsburgh (Dec. 19), Washington (Jan. 6), Richmond (Jan. 9), Charleston (Jan. 23–24), Augusta (Jan. 26), Columbus (Feb. 4), Mobile (Feb. 10), New Orleans (Feb. 14–15), and Chicago (Mar. 21–25).

WINTER 1855 NEW YORK CITY—NIBLO'S SALOON
Jan. 20	Concert
Jan. 27	Concert
Feb. 27	Concert

SPRING 1855 MONTREAL—THÉÂTRE ROYAL
Apr. 27	Concert

SPRING 1855 NEW YORK—BROADWAY THEATER
June 22	Special Appearance

WINTER AND SPRING 1856 CONCERT TOUR
Tour with E. Barili b. and Paul Julien violin. Cities visited include New York (Mar 3), Lexington, Ky. (Mar. 19), New Orleans (Mar. 29–Apr. 1), Havana (Apr. 14–May 11), Chicago, St. Anthony's, Minn. (July 16), and Minneapolis (July 17).

1857–58 CONCERT TOUR
Tour with Louis Gottschalk piano, starting in New York and covering much of the Caribbean. Cities visited include New York (Jan. 13), Brooklyn (Jan. 16), Havana (Feb. 20–26), Matanzas (Feb.), Cardenas, Cienfuegos (Mar.), Villa Clara, Trinidad Santa Clara, Porto Principe (Apr.), Santiago de Cuba (May 17–23), Havana, Port au Prince (June), St. Thomas (June 23–July 1), San Juan (July), Mayaguez (Oct.), Cabo Rojo, Ponce (Nov. 11–Jan. 7), Guayama, and San Juan (May 16–23).

AUTUMN 1859 NEW YORK CITY—ACADEMY OF MUSIC
Nov. 24	*Lucia di Lammermoor*	P. Brignoli t. G. Ferri b. E. Muzio cond.
Dec. 1	*La sonnambula*	P. Brignoli t. A. Amodio b. E. Muzio cond.

AUTUMN 1859 PHILADELPHIA—ACADEMY OF MUSIC
Dec. 8	*Lucia di Lammermoor*	G. Stigelli t. G. Ferri b. E. Muzio cond.
Dec. 14	*La sonnambula*	P. Brignoli t. A. Amodio b. E. Muzio cond.
Dec. 19	*Don Giovanni*	M. Gazzaniga s. A. Patti ms. P. Brignoli t. G. Ferri b. A. Susini bs. C. Bergmann cond.

WINTER 1859–60 NEW YORK CITY—ACADEMY OF MUSIC
Dec. 21	*Lucia di Lammermoor*	P. Brignoli t. A. Amodio b. Weinlich bs.
Dec. 22	*La sonnambula*	P. Brignoli t. A. Amodio b. E. Muzio cond.
Dec. 27	*Don Giovanni*	M. Gazzaniga s. A. Patti ms. P. Brignoli t. G. Ferri b. A. Susini bs. C. Bergmann cond.

WINTER 1860 BOSTON—BOSTON THEATER
Jan. 3	*Lucia di Lammermoor*	P. Brignoli t. A. Amodio b. E. Muzio cond.
Jan. 9	*La sonnambula*	P. Brignoli t. A. Amodio b. E. Muzio cond.
Jan. 13	*Don Giovanni*	M. Gazzaniga s. A. Patti ms. G. Stigelli t. G. Ferri b. A. Susini bs. C. Bergmann cond.
Jan. 17	*Il barbiere di Siviglia*	P. Brignoli t. G. Ferri b. A. Amodio b. A. Susini bs. E. Muzio cond.
Jan. 25	*I puritani*	P. Brignoli t. G. Ferri b. A. Susini bs. E. Muzio cond.

WINTER 1860 NEW YORK CITY—ACADEMY OF MUSIC
Feb. 6	*I puritani*	P. Brignoli t. G. Ferri b. A. Susini bs. E. Muzio cond.
Feb. 8	*Il barbiere di Siviglia*	P. Brignoli t. G. Ferri b. A. Susini bs. E. Muzio cond.
Feb. 15	*La sonnambula*	P. Brignoli t. A. Amodio b. E. Muzio cond.
Feb. 20	*Lucia di Lammermoor*	P. Brignoli t. G. Ferri b. E. Muzio cond.
Feb. 27	*Martha*	A. Patti ms. P. Brignoli t. M. Junca bs.

WINTER 1860 PHILADELPHIA—ACADEMY OF MUSIC
Mar. 5	*Lucia di Lammermoor*	G. Stigelli t. G. Ferri b. E. Muzio cond.
Mar. 7	*I puritani*	P. Brignoli t. G. Ferri b. A. Susini bs. E. Muzio cond.
Mar. 9	*Il barbiere di Siviglia*	C. Scola t. G. Ferri b. A. Amodio b. A. Susini bs. E. Muzio cond.

WINTER 1860 BALTIMORE—HOLLIDAY STREET THEATER
Mar. 12	*Lucia di Lammermoor*	G. Stigelli t. G. Ferri b. E. Muzio cond.
Mar. 14	*La sonnambula*	G. Stigelli t. A. Amodio b. E. Muzio cond.
Mar. 16	*Il barbiere di Siviglia*	C. Scola t. G. Ferri b. A. Amodio b. A. Susini bs. E. Muzio cond.

WINTER 1860 WASHINGTON—WASHINGTON THEATER

Mar. 19	*Lucia di Lammermoor*	G. Stigelli t. A. Amodio b. E. Muzio cond.
Mar. 21	*Il barbiere di Siviglia*	C. Scola t. G. Ferri b. A. Amodio b. A. Susini bs. E. Muzio cond.
Mar. 23	*La sonnambula*	G. Stigelli t. A. Amodio b. E. Muzio cond.

SPRING 1860 BALTIMORE—HOLLIDAY STREET THEATER

Mar. 26	*I puritani*	P. Brignoli t. G. Ferri b. A. Susini bs. E. Muzio cond.
Mar. 28	*Martha*	A. Patti ms. P. Brignoli t. M. Junca bs.
Mar. 30	*Don Giovanni*	P. Colson s. A. Patti ms. G. Stigelli t. G. Ferri b. A. Amodio bs. A. Susini bs. M. Junca bs.

SPRING 1860 WASHINGTON

| Mar. 31 | Concert | |

SPRING 1860 PHILADELPHIA—ACADEMY OF MUSIC

| Apr. 2 | *Martha* | A. Patti ms. P. Brignoli t. M. Junca bs. |
| Apr. 4 | *Don Pasquale* | P. Brignoli t. G. Ferri b. A. Susini bs. E. Muzio cond. |

SPRING 1860 NEW YORK CITY—ACADEMY OF MUSIC

Apr. 9	*Il barbiere di Siviglia*	P. Brignoli t. G. Ferri b. A. Susini bs. E. Muzio cond.
Apr. 11	*Don Pasquale*	P. Brignoli t. G. Ferri b. A. Susini bs. E. Muzio cond.
Apr. 16	*Lucia di Lammermoor*	P. Brignoli t. G. Ferri b. E. Muzio cond.
Apr. 18	*La sonnambula*	P. Brignoli t. A. Amodio b. E. Muzio cond.
Apr. 23	*I puritani*	P. Brignoli t. G. Ferri b. A. Susini bs. E. Muzio cond.
Apr. 25	*Martha*	A. Phillips ms. P. Brignoli t. M. Junca bs.
May 7	*Mosè*	A. Patti ms. P. Brignoli t. G. Ferri b. A. Susini bs. E. Muzio cond.
May 16	*Don Giovanni*	M. Gazzaniga s. A. Patti ms. P. Brignoli t. G. Ferri b. A. Susini bs.

SPRING 1860 BROOKLYN—PLYMOUTH CHURCH
(Concurrent with New York City season)

| May 17 | *Mosè* | A. Patti ms. P. Brignoli t. G. Ferri b. A. Susini bs. E. Muzio cond. |

SPRING AND SUMMER 1860 CONCERT TOUR
Patti was joined by A. Patti-Strakosch ms., P. Brignoli t., G. Ferri b., M. Junca bs., and M. Strakosch piano. Cities visited include Toronto (May 20), Rochester (May 25), Buffalo (May 26 & 30), Cleveland (May 31), Pittsburgh (June 1–2), Cincinnati (June 5–6), Louisville (June 8–9), Cincinnati (June 11–12), St. Louis (June 15–16), Chicago (June 19–23), probably Milwaukee, and Chicago (June 28).

SUMMER 1860 MONTREAL
Aug. 24   Concert

AUTUMN 1860 NEW YORK CITY—ACADEMY OF MUSIC

Sep. 3	*La sonnambula*	A. Errani t. (later P. Brignoli t.) A. Amodio b. E. Muzio cond.
Sep. 6	*Lucia di Lammermoor*	G. Musiani t. A. Amodio b. E. Muzio cond.
Sep. 10	*Il barbiere di Siviglia*	P. Brignoli t. E. Barili b. A. Susini bs. E. Muzio cond.
Sep. 12	*I puritani*	P. Brignoli t. A. Amodio b. A. Susini bs. E. Muzio cond.
Sep. 14	*Martha*	A. Patti ms. P. Brignoli t. E. Barili b.

AUTUMN 1860 PHILADELPHIA—ACADEMY OF MUSIC

Sep. 19	*La sonnambula*	P. Brignoli t. E. Barili b. E. Muzio cond.
Sep. 21	*Il barbiere di Siviglia*	P. Brignoli t. E. Barili b. D. Coletti bs. N. Barili bs. E. Muzio cond.
Sep. 24	*La traviata*	A. Errani t. E. Barili b.

AUTUMN 1860 BALTIMORE—FRONT ST. THEATER

Sep. 27	*La sonnambula*	P. Brignoli t. E. Barili b. M. Strakosch cond.
Sep. 29	*Martha*	F. Natali-Testa ms. A. Errani t. E. Barili b. M. Strakosch cond.

AUTUMN 1860 NEW YORK CITY—ACADEMY OF MUSIC

Oct. 3	*La traviata*	P. Brignoli t. G. Ferri b.
Oct. 5	*Linda di Chamounix*	A. Patti ms. P. Brignoli t. G. Ferri b. A. Susini bs.

AUTUMN 1860 PHILADELPHIA—ACADEMY OF MUSIC

Oct. 10	*Martha*	F. Natali-Testa ms. P. Brignoli t. K. Formes bs. N. Barili bs. M. Maretzek cond.

AUTUMN 1860 CONCERT TOUR
Essentially a series of concerts while en route to New Orleans. Patti was accompanied by G. Lotti t., E. Barili b., and M. Strakosch piano. Cities visited include Richmond (Oct. 22), Charleston (Nov. 5–13), and Savannah (Nov. 15–16).

AUTUMN AND WINTER 1860–61 NEW ORLEANS—THÉÂTRE DE L'OPÉRA

Dec. 19	*Lucia di Lammermoor*	J. Mathieu t. L. Melchissedec b. Jolly bs. E. Prevost cond.
Dec. 26	*Martha*	Pretti s. Cabel t. T. Genibrel bs. E. Prevost cond.
Dec. 31	*Il barbiere di Siviglia*	Cabel t. L. Melchissedec b. Jolly bs. E. Prevost cond.
Jan. 2	*Il trovatore*	Lacobe ms. J. Mathieu t. E. Barili b. E. Prevost cond.
Feb. 6	*Rigoletto*	Pretti s. J. Mathieu t. L. Melchissedec b. E. Prevost cond.
Feb. 14	Special Appearance	E. Prevost cond.
Feb. 18	Special Appearance	E. Prevost cond.

Feb. 21	Special Appearance	E. Prevost cond.
Feb. 25	*Les Huguenots*	Pretti s. J. Mathieu t. L. Melchissedec b. T. Genibrel bs. E. Prevost cond.
Feb. 28	Special Appearance	E. Prevost cond.
Mar. 4	°*Dinorah*[1]	L. Melchissedec b. E. Prevost cond.
Mar. 14	Special Appearance	E. Prevost cond.
Mar. 17	Special Appearance	E. Prevost cond.

SPRING 1861 HAVANA—TEATRO TACON
Apr. 1	Concert
Apr. 2	Concert
Apr. 5	Concert

SPRING AND SUMMER 1861 LONDON—COVENT GARDEN
May 14	*La sonnambula*	M. Tiberini t. J. Tagliafico bs. M. Costa cond.
May 25	*Lucia di Lammermoor*	M. Tiberini t. F. Graziani b. C. H. Zelger bs M. Costa cond.
July 4	*La traviata*	M. Tiberini t. F. Graziani b. M. Costa cond.
July 6	*Don Giovanni*	G. Grisi s. (later R. Penco s.) R. Csillag s. (later A. Ortolani-Tiberini s.) E. Tamberlik t. J. B. Faure b. G. Ronconi b. K. Formes bs. J. Tagliafico bs. M. Costa cond.
July 13	*Martha*	C. Nantier-Didiée ms. Mario t. J. Tagliafico bs. M. Costa cond.
July 27	*Il barbiere di Siviglia*	Mario t. G. Ronconi b. J. Tagliafico bs. G. Ciampi bs. M. Costa cond.

SUMMER 1861 LONDON—BUCKINGHAM PALACE
June 28	Concert	T. Tietjens s. A. Giuglini t. I. Gardoni t. C. Santley b.

SUMMER 1861 BRIGHTON
July?	Concert

SUMMER 1861 MANCHESTER—THEATRE ROYAL
Aug. 12	*La sonnambula*	M. Tiberini t. J. Tagliafico bs.
Aug. 14	*Don Giovanni*	H. Rudersdorff s. A. Caradori s. M. Tiberini t. G. Ronconi b. C. H. Zelger bs.
Aug. 16	*Martha*	H. Rudersdorff s. M. Tiberini t. C. H. Zelger bs.
Aug. 21	*La traviata*	M. Tiberini t. G. Ronconi b.
Aug. 23	*Il barbiere di Siviglia*	M. Tiberini t. G. Ronconi b. C. H. Zelger bs. J. Tagliafico bs.

SUMMER 1861 BIRMINGHAM—TOWN HALL
Aug. 27	Concert	T. Tietjens s. S. Reeves t. A. Giuglini t. C. Santley b.
Aug. 28	*Samson* (Handel)	H. Rudersdorff s. S. Reeves t. C. Santley b.
Aug. 29	Concert	T. Tietjens s. S. Reeves t. A. Giuglini t. C. Santley b.

Aug. 30   Concert   T. Tietjens s. S. Reeves t. C. Santley b.

SUMMER 1861 BIRMINGHAM—THEATRE ROYAL
Aug. 31   *La sonnambula*

SUMMER 1861 LIVERPOOL—THEATRE ROYAL
Sep. 2	*La sonnambula*	M. Tiberini t. J. Tagliafico bs.
Sep. 4	*Lucia di Lammermoor*	M. Tiberini t. G. Ronconi b.
Sep. 6	*La traviata*	M. Tiberini t. G. Ronconi b.
Sep. 7	*Il barbiere di Siviglia*	M. Tiberini t. G. Ronconi b.
Sep. 9	*Don Giovanni*	H. Rudersdorff s. R. Caradori s. M. Tiberini t. G. Ronconi b.

AUTUMN 1861 MANCHESTER—FREE TRADE HALL
Sep. 30   Concert

AUTUMN 1861 CONCERT TOUR
This tour consisted of concerts in Liverpool (Oct. 1), Leeds (Oct. 13), Manchester (Oct. 14), Birmingham (Oct. 18), Shrewsbury (Oct. 21), and Manchester (Oct. 28).

AUTUMN 1861 DUBLIN—THEATRE ROYAL
Oct. 29	*La sonnambula*	G. Galvani t. E. Manfredi bs. G. Li Calsi cond.
Oct. 31	*La traviata*	G. Galvani t. G. Cima b. G. Li Calsi cond.
Nov. 2	*Lucia di Lammermoor*	G. Galvani t. G. Cima b. E. Manfredi bs. G. Li Calsi cond.
Nov. 4	*Il barbiere di Siviglia*	G. Galvani t. G. Cima b. E. Manfredi bs. Kinni bs. G. Li Calsi cond.
Nov. 9	*Martha*	Sedlacek s. G. Galvani t. G. Cima b. G. Li Calsi cond.

AUTUMN 1861 LIVERPOOL
Nov. 11   Concert

AUTUMN 1861 BERLIN—HOFOPER
Dec. 4	*Lucia di Lammermoor*	T. Formes t. M. Zacchi b. L. Agnesi bs.
Dec. 10	*La sonnambula*	
Dec. 13	*Il trovatore*	Z. Trebelli ms. T. Formes t.
Dec. 17	*Il barbiere di Siviglia*	

WINTER 1862 BRUSSELS—THÉÂTRE DE LA MONNAIE
Jan. 15	*La sonnambula*	V. Montanari t. L. Agnesi bs. L. Orsini cond.
Jan. 21	*Il barbiere di Siviglia*	V. Montanari t. M. Zacchi b. L. Agnesi bs. L. Orsini cond.
Jan. 23	*Lucia di Lammermoor*	V. Montanari t. M. Zacchi b. L. Orsini cond.
Jan. 30	*Martha*	V. Montanari t. L. Orsini cond.
Feb. 4	*Don Pasquale*	V. Montanari t. M. Zacchi b. M. Borella bs. L. Orsini cond.

Feb. 11 *La figlia del*   V. Montanari t. L. Orsini cond.
         reggimento

LENT 1862 LIÈGE—GRAND THÉÂTRE
Mar. 3   *Lucia di*   G. Galvani t. M. Zacchi b.
         Lammermoor

LENT 1862 GHENT—GRAND THÉÂTRE
Mar. 7   *Lucia di*
         Lammermoor

LENT 1862 AMSTERDAM—STADS SCHOUWBURG
Mar. 11 *La sonnambula*   G. Galvani t. L. Agnesi bs. L. Orsini cond.
Mar. 18 *Il barbiere di Siviglia* G. Galvani t. M. Zacchi b. L. Agnesi bs. B.
                                 Mazzetti bs. L. Orsini cond.
Mar. 27 *Lucia di*   G. Galvani t. M. Zacchi b. L. Orsini cond.
         Lammermoor
Apr. 8   *La figlia del*   G. Galvani t. L. Agnesi bs. L. Orsini cond.
         reggimento

LENT 1862 ROTTERDAM—GROOTE SAAL
Mar. 15 Concert

SPRING 1862 LA HAYE—THÉÂTRE ROYAL
Apr. 5   *Il barbiere di Siviglia*

SPRING AND SUMMER 1862 LONDON—COVENT GARDEN
May 5   *La sonnambula*   I. Gardoni t. (later P. Neri-Baraldi t.) J.
                                 Tagliafico bs. M. Costa cond.
May 10   *Il barbiere di Siviglia* Mario t. E. Delle Sedie b. J. Tagliafico bs.
                                 G. Ciampi bs. M. Costa cond.
May 12   *Don Giovanni*   R. Penco s. R. Csillag s. (later H.
                                 Rudersdorff s.) E. Tamberlick t. J. B.
                                 Faure b. K. Formes bs. M. Costa cond.
June 2   *La traviata*   I. Gardoni t. E. Delle Sedie b. M. Costa
                                 cond.
June 5   *Martha*   C. Nantier-Didiée ms. Mario t. F. Graziani
                                 b. J. Tagliafico bs. M. Costa cond.
June 7   *Lucia di*   T. Wachtel t. E. Delle Sedie b. (later F.
         Lammermoor   Graziani b.) G. Capponi bs. M. Costa
                                 cond.
July 12 *Don Pasquale*   Mario t. G. Ronconi b. G. Ciampi bs. M.
                                 Costa cond.
Aug. 5   *Dinorah*   C. Nantier-Didiée ms. I. Gardoni t. J. B.
                                 Faure b. M. Costa cond.
Aug. 15 Concert

SUMMER 1862 MANCHESTER—THEATRE ROYAL
Aug. 26 *Il barbiere di Siviglia* I. Gardoni t. E. Delle Sedie b. Patriossi bs.
                                 G. Ciampi bs.
Aug. 28 *Don Pasquale*   I. Gardoni t. E. Delle Sedie b. G. Ciampi bs.
Aug. 30 *La sonnambula*   I. Gardoni t. E. Delle Sedie b.

SUMMER AND AUTUMN 1862 CONCERT TOUR
Tour included concerts in Plymouth (Sep. 3), Exeter (Sep. 4), Bath (Sep. 6), Clifton (Sep. 8), Salisbury (Sep. 9), Liverpool (Sep. 11 or 15), Brighton, Ryde, Manchester (Sep.), Sheffield, Birmingham, Newcastle, Edinburgh, and Glasgow

AUTUMN AND WINTER 1862–63 PARIS—THÉÂTRE-ITALIEN

Nov. 16	*La sonnambula*	I. Gardoni t. V. Bonetti cond.
Nov. 25	*Lucia di Lammermoor*	I. Gardoni t. O. Bartolini b. G. Capponi bs.
Nov. 30	*Il barbiere di Siviglia*	Mario t. E. Delle Sedie b. G. Capponi bs. G. Zucchini bs.
Jan. 15	*Don Pasquale*	I. Gardoni t. E. Delle Sedie b. G. Zucchini bs.
Jan. 28	*Don Giovanni*	E. Frezzolini s. Guerra s. I. Gardoni t. E. Delle Sedie b. G. Zucchini bs.

LENT 1863 VIENNA—CARL THEATER

Feb. 28	*La sonnambula*	A. Giuglini t. (later E. Carrion t.) L. Agnesi bs.
Mar. 7	*Il barbiere di Siviglia*	E. Carrion t. M. Zacchi b. L. Agnesi bs. B. Mazzetti bs.
Mar. 16	*Don Pasquale*	A. Giuglini t. M. Zacchi b. B. Mazzetti bs.
Mar. 24	*Lucia di Lammermoor*	A. Giuglini t. M. Zacchi b.
Apr. 12	*Don Giovanni*	M. Lafon s. Dalmonti s. E. Carrion t. M. Zacchi b. L. Agnesi bs.
Apr. 20	*La traviata*	E. Carrion t. M. Zacchi b.

SPRING AND SUMMER 1863 LONDON—COVENT GARDEN

May 7	*La sonnambula*	P. Neri-Baraldi t. J. Tagliafico bs. M. Costa cond.
May 9	*Il barbiere di Siviglia*	Mario t. G. Ronconi b. J. Tagliafico bs. G. Ciampi bs. M. Costa cond.
May 14	*Don Giovanni*	A. Fricci s. H. Rudersdorff s. E. Tamberlick t. J. B. Faure b. K. Formes bs.
May 28	*Il trovatore*	Lustani ms. (later C. Nantier-Didiée ms.) Mario t. F. Graziani b. M. Costa cond.
June 5	*Martha*	C. Nantier-Didiée ms. Mario t. F. Graziani b. J. Tagliafico bs. M. Costa cond.
June 6	*La gazza ladra*	C. Nantier-Didiée ms. P. Neri-Baraldi t. G. Ronconi b. J. B. Faure b. M. Costa cond.
July 9	*Don Pasquale*	Mario t. G. Ronconi b. G. Ciampi bs. M. Costa cond.
July 21	*L'elisir d'amore*	E. Naudin t. G. Ronconi b. J. Tagliafico bs. M. Costa cond.
July 28	*La figlia del reggimento*	P. Neri-Baraldi t. G. Ciampi bs. M. Costa cond.

SUMMER 1863 FRANKFURT—STADT THEATER

Aug. 19	*Il barbiere di Siviglia*	G. Gunz t. C. Pichler b.
Aug. 21	*La sonnambula*	

SUMMER 1863 MANNHEIM—STADT THEATER
Aug. 22?   *La sonnambula*

SUMMER 1863 WIESBADEN—STADT THEATER
Aug. 28   *La sonnambula*

SUMMER AND AUTUMN 1863 HAMBURG—STADT THEATER

Sep. 10	*La sonnambula*	A. Corsi t. Ruiz bs. L. Orsini cond.
Sep. 12	*Il barbiere di Siviglia*	A. Corsi t. M. Zacchi b. L. Orsini cond.
Sep. 19	*Dinorah*	
Sep. 22	*Faust* (in It.)	A. Corsi t. M. Zacchi b. L. Orsini cond.
Sep. 26	*Martha*	A. Corsi t. M. Zacchi b. L. Orsini cond.
Oct. 6	*La traviata*	A. Corsi t. M. Zacchi b. L. Orsini cond.
Oct. 10	*Lucia di Lammermoor*	A. Corsi t. M. Zacchi b. L. Ruiz bs. L. Orsini cond.

AUTUMN 1863 BERLIN—VICTORIA THEATER

Oct. 13	*Il barbiere di Siviglia*	A. Corsi t. M. Zacchi b. L. Ruiz bs. B. Mazzetti bs. L. Orsini cond.
Oct. 16	*Lucia di Lammermoor*	E. Naudin t. M. Zacchi b. L. Ruiz bs. L. Orsini cond.
Oct. 20	*La traviata*	E. Naudin t. M. Zacchi b. L. Orsini cond.
Oct. 24	*La sonnambula*	E. Naudin t. L. Orsini cond.
Oct. 28	*Don Pasquale*	E. Naudin t. M. Zacchi b. B. Mazzetti bs. L. Orsini cond.

AUTUMN 1863 MADRID—TEATRO REAL

Nov. 12	*La sonnambula*	E. Naudin t. L. Agnesi bs. J. Skoczdopole cond.
Nov. 19	*Lucia di Lammermoor*	E. Naudin t. G. Guicciardi b. A. Padovani bs. J. Skoczdopole cond.
Nov. 26	*Il barbiere di Siviglia*	Mario t. A. Guadagnini b. G. B. Antonucci bs. R. Scalese bs.
Dec. 10	*Don Pasquale*	E. Naudin t. L. Agnesi bs. R. Scalese bs. J. Skoczdopole cond.
Dec. 16	*Martha*	B. Marchisio ms. Mario t. G. Guicciardi b. J. Skoczdopole cond.

WINTER 1864 PARIS—THÉÂTRE-ITALIEN

Jan. 10	*La sonnambula*	E. Nicolini t. L. Giraldoni b.
Jan. 26	*Il barbiere di Siviglia*	Mario t. (later A. Bettini t.) E. Delle Sedie b. G. B. Antonucci bs. R. Scalese bs.
Jan. 23	*Don Pasquale*	Mario t. E. Delle Sedie b. R. Scalese bs.
Feb. 21	*Martha*	E. de Méric Lablache ms. Mario t. E. Delle Sedie b. (later L. Agnesi bs.) R. Scalese bs.
Mar. 13	*La traviata*	E. Naudin t. E. Delle Sedie b.

SPRING AND SUMMER 1864 LONDON—COVENT GARDEN

May 16	*La sonnambula*	E. Naudin t. J. B. Faure b. M. Costa cond.
June 6	*Faust* (in It.)	C. Nantier-Didiée ms. Mario t. F. Graziani b. J. B. Faure b. M. Costa cond.

332

June 9	*Il barbiere di Siviglia*	Mario t. G. Ronconi b. J. Tagliafico bs. R. Scalese bs. (later G. Ciampi bs.) M. Costa cond.
June 10	*Don Giovanni*	A. Fricci s. H. Rudersdorff s. E. Tamberlick t. J. B. Faure b. R. Scalese bs. (later G. Ciampi bs.) M. Costa cond.
July 5	*L'elisir d'amore*	Mario t. J. B. Faure b. G. Ronconi b. M. Costa cond.
July 25	*Martha*	C. Nantier-Didiée ms. Mario t. F. Graziani b. J. Tagliafico bs.

SUMMER 1864 BOULOGNE
Aug.   Concert

SUMMER 1864 LE HAVRE
Aug.   Concert

SUMMER 1864 BIRMINGHAM—TOWN HALL

Sep. 6	Concert	T. Tietjens s. S. Reeves t. Mario t. C. Santley b.
Sep. 7	°°*Naaman* (Costa)	H. Rudersdorff s. S. Reeves t. C. Santley b.
Sep. 9	Concert	T. Tietjens s. S. Reeves t. C. Santley b.

SUMMER 1864 LYONS—GRAND THÉÂTRE

Sep. 17	*Lucia di Lammermoor*
	Il barbiere di Siviglia
	La traviata

AUTUMN AND WINTER 1864–65 PARIS—THÉÂTRE-ITALIEN

Oct. 5	*La sonnambula*	E. Naudin t. (later P. Brignoli t.) G. B. Antonucci bs.
Oct. 11	*Don Pasquale*	R. Baragli t. E. Delle Sedie b. (later N. Verger b.) R. Scalese bs. (later G. Zucchini bs.)
Oct. 18	*La traviata*	E. Naudin t. M. Zacchi b.
Oct. 20	*Il barbiere di Siviglia*	R. Baragli t. (later A. Corsi t.) E. Delle Sedie b. G. B. Antonucci bs.
Nov. 6	*L'elisir d'amore*	E. Nicolini t. L. Agnesi bs. G. Zucchini bs.
Nov. 20	*Don Giovanni*	A. De la Grange s. R. Baragli t. E. Delle Sedie b. R. Scalese bs.
Nov. 27	*Martha*	E. de Méric Lablache ms. P. Brignoli t. E. Delle Sedie b. R. Scalese bs.
Dec. 18	*Linda di Chamounix*	E. de Méric Lablache ms. P. Brignoli t. (later R. Baragli t.) E. Delle Sedie b. G. B. Antonucci bs. R. Scalese bs.

LENT 1865 LILLE—THÉÂTRE MUNICIPAL
Mar. 11   *Il barbiere di Siviglia*

LENT 1865 MADRID—TEATRO REAL

Mar. 23	*La sonnambula*	R. Baragli t. L. Gassier b. J. Skoczdopole cond.
Mar. 28	*Il barbiere di Siviglia*	R. Baragli t. L. Gassier b. J. Skoczdopole cond.
	Lucia di Lammermoor	G. Stigelli t. E. Fagotti b. A. Padovani bs. J. Skoczdopole cond.

SPRING 1865 BORDEAUX

Apr.	Concert

SPRING 1865 LILLE—THÉÂTRE MUNICIPAL

Apr. 12	*Lucia di Lammermoor*

SPRING AND SUMMER 1865 LONDON—COVENT GARDEN

May 13	*Il barbiere di Siviglia*	Mario t. G. Ronconi b. J. Tagliafico bs. G. Ciampi bs. M. Costa cond.
May 20	*L'elisir d'amore*	Mario t. L. Gassier b. G. Ronconi b. M. Costa cond.
May 22	*La sonnambula*	P. Brignoli t. F. Graziani b. M. Costa cond.
May 25	*Don Giovanni*	A. Fricci s. H. Rudersdorff s. T. Wachtel t. L. Gassier b. M. Costa cond.
June 6	*Linda di Chamounix*	P. Brignoli t. G. Ronconi b. F. Graziani b. M. Costa cond.
June 8	*Don Pasquale*	Mario t. L. Gassier b. G. Ronconi b. M. Costa cond.
July 2	*Faust* (in It.)	Honoré ms. Mario t. F. Graziani b. G. Atry bs. M. Costa cond.

SPRING 1865 LONDON—SACRED HARMONIC SOCIETY

May 26	*Naaman* (Costa)	Sainton-Dolby s. S. Reeves t. C. Santley b. M. Costa cond.

SUMMER 1865 LONDON—BUCKINGHAM PALACE

June 21	Concert

SUMMER 1865 LONDON—ST. JAMES'S HALL

July 5	Concert	P. Lucca s. I. Galletti-Gianoli ms. Mario t. T. Wachtel t. P. Brignoli t. G. Ronconi b. F. Graziani b. G. Ciampi bs.

SUMMER 1865 LONDON—CRYSTAL PALACE

Aug.	Concert

SUMMER 1865 VICHY

Aug.	Concert	P. Brignoli t. R. Scalese bs.

SUMMER 1865 SPA

Aug. 21	Concert
Aug. 25	Concert

SUMMER 1865 BAD HOMBURG—KURSAAL

Aug. 31	*La sonnambula*	A. Corsi t. A. Guadagnini b. L. Orsini cond.

SUMMER 1865 BADEN-BADEN—KURSAAL

Sep. 5	Concert	
Sep. 12	*Don Pasquale*	E. Nicolini t. E. Delle Sedie b. R. Scalese bs.

SUMMER 1865 CONCERT TOUR
Cities visited include Frankfurt (Sep. 15), Wiesbaden (Sep. 18), Bonn, Düsseldorf, Crefeld, and Aachen

AUTUMN 1865 COLOGNE—STADT THEATER

Oct. 3	*La sonnambula*	
Oct. 5	*Il barbiere di Siviglia*	
Oct. 9	*Lucia di Lammermoor*	Behr bs.

AUTUMN 1865 AMSTERDAM—PALAIS DE CRISTAL

Oct. 16	Concert
Oct. 18	Concert
Oct. 21	Concert

AUTUMN 1865 COLOGNE—STADT THEATER

Oct. 24	*Faust* (in It.)
Oct. 27	*Lucia di Lammermoor*

AUTUMN 1865 FLORENCE—TEATRO PAGLIANO

Nov. 11	*La sonnambula*	A. Corsi t. Marchetti bs. V. Fumi cond.
Nov. 26	*Il barbiere di Siviglia*	A. Corsi t. G. Ferri b. V. Fumi cond.
Dec. 13	*Lucia di Lammermoor*	A. Corsi t. A. Mazzanti b. V. Fumi cond.

CARNIVAL 1865–66 TURIN—TEATRO REGIO

Dec. 21	*La sonnambula*	A. Corsi t. E. Bagagiolo bs. F. Bianchi cond.
Dec. 28	*Il barbiere di Siviglia*	A. Corsi t. A. Cotogni b. E. Bagagiolo bs. F. Catani bs. F. Bianchi cond.

WINTER 1866 MARSEILLES—GRAND THÉÂTRE

Jan. 6	*Lucia di Lammermoor*
	Il barbiere di Siviglia

WINTER 1866 PARIS—THÉÂTRE-ITALIEN

Jan. 15	*Linda di Chamounix*	E. Grossi ms. E. Nicolini t. E. Delle Sedie b. R. Scalese bs. J. Skoczdopole cond.
Jan. 23	*Don Pasquale*	E. Nicolini t. (later P. Brignoli t.) E. Delle Sedie b. R. Scalese bs. J. Skoczdopole cond.
Feb. 8	*Il barbiere di Siviglia*	P. Brignoli t. E. Delle Sedie b. J. Skoczdopole cond.
Mar. 1	*Don Giovanni*	E. Nicolini t. E. Delle Sedie b. J. Skoczdopole cond.
Mar. 8	*I puritani*	E. Nicolini t. F. Graziani b. A. Selva bs. J. Skoczdopole cond.

| Mar. 26 | *La traviata* | E. Nicolini t. F. Graziani b. J. Skoczdopole cond. |

SPRING AND SUMMER 1866 LONDON—COVENT GARDEN

May 17	*Il barbiere di Siviglia*	Mario t. G. Ronconi b. J. Tagliafico bs. G. Ciampi bs. M. Costa cond.
May 21	*La sonnambula*	G. Fancelli t. J. B. Faure b. M. Costa cond.
May 25	*Don Giovanni*	A. Fricci s. H. Sherrington s. P. Brignoli t. J. B. Faure b. G. Ciampi bs. M. Costa cond.
May 29	*Lucia di Lammermoor*	E. Nicolini t. F. Graziani b. M. Costa cond.
June 5	*L'elisir d'amore*	Mario t. J. B. Faure b. G. Ronconi b. M. Costa cond.
June 18	Concert	
June 26	*La stella del Nord*	H. Sherrington s. P. Neri-Baraldi t. J. B. Faure b. G. Ciampi bs. M. Costa cond.
July 4	Concert	
July 14	*Crispino e la comare*	Vestri ms. G. Fancelli t. G. Ronconi b. G. Capponi bs. G. Ciampi bs. M. Costa cond.
July 25	Gala Concert	

SUMMER 1866 LONDON—BUCKINGHAM PALACE

| June 26 | Concert | |

SUMMER AND AUTUMN 1866 BAD HOMBURG—KURSAAL

	Lucia di Lammermoor	G. Villani t. N. Verger b. L. Orsini cond.
	Il barbiere di Siviglia	A. Bettini t. N. Verger b. E. Bagagiolo bs. G. Ciampi bs. L. Orsini cond.
	Faust (in It.)	Z. Trebelli ms. G. Villani t. N. Verger b. E. Bagagiolo bs. L. Orsini cond.
	Don Pasquale	A. Bettini t. N. Verger b. G. Ciampi bs. L. Orsini cond.
	Martha	Z. Trebelli ms. A. Bettini t. E. Bagagiolo bs. G. Ciampi bs. L. Orsini cond.
	Linda di Chamounix	Z. Trebelli ms. A. Bettini t. N. Verger b. E. Bagagiolo bs. G. Ciampi bs. L. Orsini cond.
	La traviata	A. Bettini t. N. Verger b. L. Orsini cond.
	I puritani	A. Bettini t. N. Verger b. E. Bagagiolo bs. L. Orsini cond.
	Rigoletto	Z. Trebelli ms. A. Bettini t. N. Verger b. L. Orsini cond.
Sep. 22	*Semiramide*	Z. Trebelli ms. E. Bagagiolo bs. L. Orsini cond.

AUTUMN AND WINTER 1866–67 PARIS—THÉÂTRE-ITALIEN

| Oct. 5 | *La sonnambula* | E. Nicolini t. N. Verger b. |
| Oct. 16 | *Crispino e la comare* | Vestri ms. E. Nicolini t. F. Cresci b. G. Zucchini bs. |

Oct. 18	*Lucia di Lammermoor*	E. Nicolini t. (later G. Fraschini t.) F. Cresci b.
Nov. 1	*Don Pasquale*	Ketten t. (later I. Gardoni t.) N. Verger b. G. Zucchini bs.
Nov. 6	*La traviata*	E. Nicolini t. E. Pancani t. N. Verger b.
Nov. 24	*Rigoletto*	Zeiss ms. E. Nicolini t. F. Cresci b.
Dec. 20	*L'elisir d'amore*	E. Nicolini t. L. Agnesi bs. G. Zucchini bs.
Jan. 3	*Linda di Chamounix*	Zeiss ms. E. Nicolini t. F. Cresci b. G. Zucchini bs.
Jan. 15	*Il barbiere di Siviglia*	I. Gardoni t. N. Verger b. L. Agnesi bs. G. Zucchini bs.
Jan. 24	*I puritani*	E. Nicolini t. N. Verger b. L. Agnesi bs.
Mar. 12	*La gazza ladra*	F. Llanes ms. I. Gardoni t. L. Agnesi bs. G. Zucchini bs.

SPRING AND SUMMER 1867 LONDON—COVENT GARDEN

May 4	*Il barbiere di Siviglia*	Mario t. A. Cotogni b. J. Tagliafico bs. G. Ciampi bs. M. Costa cond.
May 16	*Lucia di Lammermoor*	G. Fancelli t. F. Graziani b. G. Capponi bs. M. Costa cond.
May 24	*Don Giovanni*	A. Fricci s. H. Sherrington s. Mario t. (later E. Naudin t.) A. Cotogni b. G. Ciampi bs. M. Costa cond.
June 7	*La sonnambula*	G. Fancelli t. J. Petit bs. M. Costa cond.
June 29	*Crispino e la comare*	Ackerman ms. G. Fancelli t. G. Capponi bs. G. Ciampi bs. M. Costa cond.
July 11	°*Roméo et Juliette* (in It.)	Marino ms. Mario t. A. Cotogni b. J. Tagliafico bs. M. Costa cond.

SUMMER 1867 LONDON—BUCKINGHAM PALACE
June 18	Concert

SUMMER 1867 DEAUVILLE
July	Concert

AUTUMN AND WINTER 1867–68 PARIS—THÉÂTRE-ITALIEN

Sep. 3	*La sonnambula*	I. Gardoni t. (later E. Nicolini t.) E. Bagagiolo bs. (later L. Agnesi bs.)
Sep. 5	*Don Pasquale*	I. Gardoni t. N. Verger bs. R. Scalese bs.
Sep. 10	*Il barbiere di Siviglia*	I. Gardoni t. F. Cresci b. R. Scalese bs. E. Bagagiolo bs.
Sep. 12	*La traviata*	I. Gardoni t. F. Cresci b. (later F. Steller b.)
Sep. 17	*Lucia di Lammermoor*	E. Nicolini t. F. Cresci b. (later N. Verger b.) L. Agnesi bs.
Sep. 19	*Crispino e la comare*	I. Gardoni t. L. Agnesi bs. G. Ciampi bs. (later R. Scalese bs.)
Sep. 26	*L'elisir d'amore*	I. Gardoni t. L. Agnesi bs. R. Scalese bs. (later G. Ciampi bs.)
Nov. 9	*Don Desiderio*	I. Gardoni t. Mercuriali b. R. Scalese bs. G. Ciampi bs.

337

Nov. 19	*I puritani*	P. Mongini t. N. Verger b. L. Agnesi bs.
Nov. 26	*Rigoletto*	E. Grossi ms. E. Nicolini t. F. Cresci b. (later N. Verger b.) L. Agnesi bs.
Nov. 30	*Linda di Chamounix*	E. Grossi ms. I. Gardoni t. L. Agnesi bs. R. Scalese bs.
Dec. 28	*Ernani*	E. Nicolini t. N. Verger b. L. Agnesi bs.
Jan. 11	*La gazza ladra*	E. Grossi ms. I. Gardoni t. L. Agnesi bs. G. Ciampi bs.
Feb. 15	*Don Giovanni*	G. Krauss s. L. Harris s. (later A. Ortolani s.) E. Nicolini t. F. Steller b. N. Verger b. L. Agnesi bs.
Mar. 1	*Il trovatore*	E. Grossi ms. E. Carrion t. F. Cresci b. L. Agnesi bs.
Mar. 28	°*Giovanna d'Arco*	E. Nicolini t. F. Steller b.

WINTER 1868 LE HAVRE
(Concurrent with Paris season)
Feb.	*Il barbiere di Siviglia*	

WINTER 1868 LILLE—THÉÂTRE MUNICIPAL
(Concurrent with Paris season)
Mar. 1	*Lucia di Lammermoor*	
Mar. 3	*Faust*	

SPRING AND SUMMER 1868 LONDON—COVENT GARDEN
May 5	*Il barbiere di Siviglia*	Mario t. A. Cotogni b. J. Tagliafico bs. G. Ciampi bs. M. Costa cond.
May 9	*Martha*	E. Grossi ms. Mario t. F. Graziani b. M. Costa cond.
May 11	*Lucia di Lammermoor*	G. Fancelli t. F. Graziani b. J. Tagliafico bs. M. Costa cond.
May 16	*La sonnambula*	G. Fancelli t. J. Petit bs. M. Costa cond.
May 18	*Don Pasquale*	E. Naudin t. A. Cotogni b. G. Ciampi bs. M. Costa cond.
May 21	*Don Giovanni*	A. Fricci s. H. Sherrington s. Mario t. F. Graziani b. G. Ciampi bs. M. Costa cond.
June 9	*La figlia del reggimento*	G. Fancelli t. G. Ciampi bs. M. Costa cond.
July 2	*Roméo et Juliette* (in It.)	Mario t. A. Cotogni b. E. Bagagiolo bs. M. Costa cond.
July 23	Gala Concert	

SPRING 1868 LONDON—BUCKINGHAM PALACE
June 19	Concert	

SUMMER 1868 LONDON—CRYSTAL PALACE
July 4	Concert	J. Van Zandt s. E. Grossi ms. Mario t. G. Fancelli t. F. Graziani b. E. Bagagiolo bs. G. Ciampi bs.

SUMMER 1868 BAD HOMBURG—KURSAAL

Aug. 15	*Lucia di Lammermoor*	E. Naudin t. N. Verger b. L. Agnesi bs. L. Orsini cond.
Aug. 18	*Don Pasquale*	E. Naudin t. N. Verger b. G. Ciampi bs. L. Orsini cond.
Aug. 22	*Semiramide*	E. Grossi ms. N. Sinigaglia t. L. Agnesi bs. L. Orsini cond.
Aug. 25	*Rigoletto*	E. Naudin t. N. Verger b. L. Orsini cond.
Aug. 29	*Il barbiere di Siviglia*	A. Corsi t. N. Verger b. L. Agnesi bs. G. Ciampi bs. L. Orsini cond.
Sep. 1	*Martha*	E. Grossi ms. A. Corsi t. L. Agnesi bs. L. Orsini cond.
Sep. 5	*Linda di Chamounix*	E. Grossi ms. N. Verger b. L. Agnesi bs. G. Ciampi bs. L. Orsini cond.
Sep. 8	*Crispino e la comare*	N. Sinigaglia t. G. Ciampi bs. L. Orsini cond.
Sep. 10	*La traviata*	N. Verger b. L. Orsini cond.
Sep. 12	*L'elisir d'amore*	A. Corsi t. N. Verger b. G. Ciampi bs. L. Orsini cond.
Sep. 15	*La figlia del reggimento*	A. Corsi t. G. Ciampi bs. L. Orsini cond.
Sep. 19	*Faust* (in It.)	E. Nicolini t. N. Verger b. L. Agnesi bs. L. Orsini cond.
Sep. 22	*La sonnambula*	E. Nicolini t. N. Verger b. L. Orsini cond.

AUTUMN 1868 PARIS—THÉÂTRE-ITALIEN

Oct. 1	*Lucia di Lammermoor*	G. Fraschini t. E. Delle Sedie b. L. Agnesi bs.
Oct. 3	*Rigoletto*	E. Grossi ms. G. Fraschini t. E. Delle Sedie b.
Oct. 10	*La traviata*	E. Nicolini t. F. Steller b.
Oct. 20	*Martha*	E. Grossi ms. G. Fraschini t. L. Agnesi bs. G. Ciampi bs.
Oct. 24	*Il barbiere di Siviglia*	E. Palermi t. E. Delle Sedie b. G. Ciampi bs.
Oct. 29	*Don Pasquale*	E. Palermi t. N. Verger b. G. Ciampi bs.
Nov. 10	*Linda di Chamounix*	E. Grossi ms. E. Nicolini t. E. Delle Sedie b.
Nov. 12	*La sonnambula*	E. Nicolini t. L. Agnesi bs.

AUTUMN 1868 PARIS—ÉGLISE DE LA TRINITÉ

Nov. 21	*Stabat Mater*

AUTUMN 1868 BRUSSELS—THÉÂTRE DE LA MONNAIE

Dec.	*Il barbiere di Siviglia*
Dec.	*Lucia di Lammermoor*
Dec.	*Faust*

WINTER 1869 LIÈGE—GRAND THÉÂTRE

Jan. 2	*Lucia di Lammermoor*

WINTER 1869 ST. PETERSBURG—IMPERIAL THEATER

Jan. 14	*La sonnambula*	E. Calzolari t. E. Bagagiolo bs. A. Vianesi cond.
Jan. 27	*Il barbiere di Siviglia*	E. Calzolari t. L. Gassier b. G. F. Angelini bs. G. Zucchini bs. A. Vianesi cond.
Feb. 1	*Lucia di Lammermoor*	A. Bettini t. (later Mario t.) F. Graziani b. Meo bs. A. Vianesi cond.
Feb. 3	*Martha*	Z. Trebelli ms. E. Calzolari t. L. Gassier b. G. Zucchini bs. A. Vianesi cond.
Feb. 5	*Linda di Chamounix*	Z. Trebelli ms. E. Calzolari t. F. Graziani b. A. Vianesi cond.
Feb. 15	*Don Giovanni*	A. Fricci s. E. Volpini s. E. Calzolari t. F. Graziani b. G. Zucchini bs. A. Vianesi cond.
Feb. 25	*L'elisir d'amore*	E. Calzolari t. L. Gassier b. G. Zucchini bs. A. Vianesi cond.
Mar. 11	*Don Pasquale*	

LENT 1869 BRUSSELS—THÉÂTRE DE LA MONNAIE

Mar. 23	*La sonnambula*

LENT 1869 LIÈGE—GRAND THÉÂTRE

Mar. 25	*Il barbiere di Siviglia*

LENT AND SPRING 1869 PARIS—THÉÂTRE-ITALIEN

Mar. 30	*La traviata*	E. Nicolini t. F. Steller b.
Apr. 3	*La sonnambula*	E. Nicolini t. L. Agnesi bs.
Apr. 6	*Il barbiere di Siviglia*	E. Palermi t. E. Delle Sedie b. G. Ciampi bs.
Apr. 13	*Martha*	E. Palermi t. E. Delle Sedie b. L. Agnesi bs.
Apr. 17	*Rigoletto*	E. Grossi ms. E. Palermi t. E. Delle Sedie b.
Apr. 20	*Linda di Chamounix*	E. Grossi ms. E. Nicolini t. E. Delle Sedie b.
Apr. 24	*Lucia di Lammermoor*	E. Nicolini t. N. Verger b.

SPRING AND SUMMER 1869 LONDON—COVENT GARDEN

May 15	*La sonnambula*	P. Mongini t. (later E. Naudin t.) E. Bagagiolo bs. L. Arditi cond.
May 17	*Don Giovanni*	T. Tietjens s. C. Sinico s. E. Naudin t. (later E. Tamberlick t.) F. Graziani b. (later A. Cotogni b.) G. Ciampi bs. G. Li Calsi cond.
May 20	*Don Pasquale*	E. Naudin t. A. Cotogni b. A. Bottero bs. G. Li Calsi cond.
May 22	*Il barbiere di Siviglia*	P. Mongini t. (later I. Gardoni t.) A. Cotogni b. A. Bottero bs. G. Ciampi bs. G. Li Calsi cond.
June 11	*La gazza ladra*	Z. Trebelli ms. A. Bettini t. C. Santley b. A. Bottero bs. G. Li Calsi cond.
July 2	*Dinorah*	S. Scalchi ms. I. Gardoni t. C. Santley b. L. Arditi cond.

July 15	*La figlia del reggimento*	A. Corsi t. G. Ciampi bs. L. Arditi cond.
July 21	*Rigoletto*	S. Scalchi ms. E. Tamberlick t. C. Santley b. A. Foli bs. G. Li Calsi cond.

SUMMER 1869 LONDON—BUCKINGHAM PALACE

June 23	Concert

SUMMER 1869 BAD HOMBURG—KURSAAL

Aug. 7	*Lucia di Lammermoor*	E. Nicolini t. N. Verger b. L. Agnesi bs. L. Orsini cond.
Aug. 10	*Don Pasquale*	E. Nicolini t. N. Verger b. L. Fioravanti bs. L. Orsini cond.
Aug. 14	*La sonnambula*	E. Nicolini t. L. Orsini cond.
Aug. 17	*Il trovatore*	A. Urban s. E. Nicolini t. N. Verger b. L. Orsini cond.
Aug. 21	*La figlia del reggimento*	N. Sinigaglia t. L. Fioravanti bs. L. Orsini cond.
Aug. 28	*Rigoletto*	E. Nicolini t. N. Verger b. L. Orsini cond.
Aug. 31	*Faust* (in It.)	K. Morensi ms. E. Nicolini t. N. Verger b. L. Orsini cond.
Sep. 2	*Il barbiere di Siviglia*	E. Nicolini t. N. Verger b. L. Agnesi bs. L. Fioravanti bs. L. Orsini cond.
Sep. 4	*Crispino e la comare*	N. Sinigaglia t. L. Fioravanti bs. L. Orsini cond.
Sep. 7	*Linda di Chamounix*	K. Morensi ms. E. Nicolini t. N. Verger b. L. Agnesi bs. L. Fioravanti bs. L. Orsini cond.
Sep. 11	*La gazza ladra*	K. Morensi ms. N. Sinigaglia t. L. Agnesi bs. L. Fioravanti bs. L. Orsini cond.
Sep. 18	*La traviata*	E. Nicolini t. N. Verger b. L. Orsini cond.

AUTUMN 1869 BADEN-BADEN—KURSAAL

Sep. 24	Concert

AUTUMN 1869 PARIS—THÉÂTRE-ITALIEN

Oct. 5	*Lucia di Lammermoor*	G. Fraschini t. F. Steller b. L. Agnesi bs.
Oct. 7	*Il barbiere di Siviglia*	Padovani t. N. Verger b. L. Agnesi bs.
Oct. 9	*La traviata*	E. Nicolini t. F. Steller b.
Oct. 16	*Don Pasquale*	E. Nicolini t. E. Delle Sedie b. R. Scalese bs.
Oct. 21	*Rigoletto*	G. Fraschini t. E. Delle Sedie b.

AUTUMN AND WINTER 1869–70 ST. PETERSBURG—IMPERIAL THEATER

Nov. 15	*La traviata*	G. Capponi t. F. Steller b. A. Vianesi cond.
Nov. 19	*La sonnambula*	E. Calzolari t. E. Bagagiolo bs. A. Vianesi cond.
Dec.	*La figlia del reggimento*	E. Calzolari t. L. Gassier b. A. Vianesi cond.
Dec. 11	*Don Pasquale*	E. Calzolari t. G. Zucchini bs. A. Vianesi cond.

Dec. 15	*Don Giovanni*	A. Fricci s. E. Volpini s. E. Calzolari t. F. Graziani b. G. Zucchini bs. A. Vianesi cond.
Dec. 31	*Faust* (in It.)	Z. Trebelli ms. Mario t. F. Graziani b. E. Bagagiolo bs. A. Vianesi cond.
Jan. 11	*Martha*	Z. Trebelli ms. E. Calzolari t. F. Graziani b. A. Vianesi cond.
Jan. 19	*Linda di Chamounix*	Z. Trebelli ms. E. Calzolari t. F. Graziani b. E. Bagagiolo bs. G. Zucchini bs. A. Vianesi cond.
Jan. 26	*L'elisir d'amore*	E. Calzolari t. L. Gassier b. G. Zucchini bs. A. Vianesi cond.
Feb. 22	*Dinorah*	Z. Trebelli ms. E. Calzolari t. F. Graziani b. A. Vianesi cond.
Mar. 3	Gala Concert	

LENT 1870 LIÈGE—GRAND THÉÂTRE
| Mar. 16 | *La sonnambula* | |
| Mar. 21 | *Les Huguenots* | |

SPRING 1870 PARIS—THÉÂTRE-ITALIEN
Mar. 29	*Linda di Chamounix*	L. Sainz ms. E. Palermi t. G. Ciampi bs.
Mar. 31	*Il barbiere di Siviglia*	E. Palermi t. F. Varesi b. L. Agnesi bs. R. Scalese bs.
Apr. 2	*La traviata*	E. Palermi t. N. Verger b.
Apr. 7	*Rigoletto*	E. Nicolini t. N. Verger b.
Apr. 17	*La figlia del reggimento*	E. Palermi t. G. Ciampi bs.
May 1	Gala Concert	

SPRING 1870 PARIS—OPÉRA COMIQUE
| Apr. 21 | Concert | |

SPRING AND SUMMER 1870 LONDON—COVENT GARDEN
May 7	*Il barbiere di Siviglia*	Mario t. A. Cotogni b. J. Tagliafico bs. G. Ciampi bs. A. Vianesi cond.
May 9	*Don Giovanni*	T. Tietjens s. J. Van Zandt s. T. Wachtel t. (later Mario t.) F. Graziani b. G. Ciampi bs. A. Vianesi cond.
May 12	*La sonnambula*	T. Wachtel t. E. Bagagiolo bs. A. Vianesi cond.
May 17	*Martha*	S. Scalchi ms. Urio t. F. Graziani b. J. Tagliafico bs. A. Vianesi cond.
May 31	*Dinorah*	S. Scalchi ms. A. Marin t. F. Graziani b. A. Vianesi cond.
June 14	°*Esmeralda* (Campana)	S. Scalchi ms. E. Naudin t. F. Graziani b. A. Vianesi cond.
July 5	*I puritani*	G. Vizzani t. F. Graziani b. G. Capponi bs. A. Vianesi cond.
July 19	*La stella del Nord*	Olma s. E. Naudin t. F. Graziani b. A. Cotogni b. A. Vianesi cond.

342

SUMMER 1870 LONDON—BUCKINGHAM PALACE
July 6   Concert

AUTUMN 1870 BRIGHTON
Oct. 6   Concert

AUTUMN 1870 AMSTERDAM
Oct. 12   Concert

AUTUMN 1870 LA HAYE
Oct. 13   Concert

AUTUMN 1870 ROTTERDAM
Oct. 14   Concert

AUTUMN AND WINTER 1870–71 ST. PETERSBURG—IMPERIAL THEATER

Nov. 1	*Dinorah*	E. Calzolari t. F. Graziani b. A. Vianesi cond.
Nov. 8	*Il barbiere di Siviglia*	Mario t. A. Cotogni b. J. Tagliafico bs. G. Ciampi bs. A. Vianesi cond.
Nov. 16	*Faust* (in It.)	E. Calzolari t. C. Everardi b. A. Vianesi cond.
Nov. 23	*Lucia di Lammermoor*	
Dec. 6	*La figlia del reggimento*	A. Corsi t. G. Zucchini bs. A. Vianesi cond.
Dec. 8	*Don Pasquale*	A. Corsi t. C. Everardi b. G. Zucchini bs. A. Vianesi cond.
	La traviata	E. Calzolari t. F. Graziani b. A. Vianesi cond.
	Linda di Chamounix	B. Marchisio ms. F. Graziani b. E. Bagagiolo bs. A. Vianesi cond.
	Rigoletto	B. Marchisio ms. A. Corsi t. F. Steller b. A. Vianesi cond.
Jan. 16	*Don Giovanni*	C. Marchisio s. E. Volpini s. P. Mongini t. F. Steller b. G. Zucchini bs. A. Vianesi cond.
Jan. 19	*Otello*	P. Mongini t. I. Corsi t. E. Bagagiolo bs. A. Vianesi cond.
Feb. 14	*La sonnambula*	

SPRING 1871 BRUSSELS—THÉÂTRE DE LA MONNAIE
Apr. 9   *La traviata*

SPRING AND SUMMER 1871 LONDON—COVENT GARDEN

Apr. 15	*La sonnambula*	P. Mongini t. E. Bagagiolo bs. A. Vianesi cond.
Apr. 18	*I puritani*	P. Mongini t. A. Cotogni b. G. Capponi bs. A. Vianesi cond.
Apr. 22	*Il barbiere di Siviglia*	Mario t. A. Cotogni b. J. Tagliafico bs. G. Ciampi bs. E. Bevignani cond.

Apr. 24	*Don Giovanni*	R. Csillag s. (later I. Fabbri s.) M. C. Miolan-Carvalho s. A. Bettini t. (later Mario t.) J. B. Faure b. (later A. Cotogni b.) G. Ciampi bs. A. Vianesi cond.
May 5	*Dinorah*	S. Scalchi ms. A. Bettini t. F. Graziani b. A. Vianesi cond.
May 12	*Otello*	P. Mongini t. A. Bettini t. F. Graziani b. G. Capponi bs. E. Bevignani cond.
June 8	*La stella del Nord*	Monbelli s. E. Naudin t. J. B. Faure b. G. Ciampi bs. A. Vianesi cond.
June 27	*Esmeralda*	S. Scalchi ms. E. Naudin t. F. Graziani b. E. Bevignani cond.
July 3	*Il trovatore*	S. Scalchi ms. Mario t. F. Graziani b. A. Vianesi cond.
July 17	*Les Huguenots* (in It.)	M. C. Miolan-Carvalho s. S. Scalchi ms. Mario t. A. Cotogni b. J. B. Faure b. E. Bagagiolo bs. A. Vianesi cond.

SPRING AND SUMMER 1871 LONDON—FLORAL HALL
(Concurrent with Covent Garden season)

Apr. 29	Concert
May 20	Concert
May 31	Concert
June 10	Concert?
June 24	Concert
July 15	Concert

SPRING 1871 LONDON—BUCKINGHAM PALACE
May 15	Concert

SPRING 1871 LONDON—ST. JAMES'S HALL
June 14	Concert

SUMMER 1871 BAD HOMBURG—KURSAAL

Aug. 8	*Rigoletto*	L. Orsini cond.
Aug. 12	*Les Huguenots* (in It.)	Z. Trebelli ms. R. Stagno t. E. Bagagiolo bs. L. Orsini cond.
Aug. 15	*Faust* (in It.)	G. Tiozzo ms. A. Bettini t. E. Storti b. P. Medini bs. L. Orsini cond.
Aug. 19	*Lucia di Lammermoor*	G. Fancelli t. E. Storti b. L. Orsini cond.
Aug. 22	*Martha*	Z. Trebelli ms. A. Bettini t. E. Bagagiolo bs. L. Fioravanti bs. L. Orsini cond.
Aug. 26	*Linda di Chamounix*	Z. Trebelli ms. G. Fancelli t. F. Steller b. E. Bagagiolo bs. L. Fioravanti bs. L. Orsini cond.
Aug. 29	*Esmeralda*	Z. Trebelli ms. A. Bettini t. F. Steller b. L. Orsini cond.
Sep. 2	*Dinorah*	L. Orsini cond.
Sep. 3	*Il barbiere di Siviglia*	L. Orsini cond.
Sep. 9	*La traviata*	L. Orsini cond.

344

Sep. 12	*I puritani*	L. Orsini cond.
Sep. 16	*Ernani*	L. Orsini cond.
Sep. 19	*Don Pasquale*	L. Orsini cond.
Sep. 23	*La sonnambula*	L. Orsini cond.

AUTUMN 1871 BRUSSELS—THÉÂTRE DE LA MONNAIE

Oct. 17	*Rigoletto*	L. Achard t.
Oct. 20	*Les Huguenots*	

AUTUMN 1871 MOSCOW—BOLSHOI TEATR

Nov. 4	*Dinorah*	A. Corsi t. G. Moriami b. E. Bevignani cond.
Nov. 18	*Il barbiere di Siviglia*	A. Corsi t. G. Moriami b. E. Bevignani cond.
Dec. 2	*La sonnambula*	A. Corsi t. E. Bevignani cond.

AUTUMN AND WINTER 1871–72 ST. PETERSBURG—IMPERIAL THEATER

Dec. 11	*Lucia di Lammermoor*	E. Nicolini t. G. Rota b. (later G. Moriami b., then F. Graziani b.) Meo bs. L. Arditi cond.
Dec. 14	*La sonnambula*	A. Corsi t. G. Rota b. L. Arditi cond.
Dec. 22	*Don Pasquale*	A. Corsi t. M. Padilla b. G. Ciampi bs. L. Arditi cond.
Dec. 27	*Dinorah*	A. Corsi t. L. Arditi cond.
Jan. 1	*Rigoletto*	Z. Trebelli ms. E. Nicolini t. F. Graziani b. L. Arditi cond.
Jan. 16	*Don Giovanni*	G. Giovannoni s. C. Sinico s. A. Corsi t. F. Graziani b. G. Ciampi bs. L. Arditi cond.
Jan. 25	*Il trovatore*	Z. Trebelli ms. E. Nicolini t. F. Graziani b. L. Arditi cond.
Feb. 2	*Il barbiere di Siviglia*	A. Corsi t. G. Moriami b. E. Bagagiolo bs. G. Ciampi bs. L. Arditi cond.
Feb. 8	*Roméo et Juliette* (in It.)	S. Scalchi ms. E. Nicolini t. F. Graziani b. G. Moriami b. E. Bagagiolo bs. L. Arditi cond.

LENT AND SPRING 1872 VIENNA—THEATER AN DER WIEN

Mar. 19	*Lucia di Lammermoor*	E. Nicolini t. F. Graziani b. L. Arditi cond.
Mar. 23	*Rigoletto*	E. Nicolini t. F. Graziani b. L. Arditi cond.
Apr. 3	*La traviata*	E. Nicolini t. F. Graziani b. L. Arditi cond.
Apr. 6	*Linda di Chamounix*	L. Sainz ms. F. Graziani b. L. Arditi cond.
Apr. 15	*Il barbiere di Siviglia*	
Apr. 20	*La sonnambula*	

SPRING AND SUMMER 1872 LONDON—COVENT GARDEN

May 4	*Dinorah*	S. Scalchi ms. A. Bettini t. F. Graziani b. A. Vianesi cond.
May 7	*Il barbiere di Siviglia*	A. Bettini t. A. Cotogni b. J. Tagliafico bs. G. Ciampi bs. E. Bevignani cond.
May 20	*Il trovatore*	E. de Méric Lablache ms. (later S. Scalchi ms.) E. Nicolini t. F. Graziani b. A. Vianesi cond.

May 28	°°*Gelmina* (Poniatowski)	E. Naudin t. A. Cotogni b. E. Bagagiolo bs. A. Vianesi cond.
June 21	*La stella del Nord*	Monbelli s. E. Naudin t. J. B. Faure b. G. Ciampi bs. A. Vianesi cond.
June 29	*Don Giovanni*	E. Parepa-Rosa s. C. Sinico s. A. Bettini t. J. B. Faure b. G. Ciampi bs. A. Vianesi cond.
July 1	*La sonnambula*	E. Naudin t. J. B. Faure b. A. Vianesi cond.
July 15	*Les Huguenots* (in It.)	C. Sinico s. S. Scalchi ms. E. Nicolini t. E. Bagagiolo bs. A. Vianesi cond.

SPRING AND SUMMER 1872 WINDSOR—WINDSOR CASTLE

June 5	Concert	
July 4	Concert	J. B. Faure b.

SUMMER 1872 BAD HOMBURG—KURSAAL

Aug. 3	*Lucia di Lammermoor*	R. Stagno t. N. Verger b. G. Capponi bs. L. Orsini cond.
Aug. 6	*Faust* (in It.)	S. Scalchi ms. R. Stagno t. N. Verger b. G. Capponi bs. L. Orsini cond.
Aug. 10	*Don Pasquale*	R. Stagno t. (later A. Corsi t.) N. Verger b. G. Zucchini bs. L. Orsini cond.
Aug. 13	*Martha*	S. Scalchi ms. R. Stagno t. N. Verger b. L. Orsini cond.
Aug. 17	*Il trovatore*	S. Scalchi ms. R. Stagno t. N. Verger b. G. Capponi bs. L. Orsini cond.
Aug. 20	*Il barbiere di Siviglia*	R. Stagno t. N. Verger b. G. Capponi bs. G. Zucchini bs. L. Orsini cond.
Aug. 24	*Rigoletto*	S. Scalchi ms. R. Stagno t. N. Verger b. G. Capponi bs. L. Orsini cond.
Aug. 27	*I puritani*	R. Stagno t. N. Verger b. G. Capponi bs. L. Orsini cond.
Aug. 31	*Linda di Chamounix*	S. Scalchi ms. R. Stagno t. N. Verger b. G. Capponi bs. G. Zucchini bs. L. Orsini cond.
Sep. 3	*Otello*	R. Stagno t. A. Rinaldini t. N. Verger b. G. Capponi bs. L. Orsini cond.
Sep. 7	*Crispino e la comare*	A. Rinaldini t. N. Verger b. G. Zucchini bs. L. Orsini cond.
Sep. 12	*La traviata*	A. Corsi t. N. Verger b. L. Orsini cond.
Sep. 17	*Esmeralda*	S. Scalchi ms. A. Corsi t. N. Verger b. L. Orsini cond.
Sep. 24	*La sonnambula*	A. Corsi t. G. Capponi bs. L. Orsini cond.

AUTUMN 1872 MOSCOW—BOLSHOI TEATR

Oct. 26	*La traviata*	E. Naudin t. A. Mazzoli b. L. Orsini cond.
Nov. 4	*Rigoletto*	L. Bolis t. F. Graziani b. L. Orsini cond.
Nov. 13	*Don Pasquale*	E. Naudin t. F. Graziani b. G. Ciampi bs. L. Orsini cond.
Nov. 15	*Linda di Chamounix*	F. Graziani b. G. Ciampi bs. L. Orsini cond.

Nov. 26   *La sonnambula*

AUTUMN AND WINTER 1872–73 ST. PETERSBURG—IMPERIAL THEATER

Dec. 9	*Dinorah*	S. Scalchi ms. I. Gardoni t. A. Cotogni b. C. E. Bosoni cond.
Dec. 12	*Lucia di Lammermoor*	A. Marin t. A. Cotogni b. G. Capponi bs. C. E. Bosoni cond.
Dec. 28	*Il barbiere di Siviglia*	I. Gardoni t. C. Everardi b. G. Capponi bs. G. Ciampi bs. C. E. Bosoni cond.
Jan. 2	*La gazza ladra*	S. Scalchi ms. I. Gardoni t. C. Everardi b. C. E. Bosoni cond.
Jan. 4	*Rigoletto*	S. Scalchi ms. A. Marin t. F. Graziani b. E. Bagagiolo bs. C. E. Bosoni cond.
Feb. 5	*Roméo et Juliette* (in It.)	S. Scalchi ms. E. Nicolini t. F. Graziani b. E. Bagagiolo bs. C. E. Bosoni cond.
Feb. 11	*La sonnambula*	E. Naudin t. E. Bagagiolo bs. C. E. Bosoni cond.

LENT AND SPRING 1873 VIENNA—THEATER AN DER WIEN

Mar. 11	*La traviata*	E. Nicolini t. F. Graziani b. L. Arditi cond.
Mar. 17	*Il trovatore*	B. Marchisio ms. E. Nicolini t. L. Arditi cond.
Mar. 27	*La sonnambula*	E. Naudin t. L. Arditi cond.
Mar. 31	*I puritani*	A. Marin t. F. Graziani b. A. Vidal bs. L. Arditi cond.
Apr. 4	*Rigoletto*	L. Arditi cond.
Apr. 9	*Lucia di Lammermoor*	L. Arditi cond.
Apr. 17	*Martha*	B. Marchisio ms. L. Arditi cond.
Apr. 24	*Dinorah*	B. Marchisio ms. A. Marin t. F. Graziani b. L. Arditi cond.

SPRING AND SUMMER 1873 LONDON—COVENT GARDEN

May 13	*Il barbiere di Siviglia*	V. Montanaro t. A. Cotogni b. J. Tagliafico bs. G. Ciampi bs. A. Vianesi cond.
May 15	*Don Giovanni*	M. Bulli-Paoli s. C. Sinico s. A. Bettini t. J. B. Faure b. G. Ciampi bs. A. Vianesi cond.
May 19	*Dinorah*	S. Scalchi ms. A. Bettini t. V. Maurel b. A. Vianesi cond.
May 28	*Il trovatore*	S. Scalchi ms. E. Nicolini t. F. Graziani b. A. Vianesi cond.
June 6	*Otello*	P. Mongini t. A. Bettini t. F. Graziani b. G. Capponi bs. A. Vianesi cond.
June 16	*Ernani*	P. Mongini t. F. Graziani b. E. Bagagiolo bs. A. Vianesi cond.
July 3	*I diamanti della corona*	Monbelli s. A. Bettini t. A. Cotogni b. G. Capponi bs. A. Vianesi cond.
July 18	*La stella del Nord*	E. de Méric Lablache ms. A. Bettini t. J. B. Faure b. G. Ciampi bs. A. Vianesi cond.
July 21	*Les Huguenots* (in It.)	C. Sinico s. S. Scalchi ms. E. Nicolini t. J. B. Faure b. A. Cotogni b. A. Vianesi cond.

SUMMER 1873 LONDON—BUCKINGHAM PALACE
July 10   Concert

AUTUMN 1873 MOSCOW—BOLSHOI TEATR
Oct. 22   *La traviata*   E. Naudin t. F. Graziani b. E. Bevignani cond.
Oct. 25   *Rigoletto*   A. Bernardi ms. E. Nicolini t. F. Graziani b. E.
                                  Bevignani cond.
Oct. 29   *Linda di Chamounix* A. Bernardi ms. E. Naudin t. G. Rota b. A. Foli
                                  bs. G. Ciampi bs. E. Bevignani cond.
Oct. 31   *Il trovatore*   A. Bernardi ms. E. Nicolini t. F. Graziani b. A.
                                  Foli bs. E. Bevignani cond.
Nov. 8   *Dinorah*
Nov. 18   *Faust* (in It.)

AUTUMN AND WINTER 1873–74 ST. PETERSBURG—IMPERIAL THEATER
Nov. 24   *Rigoletto*   S. Scalchi ms. E. Nicolini t. G. Mendioroz b. G.
                                  Capponi bs. L. Arditi cond.
Dec. 2   *Dinorah*   S. Scalchi ms. D. Filleboni t. A. Cotogni b. L.
                                  Arditi cond.
Dec. 10   *Roméo et Juliette*   S. Scalchi ms. E. Nicolini t. G. Mendioroz b. E.
            (in It.)   Bagagiolo bs. L. Arditi cond.
Dec. 23   *Linda di Chamounix* S. Scalchi ms. A. Marin t. A. Cotogni b. G.
                                  Ciampi bs. E. Bagagiolo bs. L. Arditi cond.
Jan. 7   *Otello*   L. Arditi cond.
Jan. 9   *La traviata*   E. Nicolini t. G. Mendioroz b. N. Bassi cond.
Jan.   *Il barbiere di Siviglia* A. Cotogni b. L. Arditi cond.
Feb. 4   °*Mireille* (in It.) S. Scalchi ms. E. Nicolini t. G. Mendioroz b. E.
                                  Bagagiolo bs. L. Arditi cond.

LENT AND SPRING 1874 VIENNA—THEATER AN DER WIEN
Mar. 4   *La traviata*   E. Nicolini t. A. Cotogni b. L. Arditi cond.
Mar. 10   *Il trovatore*   S. Scalchi ms. E. Nicolini t. A. Cotogni b. L.
                                  Arditi cond.
Mar. 13   *Linda di Chamounix* S. Scalchi ms. E. Nicolini t. A. Cotogni b. G.
                                  Zucchini bs. A. Foli bs. L. Arditi cond.
Mar. 21   *Lucia di*   J. Gayarre t. A. Cotogni b. A. Foli bs. L. Arditi
            Lammermoor   cond.
Mar. 24   *Il barbiere di Siviglia* J. Gayarre t. G. Mendioroz b. G. Zucchini bs.
                                  L. Arditi cond.
Apr. 1   *Rigoletto*   J. Gayarre t. L. Arditi cond.
Apr. 16   *Ernani*   F. Patierno t. G. Mendioroz b. A. Foli bs. L.
                                  Arditi cond.
Apr. 21   *Otello*   F. Patierno t. J. Gayarre t. G. Mendioroz b. L.
                                  Arditi cond.
Apr. 25   *Don Pasquale*   L. Arditi cond.
May 2   *Dinorah*   L. Arditi cond.

SPRING 1874 PEST
Apr.?   Concert

SPRING AND SUMMER 1874 LONDON—COVENT GARDEN

May 12	*Il barbiere di Siviglia*	A. Bettini t. (later L. Piazza t.) A. Cotogni b. J. Tagliafico bs. (later E. Bagagiolo bs.) G. Ciampi bs. A. Vianesi cond.
May 14	*Dinorah*	S. Scalchi ms. A. Bettini t. V. Maurel b. A. Vianesi cond.
May 23	*I diamanti della corona*	C. Sinico s. Raguer s. I. Sabater t. J. Tagliafico bs. G. Ciampi bs. A. Vianesi cond.
May 26	*Ernani*	E. Nicolini t. V. Maurel b. E. Bagagiolo bs. E. Bevignani cond.
June 17	*Il trovatore*	S. Scalchi ms. A. Marin t. V. Maurel b. E. Bevignani cond.
June 27	*Luisa Miller*	E. Nicolini t. F. Graziani b. E. Bagagiolo bs. E. Bevignani cond.
July 18	*La stella del Nord*	C. Sinico s. Cottino t. J. B. Faure b. G. Capponi bs. A. Vianesi cond.

AUTUMN 1874 PARIS—OPERA

Oct. 11	*Les Huguenots*	M. Belval s. A. Arnaud ms. P. F. Villaret t. J. Lassalle b. J. Belval bs. P. Gailhard bs. E. Deldevez cond.

AUTUMN 1874 MOSCOW—BOLSHOI TEATR

Oct. 31	*La sonnambula*	
Nov. 9	*Lucia di Lammermoor*	
Nov. 18	*L'elisir d'amore*	
Nov. 28	*Don Pasquale*	E. Naudin t. E. Storti b. C. Bossi bs.
Nov. 29	*La gazza ladra*	
Dec. 1	*Il barbiere di Siviglia*	G. Vizzani t. A. Cotogni b. J. Jamet bs. C. Bossi bs. E. Bevignani cond.

AUTUMN AND WINTER 1874–75 ST. PETERSBURG—IMPERIAL THEATER

Dec. 7	*La traviata*	J. Gayarre t. E. Storti b.
Dec. 19	*Dinorah*	G. Vizzani t. A. Cotogni b.
Dec. 24	*Lucia di Lammermoor*	J. Gayarre t. E. Storti b. E. Marcassa bs.
Jan. 25	*Il barbiere di Siviglia*	A. Cotogni b.
Feb. 19	*Rigoletto*	S. Scalchi ms. V. Capoul t.
Feb. 26	*Les Huguenots* (in It.)	B. Bianchi s. S. Scalchi ms. V. Capoul t. E. Storti b. V. Maurel b. J. Jamet bs.

SPRING 1875 VIENNA—KOMISCHE OPER

Mar. 24	*Lucia di Lammermoor*	J. Gayarre t. G. Rota b. C. Bossi bs. L. Arditi cond.
Mar. 31	*La sonnambula*	J. Gayarre t. C. Bossi bs. L. Arditi cond.
Apr. 3	*La traviata*	V. Capoul t. G. Rota b. L. Arditi cond.
Apr. 8	*Dinorah*	G. Rota b. L. Arditi cond.
Apr. 10	*Don Pasquale*	V. Capoul t. G. Rota b. G. Zucchini bs. L. Arditi cond.

Apr. 14	*Il barbiere di Siviglia*	V. Capoul t. N. Verger b. G. Zucchini bs. C. Bossi bs. L. Arditi cond.
Apr. 17	*Faust* (in It.)	V. Capoul t. N. Verger b. G. Rota b. L. Arditi cond.
Apr. 27	*Rigoletto*	L. Arditi cond.

SPRING AND SUMMER 1875 LONDON—COVENT GARDEN

May 11	*Dinorah*	S. Scalchi ms. A. Marin t. F. Graziani b. A. Vianesi cond.
May 13	*Il barbiere di Siviglia*	G. Piazza t. A. Cotogni b. E. Bagagiolo bs. A. Vianesi cond.
May 17	*La traviata*	A. De Sanctis t. (later E. Nicolini t.) F. Graziani b. A. Vianesi cond.
May 27	*Il trovatore*	S. Scalchi ms. A. Marin t. F. Graziani b.
June 1	*I diamanti della corona*	C. Smeroschi s. E. Naudin t. G. Capponi bs. G. Ciampi bs. A. Vianesi cond.
June 18	*Roméo et Juliette* (in It.)	B. Bianchi s. E. Nicolini t. A. Cotogni b. E. Bagagiolo bs. E. Bevignani cond.
June 25	*Les Huguenots* (in It.)	M. Marimon s. S. Scalchi ms. E. Nicolini t. A. Cotogni b. G. Ciampi bs. A. Vianesi cond.
July 13	*La stella del Nord*	C. Smeroschi s. E. Naudin t. J. B. Faure b. G. Ciampi bs. A. Vianesi cond.

SUMMER 1875 LONDON—BUCKINGHAM PALACE

| June 23 | Concert |

SUMMER AND AUTUMN 1875 CONCERT TOUR
Cities visited include Bristol (Sep. 14), Brighton (Sep. 18), Birmingham (Sep. 21), and Manchester (Sep. 23).

AUTUMN 1875 MOSCOW—BOLSHOI TEATR

Oct. 30	*Roméo et Juliette* (in It.)	A. L. Cary ms. E. Nicolini t. M. Padilla b. L. Colonnese b. J. Jamet bs. C. Bossi bs. E. Bevignani cond.
Nov. 12	*Il barbiere di Siviglia*	V. Capoul t. M. Padilla b. J. Jamet bs. C. Bossi bs. E. Bevignani cond.
Nov. 14	*Martha*	A. L. Cary ms. V. Capoul t. J. Jamet bs. E. Bevignani cond.
Nov. 18	*Rigoletto*	A. L. Cary ms. V. Capoul t. M. Padilla b. C. Bossi bs. E. Bevignani cond.
Nov. 23	*Les Huguenots* (in It.)	C. De Maesen s. S. Scalchi ms. E. Nicolini t. L. Colonnese b. J. Jamet bs. C. Bossi bs. E. Bevignani cond.

AUTUMN AND WINTER 1875–76 ST. PETERSBURG—IMPERIAL THEATER

Nov. 27	*Linda di Chamounix*	A. L. Cary ms. A. Marin t. A. Cotogni b. G. Ciampi bs. J. Goula cond.
Dec. 7	*Dinorah*	A. L. Cary ms. A. Marin t. (later A. De Sanctis t.) A. Strozzi b. J. Goula cond.
Dec. 15	*Roméo et Juliette* (in It.)	A. L. Cary ms. E. Nicolini t. A. Strozzi b. J. Goula cond.

Jan. 15	*I diamanti della corona*	M. Heilbronn s. E. Nicolini t. G. Ciampi bs. J. Goula cond.
Jan. 20	*Il barbiere di Siviglia*	V. Capoul t. A. Cotogni b. E. Bagagiolo bs. G. Ciampi bs. J. Goula cond.
Feb. 11	*Rigoletto*	A. L. Cary ms. J. Goula cond.
Feb. 21	*Il trovatore*	A. L. Cary ms. A. Marin t. A. Strozzi b. J. Goula cond.

LENT AND SPRING 1876 VIENNA—HOFOPER

Mar. 14	*La traviata*	E. Nicolini t. A. Strozzi b. L. Arditi cond.
Mar. 16	*Lucia di Lammermoor*	V. Capoul t. L. Arditi cond.
Mar. 18	*Les Huguenots* (in It.)	M. Heilbronn s. A. L. Cary ms. E. Nicolini t. M. Padilla b. A. Strozzi b. J. Jamet bs. L. Arditi cond.
Mar. 28	*Roméo et Juliette* (in It.)	A. L. Cary ms. E. Nicolini t. M. Padilla b. J. Jamet bs. L. Arditi cond.
Apr. 3	*Il barbiere di Siviglia*	V. Capoul t. A. Strozzi b. J. Jamet bs. G. Zucchini bs. L. Arditi cond.
Apr. 23	*Don Pasquale*	V. Capoul t. M. Padilla b. G. Zucchini bs. L. Arditi cond.
Apr. 26	°*Mireille* (in It.)	A. L. Cary ms. E. Nicolini t. A. Strozzi b. V. Hablawetz bs. L. Arditi cond.

SPRING 1876 PEST—VOLKSTHEATER
(Concurrent with Vienna season)

Apr.	*Lucia di Lammermoor*	V. Capoul t. M. Padilla b. L. Arditi cond.
Apr.	*Il barbiere di Siviglia*	V. Capoul t. M. Padilla b. J. Jamet bs. G. Zucchini bs. L. Arditi cond.

SPRING AND SUMMER 1876 LONDON—COVENT GARDEN

May 12	*Il barbiere di Siviglia*	A. Bettini t. A. Cotogni b. G. Ciampi bs. E. Bevignani cond.
May 15	*Dinorah*	S. Scalchi ms. A. Bettini t. F. Graziani b. A. Vianesi cond.
May 24	*Roméo et Juliette* (in It.)	B. Bianchi s. E. Nicolini t. A. Cotogni b. E. Bevignani cond.
May 27	*La traviata*	A. De Sanctis t. (later L. Bolis t.) F. Graziani b. A. Vianesi cond.
May 30	*Il trovatore*	S. Scalchi ms. A. Marin t. F. Graziani b. A. Vianesi cond.
June 1	*Don Giovanni*	Saar s. E. Nicolini t. A. Cotogni b. G. Ciampi bs. A. Vianesi cond.
June 22	°*Aida*	E. Gindele ms. E. Nicolini t. F. Graziani b. G. Capponi bs. E. Bevignani cond.

SUMMER 1876 LONDON—BUCKINGHAM PALACE

June 25	Concert

AUTUMN 1876 CONCERT TOUR
Cities visited include Nantes (Oct. 28), Bordeaux (Oct. 31), and Reims (Nov. 6).

AUTUMN 1876 MOSCOW—BOLSHOI TEATR

Nov. 25	*Dinorah*	A. L. Cary ms. I. Corsi t. A. Strozzi b. C. Bossi bs. E. Bevignani cond.
Dec. 2	*Linda di Chamounix*	A. L. Cary ms. A. Marin t. M. Padilla b. J. Jamet bs. C. Bossi bs. E. Bevignani cond.
Dec. 7	*Aida*	A. L. Cary ms. A. Marin t. M. Padilla b. J. Jamet bs. E. Bevignani cond.
Dec. 10	*Il barbiere di Siviglia*	A. Corsi t. A. Strozzi b. J. Jamet bs. C. Bossi bs. E. Bevignani cond.
Dec. 12	*Esmeralda*	A. L. Cary ms. I. Corsi t. A. Strozzi b. E. Bevignani cond.

AUTUMN AND WINTER 1876–77 ST. PETERSBURG—IMPERIAL THEATER

Dec. 18	*La traviata*	A. Masini t. G. Mendioroz b. J. Goula cond.
Dec. 26	*Dinorah*	Rossetti ms. J. Goula cond.
Jan. 3	*I puritani*	A. Marin t. J. Goula cond.
Jan. 10	*Roméo et Juliette* (in It.)	Rossetti ms. J. Goula cond.
Jan. 23	*Il barbiere di Siviglia*	A. Marin t. A. Cotogni b. E. Bagagiolo bs. G. Ciampi bs. J. Goula cond.
Feb. 1	*Don Giovanni*	L. Artot s. M. Heilbronn s. A. Marin t. M. Padilla b. G. Ciampi bs. J. Goula cond.
Feb. 16	*Rigoletto*	A. L. Cary ms. J. Goula cond.

LENT AND SPRING 1877 VIENNA—HOFOPER

Mar. 3	*La sonnambula*	E. Nicolini t. A. Fiorini bs. L. Arditi cond.
Mar. 9	*La traviata*	E. Nicolini t. (later A. Masini t.) A. Strozzi b. L. Arditi cond.
Mar. 15	*Semiramide*	Z. Trebelli ms. A. Oliva-Pavani t. (later E. Nicolini t.) A. Strozzi b. A. Fiorini bs. L. Arditi cond.
Mar. 20	*Roméo et Juliette* (in It.)	E. Nicolini t. A. Strozzi b. A. Fiorini bs. L. Arditi cond.
Mar. 23	*Il trovatore*	Z. Trebelli ms. E. Nicolini t. A. Strozzi b. A. Fiorini bs. L. Arditi cond.
Apr. 4	*Il barbiere di Siviglia*	E. Nicolini t. A. Strozzi b. A. Fiorini bs. G. Zucchini bs. L. Arditi cond.
Apr. 11	*Linda di Chamounix*	Z. Trebelli ms. E. Nicolini t. A. Strozzi b. A. Fiorini bs. G. Zucchini bs. L. Arditi cond.
Apr. 19	*Rigoletto*	Z. Trebelli ms. A. Masini t. A. Strozzi b. L. Arditi cond.
Apr. 26	*Don Pasquale*	E. Nicolini t. A. Strozzi b. G. Zucchini bs. L. Arditi cond.
May 1	*Faust* (in It.)	Z. Trebelli ms. E. Nicolini t. A. Strozzi b. A. Fiorini bs. L. Arditi cond.

SPRING 1877 PEST—VOLKSTHEATER
(Concurrent with Vienna season)

Mar. 26	*La traviata*	E. Nicolini t. A. Strozzi b. L. Arditi cond.
Mar. 28	*Faust* (in It.)	Z. Trebelli ms. E. Nicolini t. A. Strozzi b. A. Fiorini bs. L. Arditi cond.

SPRING AND SUMMER 1877 LONDON—COVENT GARDEN

May 15	*Dinorah*	S. Scalchi ms. A. Oliva-Pavani t. F. Graziani b. A. Vianesi cond.
May 29	*La stella del Nord*	B. Bianchi s. A. Oliva-Pavani t. V. Maurel b. G. Ciampi bs. A. Vianesi cond.
June 1	*Il trovatore*	S. Scalchi ms. E. Nicolini t. F. Graziani b. A. Vianesi cond.
June 4	*Aida*	S. Scalchi ms. E. Nicolini t. F. Graziani b. E. Bevignani cond.
June 15	*Il barbiere di Siviglia*	V. Capoul t. A. Cotogni b. G. Ciampi bs. A. Vianesi cond.
July 4	*Roméo et Juliette* (in It.)	B. Bianchi s. E. Nicolini t. A. Cotogni b. E. Bevignani cond.
July 16	*La traviata*	E. Nicolini t. F. Graziani b. A. Vianesi cond.
July 19	*Faust* (in It.)	O. Synnerberg ms. E. Nicolini t. A. Cotogni b. J. Ordinas bs. A. Vianesi cond.

AUTUMN 1877 MILAN—TEATRO ALLA SCALA

Nov. 3	*La traviata*	E. Nicolini t. L. Giraldoni b. E. Bernardi cond.
Nov. 7	*Faust* (in It.)	M. De Gourieff ms. E. Nicolini t. L. Giraldoni b. O. Maini bs. E. Bernardi cond.
Nov. 11	*Il barbiere di Siviglia*	E. Nicolini t. L. Giraldoni b. (later Giannini b.) O. Maini bs. G. Zucchini bs. E. Bernardi cond.
Nov. 13	*Il trovatore*	S. Bonheur ms. E. Nicolini t. L. Giraldoni b. E. Bernardi cond.

AUTUMN 1877 VENICE—TEATRO LA FENICE

Dec. 4	*La traviata*	E. Nicolini t. L. Giraldoni b. E. Bernardi cond.
Dec. 8	*Faust* (in It.)	M. De Gourieff ms. E. Nicolini t. L. Giraldoni b. O. Maini bs. E. Bernardi cond.
Dec. 15	*Il barbiere di Siviglia*	E. Nicolini t. V. Carpi b. O. Maini bs. G. Zucchini bs. E. Bernardi cond.

AUTUMN 1877 GENOA—TEATRO PAGANINI

Dec. 20	*La traviata*	E. Nicolini t. G. Valchieri b.
Dec. 22	*Il barbiere di Siviglia*	E. Nicolini t. G. Valchieri b.

CARNIVAL 1877–78 GENOA—TEATRO ANDREA DORIA

Dec. 26	*La traviata*	E. Nicolini t. G. Valchieri b.

CARNIVAL 1877–78 FLORENCE—TEATRO PAGLIANO

Dec. 29   *La traviata*   E. Nicolini t. V. Carpi b. M. Mancinelli cond.

Jan. 1   *Il barbiere di Siviglia*   E. Nicolini t. V. Carpi b. G. Zucchini bs. M. Mancinelli cond.

CARNIVAL 1878 NAPLES—TEATRO SAN CARLO

Jan. 19   *La traviata*   E. Nicolini t. M. Medica b. P. Serrao cond.

Jan. 25   *Il barbiere di Siviglia*   E. Nicolini t. V. Carpi b. E. Gasperini bs. A. De Bassini bs. P. Serrao cond.

Feb. 5   *La sonnambula*   E. Nicolini t. A. Silvestri bs. P. Serrao cond.

CARNIVAL 1878 ROME—TEATRO APOLLO

Feb. 15   *La traviata*   E. Nicolini t. G. Vaselli b. L. Mancinelli cond.

Feb. 18   *Il barbiere di Siviglia*   E. Nicolini t. V. Carpi b. C. Ristori bs. L. Mancinelli cond.

Feb. 20   *La sonnambula*   E. Nicolini t. A. Bettarini bs. L. Mancinelli cond.

LENT 1878 MILAN—TEATRO ALLA SCALA

Mar. 2   *La sonnambula*   E. Nicolini t. E. Marcassa bs. F. Faccio cond.

Mar. 13   *Aida*   G. Pasqua ms. E. Nicolini t. G. Moriami b. O. Maini bs. E. Marcassa bs. F. Faccio cond.

Apr. 4   *La traviata*   E. Nicolini t. G. Moriami b. F. Faccio cond.

SPRING 1878 BOLOGNA—TEATRO BRUNETTI

Apr. 10   *La traviata*   E. Nicolini t. G. Moriami b.

SPRING AND SUMMER 1878 LONDON—COVENT GARDEN

May 9   *La stella del Nord*   C. Smeroschi s. A. De Bassini t. (later A. Oliva-Pavani t.) V. Maurel b. G. Ciampi bs. A. Vianesi cond.

May 13   *Dinorah*   O. Synnerberg ms. A. De Bassini t. (later G. Piazza t.) V. Maurel b. A. Vianesi cond.

May 16   *La traviata*   E. Nicolini t. F. Graziani b. E. Bevignani cond.

May 21   *Il trovatore*   S. Scalchi ms. L. Bolis t. F. Graziani b. F. Scolara bs. A. Vianesi cond.

May 25   *Il barbiere di Siviglia*   E. Nicolini t. A. Cotogni b. F. Scolara bs. A. Carbone bs. A. Vianesi cond.

May 27   *Don Giovanni*   De Reti s. Saar s. C. Carpi t. V. Maurel b. G. Ciampi bs. A. Vianesi cond.

June 8   *Aida*   S. Scalchi ms. E. Nicolini t. F. Graziani b. E. Bevignani cond.

June 11   *Faust* (in It.)   A. De Belocca ms. E. Nicolini t. A. Cotogni b. J. Ordinas bs. A. Vianesi cond.

July 18   *La sonnambula*   E. Nicolini t. A. Carbone bs. A. Vianesi cond.

July 11   *Semïramide*   S. Scalchi ms. A. Oliva-Pavani t. V. Maurel b. G. Capponi bs. E. Bevignani cond.

AUTUMN 1878 LIVERPOOL
Oct. 10   Concert

AUTUMN 1878 DUBLIN
Oct.   Concert

AUTUMN 1878 BRUSSELS—THÉÂTRE DE LA MONNAIE
Oct. 31   *La traviata*   E. Nicolini t.
Nov. 4   *Lucia di Lammermoor*   E. Nicolini t.
Nov. 7   *Faust*   E. Nicolini t.
Nov. 9   *Il barbiere di Siviglia*   E. Nicolini t.
Nov. 11?   *Dinorah*
Nov. 13   *Aida*   E. Nicolini t.
Nov. 16   *Il trovatore*
Nov. 19   Gala Concert

AUTUMN 1878 BERLIN—KROLL OPER
Nov. 23   *La traviata*   E. Nicolini t.
Nov. 26   *Lucia di Lammermoor*   E. Nicolini t.
Nov. 30   *Il barbiere di Siviglia*   E. Nicolini t. M. Medica b.
Dec. 10   *La sonnambula*
Dec. 13   Concert

WINTER 1878–79 HAMBURG—STADT THEATER
Dec. 28   *La traviata*   E. Nicolini t.
Dec. 30   *Lucia di Lammermoor*   E. Nicolini t.
Jan. 2   *Aida*   Borée ms. E. Nicolini t. Krueckl b. Koegel bs.

WINTER 1879 LEIPZIG
Jan. 10   Concert

WINTER 1879 DRESDEN
Jan. 11   Concert

CARNIVAL 1879 NAPLES—TEATRO SAN CARLO
Jan. 22   *Lucia di Lammermoor*   E. Nicolini t. Z. Bertolasi b. C. Rossi cond.
Jan. 29   *La traviata*   E. Nicolini t. Z. Bertolasi b. C. Rossi cond.
Feb. 10   *Rigoletto*   E. Nicolini t. Z. Bertolasi b. F. Vecchioni bs. C. Rossi cond.

WINTER 1879 NICE—THÉÂTRE MUNICIPAL
Feb. 22   *La traviata*   E. Nicolini t.
       Faust (in It.)   E. Nicolini t.

LENT 1879 FLORENCE—TEATRO PAGLIANO
Mar. 4	*Aida*	V. Bartolucci ms. E. Nicolini t. A. Giacomelli b. A. Fradelloni bs.
Mar. 13	*Lucia di Lammermooor*	E. Nicolini t.

SPRING 1879 GENOA—POLITEAMA GENOVESE
Mar. 18	*Lucia di Lammermoor*	E. Nicolini t. P. Cabella b.
Mar. 23	*Aida*	G. Casali-Bavagnoli ms. E. Nicolini t. G. Belletti b. P. Povoleri bs.
Mar. 30	*La traviata*	E. Nicolini t. G. Belletti b.

SPRING 1879 TURIN—TEATRO REGIO
Apr. 2	*La traviata*	E. Nicolini t. S. Sparapani b. C. Pedrotti cond.

SPRING 1879 BRUSSELS—THÉÂTRE DE LA MONNAIE
Apr.	*Roméo et Juliette*	E. Nicolini t.
Apr.	*Aida*	E. Nicolini t.
Apr.	*La sonnambula*	E. Nicolini t.

SPRING AND SUMMER 1879 LONDON—COVENT GARDEN
May 6	*Lucia di Lammermoor*	E. Nicolini t. F. Graziani b. G. Capponi bs. A. Vianesi cond.
May 10	*Faust* (in It.)	S. Scalchi ms. E. Nicolini t. F. Graziani b. P. Gailhard bs. A. Vianesi cond.
May 13	*Aida*	S. Scalchi ms. E. Nicolini t. F. Graziani b. E. Bevignani cond.
May 16	*Il barbiere di Siviglia*	E. Nicolini t. A. Cotogni b. F. Scolara bs. Bianchi bs. A. Vianesi cond.
May 19	*Don Giovanni*	C. De Cepeda s. A. Valleria s. O. Nouvelli t. V. Maurel b. P. Gailhard bs. A. Vianesi cond.
May 22	*Dinorah*	S. Scalchi ms. O. Nouvelli t. V. Maurel b. A. Vianesi cond.
May 28	*La traviata*	E. Nicolini t. F. Graziani b. A. Vianesi cond.
June 14	*L'africaine* (in It.)	A. Valleria s. E. Nicolini t. J. Lassalle b. G. Capponi bs. A. Vianesi cond.
July 1	*Semiramide*	S. Scalchi ms. E. Sylva t. P. Gailhard bs. G. Capponi bs. E. Bevignani cond.
July 26	*La stella del Nord*	A. Valleria s. O. Nouvelli t. V. Maurel b. G. Ciampi bs. A. Vianesi cond.

SPRING 1879 LONDON—BUCKINGHAM PALACE
June 16	Concert

AUTUMN 1879 PARIS—TROCADÉRO
Oct. 23	Concert

AUTUMN 1879 BERLIN—HOFOPER
Nov. 1	*La traviata*	E. Nicolini t.

Nov. 8   *Lucia di*   E. Nicolini t.
             Lammermoor

AUTUMN 1879 DRESDEN—HOFOPER
Nov. 15   *La traviata*   E. Nicolini t. E. Degele b.
Nov. 18   *Lucia di*   E. Nicolini t. P. Bulss b.
             Lammermoor

AUTUMN 1879 BERLIN—HOFOPER
Nov. 25   *Faust* (in It.)   E. Nicolini t.
Nov. 28   *Lucia di*   E. Nicolini t.
             Lammermoor

AUTUMN 1879 HAMBURG—STADT THEATER
Dec. 1   *Il barbiere di Siviglia* E. Nicolini t. Krueckl b.

AUTUMN 1879 MUNICH—HOF UND NATIONAL THEATER
Dec. 12   *Lucia di*   E. Nicolini t.
             Lammermoor

AUTUMN 1879 STUTTGART—HOFTHEATER
Dec. 18   *La traviata*   E. Nicolini t.

AUTUMN 1879 PEST—NEMZETI SZINHAZ
Dec.   *La traviata*   E. Nicolini t. A. Brogi b.
Dec.   *Il barbiere di Siviglia* E. Nicolini t. A. Brogi b.

WINTER 1880 VIENNA—RINGTHEATER
Jan. 3   *La traviata*   E. Nicolini t. A. Brogi b.
Jan. 12   *Lucia di*
             Lammermoor
Jan. 15   *Il barbiere di Siviglia*

WINTER AND SPRING 1880 PARIS—THÉÂTRE DE LA GAÎTÉ
Feb. 14   *La traviata*   L. Signoretti t. M. Medica b.
Feb. 24   *Il barbiere di Siviglia* L. Signoretti t. M. Medica b. E. Jorda bs. E.
                                       Caracciolo bs.
Feb. 28   *Il trovatore*   G. Casaglia ms. E. Nicolini t. A. Brogi b. E.
                                       Jorda bs.
Apr. 3   *Rigoletto*   G. Casaglia ms. E. Nicolini t. A. Brogi b. E.
                                       Jorda bs.
Apr. 13   *Don Pasquale*   E. Nicolini t. A. Brogi b. E. Caracciolo bs.

SPRING AND SUMMER 1880 LONDON—COVENT GARDEN
May 15   *Roméo et Juliette*   Cottini ms. E. Nicolini t. F. Graziani b. A.
            (in It.)   Cotogni b. E. Bevignani cond.
May 18   *Il barbiere di Siviglia* E. Nicolini t. A. Cotogni b. E. de Reszke bs.
                                   (later A. Vidal bs.) G. Ciampi bs. A.
                                   Vianesi cond.
May 21   *La traviata*   F. Carpi t. F. Graziani b. E. Bevignani cond.
May 24   *Don Giovanni*   Pyke s. (later Vermi s.) A. Valleria s. E.
                                   Engel t. A. Cotogni b. P. Gailhard bs. A.
                                   Vianesi cond.

May 27	*Dinorah*	S. Scalchi ms. E. Engel t. J. Lassalle b. A. Vianesi cond.
June 8	*Faust* (in It.)	S. Scalchi ms. E. Nicolini t. A. Cotogni b. P. Gailhard bs. A. Vianesi cond.
June 15	*Semiramide*	S. Scalchi ms. I. Corsi t. P. Gailhard bs. G. Capponi bs. E. Bevignani cond.
July 3	°*Estella* (Cohen)	C. Mantilla ms. E. Nicolini t. A. Cotogni b. A. Vidal bs. E. Bevignani cond.

SUMMER 1880 LONDON—BUCKINGHAM PALACE
June 29   Concert

AUTUMN 1880 BERLIN—HOFOPER

Nov. 2	*Il barbiere di Siviglia*	E. Nicolini t.
Nov. 4	*La sonnambula*	E. Nicolini t. R. Oberhauser bs.
Nov. 8	*La traviata*	E. Nicolini t.
Nov. 17	*Il trovatore*	M. Brandt ms. E. Nicolini t. F. Betz b.

AUTUMN 1880 BRESLAU—STADT THEATER
(Concurrent with Berlin season)

| Nov. 11 | *Lucia di Lammermoor* | |
| Nov. 15 | *La traviata* | |

AUTUMN 1880 DRESDEN—HOFOPER

| Nov. 22 | *La traviata* | |
| Nov. 25 | *Il barbiere di Siviglia* | |

AUTUMN 1880 HAMBURG—STADT THEATER
Nov. 29   *Il barbiere di Siviglia*   E. Nicolini t.

AUTUMN 1880 MADRID—TEATRO REAL

Dec. 11	*La traviata*	E. Nicolini t. N. Verger b.
Dec. 17	*Lucia di Lammermoor*	J. Gayarre t. G. Kaschmann b.
Dec. 30	*Il barbiere di Siviglia*	R. Stagno t. N. Verger b. F. Uetam bs. A. Fiorini bs.

WINTER 1881 NICE—THÉÂTRE MUNICIPAL

Jan. 10	*La sonnambula*	E. Nicolini t.
Jan. 13	*Il trovatore*	C. Dory ms. E. Nicolini t. A. Carbone b.
Jan. 17	*Il barbiere di Siviglia*	E. Vicini t.

WINTER 1881 MONTE CARLO—SALLE GARNIER

Jan. 22	*La traviata*	E. Nicolini t. Berardi b. R. Accursi cond.
Jan. 29	*Rigoletto*	E. Stuarda ms. E. Nicolini t. Berardi b. Ampici bs. R. Accursi cond.
Feb. 5	*Il barbiere di Siviglia*	G. Piazza t. G. Vaselli b. Berardi b. G. Ciampi bs. R. Accursi cond.
Feb. 12	*Lucia di Lammermoor*	E. Nicolini t. Berardi b. Raguer bs. R. Accursi cond.
Feb. 19	*Don Pasquale*	E. Nicolini t. Berardi b. G. Ciampi bs. R. Accursi cond.

LENT AND SPRING 1881 PARIS—THÉÂTRE DES NATIONS

Mar. 5	*La sonnambula*	E. Nicolini t. A. Pinto bs.
Mar. 12	*La traviata*	E. Nicolini t. G. Vaselli b.
Mar. 19	*Linda di Chamounix*	G. Tremelli ms. G. Frapolli t. A. Cotogni b. A. Pinto bs. G. Ciampi bs.
Mar. 26	*Lucia di Lammermoor*	E. Nicolini t. G. Vaselli b.
Apr. 5	*Il barbiere di Siviglia*	G. Frapolli t. G. Vaselli b. A. Pinto bs. G. Ciampi bs.
Apr. 9	*Semiramide*	G. Tremelli ms. G. Vaselli b. A. Pinto bs.
Apr. 30	*Il trovatore*	
May 3	*Rigoletto*	E. Nicolini t.

SPRING AND SUMMER 1881 LONDON—COVENT GARDEN

May 24	*Semiramide*	S. Scalchi ms. I. Corsi t. P. Gailhard bs. A. Silvestri bs. E. Bevignani cond.
May 28	*La traviata*	E. Nicolini t. A. Cotogni b. J. Dupont cond.
May 30	*Il barbiere di Siviglia*	E. Nicolini t. A. Cotogni b. E. de Reszke bs. G. Ciampi bs. E. Bevignani cond.
June 2	*Il trovatore*	Z. Trebelli ms. E. Nicolini t. J. Lassalle b. E. Bevignani cond.
June 7	*Faust* (in It.)	S. Scalchi ms. E. Nicolini t. (later J. Gayarre t.) S. Athos b. P. Gailhard bs. J. Dupont cond.
June 11	*Dinorah*	Z. Trebelli ms. A. Marin t. J. Lassalle b. J. Dupont cond.
June 23	*Roméo et Juliette* (in It.)	Guercia ms. E. Nicolini t. A. Cotogni b. E. de Reszke bs. E. Bevignani cond.
July 2	*Linda di Chamounix*	S. Scalchi ms. A. Marin t. A. Cotogni b. E. de Reszke bs. E. Bevignani cond.
July 20	*La stella del Nord*	A. Valleria s. A. Marin t. A. Cotogni b. P. Gailhard bs. J. Dupont cond.

AUTUMN 1881 NEW YORK CITY—STEINWAY HALL

Nov. 9	Concert	E. Nicolini t. A. Pinto bs.
Nov. 12	Concert	
Nov. 16	Concert	
Nov. 23	Concert	

AUTUMN 1881 BROOKLYN—ACADEMY OF MUSIC

Nov. 28	Concert

AUTUMN 1881 PHILADELPHIA

Dec. 20	Concert
Dec. 23	Concert

WINTER 1881–82 CINCINNATI—MUSIC HALL

Dec. 28	*Messiah*

WINTER 1881–82 LOUISVILLE

Dec. 30	Concert

WINTER 1882 ST. LOUIS—GRAND OPERA HOUSE
Jan. 10   Concert   E. Nicolini t.
Jan. 13   Concert   E. Nicolini t.

WINTER 1882 NEW ORLEANS—THÉÂTRE DE L'OPERA
Jan. 17   Gala Concert   E. Nicolini t.
Jan. 19   Gala Concert   E. Nicolini t.
Jan. 23   Gala Concert   E. Nicolini t.

WINTER 1882 INDIANAPOLIS—ENGLISH'S OPERA HOUSE
Jan. 31   Concert

WINTER 1882 CINCINNATI—COLLEGE OF MUSIC
Feb. 18   Concert   E. Nicolini t.
Feb. 20   Concert   E. Nicolini t.

WINTER 1882 NEW YORK CITY—GERMANIA THEATER
Feb. 27   *La traviata*   E. Nicolini t. F. Salvati b.
Mar. 2   *Il barbiere di Siviglia* E. Nicolini t.
Mar. 6   *Faust* (in It.)   F. Rice-Knox ms. E. Nicolini t. F. Salvati b.
                                        A. Pinto bs.
Mar. 9   *Il trovatore*   F. Rice-Knox ms. E. Nicolini t. F. Salvati b.
Mar. 13   *Lucia di*   E. Nicolini t. F. Salvati b. A. Pinto bs.
             Lammermoor

SPRING 1882 BOSTON—GRAND HALL
Mar. 20   *La traviata*   E. Nicolini t. F. Salvati b.
Mar. 23   *Lucia di*   E. Nicolini t. F. Salvati b. A. Pinto bs.
             Lammermoor
Mar. 25   *Faust* (in It.)   E. Nicolini t.

SPRING 1882 PHILADELPHIA—CHESTNUT STREET OPERA HOUSE
Mar. 28   *La traviata*   E. Nicolini t. F. Salvati b.
Apr. 1   *Lucia di*   E. Nicolini t. F. Salvati b. A. Pinto bs.
             Lammermoor

SPRING 1882 NEW YORK CITY—GERMANIA THEATER
Apr. 3   *Lucia di*
             Lammermoor

SPRING AND SUMMER 1882 LONDON—COVENT GARDEN
May 18   *La stella del Nord*   A. Valleria s. E. Lestellier t. I. Sabater t. P.
                                        Gailhard bs. Dauphin bs. J. Dupont
                                        cond.
May 23   *Il trovatore*   A. Stahl ms. E. Nicolini t. (later G. Frappoli
                                        t.) M. Devries b. E. Bevignani cond.
May 26   *Roméo et Juliette*   Ghiotti ms. E. Nicolini t. A. Cotogni b. E.
             (in It.)   de Reszke bs. E. Bevignani cond.
June 3   *Il barbiere di Siviglia* E. Nicolini t. A. Cotogni b. E. de Reszke bs.
                                        F. Scolara bs. E. Bevignani cond.
June 8   *Don Giovanni*   E. Fursch-Madi s. A. Valleria s. A. Marin t.
                                        A. Cotogni b. P. Gailhard bs. E.
                                        Bevignani cond.

June 13	*Dinorah*	G. Tremelli ms. A. Marin t. A. Cotogni b. J. Dupont cond.
June 16	*Semiramide*	G. Tremelli ms. P. Gailhard bs. Gresse bs. E. Bevignani cond.
July 4	°°*Velleda* (Lenepveu)	A. Valleria s. E. Nicolini t. A. Cotogni b. E. de Reszke bs. J. Dupont cond.
July 10	*La traviata*	E. Nicolini t. A. Cotogni b. E. Bevignani cond.
July 13	*Faust* (in It.)	A. Stahl ms. E. Nicolini t. A. Cotogni b. P. Gailhard bs. J. Dupont cond.

SUMMER 1882 LONDON—BUCKINGHAM PALACE

| June 28 | Concert | |

SUMMER 1882 SWANSEA

| Sep. 14 | Concert[2] | E. Nicolini t. |

AUTUMN 1882 NEW YORK CITY—ACADEMY OF MUSIC

Nov. 6	*Lucia di Lammermoor*	E. Nicolini t. A. Galassi b. L. Arditi cond.
Nov. 10	*La traviata*	L. Ravelli t. (later E. Nicolini t.) A. Galassi b. L. Arditi cond.
Nov. 13	*Faust* (in It.)	E. Nicolini t. Caravatti b. Durat bs. L. Arditi cond.
Nov. 17	*Il trovatore*	A. Galassi ms. E. Nicolini t. A. Galassi b. G. Monti bs. L. Arditi cond.
Nov. 27	*Il barbiere di Siviglia*	L. Ravelli t. E. Ciampi-Cellai b.
Dec. 11	*Dinorah*	Bartlett ms. V. Clodio t. A. Galassi b. L. Arditi cond.
Dec. 13	*La sonnambula*	E. Nicolini t. G. Monti bs. L. Arditi cond.
Dec. 20	*Semiramide*	S. Scalchi ms. V. Clodio t. Durat bs. G. Monti bs. L. Arditi cond.
Dec. 22	*Linda di Chamounix*	S. Scalchi ms. L. Ravelli t. A. Galassi b. G. Monti bs. B. Corsini bs. L. Arditi cond.

WINTER 1883 PHILADELPHIA—ACADEMY OF MUSIC

Jan. 4	*La traviata*	E. Nicolini t. A. Galassi b. L. Arditi cond.
Jan. 6	*Lucia di Lammermoor*	E. Nicolini t. E. Ciampi-Cellai b. L. Arditi cond.
Jan. 9	*Semiramide*	S. Scalchi ms. V. Clodio t. Durat bs. L. Arditi cond.
Jan. 12	*Linda di Chamounix*	

WINTER 1883 CHICAGO—MC VICKER'S THEATER

| Jan. 16 | *Semiramide* | S. Scalchi ms. V. Clodio t. Durat bs. G. Monti bs. L. Arditi cond. |
| Jan. 20 | *La traviata* | L. Ravelli t. E. Ciampi-Cellai b. L. Arditi cond. |

WINTER 1883 ST. LOUIS—OLYMPIC THEATER

| Jan. 23 | *Semiramide* | S. Scalchi ms. V. Clodio t. Durat bs. G. Monti bs. L. Arditi cond. |

Jan. 26   *La traviata*   E. Nicolini t. A. Galassi b. L. Arditi cond.

WINTER 1883 CINCINNATI—COLLEGE OF MUSIC

Jan. 29   *La traviata*   E. Nicolini t. Caravatti b. L. Arditi cond.

Feb. 1   *Semiramide*   S. Scalchi ms. V. Clodio t. Durat bs. G. Monti bs. L. Arditi cond.

Feb. 6   °*Linda di Chamounix*   S. Scalchi ms. L. Ravelli t. A. Galassi b. G. Monti bs. B. Corsini bs. L. Arditi cond.

WINTER 1883 PITTSBURGH

Feb. 15   *La traviata*

WINTER 1883 WASHINGTON—NATIONAL THEATER

Feb. 20   *Semiramide*   S. Scalchi ms. V. Clodio t. Durat bs. G. Monti bs. L. Arditi cond.

Feb. 24   *La traviata*   G. Frapolli t. Caravatti b. L. Arditi cond.

WINTER 1883 BOSTON—BOSTON THEATER

Feb. 28   *Linda di Chamounix*   S. Scalchi ms. G. Frapolli t. A. Galassi b. G. Monti bs. L. Arditi cond.

Mar. 3   *La traviata*   G. Frapolli t. Caravatti b. L. Arditi cond.

Mar. 6   *Lucia di Lammermoor*   E. Nicolini t. E. Ciampi-Cellai b. G. Monti bs. L. Arditi cond.

Mar. 8   *Semiramide*   S. Scalchi ms. V. Clodio t. Durat bs. G. Monti bs. L. Arditi cond.

Mar. 10   *Don Giovanni*   E. Fursch-Madi s. L. Dotti s. G. Frapolli t. E. Ciampi-Cellai b. B. Corsini bs. L. Arditi cond.

LENT 1883 NEW YORK CITY—ACADEMY OF MUSIC

Mar. 14   *Il trovatore*   S. Scalchi ms. E. Nicolini t. A. Galassi b. L. Arditi cond.

Mar. 16   *Lucia di Lammermoor*   L. Ravelli t. A. Galassi b. L. Arditi cond.

Mar. 19   *Semiramide*   S. Scalchi ms. L. Arditi cond.

Mar. 24   *La traviata*   L. Ravelli t. A. Galassi b. L. Arditi cond.

Mar. 26   *Rigoletto*   S. Scalchi ms. E. Nicolini t. A. Galassi b. L. Arditi cond.

Apr. 6   *Don Giovanni*   E. Fursch-Madi s. L. Dotti s. G. Frapolli t. E. Ciampi-Cellai b. B. Corsini bs. L. Arditi cond.

Apr. 9   *La stella del Nord*   L. Dotti s. G. Frapolli t. Durat bs. B. Corsini bs. L. Arditi cond.

SPRING 1883 PHILADELPHIA—ACADEMY OF MUSIC

Apr. 17   *Semiramide*   S. Scalchi ms. V. Clodio t. Durat bs. G. Monti bs. L. Arditi cond.

Apr. 19   *La stella del Nord*   L. Dotti s. G. Frapolli t. V. Clodio t. Durat bs. L. Arditi cond.

Apr. 21   *Linda di Chamounix*   S. Scalchi ms. G. Frapolli t. A. Galassi b. G. Monti bs. L. Arditi cond.

SPRING AND SUMMER 1883 LONDON—COVENT GARDEN

June 16	*Il barbiere di Siviglia*	E. Nicolini t. A. Cotogni b. E. de Reszke bs. E. Bevignani cond.
June 19	*La traviata*	E. Nicolini t. M. Battistini b. J. Dupont cond.
June 22	*Semiramide*	S. Scalchi ms. G. Soulacroix b. P. Gailhard bs. E. Bevignani cond.
June 29	*Dinorah*	G. Tremelli ms. (later S. Scalchi ms.) G. Frapolli t. P. Gailhard bs. J. Dupont cond.
July 5	*La gazza ladra*	S. Scalchi ms. G. Frapolli t. A. Cotogni b. P. Gailhard bs. E. Bevignani cond.

AUTUMN 1883 NEW YORK CITY—ACADEMY OF MUSIC

Nov. 9	*La gazza ladra*	E. Vianelli ms. E. Vicini t. A. Galassi b. L. Lombardelli bs. L. Arditi cond.
Nov. 16	*La traviata*	E. Vicini t. A. Galassi b. L. Arditi cond.
Nov. 19	*Lucia di Lammermoor*	E. Vicini t. A. Galassi b. L. Lombardelli bs. L. Arditi cond.
Nov. 23	*Ernani*	L. Bellò t. A. Galassi b. E. Cherubini bs. L. Arditi cond.
Nov. 28	*Aida*	G. Tiozzo ms. E. Nicolini t. A. Galassi b. E. Cherubini bs. L. Arditi cond.

AUTUMN 1883 PHILADELPHIA—ACADEMY OF MUSIC

Dec. 10	*Ernani*	L. Bellò t. A. Galassi b. E. Cherubini bs. L. Arditi cond.
Dec. 14	*Semiramide*	G. Tiozzo ms. A. Rinaldini t. E. Cherubini bs. L. Lombardelli bs. L. Arditi cond.

AUTUMN 1883 BOSTON—GLOBE THEATER

Dec. 18	*La traviata*	E. Vicini t. A. Galassi b. L. Arditi cond.
Dec. 21	*Semiramide*	G. Tiozzo ms. A. Rinaldini t. E. Cherubini bs. L. Lombardelli bs. L. Arditi cond.

WINTER 1883 MONTREAL—ACADÉMIE DE MUSIQUE

Dec. 26	*La traviata*	E. Nicolini t. A. Galassi b. L. Arditi cond.

WINTER 1883–84 NEW YORK CITY—ACADEMY OF MUSIC

Dec. 31	*Aida*	G. Tiozzo ms. E. Nicolini t. A. Galassi b. E. Cherubini bs. L. Arditi cond.
Jan. 4	*Crispino e la comare*	I. Valerga ms. L. Bellò t. L. Lombardelli bs. V. Bellati bs. E. Caracciolo bs. L. Arditi cond.
Jan. 7	*Semiramide*	G. Tiozzo ms. L. Arditi cond.
Jan. 11	*Les Huguenots* (in It.)	E. Gerster s. J. Yorke ms. E. Nicolini t. A. Galassi b. L. Arditi cond.

WINTER 1884 PHILADELPHIA—ACADEMY OF MUSIC

Jan. 21	*Aida*	G. Tiozzo ms. E. Nicolini t. A. Galassi b. E. Cherubini bs. L. Arditi cond.

Jan. 23   *Crispino e la comare*   I. Valerga ms. L. Bellò t. V. Bellati b. E. Caraciollo bs. L. Lombardelli bs. L. Arditi cond.

WINTER 1884 BALTIMORE—ACADEMY OF MUSIC
Jan. 25   *Lucia di*   E. Vicini t. A. Galassi b. L. Lombardelli bs.
           Lammermoor   L. Arditi cond.

WINTER 1884 CHICAGO—MC VICKER'S THEATER
Jan. 28   *Crispino e la comare*   I. Valerga ms. L. Bellò t. V. Bellati b. E. Caracciolo bs. L. Lombardelli bs. L. Arditi cond.

Jan. 30   *Les Huguenots*   E. Gerster s. J. Yorke ms. E. Nicolini t. V.
           (in It.)   Bellati b. A. Galassi b. E. Cherubini bs. L. Arditi cond.

Feb. 2   *Lucia di*   E. Nicolini t. A. Galassi b. L. Lombardelli
          Lammermoor   bs. L. Arditi cond.

Feb. 5   *Roméo et Juliette*   G. Tiozzo ms. E. Nicolini t. A. Galassi b. E.
          (in It.)   Cherubini bs. L. Arditi cond.

Feb. 8   *La traviata*   E. Vicini t. A. Galassi b. L. Arditi cond.

WINTER 1884 ST. LOUIS—OLYMPIC THEATER
Feb. 19   *La traviata*   E. Vicini t. A. Galassi b. L. Arditi cond.

WINTER 1884 DENVER
Mar. 1   *La traviata*

WINTER 1884 SAN FRANCISCO—GRAND OPERA HOUSE
Mar. 13   *La traviata*   E. Vicini t. A. Galassi b. L. Arditi cond.

Mar. 18   *Il trovatore*   G. Tiozzo ms. E. Nicolini t. A. Galassi b. E. Cherubini bs. L. Arditi cond.

Mar. 22   *Crispino e la comare*   I. Vallerga ms. L. Bellò t. V. Bellati b. E. Caracciolo bs. L. Arditi cond.

Mar. 25   *Linda di Chamounix*   G. Tiozzo ms. E. Vicini t. A. Galassi b. E. Cherubini bs. E. Caracciolo bs. L. Arditi cond.

SPRING 1884 SAN FRANCISCO—MECHANICS' PAVILION
Mar. 27   Concert

SPRING 1884 SALT LAKE CITY
Apr. 1   Concert

SPRING 1884 NEW YORK CITY—ACADEMY OF MUSIC
Apr. 14   *Linda di Chamounix*   E. Vicini t. J. Yorke ms. A. Galassi b. E. Cherubini bs. E. Caracciolo bs. L. Arditi cond.

Apr. 18   *Roméo et Juliette*   G. Tiozzo ms. E. Nicolini t. A. Galassi b. E.
          (in It.)   Cherubini bs. L. Arditi cond.

Apr. 22   *Crispino e la comare*   I. Valerga ms. L. Bellò t. E. Caracciolo bs. E. Cherubini bs. L. Arditi cond.

Apr. 25   *Semiramide*   S. Scalchi ms. L. Arditi cond.

SPRING AND SUMMER 1884 LONDON—COVENT GARDEN

June 14	*La traviata*	F. Marconi t. A. Cotogni b. J. Dupont cond.
June 17	*Aida*	G. Tremelli ms. E. Nicolini t. J. Devoyod b. F. Novara bs. E. Bevignani cond.
June 21	*Il barbiere di Siviglia*	E. Nicolini t. A. Cotogni b. J. de Reszke bs. E. Bevignani cond.
June 26	*Dinorah*	S. Scalchi ms. F. Marconi t. A. Cotogni b. G. Monti bs. J. Dupont cond.
June 28	*Don Giovanni*	E. Fursch-Madi s. Latterer s. (later De Marion s.) F. Marconi t. A. Cotogni b. G. Monti bs. E. Bevignani cond.
July 3	*Semiramide*	S. Scalchi ms. I. Corsi t. E. de Reszke bs. G. Monti bs. E. Bevignani cond.
July 26	*Linda di Chamounix*	S. Scalchi ms. F. Marconi t. A. Cotogni b. E. de Reszke bs. E. Bevignani cond.

SUMMER 1884 SWANSEA

Aug. 14	Concert	

AUTUMN 1884 NEW YORK CITY—ACADEMY OF MUSIC

Nov. 10	*Il barbiere di Siviglia*	E. Vicini t. V. De Pasqualis b. L. Arditi cond.
Nov. 14	*La traviata*	E. Vicini t. I. De Anna b. L. Arditi cond.
Nov. 19	*Semiramide*	S. Scalchi ms. Bassetti t. V. De Pasqualis b. E. Cherubini bs. L. Arditi cond.
Nov. 26	*Martha*	S. Scalchi ms. E. Vicini t. E. Cherubini bs. L. Arditi cond.
Dec. 1	*Linda di Chamounix*	S. Scalchi ms. E. Vicini t. V. De Pasqualis b. E. Cherubini bs. E. Caracciolo bs. L. Arditi cond.
Dec. 12	*Aida*	S. Scalchi ms. E. Nicolini t. I. De Anna b. L. Arditi cond.
Dec. 15	*Faust* (in It.)	S. Scalchi ms. E. Vicini t. I. De Anna b. E. Cherubini bs. L. Arditi cond.
Dec. 19	*Crispino e la comare*	Saruggla ms. Bassetti t. V. De Pasqualis b. E. Cherubini bs. E. Caracciolo bs. L. Arditi cond.

AUTUMN AND WINTER 1884–85 BOSTON—BOSTON THEATER

Dec. 30	*La traviata*	E. Vicini t. I. De Anna b. L. Arditi cond.
Jan. 2	*Semiramide*	S. Scalchi ms. A. Rinaldini t. E. Serbolini bs. E. Cherubini bs. L. Arditi cond.
Jan. 6	*Martha*	S. Scalchi ms. E. Vicini t. E. Cherubini bs. L. Arditi cond.
Jan. 9	*Linda di Chamounix*	S. Scalchi ms. E. Vicini t. V. De Pasqualis b. E. Cherubini bs. E. Caracciolo bs. L. Arditi cond.

WINTER 1885 PHILADELPHIA—ACADEMY OF MUSIC

Jan. 13	*La traviata*	E. Vicini t. I. De Anna b. L. Arditi cond.

Jan. 16   *Semiramide*   S. Scalchi ms. A. Rinaldini t. E. Serbolini bs. E. Cherubini bs. L. Arditi cond.

Jan. 20   *Linda di Chamounix*   S. Scalchi ms. E. Vicini t. V. De Pasqualis b. E. Cherubini bs. E. Caracciolo bs. L. Arditi cond.

WINTER 1885 NEW ORLEANS—ST. CHARLES THEATRE

Jan. 27   *La traviata*   F. Giannini t. I. De Anna b. L. Arditi cond.

Jan. 30   *Semiramide*   S. Scalchi ms. E. Serbolini bs. E. Cherubini bs. L. Arditi cond.

WINTER 1885 NEW ORLEANS—THÉÂTRE DE L'OPÉRA

Feb. 2   *Linda di Chamounix*   S. Scalchi ms. E. Vicini t. V. De Pasqualis b. E. Cherubini bs. E. Caracciolo bs. L. Arditi cond.

Feb. 4   *Crispino e la comare*   Saruggia ms. A. Rinaldini t. V. De Pasqualis b. E. Caracciolo bs. E. Cherubini bs. L. Arditi cond.

Feb. 6   *Martha*   S. Scalchi ms. E. Vicini t. E. Cherubini bs. L. Arditi cond.

WINTER 1885 ST. LOUIS—OLYMPIC THEATER

Feb. 10   *Semiramide*   S. Scalchi ms. A. Rinaldini t. V. De Pasqualis b. E. Cherubini bs. L. Arditi cond.

Feb. 13   *Linda di Chamounix*   S. Scalchi ms. E. Vicini t. V. De Pasqualis b. E. Cherubini bs. E. Caracciolo bs. L. Arditi cond.

WINTER AND SPRING 1885 SAN FRANCISCO—GRAND OPERA HOUSE

Mar. 2   *Linda di Chamounix*   S. Scalchi ms. E. Vicini t. V. De Pasqualis b. E. Cherubini bs. E. Caracciolo bs. L. Arditi cond.

Mar. 6   *Semiramide*   S. Scalchi ms. A. Rinaldini t. V. De Pasqualis b. E. Cherubini bs. L. Arditi cond.

Mar. 10   *Il barbiere di Siviglia*   E. Vicini t. V. De Pasqualis b. E. Cherubini bs. E. Caracciolo bs. L. Arditi cond.

Mar. 12   *Faust* (in It.)   S. Scalchi ms. F. Giannini t. I. De Anna b. E. Cherubini bs. L. Arditi cond.

Mar. 14   *Crispino e la comare*   Saruggia ms. A. Rinaldini t. V. De Pasqualis b. E. Caracciolo bs. E. Cherubini bs. L. Arditi cond.

Mar. 19   *La traviata*   E. Vicini t. I. De Anna b. L. Arditi cond.

Mar. 21   *Martha*   S. Scalchi ms. E. Vicini t. E. Cherubini bs. L. Arditi cond.

Mar. 24   *Aida*   S. Scalchi ms. E. Nicolini t. I. De Anna b. E. Cherubini bs. L. Arditi cond.

SPRING 1885 CHICAGO—GRAND OPERA

Apr. 6   *Semiramide*   S. Scalchi ms. A. Rinaldini t. V. De Pasqualis b. E. Cherubini bs. L. Arditi cond.

Apr. 9   *Linda di Chamounix*   S. Scalchi ms. E. Vicini t. V. De Pasqualis b. E. Cherubini bs. E. Caracciolo bs. L. Arditi cond.

Apr. 11   *Martha*   S. Scalchi ms. E. Vicini t. E. Cherubini bs. L. Arditi cond.

Apr. 14   *Aida*   S. Scalchi ms. E. Nicolini t. I. De Anna b. E. Cherubini bs. L. Arditi cond.

Apr. 17   *Faust* (in It.)   S. Scalchi ms. E. Nicolini t. I. De Anna b. E. Cherubini bs. L. Arditi cond.

SPRING 1885 NEW YORK CITY—ACADEMY OF MUSIC

Apr. 20   *Semiramide*   S. Scalchi ms. A. Rinaldini t. V. De Pasqualis b. E. Cherubini bs. L. Arditi cond.

Apr. 24   *Martha*   S. Scalchi ms. E. Vicini t. E. Cherubini bs. L. Arditi cond.

SPRING 1885 BOSTON—BOSTON THEATER

Apr. 27   *Semiramide*   S. Scalchi ms. A. Rinaldini t. V. De Pasqualis b. E. Cherubini bs. L. Arditi cond.

Apr. 30   *Martha*   S. Scalchi ms. E. Vicini t. E. Cherubini bs. L. Arditi cond.

SPRING AND SUMMER 1885 LONDON—COVENT GARDEN

June 20   *La traviata*   F. Giannini t. I. De Anna b. L. Arditi cond.

June 23   *Semiramide*   S. Scalchi ms. G. Del Puente b. E. Cherubini bs. L. Arditi cond.

June 27   *Il barbiere di Siviglia*   E. Engel t. G. Del Puente b. E. Cherubini bs. E. Caracciolo bs. L. Arditi cond.

July 4   *Martha*   S. Scalchi ms. E. Engel t. E. Cherubini bs. L. Arditi cond.

July 7   *Faust* (in It.)   S. Scalchi ms. (later J. Macvitz ms.) E. de Méric-Lablache ms. F. Giannini t. I. De Anna b. (later G. Del Puente b.) E. Cherubini bs. L. Arditi cond.

July 11   *Linda di Chamounix*   S. Scalchi ms. E. Engel t. I. De Anna b. E. Cherubini bs. E. Caracciolo bs. L. Arditi cond.

July 14   *Carmen* (in It.)   L. Dotti s. E. Engel t. (later A. Garulli t.) G. Del Puente b. L. Arditi cond.

July 25   *Il trovatore*   J. Macvitz ms. F. Giannini t. I. De Anna b. A. De Vaschetti bs. L. Arditi cond.

AUTUMN 1885 CONCERT TOUR[3]
Cities visited include Manchester (Oct. 8).

AUTUMN 1885 ANTWERP
Nov. 23   *La traviata*

AUTUMN 1885 AMSTERDAM—PARKSCHOUWBURG
Nov. 29   *Il barbiere di Siviglia*
Dec. 2   *Il trovatore*

AUTUMN 1885 PEST
Dec. 12   Concert

AUTUMN 1885 VIENNA—MUSIKVEREIN SAAL
Dec. 16   Concert

AUTUMN 1885 PRAGUE
Dec. 19   *La traviata*

AUTUMN 1885 VIENNA—HOFOPER
Dec. 25   *Il barbiere di Siviglia* A. Schittenhelm t. W. Horwitz b. F. Von
                                      Reichenberg bs. C. Mayerhofer bs.
Dec. 31   *La traviata*   J. Müller t. K. Sommer b.

WINTER 1886 BUCHAREST—TEATRUL NACIONAL
Jan. 6   *La traviata*
Jan. 9   *Lucia di
             Lammermoor*
Jan. 12   *Il barbiere di Siviglia*

WINTER 1886 PARIS
Feb. 3   Concert
Feb. 6   Concert
Feb. 9   Concert

WINTER 1886 NICE—THÉÂTRE MUNICIPAL
Feb. 13   *La traviata*   G. Moretti t. T. Wilmant b. C. Campanini
                                      cond.
Feb. 17   *Il barbiere di Siviglia* G. Moretti t. A. Pini-Corsi b. P. Purarelli bs.
                                      Cuccotti bs. C. Campanini cond.

WINTER 1886 BARCELONA—TEATRO PRINCIPAL
Feb. 22   *La traviata*   E. Nicolini t. E. Ciampi-Cellai b.
Feb. 25   *Il barbiere di Siviglia* R. Stagno t. E. Ciampi-Cellai b. P. Meroles
                                      bs. Fiori bs.

WINTER 1886 VALENCIA—TEATRO PRINCIPAL
Mar. 9   *La traviata*   G. Rubis t. P. Ughetto b.

WINTER 1886 MADRID—TEATRO DE LA ZARZUELA
Mar. 13   Concert
Mar. 16   Concert
Mar. 19   Concert
Mar. 22   Concert

SPRING 1886 LISBON—TEATRO SAÕ CARLOS
Mar. 27   *Il barbiere di Siviglia* A. Masini t. A. Cotogni b. A. Pinto bs.
Apr. 2   *Lucia di   A. Guille t. A. Magini-Coletti b. Rossetti bs.
             Lammermoor*
Apr. 8   *La traviata*   A. Guille t. A. Cotogni b. (later A. Magini-
                                      Coletti b.)
Apr. 14   *Carmen* (in It.)   E. Borlinetto s. A. De Bassini t. A. Magini-
                                      Coletti b.

SPRING AND SUMMER 1886 LONDON—ROYAL ALBERT HALL
June 5	Concert
June 23	Concert
July 3	Concert
July 14	Concert

SUMMER 1886 LONDON—BUCKINGHAM PALACE
June 23	Concert

SUMMER 1886 LONDON—THEATRE ROYAL DRURY LANE
July 15	*Il barbiere di Siviglia* E. Nicolini t. G. Del Puente b. A. Foli bs. L. Arditi cond.

AUTUMN 1886 CONCERT TOUR
Cities visited include London (Oct. 27), Manchester (Oct. 29), Liverpool (Oct. 30), and Dublin (Nov. 2).

AUTUMN 1886 NEW YORK CITY—ACADEMY OF MUSIC
Nov. 18	Gala Concert	E. Nicolini t.
Nov. 20	Gala Concert	E. Nicolini t.
Nov. 29	Gala Concert	E. Nicolini t.
Dec. 1	Gala Concert	E. Nicolini t.

AUTUMN AND WINTER 1886–87 "CONCERT" TOUR
Tour consisted primarily of single acts of individual operas with S. Scalchi ms., A. Guille t., A. Galassi b., F. Novara bs., and L. Arditi cond. Cities visited include New Orleans (Dec. 20), Galveston (Dec. 23), Mexico City (Dec. 30–Jan. 6), Los Angeles (Jan. 20), San Francisco (Jan. 24–Feb. 9), Denver (Feb. 15–16), St. Louis (Feb. 21), Omaha (Feb. 24–28), Minneapolis (Mar. 2), Chicago (Mar. 7–12), St. Louis (Mar. 15–17), Cincinnati (Mar. 19), Cleveland (Mar. 22), Pittsburgh (Mar. 26), Detroit (Mar. 28), and Toronto (Mar. 31).

SPRING 1887 NEW YORK CITY—METROPOLITAN OPERA[4]
Apr. 11	*La traviata*	E. Vicini t. A. Galassi b. L. Arditi cond.
Apr. 13	*Semiramide*	S. Scalchi ms. F. Novara bs. A. Abramoff bs. L. Arditi cond.
Apr. 15	*Faust* (in It.)	S. Scalchi ms. E. Vicini t. G. Del Puente b. F. Novara bs. L. Arditi cond.
Apr. 18	*Carmen* (in It.)	Griswold s. E. Vicini t. G. Del Puente b. L. Arditi cond.
Apr. 20	*Lucia di Lammermoor*	A. Guille t. G. Del Puente b. L. Arditi cond.
Apr. 23	*Martha*	S. Scalchi ms. A. Guille t. F. Novara bs. L. Arditi cond.

SPRING 1887 BOSTON—BOSTON THEATER
Apr. 28	*Semiramide*	S. Scalchi ms. F. Novara bs. A. Abramoff bs. L. Arditi cond.
Apr. 30	*La traviata*	E. Vicini t. G. Del Puente b. L. Arditi cond.

SPRING 1887 WASHINGTON—ALBAUGH'S OPERA HOUSE
May 3	*La traviata*	E. Vicini t. G. Del Puente b. L. Arditi cond.

SPRING 1887 PHILADELPHIA—ACADEMY OF MUSIC

| May 9 | *Lucia di Lammermoor* | A. Guille t. G. Del Puente b. |

SPRING 1887 NEW YORK CITY—METROPOLITAN OPERA

| May 13 | Gala Concert |

SPRING OR SUMMER 1887 LONDON—ROYAL ALBERT HALL

| June | Concert |
| June | Concert |

SUMMER 1887 LONDON—HER MAJESTY'S THEATRE

| July 1 | *La traviata* |

AUTUMN 1887 CONCERT TOUR

Cities visited include Manchester (Nov. 18), Edinburgh (Nov. 23), Leeds (Nov. 25), Nottingham (Nov. 28), and Birmingham (Dec. 1).

AUTUMN AND WINTER 1887–88 LISBON—TEATRO SAŌ CARLOS

Dec. 15	*La traviata*	A. Talazac t. S. Terzi b.
Dec. 27	*Linda di Chamounix*	G. Prandi ms. O. Gennari t. F. D'Andrade b. P. Meroles bs. E. Caracciolo bs. A. Pontecchi cond.
Dec. 31	*Dinorah*	G. Prandi ms. O. Gennari t. A. D'Andrade b.
Jan. 4	*Crispino e la comare*	M. Olavarri ms. O. Gennari t. S. Terzi b. E. Caracciolo bs.
Jan. 9	*Il barbiere di Siviglia*	O. Gennari t. F. D'Andrade b. E. Caracciolo bs. G. Roveri bs.
Jan. 14	*Rigoletto*	G. Prandi ms. A. D'Andrade t. F. D'Andrade b. G. Roveri bs.

WINTER 1888 MADRID—TEATRO REAL

Feb. 4	*Linda di Chamounix*	G. Fabbri ms. F. De Lucia t. G. Vaselli b. F. Uetam bs. C. Baldelli bs. M. Perez cond.
Feb. 9	*Il barbiere di Siviglia*	F. De Lucia t. R. Blanchart b. F. Uetam bs. C. Baldelli bs. M. Perez cond.
Feb. 12	*Crispino e la comare*	G. Fabbri ms. F. Giannini t. R. Blanchart b. A. Silvestri bs. C. Baldelli bs. M. Perez cond.
Feb. 16	*La traviata*	F. De Lucia t. G. Vaselli b. L. Mancinelli cond.
Feb. 20	*Rigoletto*	G. Fabbri ms. F. De Lucia t. G. Vaselli b. L. Mancinelli cond.
Feb. 26	Gala Concert

SPRING AND SUMMER 1888 BUENOS AIRES—POLITEAMA ARGENTINO

Apr. 4	*Il barbiere di Siviglia*	R. Stagno t. S. Carobbi b. P. Cesari bs. A. Fiorini bs.
Apr. 7	*La traviata*	G. Moretti t. (later R. Stagno t.) S. Carobbi b.
Apr. 10	*Lucia di Lammermoor*	F. Cardinali t. S. Carobbi b.

Apr. 14	*Crispino e la comare*	G. Fabbri ms. P. Cesari bs.
Apr. 19	*Rigoletto*	R. Stagno t. D. Menotti b.
Apr. 25	*Linda di Chamounix*	G. Fabbri ms. A. Brasi t. D. Menotti b. F. Vecchioni bs. R. Sapio cond.
May 5	*Semiramide*	G. Fabbri ms. A. Brasi t. F. Vecchioni bs.
June 6	*I puritani*	R. Stagno t. D. Menotti b. A. Monchero bs.
June 20	°*Lakmé* (in It.)	G. Fabbri ms. F. Cardinali t. F. Vecchioni bs. R. Sapio cond.

SUMMER 1888 MONTEVIDEO—TEATRO SOLIS

July 8	*Il barbiere di Siviglia*	R. Stagno t. S. Carobbi b. P. Cesari bs. A. Fiorini bs. A. Conti cond.
July 11	*Lucia di Lammermoor*	R. Stagno t. S. Carobbi b. A. Conti cond.
July 14	*I puritani*	R. Stagno t. D. Menotti b. F. Vecchioni bs. A. Conti cond.
July 17	*Semiramide*	G. Fabbri ms. G. Moretti t. F. Vecchioni bs. A. Conti cond.
July 19	*Linda di Chamounix*	G. Fabbri ms. G. Moretti t. D. Menotti b. F. Vecchioni bs. P. Cesari bs. A. Conti cond.
July 21	°*Lakmé* (in It.)	G. Fabbri ms. F. Cardinali t. F. Vecchioni bs. A. Conti cond.
July 29	*La traviata*	R. Stagno t. S. Carobbi b. A. Conti cond.

AUTUMN 1888 LONDON—ROYAL ALBERT HALL
Nov. 20   Concert

AUTUMN 1888 PARIS—OPÉRA
Nov. 28	*Roméo et Juliette*	C. M. Agussol ms. J. de Reszke t. L. Melchissedec b. E. de Reszke bs. F. Delmas bs.

AUTUMN AND WINTER 1888–89 LONDON—ROYAL ALBERT HALL
Dec. 11   Concert
Jan. 8   Concert
Jan. 22   Concert
Feb. 28   Concert

SPRING AND SUMMER 1889 BUENOS AIRES—POLITEAMA ARGENTINO

Apr. 9	*La traviata*	C. Lanfredi t. (later E. Nicolini t.) A. Marescalchi b. R. Sapio cond.
Apr. 13	*Il barbiere di Siviglia*	A. De Bassini t. (later F. De Lucia t.) A. Marescalchi b. E. Marcassa bs. S. Reggiani bs. R. Sapio cond.
Apr. 16	*Lucia di Lammermoor*	F. Signorini t. (later E. Nicolini t.) Bacchetta b. R. Sapio cond.
Apr. 20	*Dinorah*	G. Fabbri ms. A. De Bassini t. A. Marescalchi b. G. Rossi bs. R. Sapio cond.
May 4	*Semiramide*	G. Fabbri ms. A. De Bassini t. E. Marcassa bs. G. Rossi bs. R. Sapio cond.

371

May 14	*Don Giovanni*	E. Colonnese s. V. Domelli s. F. De Lucia t. R. Blanchart b. E. Marcassa bs. G. Rossi bs. A. Conti cond.
May 31	*Linda di Chamounix*	G. Fabbri ms. C. Lanfredi t. A. Marescalchi b. E. Marcassa bs. R. Sapio cond.
June 13	*Roméo et Juliette* (in It.)	G. Fabbri ms. F. De Lucia t. R. Blanchart b. E. Marcassa bs. R. Sapio cond.
July 2	*La sonnambula*	F. De Lucia t. E. Marcassa bs. R. Sapio cond.
July 6	Gala Concert	
July 13	*La stella del Nord*	C. Lanfredi t. E. Marcassa bs. R. Sapio cond.

AUTUMN 1889 CONCERT TOUR
Cities visited include Birmingham (Oct. 14), Edinburgh (Oct. 29), Glasgow (Oct. 31), and Bradford (Nov. 11).

AUTUMN AND WINTER 1889–90 CHICAGO—AUDITORIUM

Dec. 9	Concert	
Dec. 10	*Roméo et Juliette* (in It.)	G. Fabbri ms. L. Ravelli t. G. Del Puente b. A. De Vaschetti bs. E. Marcassa bs. R. Sapio cond.
Dec. 14	*Lucia di Lammermoor*	L. Ravelli t. A. Marescalchi b. A. Carbone bs. R. Sapio cond.
Dec. 17	*Semiramide*	G. Fabbri ms. E. Vicini t. E. Marcassa bs. A. Castelmary bs. R. Sapio cond.
Dec. 21	*Martha*	G. Fabbri ms. L. Ravelli t. E. Marcassa bs. R. Sapio cond.
Dec. 24	*La traviata*	L. Ravelli t. A. Marescalchi b. R. Sapio cond.
Dec. 27	*La sonnambula*	L. Ravelli t. E. Marcassa bs. R. Sapio cond.
Jan. 4	*Il barbiere di Siviglia*	E. Vicini t. A. Marescalchi b. E. Marcassa bs. A. Carbone bs. R. Sapio cond.

WINTER 1890 MEXICO CITY—GRAN TEATRO NACIONAL

Jan. 11	*Semiramide*	G. Fabbri ms. E. Vicini t. E. Marcassa bs. A. Castelmary bs. R. Sapio cond.
Jan. 15	*Lucia di Lammermoor*	L. Ravelli t. A. Marescalchi b. R. Sapio cond.
Jan. 18	*La sonnambula*	
Jan. 22	*Il barbiere di Siviglia*	L. Ravelli t. A. Marescalchi b. E. Marcassa bs. A. Carbone bs. R. Sapio cond.
Jan. 25	*Linda di Chamounix*	G. Fabbri ms. A. Marescalchi b. E. Marcassa bs. A. Carbone bs. R. Sapio cond.
Jan. 29	*La traviata*	E. Vicini t. A. Marescalchi b. R. Sapio cond.

WINTER 1890 SAN FRANCISCO—GRAND OPERA HOUSE

| Feb. 11 | *Semiramide* | G. Fabbri ms. E. Vicini t. E. Marcassa bs. A. Castelmary bs. R. Sapio cond. |
| Feb. 15 | *La sonnambula* | L. Ravelli t. E. Marcassa bs. R. Sapio cond. |

Feb. 18	*Lucia di Lammermoor*	L. Ravelli t. A. Marescalchi b. A. Carbone bs. R. Sapio cond.
Feb. 20	*Martha*	G. Fabbri ms. L. Ravelli t. E. Marcassa bs. R. Sapio cond.
Feb. 22	*La traviata*	L. Ravelli t. A. Marescalchi b. R. Sapio cond.

WINTER 1890 DENVER—METROPOLITAN THEATER

Mar. 1	*Martha*	G. Fabbri ms. L. Ravelli t. E. Marcassa bs. R. Sapio cond.

WINTER 1890 OMAHA

Mar. 4	*Il barbiere di Siviglia*	L. Ravelli t. A. Marescalchi b. E. Marcassa bs. A. Carbone bs. R. Sapio cond.

WINTER 1890 LOUISVILLE

Mar. 7	*Semiramide*	G. Fabbri ms. E. Vicini t. E. Marcassa bs. A. Castelmary bs. R. Sapio cond.

WINTER 1890 CHICAGO—AUDITORIUM

Mar. 11	*Linda di Chamounix*	G. Fabbri ms. L. Ravelli t. A. Marescalchi b. E. Marcassa bs. A. Carbone bs. L. Arditi cond.
Mar. 13	*Lakmé* (in It.)	G. Fabbri ms. L. Ravelli t. A. Marescalchi b. E. Marcassa bs. R. Sapio cond.
Mar. 15	*Semiramide*	G. Fabbri ms. E. Vicini t. E. Marcassa bs. A. Castelmary bs. R. Sapio cond.

WINTER 1890 BOSTON

Mar. 18	*Semiramide*	G. Fabbri ms. E. Vicini t. E. Marcassa bs. A. Castelmary bs. R. Sapio cond.
Mar. 20	*Martha*	G. Fabbri ms. L. Ravelli t. E. Marcassa bs. R. Sapio cond.
Mar. 22	*Lakmé* (in It.)	G. Fabbri ms. L. Ravelli t. A. Marescalchi b. E. Marcassa bs. R. Sapio cond.

SPRING 1890 NEW YORK CITY—METROPOLITAN OPERA

Mar. 26	*Semiramide*	G. Fabbri ms. E. Vicini t. E. Marcassa bs. A. Castelmary bs. R. Sapio cond.
Mar. 28	*La sonnambula*	L. Ravelli t. E. Marcassa bs. R. Sapio cond.
Apr. 2	*Lakmé* (in It.)	G. Fabbri ms. L. Ravelli t. A. Marescalchi b. E. Marcassa bs. R. Sapio cond.
Apr. 5	*Martha*	G. Fabbri ms. L. Ravelli t. E. Marcassa bs. R. Sapio cond.
Apr. 7	*Lucia di Lammermoor*	A. Guille t. A. Marescalchi b. A. Carbone bs. R. Sapio cond.
Apr. 14	*Roméo et Juliette* (in It.)	G. Fabbri ms. L. Ravelli t. G. Del Puente b. E. Marcassa bs. A. De Vaschetti bs. R. Sapio cond.
Apr. 16	*Il barbiere di Siviglia*	G. Perugini t. G. Del Puente b. E. Marcassa bs. A. Carbone bs. R. Sapio cond.

373

SPRING 1890 PHILADELPHIA
Apr. 21   *Lakmé* (in It.)   G. Fabbri ms. L. Ravelli t. A. Marescalchi b.
E. Marcassa bs. R. Sapio cond.

SPRING 1890 NEW YORK CITY—METROPOLITAN OPERA
Apr. 25   *La traviata*

AUTUMN 1890 CONCERT TOUR
Cities scheduled include Preston (Oct. 10), Glasgow (Oct. 13), Dundee (Oct. 15), Aberdeen (Oct. 17), Edinburgh (Oct. 21), Newcastle (Oct. 24), Leeds (Oct. 27), Manchester (Oct. 29), Liverpool (Oct. 31), London (Nov. 3), Leicester (Nov. 5), Cheltenham (Nov. 7), Bristol (Nov. 10), Plymouth (Nov. 12), Exeter (Nov. 14), Southsea (Nov. 17), London (Nov. 19), and Cardiff (Nov. 21).

WINTER 1891 BERLIN
Jan.?   Concerts

WINTER 1891 NICE—THÉÂTRE MUNICIPAL
Roméo et Juliette
Lucia di
Lammermoor
La traviata
Il barbière di Siviglia

SPRING 1891 LONDON—ROYAL ALBERT HALL
June 20   Concert

SUMMER 1891 CRAIG-Y-NOS—PATTI THEATRE
Aug. 12   Gala Concert   E. Nicolini t. L. Arditi cond.
Aug. 15   Gala Concert   L. Arditi cond.
Aug. 22   Gala Concert   E. Nicolini t. L. Arditi cond.

SUMMER 1891 SWANSEA
Aug. 28   Concert

AUTUMN 1891 CONCERT TOUR
This was Patti's customary autumn concert tour of the British provinces. None of the cities visited have been identified to date.

WINTER 1892 NEW YORK CITY—METROPOLITAN OPERA
Jan. 12   Concert   G. Fabbri ms. A. Guille t. G. Del Puente b.
F. Novara bs. L. Arditi cond.

WINTER 1892 PHILADELPHIA
Jan. 18   Concert   G. Fabbri ms. A. Guille t. G. Del Puente b.
F. Novara bs. L. Arditi cond.

WINTER 1892 NEW YORK CITY—METROPOLITAN OPERA
Jan. 20   Concert   G. Fabbri ms. A. Guille t. G. Del Puente b.
F. Novara bs. L. Arditi cond.

WINTER 1892 TORONTO—HUNT PAVILION
Jan. 26   Concert

LENT 1892 BOSTON

Mar. 19	*Martha*	G. Fabbri ms. E. Valero t. F. Novara bs. A. Carbone bs. L. Arditi cond.
Mar. 22	*Semiramide*	G. Fabbri ms. A. Rinaldini t. F. Novara bs. L. Arditi cond.
Mar. 26	*La traviata*	E. Valero t. G. Del Puente b. L. Arditi cond.

SPRING 1892 NEW YORK CITY—METROPOLITAN OPERA

Mar. 30	*La traviata*	E. Valero t. G. Del Puente b. L. Arditi cond.
Apr. 2	*Martha*	G. Fabbri ms. E. Valero t. F. Novara bs. A. Carbone bs. L. Arditi cond.
Apr. 6	*Lucia di Lammermoor*	E. Valero t. G. Del Puente b. F. Novara bs. L. Arditi cond.
Apr. 9	*Il barbiere di Siviglia*	I. Campanini t. G. Del Puente b. F. Novara bs. A. Carbone bs. L. Arditi cond.

SPRING 1892 BROOKLYN—ACADEMY OF MUSIC

Apr. 23	*Martha*	G. Fabbri ms. A. Guille t. F. Novara bs. A. Carbone bs. L. Arditi cond.

SPRING 1892 PHILADELPHIA—ACADEMY OF MUSIC

Apr. 26	*Martha*	G. Fabbri ms. A. Guille t. F. Novara bs. A. Carbone bs. L. Arditi cond.

SPRING 1892 BALTIMORE—ACADEMY OF MUSIC

May 6	Concert

SPRING 1892 NEW YORK CITY—MADISON SQUARE GARDEN

May 10	Concert
May 12	Concert
May 14	Concert

SPRING 1892 LONDON—ROYAL ALBERT HALL

June 11	Concert	C. Santley b.

AUTUMN 1892 CONCERT TOUR
Cities visited include Manchester (Oct. 8), Edinburgh (Oct. 19), and Glasgow (Oct. 26).

AUTUMN 1892 LONDON—ROYAL ALBERT HALL

Nov. 10	Concert	E. Lloyd t.

WINTER 1893 MILAN—TEATRO ALLA SCALA

Jan. 20	*La traviata*	V. Maina t. A. Pessina b.

WINTER 1893 NICE—THÉÂTRE MUNICIPAL

Roméo et Juliette
Il barbiere di Siviglia
La traviata

SPRING AND SUMMER 1893 LONDON—ROYAL ALBERT HALL
June 3   Concert
July 1   Concert

AUTUMN 1893 CONCERT TOUR
Cities visited include Glasgow (Oct. 12), Edinburgh (Oct. 13), and Manchester (Oct. 26).

AUTUMN AND WINTER 1893–94 CONCERT TOUR
Cities scheduled include New York (Nov. 9 and 11, which dates are known to have been cancelled), Philadelphia (Nov. 15), New York (Nov. 18), Boston (Nov. 21–25), Rochester (Nov. 28), Buffalo (Dec. 2), Washington (Dec. 4), Baltimore (Dec. 8), Cleveland (Dec. 12), Detroit (Dec. 15), Columbus (Dec. 19), Cincinnati (Dec. 22), St. Louis (Dec. 26), Kansas City (Dec. 29), Indianapolis (Jan. 2), Louisville (Jan. 5), Nashville (Jan. 8), Atlanta (Jan. 11), Memphis (Jan. 15), Chicago (Jan. 18–19), Grand Rapids (Jan. 23), Brooklyn (Mar. 9), New York (Mar. 16), Philadelphia (Mar. 20), and New York (Mar. 22). The last concert in New York is known not to have taken place.

AUTUMN 1893 BOSTON—MUSIC HALL
(Concurrent with concert tour)
Nov. 25   °°*Gabriella* (Pizzi)   G. Fabbri ms. D. Lely t. A. Galassi b. F. Novara bs.

WINTER 1894 CHICAGO—AUDITORIUM
(Concurrent with concert tour)
Jan. 18   °*Gabriella*   G. Fabbri ms. D. Lely t. A. Galassi b. F. Novara bs.

WINTER 1894 NEW YORK CITY—CARNEGIE HALL
(Concurrent with concert tour)
Mar. 16   °*Gabriella*   G. Fabbri ms. D. Lely t. A. Galassi b. F. Novara bs.

SPRING 1894 CRAIG-Y-NOS—PATTI THEATRE
Apr.   Concert

SPRING AND SUMMER 1894 LONDON—ROYAL ALBERT HALL
May 19   Concert
June 2   Concert
July 7   Concert

SUMMER 1894 SWANSEA
July 12   Concert

AUTUMN 1894 CONCERT TOUR
Cities visited include Edinburgh (Oct. 27), Glasgow (Oct. 31), and Manchester (Nov. 5).

AUTUMN 1894 LONDON—ROYAL ALBERT HALL
Nov. 28   Concert

AUTUMN 1894 WINDSOR—WINDSOR CASTLE
Dec. 11   Concert

WINTER 1895 CONCERT TOUR
Cities visited include Berlin, Vienna, and Dresden.

WINTER 1895 NICE—THÉÂTRE MUNICIPAL
Feb. 6   *Il barbiere di Siviglia*
Feb. 13   *La traviata*
Feb. 25   *Lucia di*
            Lammermoor
Feb.   *Roméo et Juliette*

SPRING 1895 LONDON—QUEEN'S HALL
Apr. 3   Concert

SPRING 1895 LONDON—COVENT GARDEN
June 11   *La traviata*   F. De Lucia t. M. Ancona b. L. Mancinelli
                                        cond.
June 19   *Il barbiere di Siviglia* P. Bonnard t. M. Ancona b. A. Pini-Corsi b.
                                        V. Arimondi bs. E. Bevignani cond.
June 24   *Don Giovanni*   A. Adini s. H. McIntyre s. P. Brozel t. V.
                                        Maurel b. A. Castelmary bs. E. Bevignani
                                        cond.

SUMMER 1895 LONDON—BUCKINGHAM PALACE
June 14   Concert

SUMMER 1895 CRAIG-Y-NOS—PATTI THEATRE
Aug. 17   Performance in a
            mime play

AUTUMN 1895 CONCERT TOUR
Cities visited include Dublin, Belfast, Edinburgh (Oct. 12), and Manchester (Oct. 23).

AUTUMN 1895 LONDON—ROYAL ALBERT HALL
Nov. 26   Concert

WINTER 1896 MONTE CARLO—SALLE GARNIER
Jan. 25   *La traviata*   G. Masin t. H. Albers b. L. Jehin cond.

LENT 1896 NICE—THÉÂTRE MUNICIPAL
Feb. 10   *Don Giovanni*

SPRING AND SUMMER 1896 LONDON
May 12   Concert   E. Lloyd t.
June 4   Concert   E. Lloyd t.
June 30   Concert   B. Davies t. C. Santley b.

SUMMER 1896 CARDIFF
Sep. 16   Concert

AUTUMN 1896 CONCERT TOUR
Cities visited include Edinburgh (Oct. 16), Glasgow (Oct. 19), and Manchester (Oct. 28).

AUTUMN 1896 LONDON
   Nov. 21   Concert

WINTER 1897 MONTE CARLO—SALLE GARNIER
   Jan. 30   *La traviata*   G. Apostolu t. G. Caruson b. A. Vigna cond.
   Feb. 6   *Lucia di*   G. Apostolu t. G. Caruson b. Greil bs.
             Lammermoor

LENT 1897 NICE—THÉÂTRE MUNICIPAL
   Feb. 22   °°*Dolores* (Pollonnais) E. Scaremberg t.
   Mar. 7   *La traviata*
             Don Giovanni

SPRING 1897 LONDON—ALBERT HALL
   June 3   Concert
   June 29   Concert   E. Lloyd t. C. Santley b.

AUTUMN 1897 CONCERT TOUR
The only city visited that has been identified to date is Liverpool (Oct. 20).

AUTUMN 1897 LONDON—ROYAL ALBERT HALL
   Dec. 4   Concert

SPRING AND SUMMER 1898 LONDON—ROYAL ALBERT HALL
   May 26   Concert
   July 17?   Concert

SPRING AND SUMMER 1898 LONDON—CRYSTAL PALACE
   June 7   Concert   C. Butt ms. C. Santley b.
   June 25   Concert

AUTUMN 1898 CONCERT TOUR
Cities visited include Glasgow (Oct. 12), Edinburgh (Oct. 15), Manchester (Oct. 26), and Nottingham (Oct.).

AUTUMN 1898 LONDON—ROYAL ALBERT HALL
   Nov. 14   Concert

WINTER 1899 ROME
   Feb.?   Concert

SPRING 1899 LONDON—ROYAL ALBERT HALL
   May 19   Concert
   May 30?   Concert

AUTUMN 1899 CRAIG-Y-NOS—PATTI THEATRE
   Oct. 16   *La traviata*

AUTUMN 1899 CONCERT TOUR
Cities visited include Manchester (Nov. 10), Edinburgh (Nov. 17), and Glasgow (Nov. 20).

AUTUMN 1899 LONDON—ROYAL ALBERT HALL
   Nov. 22   Concert

WINTER 1900 LONDON—COVENT GARDEN
   Feb. 22   Concert   A. Alvarez t.

SPRING 1900 LONDON
May 31   Concert

SUMMER 1900 BRECON
Aug. 2   Concert

AUTUMN 1900 STOCKHOLM
Sep.   Concert

AUTUMN 1900 LONDON
Oct. 18   Concert

AUTUMN 1900 CONCERT TOUR
Cities visited include Manchester (Oct. 24) and Glasgow (Nov. 1).

SPRING 1901 PARIS
Apr.   Concert

SPRING 1901 LONDON—ROYAL ALBERT HALL
June 15   Concert

AUTUMN 1901 CONCERT TOUR
Cities visited include Glasgow (Oct. 17) and Edinburgh (Oct. 19). A concert scheduled for Manchester (Oct. 23) was cancelled.

AUTUMN 1901 LONDON
Nov. 1?   Concert

SPRING AND SUMMER 1902 LONDON—ROYAL ALBERT HALL
June 18   Concert
July 14   Concert

SUMMER 1902 BRECON
Aug. 2   Concert

AUTUMN 1902 CONCERT TOUR
Cities visited include Glasgow (Oct. 16), Edinburgh (Oct. 18), and Manchester (Oct. 22).

SPRING 1903 LONDON—ROYAL ALBERT HALL
May 28   Concert

SUMMER 1903 CRAIG-Y-NOS—PATTI THEATRE
July 31   Concert

AUTUMN AND WINTER 1903–04 CONCERT TOUR
Cities scheduled include New York (Nov. 2–7), Philadelphia (Nov. 9), Montreal (Nov. 12), Brooklyn (Nov. 17), Boston (Nov. 19–21), Baltimore (Nov. 23), Newark (Nov. 25), New York (Nov. 27), Buffalo (Nov. 30), Toronto (Dec. 3), Cleveland (Dec. 5), Milwaukee (Dec. 7), Chicago (Dec. 9–12), Detroit (Dec. 14), Cincinnati (Dec. 16), St. Louis (Dec. 18), Des Moines (Dec. 22), Kansas City (Dec. 26), Minneapolis (Dec. 30), Salt Lake City (Jan. 4), San Francisco (Jan. 7), Los Angeles (Jan. 9), San Francisco (Jan. 11), Portland (Jan. 14), Vancouver (Jan. 16), Tacoma (Jan. 18), Seattle (Jan. 21), Spokane (Jan. 23), Butte (Jan. 25), Denver (Jan. 28), Nashville (Feb. 1), Memphis (Feb. 4), Birmingham (Feb. 6), Atlanta (Feb. 8), Richmond (Feb. 11), Washington (Feb. 13), Pittsburgh (Feb. 15),

Philadelphia (Feb. 24), Chicago (Feb. 29), Indianapolis (Mar. 2), and Hot Springs, Ark. (Mar. 8).

SPRING 1904 LONDON—ROYAL ALBERT HALL
   June 11   Concert

AUTUMN 1904 CONCERT TOUR
Cities visited include Glasgow (Oct. 20) and Edinburgh (Oct. 22).

AUTUMN 1904 LONDON—ROYAL ALBERT HALL
   Nov. 17   Concert

AUTUMN 1904 ST. PETERSBURG
   Dec. 14   Concert

SPRING 1905 LONDON—ROYAL ALBERT HALL
   June 1   Concert

AUTUMN 1905 CONCERT TOUR
Unlike her usual autumn tours of the British provinces, this tour was for charity and lasted only about two weeks. None of the cities visited have been identified to date.

AUTUMN 1905 LONDON—ROYAL ALBERT HALL
   Nov. 10   Concert

AUTUMN 1905 PARIS
   Nov. 14   Concert

AUTUMN 1905 CRAIG-Y-NOS
   Dec. 4–7   Recording session

SPRING 1906 LONDON—ROYAL ALBERT HALL
   June 14   Concert

SPRING 1906 CRAIG-Y-NOS
   June   Recording session

AUTUMN 1906 CONCERT TOUR
Patti resumed her customary autumn concert tours of the British provinces. Cities visited include Manchester (Oct. 17), Edinburgh (Oct. 27), and Glasgow (Oct. 29).

AUTUMN 1906 LONDON—ROYAL ALBERT HALL
   Dec. 1   Concert

SPRING 1907 PARIS—THÉÂTRE PRIVE DE JEAN DE RESZKE
   May 25   *Il barbiere di Siviglia* G. Anselmi t. M. Ancona b. E. de Reszke
                                     bs. A. Pini-Corsi bs.

SUMMER 1907 SWANSEA
   Sep. 19   Concert

AUTUMN 1907 CONCERT TOUR
This was the last of Patti's autumn concert tours of the British provinces. Cities visited include Manchester (Oct. 16) and Edinburgh (Oct. 26).

AUTUMN 1907 LONDON—ROYAL ALBERT HALL
  Nov. 29   Concert
SPRING 1908 LONDON—QUEEN'S HALL
  May 26   Concert
SPRING 1909 PONTARDAWE—PONTARDAWE INSTITUTE
  May 6   Concert
SPRING 1911 LONDON—ROYAL ALBERT HALL
  June 1   Concert
AUTUMN 1911 LONDON—ROYAL ALBERT HALL
  Oct. 14   Concert

AUTUMN 1914 LONDON—ROYAL ALBERT HALL
  Oct. 24   Concert

Notes

1. This was the U.S. premiere of the opera and was given in the original French version as *Le pardon de Ploërmel.* All subsequent productions that Patti participated in were the Italian version with added music and recitatives.
2. This was the first of many charity concerts that Patti gave in Welsh cities such as Swansea, Cardiff, Brecon, and Neath starting in 1882 and ending in 1907.
3. These autumn concert tours of the British Isles took place practically every year from 1885 until 1907. The scope of the tours is usually much greater than is indicated by the cities listed; for example, see the Autumn 1890 tour, which is the only one for which a complete itinerary is available.
4. Although this season took place at the Metropolitan Opera, it was not given by the regular company and is therefore not listed in the *Annals of the Metropolitan Opera.*

Adelina Patti's Operatic Repertoire

by Thomas G. Kaufman

In Chronological Order by Assumption of Role

Opera and Composer	Role	City	Theater	Date
Lucia di Lamermoor, Donizetti	Lucia	New York	Academy of Music	24 Nov. 1859
La sonnambula, Bellini	Amina	New York	Academy of Music	1 Dec. 1859
Don Giovanni, Mozart	Zerlina	Philadelphia	Academy of Music	19 Dec. 1859
Il barbiere di Siviglia, Rossini	Rosina	Boston	Boston Theater	17 Jan. 1860
I puritani, Bellini	Elvira	Boston	Boston Theater	25 Jan. 1860
Martha, Flotow	Lady Harriet	New York	Academy of Music	27 Feb. 1860
Don Pasquale, Donizetti	Norina	Philadelphia	Academy of Music	4 Apr. 1860
Mosè,[1] Rossini	Anaïde	New York	Academy of Music	7 May 1860
La traviata, Verdi	Violetta	Philadelphia	Academy of Music	24 Sep. 1860
Linda di Chamounix, Donizetti	Linda	New York	Academy of Music	5 Oct. 1860
Il trovatore, Verdi	Leonora	New Orleans	Théâtre de l'Opéra	2 Jan. 1861
Rigoletto, Verdi	Gilda	New Orleans	Théâtre de l'Opéra	6 Feb. 1861
Les Huguenots, Meyerbeer	Valentine	New Orleans	Théâtre de l'Opéra	25 Feb. 1861
Dinorah,[2] Meyerbeer	Dinorah	New Orleans	Théâtre de l'Opéra	4 Mar. 1861

382

La figlia del reggimento, Donizetti	Maria	Brussels	Théâtre de Monnaie	11 Feb. 1862
La gazza ladra, Rossini	Ninetta	London	Covent Garden	6 June 1863
L'elisir d'amore, Donizetti	Adina	London	Covent Garden	21 July 1863
Faust, Gounod	Marguerite	Hamburg	Stadt Theater	22 Sep. 1863
La stella del Nord, Meyerbeer	Caterina	London	Covent Garden	26 June 1866
Crispino e la comare, Ricci	Annetta	London	Covent Garden	14 July 1866
Semiramide, Rossini	Semiramide	Bad Homburg	Kursaal	22 Aug. 1866
Roméo et Juliette, Gounod	Juliette	London	Covent Garden	11 July 1867
Don Desiderio, Poniatowski	Angiolina	Paris	Théâtre-Italien	9 Nov. 1867
Ernani, Verdi	Elvira	Paris	Théâtre-Italien	28 Dec. 1867
Giovanna d'Arco, Verdi	Giovanna	Paris	Théâtre-Italien	28 Mar. 1868
Esmeralda, Campana	Esmeralda	London	Covent Garden	14 June 1870
Otello, Rossini	Desdemona	St. Petersburg	Imperial Theater	19 Jan. 1871
Gelmina,[3] Poniatowski	Gelmina	London	Covent Garden	28 May 1872
I diamanti della corona, Auber	Caterina	London	Covent Garden	3 July 1873
Mireille, Gounod	Mireille	St. Petersburg	Imperial Theater	4 Feb. 1874
Luisa Miller, Verdi	Luisa	London	Covent Garden	27 June 1874
Aida, Verdi	Aida	London	Covent Garden	22 June 1876
L'africaine, Meyerbeer	Selika	London	Covent Garden	14 June 1879
Estella, Cohen	Estella	London	Covent Garden	3 July 1880
Velleda, Lenepveu	Velleda	London	Covent Garden	4 July 1882
Carmen, Bizet	Carmen	London	Covent Garden	14 July 1885
Lakmé, Delibes	Lakmé	Buenos Aires	Politeama Argentino	20 June 1888
Gabriella, Pizzi	Gabriella	Boston	Music Hall	25 Nov. 1893
Dolores, Pollonnais	Dolores	Nice	Théâtre Municipal	22 Feb. 1897

Notes

1. There are two versions of Rossini's *Mosè*. The first, *Mosè in Egitto*, had its premiere in Naples in 1818. It was then extensively revised for Paris in 1827, and given as *Moïse et Pharaon*. The two operas are considerably different, even as to the names of some of the principal characters, including the leading soprano. It is now customary to refer to only the first (1818) work as *Mosè in Egitto*, and to use either the French *Moïse* or the Italian *Mosè* when referring to the second version. When Patti sang *Mosè* in New York in 1860 it was billed as *Mosè in Egitto*, but what was actually given was the 1827 French version, translated into Italian.
2. When Patti sang this opera in New Orleans, in what was the U.S. premiere, it was given in French as *Le pardon de Ploërmel*. All subsequent productions that she took part in were in the Italian version (with added musical numbers and recitatives) as *Dinorah*.
3. World premieres sung by Patti are indicated in boldface type.

In Alphabetical Order by Name of Composer

Auber
  I diamanti della corona

Bellini
  I puritani
  La sonnambula

Bizet
  Carmen

Campana
  Esmeralda

Cohen
  Estella

Delibes
  Lakmé

Donizetti
  Don Pasquale
  L'elisir d'amore
  La figlia del reggimento
  Linda di Chamounix
  Lucia di Lammermoor

Flotow
  Martha

Gounod
  Faust
  Mireille
  Roméo et Juliette

Lenepveu
  Velleda

Meyerbeer
  L'africaine
  Dinorah
  Les Huguenots
  La stella del Nord

Mozart
  Don Giovanni

Pizzi
  Gabriella

Pollonnais
  Dolores

Poniatowski
  Don Desiderio
  Gelmina

Ricci
  Crispino e la comare

Rossini
  Il barbiere di Siviglia
  La gazza ladra
  Mosè
  Otello
  Semiramide

Verdi
  Aida
  Ernani
  Giovanna d'Arco
  Luisa Miller
  Rigoletto
  La traviata
  Il trovatore

Index

Numbers in bold refer to black-and-white illustrations; the color portraits are found in the central portfolio.

Author and Contributors

DR. JOHN F. CONE, former academic dean of the North Carolina School of the Arts, is adjunct associate professor of English at Fordham University's Ignatius College, where he received the Teacher of the Year award for 1992–1993. He is the author of *Oscar Hammerstein's Manhattan Opera Company* (University of Oklahoma Press, 1964) and *First Rival of the Metropolitan Opera* (Columbia University Press, 1983), associate editor of *The World's Love Poetry* (Bantam Press, 1960), contributor to *Melba: A Contemporary Review* (Greenwood Press, 1985), contributing editor and commentator of *Magnum Shakespearean Series* (Lancer Books, 1968), and contributor to *The New Grove Dictionary of American Music* (Macmillan, 1986) and *The New Grove Dictionary of Opera* (Macmillan, 1992).

WILLIAM R. MORAN, former vice president of exploration for Molycorp, a subsidiary of the Union Oil Company of California, is founder and honorary curator of the Stanford Archive of Recorded Sound. He is the author of *Melba: A Contemporary Review* (Greenwood Press, 1985); co-compiler of *The Encyclopedic Discography of Victor Recordings* (Greenwood Press, 1983–), an ongoing series; editor of *Herman Klein and the Gramophone* (Amadeus Press, 1990); and author of *The Recordings of Lillian Nordica* and a large number of articles, reviews, and discographies published in *The Record Collector, The Opera Quarterly, Recorded Sound, Record News, High Fidelity*, and other journals and books. He is the producer for RCA

Australia of *Nellie Melba: The American Recordings, 1907–1916* and is responsible for the transfers of historical discs used in the Grammy Award–winning *RCA MET: 100 Singers/100 Years.* He is a principal contributor to *Opera and Concert Singers* (Garland, 1985) and associate editor of the 42-volume reprint series *Opera Biographies* for Arno Press. He was an associate editor of the American Association of Petroleum Geologists' *Bulletin* from 1959 to 1990 and has contributed many articles, reviews, and biographies to technical and scientific journals.

THOMAS G. KAUFMAN, formerly senior manager of worldwide regulatory affairs for Warner Lambert, is now a management consultant to the pharmaceutical industry. He is a member of the editorial board of *The Opera Quarterly,* an advisor to *The International Dictionary of Opera* (St. James Press, 1993), and a contributor to *The New Grove Dictionary of Opera.* He is the author of *Verdi and His Major Contemporaries: A Selected Chronology with Casts* (Garland, 1990), and is now working on a four-volume set covering composers of the *bel canto* period. He had previously compiled the chronology of Enrico Caruso for *Enrico Caruso: My Father and My Family* (Amadeus Press, 1990). He is also the author of a large number of articles, reviews, singers' chronologies, and discographies published in *The Opera Quarterly, The Record Collector,* the *Journal* of the Donizetti Society, and other journals. He has written program notes and translated numerous opera libretti for CBS Records, the Opera Orchestra of New York, the San Francisco Opera, and other organizations.